THE DEVIL'S WORLD

The Medieval World

Series editor: Julia Smith, University of St Andrews

THE DEVIL'S WORLD

HERESY AND SOCIETY 1100–1300

ANDREW P. ROACH

PEARSON
Longman

Harlow, England • London • New York • Boston • San Francisco • Toronto
Sydney • Tokyo • Singapore • Hong Kong • Seoul • Taipei • New Delhi
Cape Town • Madrid • Mexico City • Amsterdam • Munich • Paris • Milan

PEARSON EDUCATION LIMITED

Edinburgh Gate
Harlow CM20 2JE
United Kingdom
Tel: +44 (0)1279 623623
Fax: +44 (0)1279 431059
Website: www.pearsoned.co.uk

First edition published in Great Britain in 2005

© Pearson Education Limited 2005

The right of Andrew Roach to be identified as author
of this work has been asserted by him in accordance
with the Copyright, Designs and Patents Act 1988.

ISBN 0 582 27960 7

British Library Cataloguing-in-Publication Data
A CIP catalogue record for this book can be obtained from the British Library

Library of Congress Cataloging-in-Publication Data
Roach, Andrew.
  The Devil's world : heresy and society, 1100–1320 / Andrew Roach. — 1st ed.
     p. cm.
  Includes bibliographical references (p.) and index.
  ISBN 0–582–27960–7 (pbk.)
  1. Heresies, Christian—History—Middle Ages, 600–1500. 2. Christian sociology—
History—Middle Ages, 600–1500. I. Title.
BT1319.R63 2005
273′.6—dc22
                                                                    2004063815

10 9 8 7 6 5 4 3 2 1
09 08 07 06 05

Set by 35 in 10.5/13pt Galliard
Printed and bound in Malaysia.

The Publisher's policy is to use paper manufactured from sustainable forests.

CONTENTS

CONTENTS

LIST OF MAPS AND PLATES

Maps

1. The Spread of European Heresy
2. Languedoc and Lombardy

Plates

1. Medieval manuscript illumination of troubadours from Alphonse le Sage's *Las Cantigas*, *c*. thirteenth century.
2. Castello Scaligero, Sirmione, on Lake Garda: last refuge of the Italian Cathars, captured 1276.
3. Plan scénographique de 1550: Archives municipales de Lyon. Sixteenth-century plan of the city of Lyon, showing cathedral, fortified ecclesiastical quarter, and cathedral wharf from the time of Valdes.
4. Saint Dominic Sending Forth the Hounds of the Lord, with Saint Peter Martyr and Saint Thomas Aquinas, *c*.1369 (fresco) by Andrea di Bonaiuto: the scene shows Thomas using books to convert heretics as well as making the punning reference to 'domini canes', dogs of the Lord.
5. The staircase under which lived Saint Alexis, the inspiration for Valdes of Lyon. Staircase now in the church of Sant'Alessio, Rome.
6. Italian fresco with Saint Francis of Assisi, without halo or stigmata; probably the earliest picture.
7. View of Carcassonne from the west side, state of the fortifications and the city in 1853 before 'restoration'.
8. Saint Francis of Assisi: Cimabue's fresco in the Lower Basilica, Assisi.
9. Saint Francis Releases the Heretic, 1297–99 (fresco) by Giotto di Bondone: a posthumous miracle of Saint Francis (flying left!). Giotto's painting depicts the penitent heretic (Pietro d'Alife) with some dignity; earnest, bearded and barefoot.
10. Montségur Castle, Languedoc, by Simon Marsden: a besieger's view of the Cathar redoubt captured in 1244.
11. Saint Peter Martyr (oil on panel) by Vittore Carpaccio, *c*. fifteenth century.
12. Ruined Arena, Verona. Execution site of heretics captured at Sirmione.
13. Keeping the customers happy: the Bishop of Paris Blessing the Lendit Fair in the fourteenth century.
14. The Porziuncola (Portiuncola), Assisi. First home of the Franciscans. Now completely endorsed in church of Santa Maria degli Angeli.
15. Interior of Franciscan church of Santa Croce, Florence.

ACKNOWLEDGEMENTS

The publishers are grateful to the following for permission to reproduce copyright material:

Financial Times for use of an extract derived from Richard Tomkins' article 'Christ replaces Coke as the focus of youthful longing' (30 July 2004); the Bridgeman Art Library for use of images BAL130097, BEN113975, XIR63359, BAT201228, XIR217771 and MES97834; the Bridgeman Art Library and Bibliothèque nationale de France for use of image BAL52371; the Bridgeman Art Library and Simon Marsden for use of image TMA220587; Archives municipales de Lyon for use of Plan scénographique de 1550; Corbis for use of images WN001950, CS004509, IH64074, and SL003793; Eva Duve for image of the Porziuncola (Portiuncola), Assisi; Helena Bruce for image of the staircase under which Saint Alexis lived, Sant'Alessio, Rome.

In some instances we may have been unable to trace the owners of copyright material, and we would appreciate any information that would enable us to do so.

SERIES EDITOR'S PREFACE

The history of medieval heresy intrigues and appals. Combining tales of defiance and repression, principle and expedience, conviction and cravenness, it invites us to think equally hard about the role of belief and the power of institutions in human actions. In the pages that follow, Andrew Roach helps us to do this by exploring what makes beliefs 'work' in specific social milieux. Moving gracefully between the Balkans, France, Italy and the Rhineland, he draws on his own detailed knowledge of religious and archival sources to offer us a fresh and invigorating look at religion in action in the twelfth and thirteenth centuries.

Against a backdrop of the rise of a market economy associated with the growth of towns and long-distance trade, we are invited to view religion from the perspective of its lay consumers, rather than its clerical providers. What did people want? For what purposes? Where could they most conveniently get it? How much did it cost, in social and political, as well as in economic terms? Dr Roach's argument is that the twelfth century saw the end of the Roman Catholic Church as a monopoly provider; thereafter consumers could pick and choose among competing goods in what he terms the 'spiritual market place'. Here many different preachers set up stall, some acceptable to the papal church, others not. He compares their tactics of persuasion and the currencies in which they bargained as well as analysing the consumers whom they attracted – urban and rural, rich and poor, men and women. In towns and villages, on the roads and in the mountains, we meet ordinary folk and colourful characters – preachers, missionaries, inquisitors, devout lay men and women, local rulers, whose fears, beliefs and aspirations form the substance of this book.

Andrew Roach offers the striking conclusion that that the successful repression of most heresy in the course of the thirteenth century did not eliminate choice, as we might expect. Far from it: by the early thirteenth century, such a wide range of styles of Christian observance were available within the Catholic Church itself that the exercise of choice no longer necessarily forced the consumer outside it. The argument that pluralism and choice, rather than homogeneity and obedience, characterised the Church of the high middle ages is a vote for the autonomy and individuality of religious expression in an age more frequently presented as one of group solidarity and conformity. I welcome this addition to the Longman Medieval World for the challenges it brings to our assumptions about religion and belief in the Middle Ages.

Julia M. H. Smith

PREFACE

In 1995 Longman contracted me to write a short history of heresy in relation to the twelfth- and thirteenth-century Church. The end product has been nine years in the making for which my only excuse is that I am a slow worker, have got married, become a father and moved into a respectable house with a small lawn. During this time 'the book' has held much of the status as I imagine bread blessed by a Cathar *perfectus* did in the middle ages; stale and mouldering at the back of the cupboard, I could neither show it off nor throw it away and forget about it. Only at this stage in the process do I realise how many friends this book has made me, how many interesting conversations it has triggered, how many confidences have been shared because of it. This is where my real debt of gratitude lies and why I suspect I may try another one before too long.

In the meantime my sincere thanks to everyone who has helped me to produce this one. The staff of Oxford, Cambridge and Glasgow university libraries were unfailingly helpful, as were the librarians and archivists of the Vatican, although my tip is not to turn up there saying you are interested in heresy. My stay in Rome was made infinitely more congenial thanks to being able to be part of the American Academy there. I owe a great debt to two further institutions: the Historisches Seminar at Johannnes Gutenberg-Universität, Mainz, suggested an exchange with the Glasgow History department in 2001–2, so that for four months I was able purely to teach and write, a luxury most British academics can only dream of. I have also been able to spend extended periods at Saint Deiniol's Library, Hawarden, for some of the time on a Moorman scholarship. It is a place of divine learning and serious fun; I benefited from both. Research visits were made possible by grants at various times from the British Academy, the Arts and Humanities Research Board, the Carnegie Fund, the Royal Society of Edinburgh and History Department of the University of Glasgow who also granted me study leave. I am grateful to all these bodies. In addition, thanks are due to Jack Baldwin who allowed me three months living in a real medieval tower in Morricone, Eva Duve who started me thinking about the illustrations and Alison Peden who patiently scanned them.

An extended family of friends and colleagues have either read parts of the text or been willing to discuss matters of belief and heresy over the years. I learnt much from the views of all of the following: Stuart Airlie, John Arnold, Malcolm Barber, Peter Biller, William Burgwinkle, Sam Cohn, Marilyn Dunn, Simon Fowler, Sharon Gauld, Hilary Greer, Sarah Hamilton, Annette Handrich, Jill Kirkwood, Malcolm Lambert, the late Michael Kennedy, Elizabeth McCahill, Steve Marritt, Lily Mo, Jim Murphy, Sandy Murray, Paul Ormerod, Daisy Roach, John Roach, Jonathan Shepard, Jim Simpson, Graeme Small, Matthew Strickland, the late John Thomson, Simon Tugwell and Sue Vice. Despite their best efforts, I am sure there are still errors for which I am, of course, responsible; please e-mail me if you spot one.

A much smaller group have had the dubious privilege of being close to me throughout the writing process. David Bates was both an understanding boss and perceptive editor, Heather McCallum was unfailingly courteous and patient throughout her time at Longman as deadlines came and went. Her successors processed the manuscript with efficiency and enthusiasm. Nicola and Jonathan Shepard put me up in both Cambridge and Oxford at various times over the years and helped with innumerable acts of generosity and kindness. For help with the index, I thank John Roach and Helena Bruce. My parents, John and Beryl Roach, and my aunt, Pat Ellerby, encouraged me with this as they have everything else in my life. My thanks to them all.

Finally, for the reader who has got this far, two people's presence lie behind each page: my daughter Imogen who helped me get this in perspective; it is, after all, only a book, and Helena, dearest of all to me, who has been willing to share her life with *The Devil's World* as well as its author and to whom it is respectfully dedicated.

University of Glasgow
St Andrew's Day, 2004

ABBREVIATIONS OF SOURCES
MOST FREQUENTLY CITED

AASS	*Acta Sanctorum quotquot toto urbe coluntur: . . . notis illustravit Joannes Bollandus*, 67 vols (Paris, 1863–1983)
AFH	*Archivum Franciscanum Historicum*
AFP	*Archivum Fratrum Praedicatorum*
Annales ESC	*Annales: Economies, sociétés, civilisations* now *Annales, histoire, sciences sociales*
Barber, *Cathars*	M. C. Barber, *The Cathars: dualist heretics in Languedoc in the high middle ages* (Harlow, 2000)
Biller & Hudson	P. Biller and A. Hudson (eds), *Heresy and Literacy, 1000–1530* (Cambridge, 1994)
CEHE	*Cambridge Economic History of Europe: planned by the late Sir John Clapham and the late Eileen Power*, 8 vols (Cambridge, 1960–89)
Doat MS	'Fonds Doat', Bibliothèque Nationale, 258 vols (Paris, 1669)
DMA	*Dictionary of the Middle Ages*, ed. J. R. Strayer, 13 vols (New York, 1982–9)
FAED	*Francis of Assisi: Early Documents*, eds R. J. Armstrong, J. A. W. Hellmann, W. J. Short, 4 vols (New York, 1999–2002)
Fontes	*Fontes Franciscani*, eds E. Menestó *et al.* (Assisi, 1995)
Fournier	*Le Registre de Jacques Fournier, évêque de Pamiers (1318–1325): Manuscrit no. Vat. Latin 4030 de la Bibliothèque Vaticane*, ed. J. Duvernoy, 3 vols and Errata (Toulouse, 1965)
G & L	*Petri Vallium Sarnaii monachi Hystoria albigensis*, eds P. Guébin and E. Lyon, 3 vols (Paris, 1926–39)
JEH	*Journal of Ecclesiastical History*
Mansi	*Sacrorum Conciliorum nova et amplissima collectio*, ed. J. D. Mansi, 53 vols (Paris, 1759–1927)

MGH SS	*Monumenta Germaniae Historica: Scriptores*
MOPH	*Monumenta Ordinis Fratrum Praedicatorum Historica*
PL	*Patrologiae cursus completus . . . ab aevo apostolico ad tempora Innocentii III, anno 1216 . . . series Latina,* ed. J.-P. Migne (Paris, 1844–64)
TRHS	*Transactions of the Royal Historical Society*
WEH	*Heresies of the High Middle Ages,* eds W. L. Wakefield and A. P. Evans (New York, 1969, reprinted 1991)

TIMELINE

909	Foundation of Cluny
c.970	Cosmas the Priest reports on Pop Bogomil
1072–84	Otfried de Watten *fl.*
1073–85	Pope Gregory VII
1079–1142/4	Peter Abelard
1090–1153	Bernard of Clairvaux
1095	Launch of First Crusade
1097–1104	Trial of Basil the Bogomil in Constantinople
c.1100–55	Arnold of Brescia
1112–*c*.15	Tanchelm of Antwerp *fl.*
1115–40	Aibert of Crespin, *fl.* as hermit
1116–45?	Career of Henry of Le Mans
1122	Concordat of Worms
1135	Council of Pisa
1152–90	Reign of Frederick Barbarossa
1162	Destruction of Milan
c.1170	Council of Saint Félix?
1170–1221	Dominic of Calaruega
1173–1205/18?	Valdes of Lyon *fl.*
1179	Third Lateran Council
1181–1226	Francis of Assisi
1184	Council of Verona
1187	Fall of Jerusalem
1190s–*c*.1250	Nazario,Cathar bp. of Concorezzans *fl.*
1198–1216	Pope Innocent III
1199	*Vergentis in senium*
c.1200–*c*.1240?	Belesmanza, Cathar bp.of Albanenses *fl.*
1206	Death of Amaury of Bène
1209–29	Albigensian Crusade
1215	Fourth Lateran Council
1218	Waldensian Council of Bergamo
c.1218–74	Bonaventure of Bagnoreggio
1229	Treaty of Paris/Meaux
1231–5	First inquisitors operating
1240s	John of Lugio, *Book of the Two Principles*

1242	Massacre of Avignonet
1244	Fall of Montségur
1250	Rainerius Saccone, *'Summa' on the Cathars and Poor of Lyon*
1256	William of Saint Amour, *On the Perils of the Most Recent Times*
c.1260–1300	Gerard Segarelli *fl.*
1269	Gerard of Abbeville, *Against the enemy of Christian Perfection*
1274	Second Council of Lyon
1294–1303	Pope Boniface VIII
1296–1321	Autier Cathar revival
1300–07	Fra Dolcino *fl.*
1321	Death of Cathar William Belibaste
1370s	John Wyclif teaching at Oxford

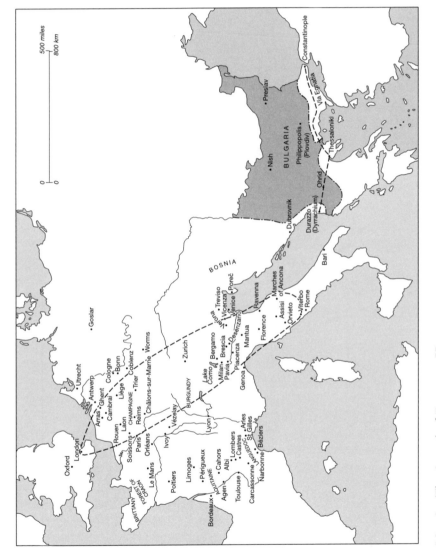

Map 1　The Spread of European Heresy

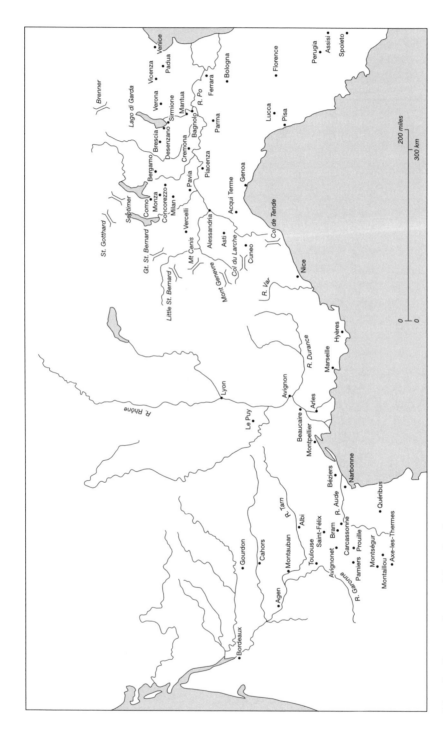

Map 2 Languedoc and Lombardy

· xviii ·

INTRODUCTION

O n July 30, by curious coincidence, the day after submitting the first draft of this book to the publishers, I read the following in the *Financial Times.*

> Cool Christianity is the cult brand epitomised, making its customers feel part of a community and instilling a sense of ownership that verges on the fanatical. Old Christianity used to be about serving God in this world with the promise of uncertain rewards in the hereafter. Now, provided you can afford the merchandise, the rewards are up-front: loud music, multimedia entertainment, a cool image and a comforting sense of spirituality. And like all the best cult brands, cool Christianity begets proselytizers who spread the brand message by word of mouth without the need for advertising.
>
> You've guessed what comes next. Far from brands being the new religion, it seems to me that religion is the new brand.[1]

Two thousand years of one of the world's most dynamic religions is written off as 'old Christianity'. Yet the writer has a point in that Christianity is a brand of the most potent type, a form of self-expression, and the tone of surprise in the article may come from the fact that there is surprisingly little written on the history of the consumer's experience of religion.[2] In truth, for most people, a large part of organised Christianity has always been the 'up-front' rewards; the comforting spirituality, the sense of fellowship, even music and entertainment. This book is about the emergence of choice in a broad economic and cultural context from the eleventh century to the end of the thirteenth. In the underdeveloped Europe of this period there was a poor selection of material goods and so people developed and practised their skills as consumers on the variety of forms of religion on offer. In so far as the word $\alpha\iota\rho\varepsilon\sigma\iota\zeta$, 'heresy', means 'choice' this is also a study of heresy in society, how consumers often drew on their own resources, finding new sources of supply and by-passing old ones. The end result was the gaudy religious market of the fourteenth century, with its variety of religious orders, painted churches and flagellants. This is not to suggest that medieval Christianity was in some sense not genuine, only that lay consumers had a very clear idea of what they wanted for themselves and loved ones, namely long and healthy lives, followed by salvation after death. Religion's job was to provide this and some form of spiritual involvement en route and lay people expected to use the usual means of obtaining influence: money, family connections and prestige.

Even the distinction drawn by the *Financial Times'* correspondent between 'up-front rewards' and those 'in the hereafter' may be misleading. The act of choice itself became a significant spiritual experience for the believer. The Albigensian or Cathar heretics believed that this world and all that was in it was made by the devil which accounted for all the evil within it. Far from making them an unworldly religion, focusing on an afterlife, Cathar theology foregrounded this world. Many of them believed it was eternal, just like the next. Certainly the human soul was trapped in it, doomed to wander from body to body until it came across the Cathars by whom it could be released. The relationship between the Cathar heresy and the act of choice gave the book its title.

One reason for the lack of scholarship on this subject is that the roots of 'consumption', the selection, purchase and use of goods and services, have always been seen as post-medieval processes. The idea that the 'supply side' of history has been over-studied at the expense of demand factors first emerged with regard to the Industrial Revolution: who was buying all these manufactured goods and why? Since then historians have attempted to identify the roots of what has inevitably been termed 'the consumer revolution'. Elite consumption, it has been suggested, had its origins in sixteenth-century politics, when the demands of the court favoured fashion as a way of grabbing attention, over 'patina', the slow accumulation of goods to emphasise generation-spanning social status. An explanation owing more to economics is that *mass* consumption derived from social emulation in the eighteenth century. A combination of relative closeness of social ranks in Britain in particular, women's control over household expenditure and the increasing ability to express social status through newly manufactured goods allowed 'keeping up with the Joneses' to become a way of life. Along with explaining 'consumption' there have also been attempts to analyse the 'consumer'. One recent study has seen 'consumerism' as a hidden collective political movement, as powerful as 'trade unionism' over the last two centuries. In contrast, one could see consumerism emerging in the late eighteenth century as part of the Romantic cult of the individual, who inhabits 'not just an "iron cage" of economic necessity, but a castle of romantic dreams', striving through his or her conduct, 'to turn the one into the other'. The individual is duty bound to develop their own uniqueness through purchasing self-gratification.[3]

There are two ways a medievalist can critique these theories. Unhelpfully, it can be pointed out that none of the key factors are new in the periods to which their great importance is ascribed. Social emulation is hardly a novelty in the eighteenth century, indeed anyone reading the Paston letters or the *Merchant of Prato* might assume it was an obsession of the middle ages. Likewise, court fashion has been considered and criticised since the days of Henry Curtmantle. Elizabeth I's parsimony in getting her nobles to pay for court splendour harks back to her itinerant medieval predecessors before the brief era of royal largesse which followed the dissolution of monasteries. Finally, and most interestingly, Christianity has always been a doctrine of individual salvation. It may be articulated in collective terms such as the medieval 'three orders', where those who pray bear the responsibility for saving those who labour and those who fight, or the sixteenth-century doctrine *cuius regio, eius religio*, meaning that the ruler's faith dictated their subjects' religious allegiances, but pre-Reformation Christianity had the sunny confidence of the probability of each soul being saved, exactly the characteristic attributed to the post-Calvinist Church of England of the eighteenth century as a prerequisite of the development of the Romantic consumer. To be fair, most of the authors referred to above have already thought of such criticisms and made some attempt to establish the distinctiveness of the period they study.

A more profitable approach may be for medievalists to outline how some of the defining characteristics of the consumer are already in place by 1300. Many of the techniques deployed at that time in choosing between heresy and orthodoxy were to become essential for people to make choices of material goods in later centuries. For a start, it is a commonplace among historians and contemporaries alike that in most medieval households the religious tone was set by the women. However, it is also undeniable that consumption in its modern form was unrecognisable in the middle ages. There was simply not the volume of manufactured goods to choose from. This did not mean that large sections of society were cut off from making purchases in the market. As is shown in chapter 2 the economy was rapidly 'commercialising' in the twelfth century. Even many of the peasantry did not make their clothing from the cheapest cloth available and for service industries like higher education or troubadour entertainment there was a competitive market in the late twelfth century which extended beyond the aristocracy to merchants, urban dwellers and rural minor nobles of even modest means.

The most widely used 'service industry' of all was religion. As the first chapter shows, the laity were in contact with the Church in all aspects of their life. They would have been acutely aware of the tithes and offerings they gave and what they received for them. What is clear even from the accounts of the late eleventh and early twelfth century is that unauthorised preachers with unorthodox teachings were already attracting wide audiences among the laity. When organised heretics such as the Cathars and Waldensians appear in chapter 3, their heretical teachings are not as important as the fact that they embody and can therefore shape the laity's idea of holiness. These matters were clearly subject to fashion. The rare quantitative evidence of how much was spent on religion, such as the analysis of Genoese wills in chapter 2, shows drastic changes of taste, particularly in the early thirteenth century, when the arrival of the friars ruined several existing religious institutions and put severe pressure on the parishes which had been used to receiving the bequests of the faithful.

Religion was also a 'leisure pursuit' open to all classes, in the sense it was something participated in outside work. Recent research has concluded that even the medieval peasantry had some unenforced leisure, some of which was spent in devotional practices. Glaber records a peasant making his way to morning service, many more attended Sunday morning Mass. Motivation was mixed: an observation from an early twentieth-century source that

> Sport was not allowed, there was only church, so people went to church. There were very few people in the village who didn't go, it was a way of passing the day.

seems an echo of medieval condemnations of sleeping, gossiping and girl-watching in the audience. Still, people went, and in towns, inspired by the Dominicans and Franciscans, many went on weekdays too. Sermons were a different matter; a famous preacher like Francis of Assisi or the confrontation between prelates and heretics at the Council of Lombers could bring crowds from miles around. As preaching gained in popularity in the thirteenth century, it could take place at various times of day, particularly after Mass or the late afternoon and it could happen within the church or outside in the cemetery or the nearest square: the church bells rang to announce sermons, even sometimes by heretics.[4] There was more at stake here than edification; the preacher received offerings for his support immediately afterwards. The group to which he (or occasionally she) belonged had its reputation reinforced or diminished by the preacher's words, which affected popularity and bequests. This competition for souls between heresy and orthodoxy is described in chapter 5 and was one which the Church could only win with the help of inquisitors as related in chapter 6.

Over the course of this period the consumer of religion was transformed. In external terms, popular religion had greatly increased opportunities for social emulation with the expansion of guilds, pilgrimages and acts of devotion. It was not so much that any of these were new, it was that they now catered for a far greater range of purses. Instead of a few important centres of pilgrimage, there were literally hundreds by 1300; lay people could make offerings ranging from lighting a candle through to founding a monastery, and new products continued to emerge and be refined such as mystery plays and indulgences. Politically, too, it had become important to be seen to be active in religion, both to refute charges of heresy and because fraternities and parish guilds now had conspicuous influence; the stories of action by a congregation in chapter 7 are even reminiscent of the organised actions on behalf of the consumer by the Co-operative movement or Consumers' Association. However, where perhaps medieval religion may really foreshadow the modern consumer is in the internal dynamic of emotions.

In an important work Colin Campbell, a literary scholar, described the 'romantic' consumer who 'enjoys' emotion, in the sense that feelings are not suppressed, but are controlled and appreciated, for their own sake. The hedonism is not in sensations, such as having more food, drink, sex, singing and dancing, but in taking pleasure from an experience, the 'thrill'. Crucially, according to Campbell, while in pre-Reformation 'Roman Catholicism symbols served to arouse . . . powerful emotions, their control was kept firmly in the hands of priesthood, and hence situationally located in communal ritual.' In this model, individual control of emotion begins with Protestants and puritans in particular.[5]

Up to a point. In the mid twelfth century rewards focussed on the afterlife. In a famous recruiting letter for the Second Crusade in 1146, Bernard of Clairvaux addressed:

> Those of you who are merchants, men quick to seek a bargain, let me point out the advantages of this great opportunity. Do not miss them. Take up the sign of the Cross and you will find indulgence for all the sins which you humbly confess. The cost is small, the reward is great and the gain will be God's kingdom.

Bernard offers a definite, if intangible, reward in return for the investment. Cathar doctrine of a few decades later promised more or less the same. Given the performance of the correct ceremonies at the deathbed, the believer found 'salvation'. To highlight what that meant the early Cathars gave a description of the 'land of the living' as they termed paradise:

> There are cities and suburban castles [sic], villages and woodlands, meadows, pastures, sweet water and salt, beasts of the forest and domestic animals, dogs and birds for the hunt, gold and silver, vessels and bedding of various types.

Campbell's point about pre-Reformation unrestrained hedonism would seem to be excellently brought out by the next sentence which promises sex, drinking and games.[6]

By 1300 religion had undergone quite radical change. On one level rewards were far more 'up-front'. Membership of the local fraternity would get you power and influence. If a witness of the Autier revival is to be believed, membership of the Cathars would make you rich. On another level religion was far more about participation; in sacraments such as Mass, confession, baptism and marriage, in living in informal religious communities, in candlelit processions or indeed flagellatory ones. Given that all these aspects of religion have a variety of motives, the strangest to the modern observer is flagellation. A familiar inter-pretation is eschatological, that people were drawn to such gatherings because they believed the end of the world was nigh and they had to do penance for their sins. More recent research has stressed the ritualistic nature of these movements or 'revivals' which clearly fall into the same category as early medieval Peace movements in that high religious excite-ment can obscure a reasonably straightforward socio-religious programme centring on peacemaking and political amnesty. Contemporaries professed ignorance of the origins of such movements, but centred them firmly in the laity: they may even have been public performances by established flagellant confraternities. After the experience they went home to get on with their lives. So while these were undoubtedly collective activities matching Campbell's model of pre-Reformation religion, there is at least the suspicion that flagellation was a controlled end in itself and that such parades were not hysterical outbursts, but a premeditated, 'thrilling' experi-ence of catharsis of the soul for the limited number of participants who wished to take part. Such a view is not undermined by the usual contem-porary word for such events, *devotio*, also being employed for pilgrimage enthusiasm and most famously of all for the informal semi-monastic communities in late fourteenth-century Holland, the *Devotio Moderna*.[7]

Many of the other forms of late medieval religion mentioned above could also be counted as 'pleasure seeking' in Campbell's sense of re-quiring a control of emotion, to experience pleasure. While activities were largely communal in form contemporaries recognised their value as individual experience. As for the idea that such matters were 'firmly in the hands of the priesthood', it was only in the sense that such groups of individuals required a priest to give the ceremonies legitimacy; control remained with those who paid. There is no space here to explore the wilder shores of late medieval religion, such as mysticism, in relation to the development of the Romantic consumer, but my point should now be clear. There is a long way to go before the convulsion in demand for material goods and the advent of the modern consumer, but ideology, motives and techniques for consumer choice in religion were all in place by 1300. The Reformation marked the end of the story rather than the beginning, so that in the late seventeenth and eighteenth centuries when religion was less of an issue and production and distribution of goods greatly improved, consumers were equipped to articulate both material and spiritual wants through their choices.

This book is by no means the first study of the relationship between religion and economic change in this period. Lester Little's *Religious Poverty and the Profit Economy* looked at the 'supply side' in terms of religious institutions which responded to the new realities in society by adopting poverty as a guiding principle. It remains a stimulating thesis, even if my own researches would suggest that poverty was more central to the concerns of clerics rather than laity. In the mid thirteenth century no Inquisition witness praises the Cathars for their poverty, except as an implicit part of a 'good life'. On the other hand, accounts of Francis of Assisi from the second half of the century written by the more radical of his followers repeatedly stress the saint's poverty, contemporary with its emergence as a topic of acrimonious debate between friars and secular clerks at university. A further emphasis on the changes among *clerici* is found in R. I. Moore's *The First European Revolution, c.970–1215.* In his thesis, the disorder of the earlier part of the period was not what it seemed, carrying with it a surprising amount of continuity in ruling class from the Carolingian world. Order was restored by the crushing of the 'little community' by the larger in the shape of a centralised secular power and the Church. The men who dominated both were literally inter-related and drawn from a relatively small number of influential families. He sees the twelfth century as one in which the 'clerks', that ubiquitous class of educated men which ran both Church and State, marginalised both peasants and warrior aristocracy to seize a power they never lost.

The clarity of Moore's vision of the world of the eleventh century can not banish doubts about his view of the twelfth, particularly in the light of what happened just outside his period of consideration which ends in 1215. First, active heresy is marginalised in Moore's analysis. At best heretics are doomed cavalry riding out to face ecclesiastical panzers, or they may even be invented enemies to justify further regulation and repression. This seems to do an injustice to the thousands who were prepared to go to the stake for their beliefs and to the real fear of heretics throughout the thirteenth century. High calibre figures were appointed as inquisitors as late as 1300, suggesting genuine insecurity at a point when the 'revolution' should have been secured. Moreover, as this study intends to show, religion in 1300 was more varied and local-ised than is accounted for in Moore's analysis. The 'little community' had reasserted its position through pilgrimage, parish guilds, informal communities and occasionally through heretical movements. Moore himself admits that the weakness of the definition of this process as 'revolution' is that 'the people who exercised power in the eleventh and twelfth centuries were overwhelmingly the biological descendants of those who had held it since the eighth': it was a reorganisation of the sources of power. If this is so, then the real change came in the thirteenth century, when in both political and religious terms power broadened to include men and women who had previously been outside these elites.[8]

Heretics were a vital factor for change between 1100 and 1300. The religious movements of the eleventh century described in the first chapter, such as the Peace movements, the course of reform in Milan and the First Crusade, did little more than remind lay people that they did have a role in the Church. The expansion in economic choices in goods, entertainment and learning which make up chapter 2 perhaps educated them in making choices even about non-material matters, but the crucial contribution came (in chapter 3) with the arrival of the Cathars. As a missionary Church the Bogomil-Cathar movement had to earn its support among the laity. In all probability, early Bogomil missions failed, twelfth-century ones succeeded when they concentrated on giving the laity what they wanted: a lifestyle they could respect and a sure route to salvation. Cathar organisation became geared to supply this. Having made the initial mistake of trying to establish bishoprics and a universal church on the Catholic or orthodox model, they learned to operate at com-munity level with the essential priority being to give believers access to a known 'good man' on their deathbed to ensure their salvation. This occurred best where secular authority was also fragmented such as southern France, north Italy or the Rhineland, but the Cathars even had an impact in areas where their missions failed, such as England. Chroniclers there recorded outbreaks of heresy on the Continent and were uncomfortably aware that they had only been saved by the heavy hand of Henry II's government.

The Waldensians too tapped into a deep-seated change in the laity's requirements of a Church. The attempts of Pope Alexander III in conjunction with the archbishop of Lyon to keep Valdes in the Church and the insistence of local clergy and many of the prelates of Third Lateran Council to force him out stemmed from a common realisation of Valdes's popularity and the lack of any alternative within the Church. Once again, without official patronage, the Waldensians had to build their own local structures and not surprisingly within a few years these turned out to vary greatly from place to place. Chapter 4 briefly examines some of the responses to come out of the Church. Centrally directed projects, such as the attempt to eliminate heresy by the clumsy brutality of crusade or even the imaginative legislation of the Fourth Lateran Council, proved less effective than friars of the Franciscan and Dominican orders which sprang, respectively, from the enthusiasm of a layman and the initiative of a provincial cleric.

The advent of an orthodox alternative led to an exciting period in the early thirteenth century when lay people in many parts of Europe could choose their own expression of religion from a range on offer. The mature and established Cathar Church faced the flowering of the Franciscans and Dominicans. The result was an unpredictable mixture, as many patronised both orthodox and heretical movements. The consensus grew within the Church that this was a battle which could not be won; heresy may have been weakened, but could not be destroyed without repression. Even when this emerged in the form of the Inquisition, which is examined in chapter 6, the 'consumer' still had a surprising amount of power. In order to break down communities and realise the capture of leading heretics, inquisitors had to deal with individuals, they had to persuade enough of them to confess voluntarily in order to bring pressure on the recalcitrant, they had to safeguard informants and they had to keep track of penitents. Above all, evaluation of the information inquisitors were given depended on understanding the lay mentality. Repression required the best pastoral care of all.

In the event lay ideals shifted in the late thirteenth century. Heretical movements and several orders of friars meant a glut of wandering preachers, all claiming to represent a way of life based on the apostles of the New Testament. Increasingly disillusioned by vicarious routes to salvation, the laity turned instead to ways in which they could seek more active participation in religion. Men and women took advantage of Franciscan and Dominican tertiary orders which enabled them to live a religious life within their own homes; guilds and fraternities sponsored parish churches and organised processions. Even the revival in heresy took place indoors, sometimes over dinner or reading books. The religion of 1300 had ceased to be something which was bought or even supported from a distance, it had become a lifestyle choice.

As for the heretics, they found niche markets, whether among the outsiders in the cosmopolitan university city of Bologna or the remote mountain communities of the Alps and Pyrenees. They could survive by blending into the background and satisfying the changing needs of their supporters. The result was that success made the Waldensians unrecognisable; the Cathars kept a clearer sense of identity and were brutally persecuted as a consequence. The obvious legacy of the heretics was that they raised society's awareness of religious issues and forced the Church to define its beliefs and inform the laity. More valuable to lay communities was the knowledge the heretics bequeathed of how to create different structures of religious organisation on their own.

chapter 1

THE MONOPOLY: 900–1135

In the eleventh century the laity was the consumer of a service from a monopoly provider, charged more for a product which the provider itself admitted was inferior, yet unable either to provide the service for themselves or seek out an alternative. Moreover, the provider was keen to limit perceptions of the product. When the Church had become institutionalised as the imperial faith, the Council of Constantinople announced in 381:

> The Faith of the three hundred and eighteen fathers assembled at Nicaea . . . . shall not be set aside, but shall remain firm. And every heresy shall be anathematised . . .

The early Church had eliminated choice in favour of doctrinal unity even if this meant outlawing the writings of many influential teachers such as Arius (d.336), Pelagius (d.425) and Donatus the Great (d.355). The struggle with their various followers had been painful and was commemorated in the writings of men whose words were to dominate the succeeding centuries, such as Augustine of Hippo (d.430).

The emphasis on doctrinal unity persisted through the subsequent centuries in which the Christian faith spread throughout Europe. Local bishops found that their religion was threatened less by the remnants of paganism than by the unauthorised forms of Christianity, feeding on popular enthusiasm, curiosity and often credulity. There were cases of prophetesses offering cures for plague in the name of Saint Martin and unauthorised 'bishops by grace of god' claiming to know the contents of letters dropped from Heaven by Christ himself. Relying on their considerable secular power and the mastery of a corpus of already ancient texts, bishops strove to establish a 'correct' form of Christianity. In this they were helped by the newly resurgent Carolingian imperial authority which relied on the Church for much of its legitimacy. The religion they established was liturgical, grand and deliberately derivative. Preaching was limited to homilies translated from the Church fathers, the only saints which could be venerated had to be respectably dead for centuries and theological speculation was frowned upon. An attempt to discuss predestination in the mid-ninth century ended in embarrassment and confusion: the advantages of it to bolster the authority of the purveyors of the clerical monopoly were outweighed by the demoralising effect of the laity.[1]

Religion was then the responsibility of the Church, but in a sense there was no such thing as 'the Church'; the popes in Rome, enmeshed in Italian politics, local bishops who had inherited many of the responsibilities of secular government at the disappearance of the Roman Empire and the isolated elite in monasteries had little in common. There were examples of great spirituality in all of them, but there was also mutual suspicion and an insistence on local autonomy. There were certainly no clear lines of authority and a wide diversity of practice. As in many monopoly providers this was in many ways very comfortable for those who were a part of it. Neither their superiors nor their lay customers expected much from them and they were rarely disappointed.

There was, at least, doctrinal uniformity. The relatively small number of clerics actively involved in intellectual debate effectively policed themselves and disputes rarely left academic circles. There was a common feeling among clerics that the laity should be kept at arm's length spiritually and physically. Those whose role in life was to fight or to labour should do exactly that and leave their salvation in the hands of those who prayed and were qualified to deal with such matters. When it came down to buildings, the isolation of the clergy performing ceremonies in the chancel or choir of the church at the east end, cut off from the laity in the larger nave to the west, was mirrored by the isolation of monks from society in general, praying for the sins of the world from behind high walls. In terms of participation in the spiritual community of the Church, lay input was minimal. Any significance they had was only as witnesses to what was done on their behalf. But in that lay the key to change as the witnesses started to articulate what it was they wanted to see.

There are three stages to the breaking of any monopoly and these correspond to the remaining sections of this chapter. In the first place consumers have to be actively interested in the product on offer and not just take it for granted. Between 900 and 1100 the Church slowly built up a consciousness of the lay role in religion through Cluniac monasteries, the movement for clerical reform and the preaching of the First Crusade. Then people have to become dissatisfied with the existing provider. Evidence for this is difficult to gather, but the growth in taxes and emphasis on the sacraments at parish level, particularly where this brought about drastic change from existing practice, may have made lay people aware of the Church's shortcomings. The growth of pilgrimage encouraged competition between shrines and gave travellers some index of performance of the Church in their local area. Finally, there has to be some viable alternative and though this was only really provided by the emergence of the Cathar and Waldensian organisations, the first stirrings can be seen in the followings of the charismatic preachers of the twelfth century.

Monks, popes and 'people'

The eleventh and early twelfth century saw the emergence of the laity, the troublesome 'people' recorded by clerical writers. Laity and clerics had always been closely entwined. Monks and leading secular clergy were mostly drawn from the European aristocracy and shared their inclination to rule. Secular rulers were the fathers, brothers and sisters of clerics and took on the role of protectors and benefactors. In return dubious claims to governance were legitimated and prayers offered for clouded characters. At a lower level the Church was enmeshed with the life of lay society besides religion; because over 20 per cent of land in western Europe was in the hands of ecclesiastical institutions, the local church or monastery could be your landlord or your employer. In urban communities chapters of cathedral clergy controlled house rents and market tolls. Since many folk were tied to the land they often found themselves handed over in property transactions or obliged to work on the estates of a bishop or abbey. Where secular government was weak the Church could act as a secular lord with responsibilities for defence, justice and public order. The wielding of effective political and economic power by ecclesiastical institutions ensured that any expressions of dissatisfaction usually occurred at local level.

Juxtaposed with the Church's responsibilities within secular society were the duties of the spiritual elite to the men and women around them. With varying degrees of enthusiasm the various component parts of the Church acknowledged their obligation to provide pastoral care in the sense of preaching, administering the sacraments and giving fatherly (and occasionally motherly) advice to believers. This need linked the middle ages with the early centuries of the Christian Church, and in the tenth century took the form of a calling for reform from within the Church itself. There was no desire to break the monopoly, but there was concern to improve the moral character of those providing it. In the search for support reformers turned to the laity and were able to mobilise forces in society not previously involved in religion. The monastery of Cluny on the Rhône was founded in 909 and proved to be notably innovative in bringing together monks with outsiders. At its heart was a very old-fashioned idea of prayer and ceremony as an almost magical series of acts and incantations; if these were completed precisely God's approval would be gained both for the monastery and society as a whole.[2] Consequently, although like all monks the Cluniacs were devoted to poverty in their personal lives, they made sure their worship was a rich and sensuous experience with a chandelier above the high altar and rare spices perfuming the incense.

If it was hoped that God would be impressed by this form of devotion, many on earth certainly were. In the absence of a strong royal protector, Cluny looked to the local lay aristocracy for both patronage and protection and was therefore forced to live on its reputation. Supporters had to be confident that the religious ceremonies were being performed correctly and that discipline was being maintained. The abbey inspired many offshoots throughout France, but they were termed priories to emphasise the controlling influence of the mother house and its abbot, while in turn Cluny had itself placed under the direct authority of the pope. Moreover, each monk was supposed to make the journey to the mother abbey to make his profession. This looks a little like modern branding and indeed Cluny very consciously made a virtue of its name. Moreover, the Cluniac order formed a loosely organised corporation within the Church, offering lay supporters a conscious choice of association with it.

Lay nobles were admitted into the order often late in life, even though they had not the Latin education necessary to play a full part in services and sometimes despite horrible crimes committed 'in the world'. Those who were unwilling to take on such a commitment in this life could at least benefit in the next since the Cluniacs also allowed the burial of lay benefactors within the monastic precincts. Again an innovative practice tapped into very ancient roots. In western Europe the dead were often quite close to the living. The design of the monastic cloister demonstrated a reliance on the dead. On the first floor, the living monks slept and stumbled to their night services. Beneath the ground slept dead founders and prominent previous abbots. Above them in the chapter house on the ground floor the abbot presided over the daily reading of a chapter of the Rule and, hopefully, a meeting of the combined wisdom of the living and the dead. The idea was given new urgency by the recently articulated doctrine of purgatory, a kind of fiery antechamber to heaven. Prayers for the dead now could be helpful in the specific context of shortening the time deceased friends and relatives spent there paying for their sins. Cluny promoted a day of prayer for the dead on November 2, All Soul's Day. This deepened the unity between the abbey and the aristocratic society to which it appealed because its monks were the brothers and uncles of the knightly class which dominated lay society. The very success of the monastery and its dependants did rather emphasise the belief of many that the only certain salvation was within the monastery walls. Other members of the laity could only look on enviously.

Cluny made the most of its links with the papacy. Two of its monks ascended to the see of Saint Peter and the monastery and its many daughter houses played their part in the revival of papal prestige. Popes of the eleventh century set about reasserting their leadership in reforming the Church and to this end they did not merely issue edicts from Rome, but instead criss-crossed Europe holding synods and councils. Leo IX preached at Reims in 1049, Paschal II was at Troyes in 1107. Between them the crusading Pope Urban II completed a full preaching tour of southern France and north Italy. More than any century before the twentieth it was possible to have seen the pope and heard his words.

The two issues which concerned the papacy above all were simony, the taking of money for ecclesiastical positions and nicolaitism, priests marrying instead of living lives of celibacy.[3] Both these issues were raised not just for the moral benefit of the clergy. Cluniac monks and successive popes addressed the paradox that the surest way to win general lay support and respect was to emphasise ecclesiastical independence of the grubby bullying and concerns of the lay world. Moves against simony were designed to allow monastic and cathedral chapters to elect their own candidates free from interference, whereas the encouragement of clerical celibacy was an attack on the large number of ecclesiastical posts or benefices run effectively as family businesses, passed down from father to son. Both issues grew from Cluny's insistence on its own autonomy and contemporary interest in how the Church had been run under the first popes. What was striking was the wider concern among the laity about such matters.

The most famous clashes took place at Milan, on the Lombard plain, the largest city in western Europe and a major economic centre. In the late 1050s Milan's sophisticated lay population started a boycott of sacraments from their own clergy, who for centuries had openly married and paid the archbishop on receiving a new appointment.[4] With papal backing, the protesters were organised by one Ariald, the descendant of a rural knight. Many of his supporters came from the *vavassores*, or newly arrived lesser nobility, and the *cives*, an assortment of merchants and notaries. Together these so-called *Patareni* represented a threat, not only in the religious sense but as major powers in the government of the city, to the older aristocracy from whom the archbishop and his cathedral chapter were drawn.

The campaign against simony moved on to larger targets. In the eyes of the reformers the most glaring abuse of ecclesiastical office was that prelates with souls in their care could be appointed by lay rulers and used as government officials. In formal terms the issue hinged on who would invest bishops with the ring and staff which marked their office. During the pontificate of Gregory VII between 1073 and 1085 the logic of the boycott used in Milan hardened into a two-pronged ideology. First, Gregory attacked those churchmen who benefitted from the arrangement:

> Those who have been promoted by the simoniac heresy, that is, by the intervention of money, to any rank or office of holy orders may no longer exercise any ministry in holy church . . . Nor may those who are guilty of the crime of fornication celebrate masses or minister at the altar in lesser orders.

But who was to enforce this draconian commandment?

> If they [the clergy] disregard our rulings . . . the people may in no wise receive their ministrations, so that those who are not corrected from the love of God and the honour of their office may be brought to their senses by the shame of the world and the reproof of the people.[5]

Gregory then turned to the greatest simoniac of all, the Emperor Henry IV who had been accustomed to nominate his own bishops. He deposed and excommunicated him in 1076, explaining that 'it is fitting that he who strives to lessen the honour of your Church should himself lose the honour which seems to belong to him'.[6]

At a stroke, Gregory and those who supported him dispensed with two important elements of the Church's monopoly position. In the first place they conferred an important role on the consumer to judge who was of suitable moral character to minister to them and this could potentially destabilise any spiritual figure, not least the pope himself. At the same time the rejection of the lay ruler distanced the Church from the coercive support of the secular power. Formal co-operation between ecclesiastical and secular government could no longer be taken for granted.

Exactly how the laity became informed about these issues is little known. Preaching by informed religious figures was rare and although, centuries before, Carolingian church councils may have expected priests to preach it was at best limited, and following the collapse of the Carolingian state may have disappeared completely. The traditional preachers of the Church were bishops; however there are few sermons from this period and even notable exceptions such as Fulbert of Chartres and

Anselm of Bec in the eleventh century seem to have preached only to a limited public.[7] It is possible that the first widespread preaching to the laity which involved them in religious reform came during the late tenth and early eleventh century with the so-called 'Peace of God' movement.[8] These were assemblies around the year 1000, mainly in the Poitou, Limoges and Berry areas of western France, primarily to restrict violence and robbery by powerful laymen taking advantage of the collapse of central authority in the country. In an attempt to enlist divine support restrictions were also proclaimed on clerical marriage, simony and priests bearing arms. Some of the prelates present could be as predatory as any lay man, often defending family interests with violence and blurring ecclesiastical and personal property, so ideas of clerical purity connected seamlessly with the aim of bringing robbers under the authority of the law.[9]

The most famous chronicler of the councils was Ralph Glaber, a monk who left a vivid generic account of them around 1033. Summoned by bishops, abbots and 'other devout men', people came – rich, middling and poor. Bodies of saints and innumerable caskets of holy relics added to the solemnity of the occasion and concentrated the Church's spiritual firepower. At the climax:

> The bishops raised their croziers to the heavens, and all cried out with one voice to God, their hands extended, 'Peace! Peace! Peace!'

For all the transcendental fervour both clergy and laity had vital but prosaic outcomes in mind. It was understood that the council would reassemble in five years and in the meantime the main benefit was four years of abundant harvests and low prices of all foods except meat and exotic spices after a long, grim famine. This really was a 'peace dividend', obtained by co-operation between heavenly and earthly powers. There were also health benefits. Glaber certainly implies miraculous cures, but his descriptions of straightening of limbs achieved through breaking skin, tearing flesh and much bloodshed suggests the ghastly business of medieval surgery in action and recipients may have benefited from an accumulation of clerical medical expertise at the assembly, rather than the direct intervention of God.[10]

In the end the influence of the Peace councils was limited. They were mainly confined to one area and faded around the middle of the eleventh century, but their model of society coming together under religious leadership to achieve common goals was to prove persistent in medieval society and within a generation was to have its most startling result in the First Crusade. It was this event which really proved the power of preaching. Starting at a huge assembly at Clermont in southern France in November 1095, Pope Urban II was able to mobilise whole sections of the lay population to make an armed pilgrimage to Jerusalem. In doing so he not only increased the prestige of his own office, but sanctified the role of knighthood and institutionalised the haphazard world of pilgrimage. The crusading contingent included not just the 'princes' who Urban had addressed, but also men who were not knights as well as women and children.

The message did not just come from Urban. Along with the bishops who were active after the council, such as Adhémar of Le Puy, there were also unauthorised preachers, such as Peter the Hermit, whom William of Tyre described as a priest from Amiens. The message rippled out across Europe, by 'rumour' according to the anonymous *Gesta Francorum*. The same author also clearly understood, quite contrary to the limited spiritual privileges probably promised by the pope, that those killed on the crusade would go straight to heaven.[11]

The First Crusade engaged the laity as never before. Its heterogeneous character may have caused embarrassment to the professional warriors in the party, such as when Peter the Hermit's band turned to crime in the Greek capital, Constantinople, but the implication of the fall of Jerusalem in 1099 was that God had supported the movement all along. The tone of letter to the pope reporting the news shows unprecedented confidence in God's approval of an essentially lay army:

> Multiply your supplications and prayers in the sight of God with joy and thanksgiving since God has manifested His mercy in fulfilling by our hands what He had promised in ancient times . . .[12]

The momentum may have come to a halt in the early years of the twelfth century. The consolidatory campaign of 1101 was widely preached, but targeted much more at knights and nobles who could defend the newly won kingdom, rather than the broader population. Its defeat in Asia Minor enhanced a sense of spiritual anticlimax as contemporaries concluded that God was expressing his displeasure at the manifest sins and pride of Christians in the West.[13]

Small worlds and wide worlds: parishes and pilgrimage

Dramatic as these events were they were not as influential as changes in individual churches and parishes throughout Europe. People came into greater contact with the Church, but not always in a good way. More taxes were gathered from them and their growing interest in the fate of their own and their family's souls came at considerable cost. The equally thriving enthusiasm for miracle cures for bodily sickness was also exploited by churchmen as much as it was encouraged. Even the drive for reform, by attempting to standardise practice, often only raised issues which had been taken for granted for generations.

Probably the most universal experience of the Church was paying its taxes or tithes. By the eleventh century the tithe had already been paid for hundreds of years and was based on the idea that it was a form of support for the priest. By the eleventh century, the priest was lucky if he saw between a quarter or half of it, since the collector was often the bishop and he had the competing claims of his own household, hospitality and church fabric to manage. Since the tithe was a tax it did not have to actually have any relationship to the Church as an institution at all. Secular lords often appropriated tithes, and in an extreme case, the archbishop of Milan in 983 bought himself the support of a host of minor nobles by granting them the tithes of the district.[14]

At first sight tithes resemble an income tax in that they were paid at the rate of a tenth on crops, often termed the 'major tithe'. There were also the smaller tithes, consisting of a tenth on things nourished by the land (cattle, milk or wool) and, in addition, a tenth of what was produced by the labour of hand or brain. In fact it more closely resembled a property tax, it was based on where you lived and though nominally assessed every year, like all other medieval taxes, it rapidly became fossilised at a customary sum. This was particularly true of the tithe on items made or traded, where the difficulty of assessment meant that the Church was fortunate if it received a contribution at all, although it constantly attempted to enforce its rights.

Property taxes are notoriously unfair in that they penalise those that remain quietly living their lives in one place whereas those who are in constant motion frequently get away with paying very little. There was surprisingly little open resentment of tithes, but a variety of attitudes to paying them:

> When the grapes had been harvested at the villa of Brildel, it was customary for the priest together with the manager and his assistants, to collect from each house the tithe which the parishioners owed. Some paid their tithes joyfully and reverently, as suited the blessing they had received; others hardly gave anything, holding back and arguing; worse were those who blasphemed and gave nothing. Some men who lived outside the parish bought the vineyards of the poor parishioners and trusting in their strength gave abuse rather than tithes. We discussed these troubles of the church first with our equals then with the parishioners and decided at their request that each man must pay what he owes in his own vineyard at the time of the harvest.[15]

This 1154 example from Trier in Germany, although quite late, illustrates the point. Collection was a chore and could only be accomplished with a certain degree of negotiation.

Bishops became aware of the potential of the asset in the eleventh century. In 1033 the bishop of Arezzo in Italy warned merchants in his diocese that they too were liable to pay tithes, not just peasants. The drive to recover tithes which had fallen into the hands of powerful lay men was an integral part of the reformers' drive against simony and there came a steady trickle of tithes donated or sold back to bishops or monasteries. The new ecclesiastical owner usually proved as exacting as a secular lord, if not more so, since monasteries and bishoprics had the record-keeping skills and staff to ensure a higher collection rate. This is what may have caused trouble: since the property generally changed very slowly, people became annoyed and alarmed when the tax increased or collection became more rigorous. Many of those affected were relatively prosperous and articulate local laity who may also have started to ask what they received in return for their payments. Recovery of tithes by churchmen began about 1040 and continued until 1140, peaking around 1080–1100, but in Italy the peak occurred later in the 1140s and 1150s.

One of the most difficult questions of this period is what the attitude of the Church to parish laity was. There is enough evidence to make a case that the aims of the reformers were to provide a purified priesthood to say Mass with little attempt do anything more. This older vision of the Church saw parishioners primarily as property. Theobald, archbishop of Canterbury, wrote in the mid twelfth century to the monks of Coggeshall in Essex who had just driven a community of parishioners from their homes. His concern was not to do with the spiritual welfare of the individuals involved, but the loss of tithes due to the prior of Rumilly le Comte which would result. This seems to show the medieval Church at its worst. Essex villagers being evicted in the name of spiritual solitude, and their parish apparently anyway in the hands of a community of foreign monks whose primary regard was the income.[16]

On the other hand, if the laity were of such little account why did the Church make such an effort to be represented at local level? Parishes were convenient sources of revenue, but money was still invested in churches themselves and providing clergy to conduct services. Much depended on local circumstance. In Germany, from a sample of 57 towns, two-thirds had a single parish church outside the walls. The church had predated the town as part of a rural parish and subsequent development had proceeded without anyone seeing the need for further churches. By contrast, London developed with over 100 churches by the end of the twelfth century, each one the centre of a small community, perhaps three and a half acres defined by a street or crossroads.[17] Groups of neighbours were sometimes responsible for building a church or, as in York, an enterprising priest, Roger, organised the building of Saint James outside Micklegate on the site of a wayside cross. This was true pastoral care or 'care of souls' as medieval documents had it, making sure each believer had access to a priest. Most communities varied between these extremes. In Lille, in the busy area of north-west France, parishes developed slowly; a fourth church added to three existing ones in 1144, two more in 1233 and a further one in 1273 to make seven in all. A similar pattern can be observed in the south, with Toulouse's single parish of 844 probably not being added to until the eleventh century, rising to five by 1200 and seven shortly afterwards.[18] Italy was different again. The *pieve* consisted of a mother church defined by its font or baptistery and churches serving local communities over a wide region. All tithes would be initially payable to the mother church. This gave Italian 'parishes' a dual focus with the local churches dependent on the income redistributed by the mother church. Only in the course of the twelfth century did parishes on the pattern of northern countries emerge.

Ironically, the reforms of the eleventh century may have hindered the Church's ability to respond flexibly to the growth in settlement which was occurring. One method of improving clerical morality was to organise the clergy of a town into a neo-monastic collegiate institution where discipline could be enforced, but these often created powerful vested interests which resisted all change, especially new parishes carved out of existing ones. Good examples can be cited from the areas which were to become notorious for heresy. In southern France at the end of the eleventh century the church of St Nazaire in Carcassonne was converted to a community of canons, clergy living under a rule, who took an iron grip on the ecclesiastical organisation of the town.[19] In nearby Cahors around the same time the canons were given full rights over the revenues due to all the town's churches.[20] In Italy where the average bishopric was smaller in area than in northern Europe there was a particular reluctance to devolve responsibility. The twelfth and thirteenth centuries saw the cathedral baptisteries at the height of their power. Even in quite small towns such as Monza near Milan the church of San Giovanni had rights over 21 chapels as well as another baptistery with seven more churches dependent on it in turn. In any case, for historical reasons over half the major churches in north Italy, including San Giovanni, already had a collegiate structure which owed nothing to the drive for moral reform among the clergy.[21]

For all its failings and variations the parish structure ensured that in return for their tithe the laity at least got access to a church within walking distance. In places they obtained rather more leverage; in Genoa, the city's government or *commune* became the agent of religious reform by prohibiting laymen from possessing tithes, while some Italian and German parishioners had the right to elect their priest, such as at Santa Maria Novella in Florence where a well-established arrangement was recognised in 1197.[22]

Whether appointed or elected the appeal of the Church depended on how parish clergy related to his parishioners. The chief function of the priest was to make five sacraments available to the laity: baptism, confession and penance, marriage, last rites and the Eucharist. Elemental was the Eucharist, the central moment of Mass. It was held weekly on Sunday afternoon and emphasised the miracle in which God through the agency of the ordained priest turned bread and wine into the flesh and blood of Christ. In one sense its popularity can be seen in the period 1000–1200 when the number of private Masses increased and more altars were erected. There was an element of demand from the laity in this as the number of Masses sponsored by lay fraternities and other patrons grew, often on behalf of departed relatives and colleagues. The boycott of Milanese churches, which was so effectively used by Ariald in the mid eleventh century, presupposed a healthy regular attendance and Abbot Suger's tales from Paris of women standing on their menfolk's heads to see Mass celebrated and relics presented suggests an excitement reminiscent of a rock concert. Away from big cities and special occasions the situation may have been different. A more reluctant laity is assumed in canon 21 of the Fourth Lateran Council of 1215 which commanded all Christians to take communion at least once a year. It may be that the laity liked the idea of Mass going on, but that numbers actually attending gradually declined over the twelfth century. As the sacred status of the priest was emphasised, the laity's role in the ceremony diminished. The wine was increasingly reserved for the priest so the laity had to be content with the bread alone. Legislation insisting on the Elevation of the Host in the early thirteenth century suggests that celebrants had neglected even to show people that the miracle was being performed.[23] When the laity did realise what was happening, the physics of the process fascinated them; just how large was the body of Christ?

A similar marginalisation of the laity occurred in other sacraments. Baptism had once been a great communal event with all the babies born in the intervening period attending twice-yearly ceremonies on the eves of Easter and Pentecost, often at the local cathedral or a dedicated baptistery. It was combined with first communion where the priest administered wine to the tiny mouth by soaking a leaf or his finger, but in the twelfth century all this disappeared as baptism became a more private event, performed within a few days of birth, excluding the first communion, and a monopoly of the parish priest.[24] No baptisteries were built in France after the eleventh century, instead throughout Europe the font inside the parish church became the centre of the ritual. It is easy to see the material benefits for local clergy. Conferring baptisms was one of the defining features of a parish and in areas where the parochial structure was still fluid, a record of administering baptism might increase the status of a church. Moreover, since an offering or payment to the priest was customary it made economic sense for an incumbent to spread baptisms throughout the year. Only in Italy did the twice-yearly ceremonies performed by the bishop at the baptistery persist well into the twelfth century, and beyond in some towns.[25]

The changes did have a spiritual dimension. Churchmen concerned with pastoral care in the early twelfth century worried about the fate of babies dying unbaptised and this in turn was due to a growing awareness that children were born in a state of sin.[26] Many parents did not share this concern and, faced with another trip to the priest, wondered instead how a newborn baby could possibly be sinful. Certainly there were plenty of preachers who denied the validity of infant baptism in the twelfth century and the controversy was still alive in the thirteenth when the holy woman Marie d'Oignies rammed home the official doctrine by driving out an unsuspected demon in a newborn baby before its baptism.[27]

After baptism the next life-changing sacrament was confirmation, carried out by the bishop of the diocese, when a child reached the 'age of discretion' (an elastic phrase which could vary from place to place), between seven and fourteen years. Its spiritual content was limited, with cases of bishops administering the sacrament from horseback.[28] This meant that the next meaningful contact with the priesthood after baptism might be on the deathbed.

A sick or dying parishioner may have received a visit from the local priest for a last communion, but this varied with locality and indeed the social status of the person afflicted. Again attention shifted from the dying person's participation and concentrated on what was done to them, namely the priest anointing the areas of the body of the five senses with blessed olive oil. After you died, however, your relatives were obliged to lay you to rest in the local cemetery. From the eleventh century the parish church assumed more significance here too, taking a much more active role in interment, closing down distant burial sites and insisting that the dead be buried in the churchyard or nearby cemetery. These were often near the centre of the settlement and became the venue for markets and other social activity. In death, as in life, social position was everything: very few got to lie undisturbed within the church compared with those whose bones were crammed into the overcrowded churchyard to be dug up a few years later and stored in the charnel house. Again there was room for dissent here and the Cathar heretics of the later twelfth century successfully ran their own graveyards.[29]

For all the organisational achievement of even this degree of pastoral care, to the modern observer it seems rather mechanistic and there is evidence that some contemporaries also sought a more personal contact with a spiritual figure, to provide reassurance of absolution for the inevitable messiness of relationships and to make a personal contribution to their chances of heaven. Private confession and penance was the relationship between believer and priest which was to change the face of organised religion, but as yet it was in its infancy. A delegation of preaching clergy from Laon who toured southern England in 1113, carrying their relics to raise money to rebuild their destroyed cathedral, excited great enthusiasm. Miraculous cures were recorded after supplicants had then confessed to their local parish priest.[30]

Balancing the lay desire to participate in religion was a dislike of regulation, best shown in attitudes to marriage. In the second half of the eleventh century reforming churchmen looked for a greater spiritual element in the solemnisation of marriage. This was an innovation because before this period it was by no means clear that marriage could be a sacrament; it was in effect licensed sex and viewed rather dimly by the avowedly celibate spiritual elite in monasteries and the higher ranks of the clergy. For those with property marriage was a means of transfer of wealth across generations and between families. The reformers insisted on marriages celebrated in public and within new bounds of 'affinity' which stretched to an improbable seventh degree of relation. Such changes made life awkward in that marriage to extended kin, which had been a good way to keep possessions within the family, was now technically an offence and secret marriages could no longer be simply denied. Lower down the social scale there was every incentive to keep unions informal and as private as possible. On manorial estates marriage already incurred secular dues for a peasant woman or a villein withdrawing from the holdings of a lord. The intervention of the Church could well be thought of as interference in a matter that people could organise perfectly well themselves. Yet from the late eleventh century liturgies emerged to enable couples to be married *in facie ecclesie* ('in the face of the Church'), quite literally, since the key part of the ceremony took place at the church door.[31]

The result was a compromise in that it was agreed that religion had some role in marriage which varied from place to place. In the south of

France the priest 'handed over' the bride to her husband. Marriage prayers from late eleventh-century northern Italy are clearly an ecclesiastical 'bolt on' to a ceremony which had been conducted elsewhere and could be completed in minutes. Whatever the limitations, marriage allowed participation in a sacrament at a time when the role of the laity was being reduced to that of witnesses, and that was a liberating aspect. Near the beginning of the ceremony and crucially important, the priest had to obtain the consent of both parties. Uniquely it was a sacrament of which the laity could partake, but the clergy could not.[32]

All these sacraments were charged for. This was not supposed to be the case. Given the sensitivity over simony, the payments were described as 'offerings' and legislation on tithes was carefully framed so that there was no implication that they were a fee for sacraments received.[33] In reality, there was a scale of fixed charges, not only for the sacraments, but also for 'churching' or purifying a woman after childbirth and blessing those about to set off on pilgrimage.[34] The Church wanted the respect of a much broader swathe of society for its newly reformed priesthood, indeed it depended on it for physical safety and financial security. To some extent the feeling was reciprocated by the laity, from the *nouveau riche* followers of Ariald in Milan to Glaber's devout peasant walking to matins.[35] But while the laity were mere witnesses, the quality and purity of the purveyor of the sacraments became vital. Priests were neither wholly *shaman* performing magic, nor learned profession-als. They stood somewhere between the two. By 1215 the Fourth Lateran Council compared them to doctors, but pharmacists would be a better analogy, since they made a living selling spiritual goods, reliant on other people's learning and their own standing in the community.

Part of the problem was that contemporary churchmen were always liable to be compared with those of the past. Just as the dead abbots literally underlay the deliberations in Cluny's chapter house, so lay be-lievers and clergy were surrounded with corpses and relics of the giants of the faith. The holy dead clung to the living, conferring through their often scattered bones, clothing and possessions, protection, health and a word in the right celestial ear for believers willing to display their devo-tion specifically to them. Often this was through pilgrimage; although reverence for relics went back to the beginning of Christianity, it was no surprise to find sacred journeys increasing in length and importance in the eleventh century. The most important Christian site, Jerusalem, became relatively accessible either overland through the Balkans and Anatolia or by sea across the eastern Mediterranean, and the journey was promoted by the Cluniac movement which set up hospices along the route and were even willing to make loans to would-be pilgrims. Large-scale expeditions began in the 1020s, but these were dwarfed in 1064–5 when some 7000 German men and women made their way to the Holy City. Motives for pilgrimage were varied; professional warriors sought to atone for their deadly way of life, the sick sought cures, the healthy a guarantee of salvation.[36]

Pilgrimage was an early way of allowing the laity to taste a little of the magic of monastic devotion. Comparative study of sacred journeys across several religions has given a three-stage model of the experience. First, like entering a monastery, there is a separation from the spatial, social and psychological *status quo*, then pilgrims move into marginal or liminal space, crossing a threshold to create a new set of social relations in which a religious experience can take place. Of course, the difference is that, unlike monks, pilgrims return to where they came from, but as changed, renewed human beings. From the words of Raymond of Saint Gilles already quoted, this does seem to be what happened on the armed pilgrimage of the First Crusade, allowing it to become a collective theophany, a manifestation of the divine.[37]

Jerusalem was not the only target for pilgrims. Rome was an un-rivalled store of relics in the West, including those of the apostles Peter and Paul, underpinning papal authority, but even its popularity was challenged by the development of the tomb of the apostle James at Compostella in remote Spanish Galicia. From the discovery of the bones in the ninth century the numbers making the journey grew until by the end of the eleventh century it was second only to Jerusalem itself. Significantly, lay people, in particular Pelayo, a quasi-monastic lay hermit, played a large part in the legend of the apostle's discovery. It is they who saw a new star and heard angelic voices pointing to the place's spiritual significance, the bishop was riven by doubt and had to fast before being allowed to make the discovery.[38]

The very routes to the site became sacred and the southern French shrines of Saint Gilles and Rocamadour rose on the back of the Compostella pilgrimage. The Church began to regulate the experience far more with Urban II issuing indulgences or remissions of penance due, if the penitent visited certain shrines. At Compostella more efficient exploitation of the relics defrayed the construction costs of a new cathedral started in 1122. To commemorate the pilgrim's journey, badges were produced in a distinctive shell shape; the earliest date from the late eleventh century. Their sale was not a Church monopoly as was to be the case at most shrines, but pilgrims did have to pay the custodians of the shrine to be allowed to touch the relic with their badge and thereby obtain a little of the saint's power to take away with them. As the twelfth century wore on it became necessary to obtain a pilgrimage badge from a shrine to gain the spiritual benefits desired or to prove that a penance had been completed.[39]

This process answered a deep spiritual need by the laity for tangible involvement in their own salvation. Unwittingly, however, the Church created a market in shrines and measurable criteria of their effectiveness for consumers. Remission of penance started to be issued by popes and local bishops for visits to sites so that potential pilgrims knew exactly what they were getting. Trade-offs were encouraged. William of Malmesbury in the 1120s suggested that two trips to St David's in Wales might be the equivalent of a visit to Rome, supposedly on the authority of Pope Calixtus II. By the second half of the century such was the trade in pilgrims' badges that these now acted like little relics themselves, able to cure third parties at home. Above all there was now furious competition between the shrines. Although antiquity was an essential feature of most pilgrimage venues, there was nothing to stop a site from being 'relaunched' by, for instance, rebuilding the actual church containing the relic and hiring a biographer to write a new life of the saint and the many miracles which had occurred before and after his death, as happened at Glasgow cathedral's shrine to the obscure Celtic Saint Kentigern (Mungo) at the end of the twelfth century.[40]

Glasgow's project was slick and successful. Far more revealing of an intelligent laity able to make spiritual choices for themselves was an early failure to develop a pilgrimage site at Limoges. On August 3, 1029 the relics of Saint Martial were due to be transferred from a nearby monastery to the cathedral where a new liturgy would be sung to celebrate the recent declaration that he had not just been a Christian missionary from Roman times, but one of the companions of Jesus Christ himself. The monks had carefully fostered the upgraded saint's cult with the laity; a new life stressed the saint's encouragement of lay participation in Mass and confession, his role in the construction of rural churches and his endowment of a hospital for the poor in Limoges.[41] In anticipation of visiting crowds from near and far, a new basilica had been built with an ambulatory around the shrine to allow the efficient circulation of pilgrims at the saint's tomb. But for various reasons the new cult failed to thrive. The monastic chronicler and publicist for the saint, Adhémar of Chabannes, recorded an embarrassing confrontation with Benedict of Chiusa, described as a 'travelling Lombard prior', who suggested that the cult of Saint Martial was in fact a vehicle for the monks' greed, to the noisy delight of his audience. Extensive research on the incident has suggested that politically volatile knights of the lower aristocracy may well have been present, stirred up by jealous clergy from neighbouring institutions. Moreover, Adhémar and his colleagues may have been naïve.

For all their promotion of the new cult, there may have been resentment of the new basilica and the ceremonial lavished on the saint on the part of those who had had to pay for it, namely monastic employees, tenants and priests in parishes where the monastery controlled the tithe. Not only did the charges of monastic greed seem justified, but the emphasis given to Martial's concern for the laity only underlined contemporary shortcomings in that department. Finally, relics had to deliver: where were the miraculous cures which were proof of sanctity and divine approval of the cult? Benedict's companion was a doctor (*medicus*) and was perhaps disproving the saint's cures by doing better himself. At any rate Benedict declared their saint a fake and predicted disaster for the town and its monastery. Adhémar himself blamed none of the above, but hinted at the responsibility of shadowy 'Manichaean' heretics whose presence in the area he had recorded the year before. Certainly this could be the reasoning of a man who preferred to blame foreign subversives rather than look for reasons for failure closer to home, but given that the people of Limoges had a framework to question the worship of relics so early and that we know so little of what shaped lay opinion in the early eleventh century, it could be that Adhémar was one of the first churchmen to stumble across the dualist heresy which was to sweep Europe a century later.[42]

Books about heresy often imply that orthodox religion was a failure. The Church of this period was not. Its crusades inspired thousands, its monasteries had to turn away men and women wanting to join. Most impressively of all the parish system meant that all Christendom was now a participant to some extent in organised religious life. But the reform movement had created criteria by which many aspects of the Church could be judged, provided that the laity were informed enough to make that judgement. From there it was a short step to making choices when offered a greater range of spiritual guides.

The preachers

In the last years of the eleventh century a series of influential figures began specifically to target their calls for reform to the laity, risking the fury of local churchmen. The region in which the majority of this activity took place was modern northern France and southern Belgium, areas already famous for their lucrative textile production and precocious urban growth. One Ramihrdus of Douai took up preaching against simony and clerical marriage in 1076 or 1077 and, when arrested, embarrassed the bishop at Cambrai by alleging that even he was up to his neck in simony and other avarice. Some of the bishops' officials took action and burnt Ramihrdus, thus provoking a papal inquiry. Within months the bishop had resigned, while Ramihrdus was still revered by local weavers 50 years later.[43]

Less well known is the case of Otfried de Watten, a notary who was religiously inspired to restore an abandoned church in the marsh and forest of Watten, north of Saint Omer in 1072. He too attracted lay followers, but felt he needed the protection of higher authority and made his way to Rome and Pope Gregory VII. He emerged with the right 'to preach the word of God everywhere' so that the memory of Gregory would be perpetuated. Moreover he also received 'the power of binding and loosing', that is of confessing sins, suggesting an interest in penance. Such a privilege enraged the clergy of his local diocese of Thérouanne, who forced him to flee to Ghent where he took refuge with the monastery of Saint Peter until his death in 1084.[44]

There were others, such as Arnould de Tiegem, reconciling fomenters of violence in Flanders and promoting the Church's new ideas on marriage, or Wéry, a monk of Ghent who converted five brigand knights and with them set up a community to provide hospitality for travellers. The achievements of these preachers were overshadowed first by the uneasy reputation of their patron, Pope Gregory, after his death in 1085 and then by the First Crusade, despite the fact that the great lay preacher who recruited in northern Europe, Peter the Hermit, came from Amiens and on his return from the East turned to similar themes preaching the virtues of peace and also of marriage, especially of prostitutes, to ensure their salvation.[45]

One figure who spanned the period between Gregorian reform and the growing diversity of preaching in the twelfth century was Aibert of Crespin. His father was from a modest knightly family and Aibert had a conversion experience when he met a *jongleur* telling the story of St Thibaut of Provins, a noble who entered a monastery earlier in the century. Aibert's career contained a striking change of direction; after almost 25 years in the strict Benedictine monastery of Crespin, around 1115 he retreated to the marshes of the Haine at Scopignies and began preaching and attracting followers. He became an ordained priest and sought and received permission from Pope Paschal II to hear confessions and reconcile penitents. Aibert became a sort of living relic, attracting pilgrims from distant parts. Not surprisingly, local clergy saw him as a threat to their livelihood. Although an inquiry by two abbots concluded favourably, Aibert still felt it necessary to gain a renewal of privileges from Innocent II in 1131, including a guarantee of safety for pilgrims to him on pain of excommunication. His popularity was a standing indictment of local ecclesiastical institutions, yet when he died in 1140 he left a thriving cult which was eventually to lead to his canonisation.[46]

What pushed preachers calling for reform into inviting the laity to consider radical alternatives to the established Church may have been high politics. In 1111 the reforming Pope Paschal II, under pressure from Emperor Henry V, agreed to allow the emperor, a lay ruler, to appoint or invest bishops throughout Germany. Inevitably it would be difficult to stop other rulers claiming the same right and almost 30 years of struggle by reforming churchmen within the Church would be lost. Lay rulers could once again regard ecclesiastical posts as their personal patronage, tantamount to legalised simony. Such a settlement may well have enraged one Tanchelm, an obscure priest or possibly monk who had moved to Antwerp on the river Scheldt after beginning his career preaching in the salty marshes of Zeeland. Tanchelm had been part of a delegation to Rome which unsuccessfully petitioned Pope Paschal to have the ecclesiastical jurisdiction of the town transferred from the imperial diocese of Utrecht to Tournai or Thérouanne in the county of Flanders, whose ruler was more sympathetic to reform. Shortly afterwards the first stories of Tanchelm's preaching began to circulate.[47]

The most important account of his work is a poisonously hostile letter from the enraged canons of Utrecht to the archbishop of Cologne, seizing the opportunity to discredit those who had wished to transfer the town. It describes lurid orgies and borrows material from the sixth-century writer Gregory of Tours, but even so, the appeal of Tanchelm was clear. He not only filled a vacuum in pastoral care, but gave a role for the laity in his movement. Most of all he knew how to make preaching an event; dressed like royalty and with followers carrying swords and banners he addressed huge audiences from rooftops or in fields. He attacked all secular clergy from the pope downwards, reserving especial scorn for churches and priests whose corruption rendered their sacraments worthless. Tanchelm claimed to be filled with the Holy Spirit like Christ himself, and perhaps distributed some sort of sacrament to be drunk at these assemblies, contemptuously dismissed by his enemies as his bathwater.

Tanchelm courted popular appeal by advocating the non-payment of tithes, but he was not proposing poverty for the Church, merely that it should be worthy of the wealth given to it. In a typically outrageous gesture Tanchelm publicly betrothed himself to a statue of the Virgin Mary, called upon his audience to pay the expenses of the betrothal feast and marriage and then had men and women competing as to which sex could contribute the most. Behind the scenes rather more regular means of support were organised. One of his followers, a former priest, succeeded in driving out the clerics serving Antwerp's single church and usurped the tithes. Tanchelm then received influential lay help when a blacksmith organised a fraternity or guild among twelve townsmen and one woman, supposedly echoing Christ's disciples and Mary Magdalene. Tanchelm appears as a slightly old-fashioned figure with his sumptuous worship perhaps reminiscent of the riches of a Cluniac monastery. His modest guild can have given only limited political protection and he also appeared to have made enemies. While he remained in the town he was safe and for three years he dominated Antwerp's religious life, then an ill-advised attempt to spread his message into the surrounding country-side ended with a fatal blow to the head from a priest while travelling by boat.[48]

So flamboyant a character was not easily forgotten and there were stories of a persistent cult, but Tanchelm was a one-off. Nevertheless, the issues he raised were echoed in the teaching of an equally charismatic yet more thoughtful preacher who emerged a little later in Le Mans, some hundred miles south-west of Paris. Henry of Le Mans, also known by historians as Henry of Lausanne and Henry the Monk, was in appearance the archetype heretic. The Le Mans chronicler described a tall young man with unkempt beard and cropped hair who dressed austerely and even in mid-winter strode around the town barefoot. When Henry addressed a crowd even his detractors had to concede he was remarkably fluent; for his admirers he could move a heart of stone to repentance. Henry's origins are even more mysterious than Tanchelm's, perhaps a monk or a minor cleric, and like him he emerged from Paschal's attempt to settle the dispute over investitures. In 1116 Bishop Hildebert of Lavardin, himself a noted reformer and preacher, left for a gathering of clergy in Rome to challenge Paschal's agreement, but before he went he licensed Henry to preach in the town.[49]

In the bishop's absence Henry turned on clerical corruption, while still able to gather enough clerics around him to set up a stage for himself. The Le Mans chronicler was hostile and contemptuously reported that he appealed to matrons and adolescent boys. Taken in conjunction with his supporters among the clergy who wept openly at his pronouncements this was a powerful mix of energy and influence. Henry attempted a radical programme of pastoral care for Le Mans, combining social conservatism with an attempt to bring the socially excluded back into the community. From his standpoint of austerity he denounced the materialism of the marriage dowry, declaring that the naked should marry the naked, the sick should marry the sick and the poor should marry the poor. There is the implication that people should not marry for social status, as was so common in burgeoning commercial towns like Le Mans in the early twelfth century. Discontented husbands and urban clergy were a prime market for prostitutes and Henry then turned his attention to this social problem which was relatively new in the provincial towns of northern Europe. At a great ceremony, pointedly held outside the town's prominent monastery, he persuaded street women to cast aside their old clothes and repent while he called for young men to come forward and marry them. Each bride received sufficient dowry to buy a modest set of new clothes with money Henry had gathered from his followers. Despite this element of planning, the scheme was short-lived; with great satisfaction the chronicler tells us that the men soon left their 'wives' destitute and they returned to their former lives or worse.

Dangerous forces had been unleashed; Henry's highlighting of clerical corruption almost led to a massacre of clergy on two occasions and was only prevented by the intervention of the local secular ruler, Fulk V, Count of Anjou. His protection also enabled a sentence of excommunication to be read out in Henry's presence. When Hildebert finally returned from Rome, there was initial resistance to his entry by the townspeople who claimed that Henry was now their spiritual leader. Subtler tactics were called for. Rumours of amorous liaisons shook Henry's reputation and after a fire in the suburbs, Hildebert felt sufficiently strong to enter the city and bring Henry to debate. When the latter claimed to be a deacon, but was unable to say the divine office, Hildebert regained control. Even so it was a measure of Henry's popularity that Hildebert moved cautiously and did nothing more severe than expel him from the diocese. There are no records of any measures against his followers, although some were publicly forgiven.[50]

Apart from an isolated case at Ivoy in Ardennes, there were no further cases of heresy recorded for almost 15 years.[51] Both Henry of Le Mans and another popular preacher, Peter of Bruys, may have been active during this period, but if so nobody considered them worth arresting or recording. It is tempting to ascribe the decline in accusations of heresy to the lowering of tension which followed the Concordat of Worms in 1122, a compromise which satisfied most imperialists and also reunited the reformers. Bishops and abbots were to be canonically elected and invested with the ring and staff of authority from the pope, but the candidate was to do homage for feudal lands to the emperor, who was also permitted to be present at the election. As with most political compromises it was not altogether clear how much had been given up until the system was seen in operation, so the reformers may not at first have realised the extent to which imperial influence over ecclesiastical appointments was to persist.

In the changed atmosphere there were real achievements. The Church structure in imperial towns could now be modernised and, as in

Tanchelm's day, the canons of Antwerp were evicted from their church, this time to build a second one to cater for the town's growing population. Norbert of Xanten, a former cathedral canon from the Rhineland who had taken up a life of poverty and preaching, was invited to minister to the town. Heresy was to some extent in the eye of the beholder and a close watch was kept on Norbert and his followers.[52]

Many reformers turned back to the traditional fountain of purity within the Church, monasticism, in particular the newly formed Cistercian order and its leader Bernard of Clairvaux. For the last time monks and the secluded life they offered became the centre of western Europe's spiritual experience.

This did not mean that there were not more radical opinions out there in the loosely policed world of the early twelfth century, or that the laity were not listening to them, only that there was little political mileage in embarrassing superiors by reporting them. This changed after 1130 when a disputed papal election opened up a conflict between the rival popes Innocent II and Anacletus II. Once again the activities of Henry came under scrutiny. He had moved into southern France to continue his preaching, an area where there was little effective secular or ecclesiastical authority. He was also now being taken more seriously. The source which survives is an account by one 'William the monk', of a possibly fictitious debate between himself and Henry around 1132–3. While the tone is still hostile, Henry's beliefs are reported in some detail.

From William's document it would now appear that Henry had put his doctrines into writing and broadened his appeal, although William still scornfully refers to him preaching in fields and meadows. Henry continued to denounce priests unworthy to confer the body of Christ, the Church's interference in marriage and infants unnecessarily baptised. But there were also new teachings such as that there was no need for churches of stone or wood, for bishops or priests to have benefices or even for prayers for the dead. Some of these points left William struggling to find convincing replies. He had no answer to why bishops had to have the paraphernalia of their rank, the ring, mitre and pastoral staff, except to say that they are sanctioned by 'authority'. Likewise the best defence he could make of bishops' wealth is that early Christians gave up their possessions by laying them at the feet of the apostles. Rather feebly he also added that after all the sin of avarice for bishops is committed not in possessing, but in wanting to possess. There is an almost audible shudder when he considers the prospect of raving old men and wretched peasants preaching.[53]

Shortly after William's attack appeared Henry was arrested and ordered to appear before the Church's Council of Pisa in 1135. Even now there was no formal condemnation and Henry was still seen as a possible asset. Dominated by monks, the Council ordered monastic confinement to curtail Henry's excesses, but the monastery was the Cistercian head-quarters at Clairvaux and Henry was enrolled as a Cistercian monk armed with letters from St Bernard, no less. The attempt at rehabilita-tion failed and Henry did not stay long, but once again no further action was taken for almost a decade.

Henry's career to date showed the change in attitudes to religion over the decades between the 1070s and 1130s. The reformers' interest in regulating the clergy's sexual and financial activity had broadened to become a far wider question of lifestyles within the Church. Above all they had involved the laity and raised expectations. Preaching, pilgrim-age and the growth of parishes had all opened minds as to the sheer diversity of forms of religion. The remainder of the twelfth century was to see the growth of that critical faculty and in some areas the adoption of alternatives to orthodoxy.

chapter 2

THE NEW ECONOMY: MARKETS, TROUBADOURS, UNIVERSITIES AND HERETICS

T he middle ages have a largely undeserved reputation for economic stagnation. In the twelfth century the European economy grew steadily and brought about rapid change in every aspect of society. For lay consumers, even of quite modest means, there were unprecedented choices available as a result of economic prosperity. Knights, business-men and the new breed of secular bureaucrats could afford better clothes and food than previous generations. Moreover, even in provincial towns a far wider range of these things were available to them through a growing number of fairs and markets. Less tangible goods were also on offer; a market in entertainment emerged through itinerant troubadours and – not least – in ideas from the fledgling universities. Songs and knowledge were also better distributed. The troubadours' declarations of love were made in the Provençal language of southern France, but understood and celebrated throughout Europe. The former students of Bologna and Paris took up posts in the Church and secular government throughout Christendom. The implications for the spread of heresy are obvious: new ideas were less suspected, new faces less unwelcome. In the twelfth century people started to make spiritual choices because they already had to make choices in other aspects of their lives.

The economic revival

I Rich and Poor
It is still uncertain what triggered the long-term economic growth which began around 1000: viable European settlements in Greenland and a population of 80,000 in Iceland suggest a warmer climate and longer growing season in northern Europe.[1] Although hardly a time of peace there were no devastating interventions such as those of the Vikings, Magyars or Saracens. The physical difficulty of a shortage of cash as a means of exchange was eased by discoveries of silver, first in the Harz

mountains at the end of the tenth century and then at Freiberg in the 1170s.[2] What may have been underestimated in older models of the medieval economy was the degree of commercialisation in society. Especially in the more fertile areas of Europe, cities could be fed from a comparatively small proportion of the area of the surrounding countryside, allowing spare capacity for growth and fierce price competition among producers.[3] The number of towns in Europe grew from just over 100 at the beginning of the tenth century to nearer 5000 by 1300.[4] The character of this urban expansion was just as important. Towns may have contained as much as 20 per cent of the medieval population in England, far more in medieval Italy where town:country ratios of 5:7, such as in the region of Bologna, were not unusual in the later thirteenth century. These figures are characteristic of developed societies today, but the towns themselves more resembled the crowded settlements of the developing world. Most people, rich or poor, had more than one occupation. Dating from the early twelfth century, the much quoted Charter of Lorris, a small town near Orléans, assumed that most of the inhabitants would be involved in agriculture as well as trade and also insisted on the citizens helping to take the king's wine to Orleans once a year.[5] In larger towns underemployment was a persistent problem with poorer men and women working as servants or labourers on a casual basis and getting by as best they could for the rest of the time with begging, petty theft or prostitution.[6] Nevertheless, townspeople ate better than those in the country. Far more of the bread was white, the animals slaughtered were younger, fresh fruit was more available and more ale and wine was consumed. Fear of disorder meant that low quality food and remnants were often made available cheaply to the poor.[7]

The experience of the consumer in medieval Europe is still open to question. What is certain is that much consumption was automatically conspicuous. Clothes for formal occasions were brightly coloured and as expensive as possible. Feasts were an important affirmation of social status and tended to the exotic. To satisfy these tastes a rather better network for distribution existed than was once thought. Recent evidence from England suggests that the quality of roads and the number of bridges has been underestimated. It would be surprising if this were not also true in Europe, particularly where there had been an extensive transport network under the Romans.[8] Moreover, there was a crucially important institution bringing consumers and retailers of long and short distance to trade together, the fair. It not only made available a greater range of goods, but allowed consumers to deal direct with merchants. Prices often undercut those of established businesses in the nearest big city. Saint-Gilles in southern France was far from a premier port in international trade, but at its fair in early September around the saint's feast day, Italian merchants mingled with pilgrims and native inhabitants from town and country. On sale was local produce such as wine, corn, salt and fish as well as manufactured woollen cloth and imported silks and perfumes. Most important of all was the number of 'spices' available, a category broad enough to include not only vital cookery ingredients such as pepper and ginger, dried fruit (currants, figs and dates), cinnamon and cardamon, but also dyestuffs and rare textiles such as Calabrian cotton and indigo and even pharmaceuticals such as quicksilver and the bright clear red resin known as 'dragon's blood'.[9] Spices should not be thought of as dominating medieval food, more usually flavourings were supplied by domestically produced garlic, onions, mustard or vinegar, but, as today, they added something exciting for special meals. In this role they were used by a broader cross-section of society, although many could only afford occasional small quantities.[10]

Finally, money itself had become a commodity. The regularity of fairs, particularly the major cloth fairs, enabled gradually more sophisticated credit arrangements to evolve. For large amounts of cash Jewish moneylenders were available, but it seems certain that they were only the top of the pyramid, at the base of which were Christian moneylenders advancing smaller sums to local clients. Lending money at interest, or usury as it was disparagingly termed, was strictly illegal according to canon law and its practitioners were vulnerable to popular resentment, however the scale of resentment only showed how much they were used and the medieval economy would not have functioned without them.

In the years after 1100, people of all ranks in society had experience of being consumers and making recognisable consumer choices. This is not to say that life was easy: bad harvests and warfare could still spell disaster and few had much cash to spare, but if you did have money or your credit was good there were ways to spend it. Much depended on where in Europe you lived.

II Region

The engine of economic growth came from what is still the richest area in Europe, known to marketing analysts as the 'big banana', running from London and the south-east of England, through northern France and the Low Countries, sweeping through Burgundy and western Germany, Switzerland and north Italy, petering out just north of Rome.[11] Even within this area, prosperity was patchy, leading to boom town growth in the good years and catastrophic recessions in the bad. And prosperity brought its problems: its distribution was not even, so the poor, particularly in the fast-growing towns, became more noticeable.

There were strains on well-to-do society also. Riches could come quickly, children made wealthier than their parents' dreams, and yet the newly enriched often found themselves despised by their social superiors and hated by those they had left behind. Urban attempts at self-government or 'communes' in the early twelfth century were often undermined by alliances between former aristocratic rulers, traders of modest means and the poor. Such envy and social tension was expressed even more crudely in the attacks on Jewish moneylenders which began in the late eleventh century. Insidiously, there arose a mistrust of wealth itself, as being ill-gotten gains. In the second decade of the twelfth century the preacher Henry of Le Mans avoided the golden robes worn by his contemporary Tanchelm in Antwerp and this may be one reason why his career of over 30 years contrasts with Tanchelm's sudden and violent death.

Despite fragmentary evidence, certain dates stand out in the fitful evolution of the institutions of European trade. Although there are references to fairs dating back to Carolingian times, the great cloth fairs of Champagne, east of Paris, only become clearly visible around 1114, under the control of the counts of Champagne and taking advantage of the renewed prosperity of the Flemish cloth industry. The fair founded between 1109 and 1112 at nearby Saint Denis outside Paris, looks like an attempt on the part of the abbey and Louis VI of France to cash in on the expanding trade. Yet it was only in 1148 that money-changers from Vézelay were mentioned at the fair at Provins, and 1172 when merchants from Milan are first recorded going to the fairs to buy wool and cloth.

The appearance of the Milanese showed that the economy in southern Europe was also developing. Merchants may have gone from Asti into northern France as early as 1074, but Italian businessmen mainly concentrated on the Mediterranean, achieving notable expansion into the Byzantine Empire. The Venetian presence in Constantinople was established by preferential tariff rates in 1092, the Pisans in 1111 and the Genoese in 1155. By the first half of the twelfth century all three cities also had direct links to the Middle East through Egypt and the crusader ports.[12] The economic expansion of north Italy was not confined to coastal cities. Milan emerged as a major trading city at the confluence of routes over the Alps, also manufacturing textiles and metalwork. The cities along the Po, such as Cremona, Piacenza, Pavia and Verona became centres of cloth and money-changing.

In the second half of the twelfth century, these two dynamic areas of expansion came together. Overland trade between north and south had traditionally gone through the Alps via the Great or Little Saint Bernard passes, developed since Roman times. But, around 1150, the Mont Cenis pass started to become a popular trade route because it offered a quicker road from Italy to Lyon and access to the Rhône-Saône river systems, which in turn led to the fairs of Champagne. In addition, the opening of the Simplon and Saint Gotthard passes around 1235 created a fast overland route between Italy and western Germany.[13] The competition between routes and passes was keen. Carters and boatmen in France lowered prices to respond to the opening up of the Saint Gotthard and at one stage in 1318 the del Bene company of Florence were paying less per mile to transport their cloth overland from Paris to Marseille than they were to transport it from Marseille to Pisa by sea. Routes were consciously promoted and the Church had a role to play in this. Bishop Guido of Coira (1096–1122) founded a hospice high on the Septimer pass, with the support of local communities, as much to attract travellers as for any religious purpose.[14]

Outside these favoured areas development was far more patchy. The area of southern France or Languedoc which was to become the heartland of the Cathar movement saw contrasts. It had natural advantages such as routes between the Mediterranean and the Atlantic and a road system inherited from the Romans, but expansion in economic activity in the first half of the twelfth century was at first confined to the coast. Trade in the area was dominated by the fleets of the Genoese and Pisans who operated through ports such as Montpellier and Narbonne. The Jewish traveller, Benjamin of Tudela, described on a visit to Montpellier how, in 1165:

> People of all nations are found there doing business through the medium of the Genoese and Pisans.[15]

The southern French ports were to find the opportunity to extend their activities when open warfare broke out between the Italian rivals in the mid 1160s. Both cities looked for support and local rulers took full advantage. Occasionally this could backfire as in 1166 when the fair of Saint-Gilles was disrupted by a pitched battle in the harbour between the Pisan and Genoese fleets, but there were also important concessions gained. The southern French towns were able to establish formal relations with both and a series of trade agreements allowed their ships a role in western Mediterranean trade. On the whole the Genoese were the dominant power and they strictly limited the spheres of activity: an agreement of 1166 stated that only one ship a year of bona fide pilgrims was to leave from Narbonne to the Holy Land and, in theory at least, all men and goods entering Narbonne had to have the permission of the Genoese consuls.[16] The growth of heresy in Languedoc and north Italy took place against a background of increasing economic links between the two regions.

The nature of the exchange was that southern France imported Italian manufactured goods such as cloth, iron and steel products and spices, while exporting bulky lower value produce such as grain, wine, wool and olive oil.[17] Some from Languedoc took advantage of the opportunities in Italy. In the 1180s notarial records first document the presence of southern French traders based in Genoa. Some were relatively modest men like Peire de Tolosa, who was in business with a Genoese merchant to trade in Sicily and then import goods into Genoa, with the Italian putting up most of the capital and Peire doing the travelling. The will of Arnaud de Narbonne suggests greater prosperity. He donated money to a number of Genoese religious institutions as well as to members of his family from southern France. He also arranged for his Saracen maid or slave to be freed on his death. Such servants were expensive so this was the generosity of a wealthy man.[18]

In the southern French interior growth was slower. Toulouse was the only major inland town functioning as a financial centre as well as making and dyeing basic quality cloth for home consumption and export to the Iberian peninsula, but it was only the size of a middle-ranking Italian town. For most of the twelfth century the counts of Toulouse chose to spend their time and take their title from the eastern end of their possessions at Saint-Gilles. However, in the second half of the twelfth century a number of fairs appeared in the region, including two at Carcassonne, totalling over three weeks of trading.[19] Recognition and representation for the business community gradually spread inland in conscious imitation of the custom in Italy, but it came later and achieved less. The first evidence that southern French towns wanted communal self-government comes from Montpellier in the 1140s. By the 1170s Toulouse had also elected consuls, although autonomy was only achieved in the 1190s. Even then subsequent attempts by the city to gain control of the surrounding countryside to form a *contado* or city-state on the Italian model were unsuccessful. The minor nobles of the region were stubborn defenders of their rights and even small villages had their own ambitions for autonomy.[20]

As an integral part of society, the Church was in a position to encourage or inhibit economic expansion. Not only were fairs closely linked to religious festivals, such as the one at Saint-Gilles, but local ecclesiastical institutions were major stakeholders. Typical was the fair at Lodève, inland from Montpellier, where the rents of traders were shared between the bishop, the chapter and various local nobles. One bishop of Lodève was killed in the course of a dispute with the 'consuls' of the town in the early years of the thirteenth century, showing how dangerous it was to become unpopular with a community dependent on trade and looking for greater self-determination.[21]

The violent action against the region that was undertaken by the Albigensian crusade between 1209 and 1230 did not destroy its prosperity. Although Toulouse, Carcassonne and Avignon suffered badly at different stages of the war, all three towns maintained their prominence in the thirteenth century. In the years 1230 to 1250 more than 400 new towns or *bastides* were founded and, though not all of them were successful, they helped to stimulate trade and urban society. Further fairs were founded, particularly in the small towns in the hinterland of Narbonne and Montpellier. Only towards the end of the century did the southern French economy begin to fail, hamstrung by high taxation from the French crown and clumsy attempts to divert trade through the new royal port of Aigues Mortes.[22]

III The Church

As with the laity, many individuals in the Church found choices and opportunities in the new economic wealth, but many of the institutional components found it less easy to adapt. The cathedrals of the period are often taken as monuments to an age of faith, but it is worth remembering that traditionally bishops had been rich men in their own right, from prominent families with private lands. Moreover, their position within towns meant that they also had considerable secular rights; cathedral construction may indicate an ability to extract income and labour rather than popular enthusiasm.[23] Nevertheless, bishops were the class within the Church to whom many looked for reform. With characteristic economic astuteness, the eleventh-century reformers Peter Damian and Fulbert of Chartres both called upon the Church to alienate treasures to buy land to secure independence from lay interference, but like much of the medieval aristocracy, bishops were in a difficult position since their wealth was difficult to mobilise in any liquid form. Until the major Italian mints started to produce coinage from the 1120s, reforming churchmen were often reduced to using gold and silver religious objects, books furs, cloths and even swords to purchase land. When wealth did increase, and money became more readily available, rather than investing in the pastoral care provided by the episcopacy, most influential donors still followed the advice (given by Fulbert of Chartres a century before) to donate to communities living under a rule; 'purify those who are poor, namely monks and regular canons'.[24]

Were they really poor? Up to a point: Guibert of Nogent, writing around 1115, reveals both how poverty was embraced and also misunderstood in his account of the foundation of the Carthusians. Bruno, an administrator and academic in the church at Reims, leaves the city, disgusted at the conduct of the new archbishop. Deep in the mountains near Grenoble in 1084 he founds a community of monks which became the mother house of the Carthusian order. Writing 40 years later, Guibert is keen to show that they have maintained their founder's wish to renounce the world. He reports that the count of Nevers had made a gift to the monks of silver vessels, which the monks promptly returned, thereby shaming the count into giving the no less valuable gift of 'a large quantity of hides and parchment'. Guibert admits that the Carthusians are accumulating 'a very rich library'. Peter the Venerable noted that much of the Carthusians' manual work was in book production and wrote to the monastery at La Chartreuse for a new copy of the letters of Saint Augustine since the greater part of Cluny's own had been eaten by a bear. Peter quietly 'paid' for this with some books from Cluny's library and a crucifix with the image of Christ. As has been seen, both books and ornaments could be used as currency, although perhaps there was no need to use them as such since Guibert also says that the fields were little cultivated and that the monks bought in produce from the profits from their sheep fleeces. With 20 lay brothers at the bottom of the hill, as well as servants who tended to the estate, Guibert's account of poverty starts to look like a story of privilege.

As for the other order mentioned in the story, the monks of Cluny had never pretended to be poor in a personal sense. They performed a conscientious round of services amid great opulence, as this was what many of their patrons wanted. They found themselves in difficulty as spiritual fashions changed. With more prosperity in society in general Cluny's conspicuous riches looked much like those of the less reputable *nouveau riche* individuals and institutions. When Peter tried to introduce a more austere regime in 1122, he provoked a violent division among the monks. Guibert felt that monastic life no longer commanded the prestige it once did among the laity. He grumbled that whereas nobles and their wives gave generously of their property and set up ecclesiastical endowments a generation before, their sons now withdrew such gifts or demanded payment for their renewal.[25]

In the short term Guibert was wrong and traditional monasticism was to have a last flowering of spiritual excitement. A small group of monks in Burgundy who had withdrawn from the world into a life of poverty in 1098 were about to be saved from extinction by the remarkable leadership of Bernard of Clairvaux who entered their house at Cîteaux in 1112. Clothed in their white habits, these Cistercian monks attempted a much stricter interpretation of the ancient monastic rule of Saint Benedict. Bernard's withering attack on the wealth of Cluny is well known. He criticised the comfortable clothing and rich food within its cloister, and yet Bernard was also to provide a critique of the isolation and solitary life which the Cistercians craved. A nun of the convent in the prosperous Champagne town of Troyes had proposed 'to fly riches, crowded towns and delicate meats' to live in the 'desert' with a few others or possibly alone, much as the early Cistercians had done. Bernard was horrified:

> For anyone wishing to lead a bad life the desert supplies ample opportunity. The woods afford cover and solitude assures silence. No one can censure the evil no one sees.[26]

Certainly there were others within the Church that had their doubts about the Cistercian movement. It made little progress in Italy until the visit of Bernard himself in 1133. In Milan, the resentment was partly due to the papal schism, in which the city favoured Anacletus II, whereas Bernard was promoting his candidate, Innocent II.

There are also hints that economic factors were at work to undermine the Cistercians. Bernard's attentions had resulted in the reconciliation of Milan with Innocent and the foundation of the Chiaravalle monastery in the marshy ground to the south of the city in the summer of 1135. But, even by September, there were rumours that the loyalty of Milan and the nearby town of Cremona was wavering. Bernard fulminated:

> The opposition of Cremona has hardened, their prosperity is their undoing; the Milanese have become arrogant, their over-weaning self-confidence deceives them.[27]

The archbishop of Milan returned the compliment by describing the monks in their white and grey capes as 'heretics'. This attitude was not just blind conservatism or hypocrisy, but the working out of a different tradition of reform. Since the era of Gregory VII the Milanese Church had gained an independence from lay interference and the corrupting sin of simony by becoming a rich and powerful force in its own right. The older cardinals who supported Anacletus in the 1130s were the survivors of this vision of reform. But younger reformers like Bernard despised wealth. Instead they took a more sophisticated view of the laity, placing more emphasis on an austere lifestyle to gain their respect. There was enough common ground between Bernard and the ragged preacher Henry of Le Mans for the latter to be offered a place at Clairvaux when he was prosecuted in 1135. Significantly he did not stay long.[28]

By then the Cistercians were being criticised for their cupidity. In 1159 despite needing the monks' support in another disputed election, enough complaints had reached Pope Alexander III for him to write two admonishing letters to the order. The most eloquent criticism which survives comes from Walter Map, a secular clerk towards the end of the century, who had little time for the 'white monks'. With an audience of

Table 2.1 Percentage of land owned by the Church

	1076–1100	1101–25	1126–50	1151–75	1176–1200
Southern France	29.7	19.5	15.6	10.1	11.7
Italy	23.5	18.6	18.2	14.6	14.9
'European' average	23	19	18	14	14

fellow clerical bureaucrats in the English royal court, Map was snide and insinuating on a wide range of issues. He accused the Cistercians of eating chicken and bacon, of destroying churches and razing villages to create solitude for their houses. There were crude hints about homosexual practices, but above all Map singled out their greed. According to him, the Cistercians refused to possess churches, but were willing to accept rights of presentation from a patron, insert their own vicar and then collect an annual pension from him. The meanness of the Cistercians' charity was contrasted with their lavish entertainment of potential benefactors. The monks would try any means to gain possession of land they coveted, up to and including murder. He summarised the Cistercian philosophy as: 'No man can serve God without Mammon.'[29]

Map's perceptions may have been given added bitterness by the fact that the Church as a whole was probably becoming poorer in the twelfth century. Research dating back to the 1960s attempted to calculate the percentage of Church property using the evidence of neighbours recorded in charters dealing with the transfer of lands. While too much reliance cannot be placed on the absolute figures, the trend is clear enough: Church lands declined over the course of the twelfth century, particularly in southern France and, to a lesser extent, in Italy (see Table 2.1).[30]

It is possible that since the total amount of cultivated land was increasing, the figures only show that the Church was not attracting new donations rather than actually losing lands. It may also be that in Italy in particular, the Church was realising assets through the sale of land in the new economy, but it is difficult to escape the conclusion that, especially in southern France, land was simply being seized. Anecdotal evidence hints at a crisis. There is the famous story that Fulk of Marseille, the newly appointed bishop of Toulouse, found only 96 *sous* in his treasury and had to water his four mules at the well in his house for fear of creditors seizing them if they were taken down to the river. It is substantiated by the history of bitter litigation with vassals and the loss of tithes to nobles and monasteries which stretched back over the previous half-century.[31] A similar picture is painted of the diocese of Orvieto in the early thirteenth century. In 1228 the new bishop took inventory of a lame mule, an old set of vestments, two chests, some sacks of grain and nine wine casks, seven of which were empty. The public face of this poverty was humiliating, with so much grass growing in the cathedral that it resembled a meadow. In this case, the despoilers of the bishop's revenues were the cathedral canons, and much of the wealth ended up in the hands of the prominent local families to whom they were related.[32] Of course for every case like Toulouse or Orvieto there was the ostentatious wealth of an archbishop of Lyon or Milan, but this variation may have only made matters worse. A study of the energetic bishops of Agde and Maguelone (Montpellier) reveals substantial investments in fortified churches in the twelfth century, despite the practice being forbidden at the Third Lateran Council of 1179.[33] While it is almost too easy to say that the Church in southern France felt itself literally under siege from a rapacious local nobility, priorities had definitely become very muddled.

One way in which the flow of property could be redressed was by charity from the laity. In Genoa bequests show changes in lay tastes and also growing generosity. As can be seen in Figure 2.1, the major increases went to social charity and the Franciscan and Dominican friars when they arrived. Within the broad category of 'social charity', donations for the upkeep of the poor rose substantially from 3.3 per cent of all bequests to 15.4 per cent in the period 1227–53. The major losers were the monasteries and city churches, particularly as they would also have been responsible for most of the Masses for the dead and those said on the anniversary of the testator's death, the revenue from which was also declining. It should be noted that their problems would have been compounded by a period of inflation which would have increased their expenses in the decades either side of 1200. Above all, the Genoese evidence shows how discerning lay donors had become. They abandoned age-old institutions to give money to new causes in accordance with social need and their own consciences and were prepared to switch again to the more directly spiritual pastoral care provided by the friars.

A similar situation was to be found in Toulouse: the proliferation of religious foundations before and after the troubled years of the Albigensian Crusade show how the Church was effectively fragmenting into competing strands. As in Genoa, social charity increased in the early thirteenth century and of the town's 22 leper houses and hospitals recorded in 1250, no less than eleven were founded in the latter twelfth century and the first decade or so of the thirteenth. The result was that here, too, the parish clergy lost out: a complaint from around 1200 blamed the decline in offerings received by parish priests on feast days as much on the building of new churches as on the abundance of heretics in the town. Around 50 years later priests were allegedly putting pressure on

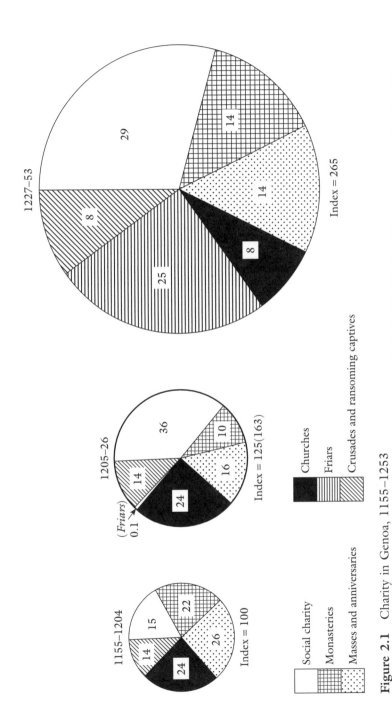

Figure 2.1 Charity in Genoa, 1155–1253

Source: S. Epstein, *Genoa and the Genoese, 958–1528* (North Carolina, 1996), 92, 117, 130. Epstein's figures are drawn from 'small, but representative' samples of wills. 'Social charity' includes donations to hospitals, lepers and paupers and money given for the maintenance of bridges and to provide dowries for poor women. The figures for crusades and the ransoming of captives reflect Genoa's links with the crusades and Muslim regions. The index is taken from Epstein's totals of money bequeathed and the figure in parentheses includes one large and uncharacteristic donation which has been left out of the percentage calculations.

parishioners into making offerings by, for example, refusing to remarry a widower until he had made an offering on behalf of his dead wife. By then the laity had a large variety of religious institutions competing for their favour. Pastoral care probably improved in Toulouse in this period, but was largely unregulated, so movements within the Church took their places in the spiritual marketplace alongside the heretical.[34]

The Troubadours and vernacular culture

The rise of troubadour culture not only illustrates that consumer choice could now be applied to more abstract concepts like entertainment, but also offers a parallel in how a cultural trend might be disseminated across Europe. This is all the more striking because northern Italy and southern France where the troubadours found most popular favour were also the regions synonymous with heresy.

One of the fruits of the economic expansion of the twelfth century was an increasingly elaborate court culture and the growth of entertainment in the vernacular for the court's inhabitants. Guilhem IX, Duke of Aquitaine (1071–127), started to compose songs in his native Provençal, the distinctive language of southern France. In doing so he became the first recorded troubadour. Despite the fact that Guilhem was one of Europe's foremost nobles and that this class continued to compose, the troubadour tradition gradually became professionalised. Often writing both words and melodies, the poets not only produced love songs (*cansos*), but also coruscating commentaries on contemporary mores (*sirventes*).

The origin of this material has been much debated. It owed something to the Latin culture of the Church and the increasing interest in classical literature, and perhaps more to the Hispano-Arabic love poetry on the other side of the Pyrenees. The movement was slow to catch on; just five troubadours are known to have been active before 1150 and even after then reliance on noble patrons limited numbers at the top of the profession. But troubadours became fashionable far beyond southern France and crossed linguistic divides to reach England and Germany, as well as northern France. The trade was organised, very approximately, into the *trobador* who composed material and the *joglar* who performed it, although *joglar* are also found dancing, playing instruments and telling jokes. There was an overlap between the two, but the title of *trobador* was a badge of honour, with perhaps half of the known troubadours of the twelfth century from the upper or lower nobility, as opposed to around a sixth from merchant families.[35] A few were clerics, but many more seem to have had some sort of ecclesiastical training. A few women were also composers, mainly from noble families. The very existence of these poets was a sign of prestige and economic affluence and they became a choice commodity for those who could afford them.

Writing around 1159, the English churchman John of Salisbury was struggling to come to terms with the new fashion:

> The singing of love songs in the presence of men of eminence was once considered in bad taste, but now it is considered praiseworthy for men of greater eminence to sing and play love songs which they themselves with greater propriety call *stulticinia*, follies.[36]

However, his distaste for the 'procession of mimics, jumping or leaping priests, buffoons and other gladiators, wrestlers, sorcerers, jugglers, magicians and a whole army of jesters' is obvious. Indeed they were all part of a culture of quite jaw-dropping excess. During the 1170s and 1180s, there were a number of prestigious feasts organised across Europe which highlighted the wealth of patrons and what it could buy. The most notorious of these was held at Beaucaire near Avignon to celebrate the reconciliation brought about by Henry II of England between Raymond of Toulouse and Alfonso, King of Aragon, in 1174. The kings were in fact absent, but one account has nobles such as Guilhem the Fat of Martello bringing 300 knights and cooking all the food from the kitchen with expensive torches of wax and pitchpine, while Raimon of Vernoul burnt 30 horses in a fire because of a boast. Finally, supposedly 30,000 sous worth of coin were ploughed into the castle grounds, an ostentatious example of truly disposable income. Professional entertainers were an important part of the festivities and one Guilhem Mita was crowned 'King of all minstrels'.[37]

Such was the popularity of troubadour output that during the last decades of the twelfth century it was possible to make a living from 'touring the courts' (*anar per cortz*) in southern France and the number of writers and performers increased accordingly. There were also a number of entertainers hustling for business in towns. By 1204 they could be such a nuisance that in Toulouse *joglar* were prevented from entering homes without the householder's permission, except during weddings.[38]

In times of hardship the culture proved its ability to spread and evolve. In the 1190s there were important changes in the court society on which the troubadours depended. Some major patrons died, such as Barral, Viscount of Marseille in 1192, Raymond V of Toulouse in December 1194, and Alfonso II of Aragon in 1196.[39] Along with them a generation of troubadours died or ceased composing, among them Guiraut de Bornelh, Bertran de Born and Arnaut Daniel. Some time between 1195 and 1200 the troubadour Fulk of Marseille became a Cistercian monk, thus beginning a transformation which was to see him emerge in 1205 as bishop of Toulouse and scourge of heresy. Around 1200 it may well have appeared more difficult for anyone who hoped to make a living composing and performing, and the position deteriorated when the Albigensian Crusade struck the southern French courts in 1209.

The answer to the dearth of patronage was a growing presence in the affluent courts of north Italy. These had been aware of troubadour poetry as early as 1157, when a Lombard, Peire de la Cavarana, composed a *sirventes* in Occitan against the Germans and Frederick Barbarossa,[40] but southern French troubadours apparently only started to find patrons on the other side of the Alps around 1190. The evidence for this comes mostly from the *vidas* or potted biographies of troubadours prepared in Italy in the mid thirteenth century. Often concerned with tales of love won and lost they must be treated with caution as historical sources, but they do attempt to give the place of origin and social status of the poet along with the names of some of his patrons and these aspects have proved to be reasonably accurate when they can be checked.[41] The *vida* of Peire de la Mula claimed patronage for the poet from Ottone, Count of Carretto, and ruler of Genoa in 1194, as well as from the courts of Montferrat and Cortemiglia. Peire Vidal, after visiting the courts of Toulouse, Marseille and Aragon, went to Lombardy in the early 1190s and visited the minor courts of Lombardy and Piedmont as well as that of Boniface of Monferrat.[42] Boniface was the crucial figure in the spread of troubadour culture to Italy. When he set out for the Fourth Crusade in 1202 he was patron to two leading troubadours, Gaucelm Faidit and Raimbaut de Vaqueyras. His brother-in-law, Albert, Marquis of Malaspina, was also a patron, featuring in a poem composed by Raimbaut de Vaqueyras in 1195.[43]

The ravages of the Albigensian Crusade further reduced the patronage network of southern French nobles until the peace of 1229. Of the 40 *trobador* active during the period with *vidas*, eight moved to Italy to join those who had already left.[44] Eight more moved to Spain in the same period. There was a distinct pattern to the departures: at first only Aimeric de Péguilhan left the area in the first months of the crusade, possibly obliged to because of a reputation for heretical sympathies.[45] The disastrous defeats suffered by the south between 1211 and 1214 prompted another four troubadours to leave for Italy and at least one, Peirol, the troubadour knight who could no longer maintain his status, suffered economic hardship.[46]

Provençal poetry and song became fashionable with Italian patrons, but most of the troubadours who left during the crusade returned to southern France in the 1220s. It was left to a later generation to exploit the taste on a systematic basis. First, they sold a poetic medium: Uc

Faidit wrote a Provençal grammar for two Italian nobles around 1240. They also promoted the authors: Uc de Saint Circ (who may have been the same person) wrote the biographical *vidas* and *razos*, fanciful stories explaining the creation of individual songs in the mid 1250s. Interestingly these did not just provide information, but projected the image of an archetypal troubadour in much the same way as the paradigm of the holy man was set out by contemporary writers on religion. Most importantly the first manuscript collections of songs were made in north-east Italy from 1254. The obvious shift of oral to written culture was part of the conscious marketing and commodification of the troubadours' output, and marked the culmination of a process which seems to have started with song sheets circulating from the mid twelfth century, none of which have survived.[47] By the mid thirteenth century native Italian troubadours such as Lanfranco Cigala and Sordello could write poetry in courtly Provençal so that imports were unnecessary, and of the 14 later southern French troubadours whose *vidas* have survived, only one is recorded as travelling to Italy. This was the enterprising Uc de Saint Circ who evidently combined creativity with commerce and was convicted of usury there in 1257.[48]

Despite the contempt for usurers and money which pervades the troubadour corpus it should be no surprise to see troubadours exhibiting entrepreneurial flare. Increasingly they had origins among the prosperous burgesses and merchants of the towns. From the evidence of the *vidas*, the proportion of *trobador* from business backgrounds peaked in the later twelfth century and first half of the thirteenth. Besides Uc de Saint Circ, there was Pistoleta who gave up his career as a *joglar* to become a successful merchant, Fulk of Marseille who famously was a merchant's son, or there were the *joglar* from southern France, Lombardy and Tuscany who were paid in 'innumerable rolls of cloth' at the court of the ruler of Genoa in 1227.[49]

Nobles too could be involved in entrepreneurial activity so it is best not to make too much of troubadour's social origins, yet one other group clearly stands out as providing a substantial proportion of their number. Becoming a *trobador* offered an opportunity for some clerics to use their education in a secular market. Aspects of popular religion such as pilgrimage had always been a part of troubadour subject matter, and overtly religious material played a greater role in the output of the thirteenth century. This retreat from the eroticism of the *canso* may reflect the growing lay interest in spiritual issues which the troubadours had a vested interest in tapping into for patronage from influential lay men and women. Troubadours needed the support of the laity as much as those more formally committed to the religious life. This is why it used to be thought that there was some sort of association between troubadours and Catharism.[50] Heretics and *trobador* shared many of the same preoccupations: Peire Cardenal could address theological issues close to the dualism of the Cathars, such as why God did not dispossess 'devils', since it was within his power, and once done, he would have more souls.[51] Both poets and preachers relied on the protection of individual patrons, but if any troubadours did harbour heretical sympathies they were too shrewd to alienate potential custom by declaring them in verse.[52]

There were, however, plenty of courts where both heretics and troubadours received patronage. Azalais, wife of Roger II Trencavel, supported numerous troubadours of whom the best known was Arnaut de Mareuil, and her husband was a notorious defender of heretics.[53] Raymond-Roger, Count of Foix, was Peire Vidal's *comte ros* or 'red count', while his wife and sister both became public supporters of the Cathars.[54] Perhaps the closest association was Bertrand de Saissac, guardian of Roger II's son, praised for his generosity by the troubadour Raymond de Miraval, and trusted adviser to local Cathars according to a chronicler of the Albigensian Crusade.[55] A generation later in north-east Italy Ezzelino da Romano was accused of supporting both troubadours and heretics although evidence of his favour for either is thin.[56]

Troubadour culture provided a model for heretical movements in how to obtain influence. In economic terms, the troubadours were a development of the service sector of the twelfth century. Like many other workers in the new economy they held more than one job, combining singing and composing with other roles as fighters, merchants or bureaucrats, and because their success depended on mastering changing fashions, their profession demonstrates how ideas could be transmitted in the secular sphere from one part of Europe to another. Moreover, because they often derived from the very social groups they served, they understood the aspirations of their 'customers' and devised an ideology specifically for them. Francis of Assisi was to be described as 'God's troubadour', but in reality he was only stealing the title from the Cathar and Waldensian heretics.

The twelfth-century renaissance and heresy

Another forum for new ideas against a background of markets and choices was the university. The reformed Church of the eleventh century demanded more educated clergy. The result was the growth of the schools attached to cathedrals all over western Europe and, in some places, the emergence of more advanced places of learning that the thirteenth century would learn to call universities. Despite the obscurity of the origins of these schools their development was rapid, so that by the 1120s certain teachers and places were singled out. The consumers of this education were often the sons of the aristocracy and, in effect, receiving the tithe income which came with ecclesiastical posts compensated the aristocracy for giving up lay rights over churches.[57] Particularly in northern Europe, the upper reaches of the Church was a promising career which gave an income for life. Although the supply of benefices was increasing, it was quickly outstripped by demand. The requirement to be noticed at the most reputable and best connected schools forced many to travel far in search of education and north of the Alps Paris was the paramount centre of learning. The city was the seat of a bishopric and the royal court as well as the influential abbeys of Saint Denis and Saint Victor. Naturally, it was also within the 'big banana' of European prosperity.

Life at a medieval university most of the time was less exciting than we might imagine. Some intriguing ideas were discussed by a small elite and then reported for posterity, but the vast majority of masters and students were diligent, careerist churchmen destined to be the cogs in the wheels of ecclesiastical and secular government. These men were to shape our views of heresy. When they confronted heretics, it was in formal debates. In giving accounts of heretics they emphasised their own theological outlook and training. The wider impact of university education was the growth of a common Latinate culture, an increase in the production and accessibility of manuscripts. The growth of education was not confined to higher learning. Hugh of Saint Victor's *Didascalicon* suggested that household management and statecraft were an integral part of wisdom and proposed a sort of shadow curriculum in practical skills: fabric manufacture, armaments, agriculture, food production, even popular entertainment. Commerce is particularly favoured as a branch of rhetoric and a means of reconciling private good and common benefit.[58] John of Salisbury, recalling his own time as a student around the 1140s, gives a glimpse of a wider educated public:

> Meanwhile I took as pupils the children of nobles, who in return provided for my material necessities [. . .] In this capacity, because of my duties and the insistent questions raised by the youths, I was forced frequently to recall what I had previously heard.[59]

At the other end of Europe's zone of prosperity, educational facilities were more established. By 1050 on the eve of the struggles for reform in Milan, the cathedral had two schools in the north transept of the cathedral of Saint Ambrose which the city clergy could attend. They dealt with the advanced study of the liberal arts, that is the *trivium* of grammar, logic and rhetoric, supplemented by the *quadrivium* of arithmetic, astronomy, geometry and music. In the cathedral forecourt were two further schools where the choirboys were trained and received a basic education. The source of this information is the chronicler Landulf who hints that these schools should be set in a wider context, since he set up independently as 'a lector, scribe, and teacher of the young, taking part in public life and composing letters for the rulers of the city'.[60]

Italian cities do seem to have maintained a tradition of secular learning, particularly in the all-important art of letter writing, the *ars dictaminis* which was learnt by notaries, the forerunners of professional lawyers. Italian education was a commercial venture; tutors taught for a living and their customers learnt the skills which would help them navigate the legal system which governed business life. The one area of expertise which emerged, and emerged quite suddenly, was in law at Bologna. From a situation in the mid 1120s where it had the usual education facilities for a town of its size, by 1140 it had become a recognised centre for both civil and canon law. Once again, the rapidly growing economy of the early twelfth century had its effect, creating a demand for lawyers to solve political and commercial disputes. However, for advanced learning (and preferment) in theology or the liberal arts Italians had to travel north, so at least some of the capital which had flowed south with the balance of trade was returned, and Paris became a genuinely cosmopolitan centre of learning.

Somewhere within the demand-led educational structures of twelfth-century Europe was genuine intellectual curiosity and students were encouraged to develop as much discernment in their studies as they had as educational consumers. The most famous teacher of all, Peter Abelard, commented in the preface to his *Sic et Non* ('*Yes and No*'), written in the early 1120s, that the Church Fathers 'must be read not with a requirement to believe, but with the freedom to judge'.[61]

Abelard had been born on the borders of Brittany around 1079, the son of a Poitevin knight, and started his teaching in Paris in the first decade of the twelfth century. He was already notorious, having de-nounced his teachers and seduced his pupil, Heloise, the niece of a canon of Notre Dame, for which he was repaid by the canon arranging for him to be beaten and castrated. This was around 1118, and by this time he had married Heloise who had given birth to a son. In the circumstances the couple were forced to separate and Abelard became a monk, but continued to teach until two years later when he was accused of heresy.

Abelard's first trial for heresy at Soissons in 1121 was mainly a matter of academic humiliation for his attempts at logical analysis of the

Trinity. His book on the subject was symbolically burnt and Abelard was formally placed in perpetual confinement, but there were hints that this was a negotiated result and within a year he was free and later able to produce a second and then a third edition, incorporating it within a much broader work, the *Theologia*. Abelard insisted that he wrote 'at the request of our students'. His thoughts on the Trinity were composed because students asked for 'human and logical reasons ... something intelligible rather than mere words'. This may be nothing more than writer's vanity, but it was true that the schools were ruthlessly competitive and a good teacher needed to be seen to be satisfying consumer demand in order to make a living.[62]

It was Abelard's ability to propagate his ideas as much as his theology which was to lead him into trouble again 20 years later. After a chequered career which had seen him as a monk, an unsuccessful abbot and a gregarious hermit, he returned to Paris around 1133 and set about a fertile period which was to see the emergence of new versions of the *Theologia* and a book on ethics, subtitled *Scito te ipsum* or '*Know yourself*'. He had already completed an autobiography, remarkable for both its modern tone and breathtaking arrogance, which is an important source for conveying the atmosphere of the schools in the first third of the twelfth century.

In 1139, Abbot William of Saint Thierry, perhaps having already taken on the role of guardian against heresy, if he was the same 'William' who had debated against Henry of Le Mans, wrote to Bernard of Clairvaux as the most powerful Cistercian monk in Europe, a close ally of Pope Innocent II and an old friend. Again the complaints against Abelard were obscure; what had really startled the two monks was the degree to which the issues Abelard raised had escaped into the community at large. William warned that Abelard's teachings were being broadcast far and wide, crossing the seas and the Alps, even reaching Rome itself. Bernard took up the theme:

> Catholic Faith, the childbearing of the Virgin, the Sacrament of the Altar, the incomprehensible mystery of the Holy Trinity, are being discussed in the streets and market places.

He and his supporters repeatedly claimed that the faith of simple people was being corrupted by Abelard's teaching.[63] These claims could be dismissed as exaggeration, particularly in the light of Bernard's misjudgement of the public mood in his later preaching campaign against heresy in 1145. But his allegations may contain an element of truth. One of Abelard's disciples was the already troublesome Arnold of Brescia, later to be burnt for heretical beliefs and although none of Abelard's teachings were taken up directly by Arnold or any other popular heretic, Abelard did in a sense provide the intellectual underpinning for many of the issues which surfaced at a popular level.

The most obvious example of the above was Abelard's assertion in *Scito te ipsum* that the intention or consent to sin was the main determinant of guilt, more so than the sinful action committed. He applied this principle to various situations including that of the day-old infant who cannot possibly therefore inherit the *guilt* of original sin, only the punishment.[64] Abelard was far too canny to spell out that this may make infant baptism irrelevant, but the implication was obvious and condemnation of infant baptism became a commonplace of twelfth-century heresy. Again, Abelard worried about the nature of Christ, for how could the man of flesh also be the Christ in the Trinity? The dualist Cathars were to return to this issue, insisting that the Christ recorded in the Bible was only present 'in a spiritual sense' or had been born in the 'land of the living', different from this earth.[65]

Partly due to his high profile, Abelard's ideas had spread beyond those who had actually read him to create a 'textual community' of those aware of his ideas that drew in almost all Europe. Heloise was aware she was not her husband's only admirer.

> What king or philosopher could match your fame? What district, town or village did not to see you? When you appeared in public, who did not hurry to catch a glimpse of you, or crane his neck and strain his eyes to follow your departure?[66]

A more detached view, analysing the distribution of Abelard's manuscripts, comments that they spread far and wide with great speed.[67]

Besides Abelard's boasts of students flocking to him and the claims of many to have been his pupil, there is even evidence of the circulation of his ideas in vernacular literature. The strange and brilliant version of the Tristan love story by the northern French poet Béroul is difficult to interpret sympathetically without a rudimentary knowledge of Abelard's emphasis on intentions rather than deeds. Tristan and Yseut are forced into an adulterous love affair by the accidental administration of a love potion. They go to great lengths to keep their liaison from Yseut's husband, King Mark, to whom they both owe loyalty and affection. Their motives contrast with those of the barons and the evil dwarf magician at the court, who under the guise of doing their duty to their lord by telling of his wife's infidelity are really pursuing their own selfish agenda. The lovers are true to themselves and true to their obligations, although to the outside world they are committing mortal sin. As Abelard put it:

For [God] sees excellently where no one sees, since in punishing sin he pays no attention to the act, but to the spirit, just as we, conversely attend, not to the spirit which we do not see, but the act which we recognise. Consequently often, through error or coercion of the law . . . we punish the innocent or free the guilty. God is said to be the knower and tester of the heart and reins, that is of whatever intentions originate from the affection of the soul or the weakness or pleasure of the flesh.[68]

Given the diffusion of a variety of Abelard's ideas, Bernard was probably right to concentrate on the most important. A long list of 19 propositions supposedly taught by Abelard had been prepared prior to a council of Churchmen at Sens in early June 1140, but Abelard pre-empted the Council by appealing to the papacy. Bernard responded with a letter to Pope Innocent II. He considered four of the articles in some detail, but he emphasising just two points above all. First, that the intellectual enterprise in which Abelard was involved was itself inimical to faith: as he said: 'for that faith in God has no merit, if human reason provides proof for it'. Secondly, Bernard seized on the idea that Abelard defined faith as 'private judgement' (*aestimatio*). This was crucial to the development of the believer as a consumer of religion. The 'infallible proofs' of faith Bernard cites are public truths,

Commended by divine miracles and revelations, established and consecrated by the Son of the Virgin, by the blood of the Redeemer, by the glory of Him rising again.[69]

The most accessible miracle was the one regularly repeated by priests who transformed bread and wine into the body and blood of Christ. For people to choose different forms of religion, even heretical groups, there had to be more emphasis on a person's private faith and internal decision-making processes. Up to a point, it did not matter whether Abelard had taught these things or not. Bernard had successfully identified danger-ous ideas at large and was determined to destroy them. As for Abelard, he was condemned by Innocent II on the strength of Bernard's letter, only to be saved by Peter the Venerable, abbot of Cluny. He remained under the abbot's protection until his death at the monastery of Saint Marcel near Chalon-sur-Saône 18 months later.

Abelard personified the rapid changes occurring in the early twelfth century. He took advantage of economic prosperity to make a living from teaching in and around Paris. In doing so he achieved fame far beyond the young churchmen who were his students, to reach society at large. He used this to push back the frontiers of what could be said and debated. However, he paid the penalties of his boldness. In his personal life he suffered for having a relationship with a woman which would have been routinely accepted just 20 years before, while his career was interrupted twice by clumsy attempts to silence him.

Yet the real danger to orthodoxy came not so much from celebrated radical thinkers, but from their students who could slip into society almost unnoticed. By the time Amaury of Bène was teaching at the end of the twelfth century, the University of Paris had taken shape in the sense that a *universitas* or guild of masters had set up a closed shop and the cut-throat competition of earlier in the century had come to an end. In 1215 the papal legate, Robert de Courson, marked the beginning of the university's institutional history by issuing a set of statutes, but the Capetian King Philip II had already acknowledged the importance of the academic community's presence by a charter of 1200 which protected scholars from arbitrary arrest by city officials. A consensus had developed that masters had a fair amount of latitude in what they taught as long as it remained within the confines of the schools. This makes the case of Amaury more surprising. Sources are vague as to what his teachings were, although his insistence that to be saved one had to be a 'limb of Christ' suggested some idea of mystic union. Accused of heresy, like Abelard he appealed to Rome, but was nevertheless condemned and forced to return to Paris and recant. The episode seems to have broken Amaury who died shortly afterwards, although he was still respectable enough for a monastic burial.[70]

This peaceful rest did not last, unfortunately. Four years later, in 1210, he was exhumed and excommunicated. The reason was the arrest of 14 men claiming to be his supporters after they had been infiltrated by Ralph of Namur, an ecclesiastical official. A number of features made the case unusual. The group contained no fewer than nine students of theology, including one current lecturer in the faculty of arts. These were not discontented academics, although they had all studied in the schools. Only one of them lived in Paris itself, and at least six were working priests. They had quite deliberately taken their teachings into the area outside Paris, into the dioceses of Langres and Troyes on the trade routes to Italy and the fairgrounds of Champagne.[71]

Amalricians, as their opponents called them, singled out the issues at the interface between clerics and laity, they denied that baptism, confession, or the miracle of the Eucharist helped salvation and they mocked pilgrims who kissed the bones of saints. Having dismissed the duties of priests as irrelevant, they turned their attention to sin and, in distorted echoes of Abelard's teaching, taught that nothing could be a sin as long as it was done in a spirit of love. One chronicler made the rather cheap comment that they used this to seduce women, but others remarked on their female followers and their appeal to widows and the unsophist-

icated. In fact the secret of their popularity may lie in their empower-
ment of the laity. One David of Dinant seems to have been associated
with the group and he produced theological works in French, while the
group created their own version of the Lord's Prayer. They insisted that
paradise lay in the knowledge of the Truth since whoever knew God
could not sin. This was essential since their vision of the future was not
optimistic. Four plagues were prophesied – the people would starve in a
famine, the nobles would kill each other, the earth would swallow up
the inhabitants of towns and fire would consume the prelates of the
Church. There is just a hint of academic disdain here for the hopeless
peasants, quarrelsome aristocrats, greedy townspeople, and corrupt
churchmen inhabiting the world outside the schools. The lack of confidence in the existing social structures was balanced by a naïve belief in
the king of France, coincidentally a keen supporter of the university, to
whom had supposedly been given the knowledge and power of the
scriptures. Armed with their learning the group were ready to embrace
the idea of change; for them the age of the Spirit had begun, a belief
also contained in the fashionable but as yet undeveloped theories of the
Calabrian mystic, Joachim of Fiore.[72]

In seeking to end the group's influence outside the university the
ecclesiastical authorities showed none of the hesitancy with which they
had approached the world of scholarship in the 1140s. Once Ralph had
collected enough evidence he returned to the bishop who ordered the
arrest of the suspects. After interrogation of the individuals, a provincial
council passed sentence and stripped the heretics of their clerical status.
Ironically, in the light of their admiration for Philip II, the execution
was carried out by express order of the king. Ten were burnt in the field
named Champeaux, just outside the walls of Paris. Four others were
sentenced to a penance of life imprisonment in a monastery. Accounts
vary as to the fate of Amalric's body, but it was exhumed and probably
burnt.[73]

The case received more attention than it merited, probably because
of the panic which followed the rise of the Cathars. Chroniclers recorded
the incident in Germany and Scotland as well as several in France and
the group inspired a detailed refutation in the tract, *Contra Amaurianos*
(*'Against the Amalricians'*). What struck contemporaries was that the
men involved were the winners of the changes of the last century,
educated men with benefices in one of the richest areas of Europe.[74]
The commitment of the heretics to spreading their doctrines was
impressive. One of those later burnt, John, priest of Cones, left his
parish warning his flock not to believe any other doctrines than the ones
he had taught. It is therefore slightly surprising to find that only one

other Amalrician was ever recorded: another man with some academic background who was burnt in Amiens two years later. One reason may have been that for all the advantages they enjoyed over dissident preachers a century earlier, in times of prosperity, ease of communication and availability of texts, the followers of Amaury made little attempt to organise. They simply took up their places in the Church's structure and started to preach. Winning over someone's private faith was one thing, getting them to express it and participate required more thought about building communities of belief. At least one of the group's prophecies came true; the *Contra Amaurianos* reported them as preaching that within five years 'everyone will be Spirituals', filled with the Holy Spirit. The time-scale may have been ambitious, but it was an uncannily accurate description of the religious movements both orthodox and heretical which were to dominate the rest of the century.[75]

chapter 3

A WORLD OF CHOICES: ORGANISED HERESY IN EASTERN AND WESTERN EUROPE

Just as there were more consumer goods to choose, more entertainers to patronise and more centres of learning from which to receive ideas, the laity started to experiment with a range of forms of spirituality. In the first half of the twelfth century these mostly remained orthodox. The few figures who tested the boundaries of tolerance with their spirituality made little wider impact since sooner or later they were overwhelmed by the local Church hierarchy or institutionalised their teaching along existing lines. In other words they founded monasteries or met violent ends. Cumulatively their careers were significant, but individually they were shooting stars, puzzled over by chroniclers much as they analysed rare natural phenomena. The situation changed in the second half of the century with the arrival of the Cathars; they were as concerned to offer organisational and doctrinal alternatives to the Church as they were to make criticisms of it. The laity were emboldened by a world of choices and were now more confident in their judgements, particularly of what constituted a spiritual lifestyle. This allowed a preacher such as Valdes of Lyon, disapproved of by the Church, even if basically orthodox, to establish a movement which could survive persecution and the death of its founder. In both southern France and Italy there was little authority to suppress new religious movements and in the latter the most sophisticated lay audience in Europe was quick to embrace them.

The Bogomils

The fundamental doctrinal alternative to the Church was a dualist religion which came from outside the West and exploited the twelfth century's receptiveness to new ideas. The inspiration behind the Cathars had its medieval origins faraway in Bulgaria. In modern history the country has often been regarded as something of a backwater, indeed even in the middle ages Byzantine Greek writers described the place as a 'filthy marsh' and the inhabitants as 'frogs', monsters, or 'barbarian slaves who smell of sheepskin'.[1] This disguises a 'new frontier': the medieval state was far larger than modern Bulgaria and at its height under Tsar Symeon (893–927) stretched from the Adriatic to the Black Sea and from the hills above Greek Thessalonika to the unfolding Russian steppes. Exports of cattle, linen and honey along the Danube or along the old Roman Via Egnatia between Constantinople and the Adriatic coast gave it links to both East and West. In the foothills of the Balkan mountains, Symeon was able to build himself a capital at Preslav, the towering ruins of which are impressive even today.

Bulgarian religious culture was lively to the point of dangerous. Conversion to Christianity in the 860s was a confused convergence of missionaries from Constantinople, Carolingian Germany and Rome in competition. Symeon, having unambiguously accepted the Byzantine orthodox version of Christianity, strove to establish it with an extensive programme of church building, but did so on the back of a violent pagan reaction, and beneath the surface Bulgaria remained a melting pot of religious traditions. Stimulated by new wealth and religious controversy, in Preslav there was a precocious production of original works and translations in Slavonic. To the south-west, Archbishop Clement of Ohrid created a major religious centre on the shores of its lake and allowed preaching and teaching to take place in Macedonia in the early years of the tenth century using his native Slavonic vernacular.[2]

Symeon's church-building efforts were patchy and parish priests had a poor reputation, not least because the eastern tradition allowed them to marry. Real spirituality was held to reside in monasteries and, like the enthusiasm for Cluny among their western contemporaries, the Bulgarian aristocracy invested heavily in monastic foundations. Monks in the orthodox Church could fulfil a rather greater variety of roles than their western counterparts and could even act as missionaries to the mass of the laity as Clement directed from Ohrid, but most lived in exclusive foundations such as the one established by John of Rila around 930 in the remote beauty of the valleys south of modern Sofia. Even more so than in the West, monasteries held the key to salvation and guarded themselves from pollution by the laity. John characteristically refused to see Symeon's successor, Peter (927–69), who had travelled to pay his respects.[3]

Those lacking the social status to become monks or found houses evidently looked elsewhere. Cosmas the Priest, an otherwise unknown writer, described the practices of another priest, Bogomil or 'lover of

God' and his followers, shortly after the death of Tsar Peter. The heretics in Cosmas's piece act a lot like monks. They fast and keep vigils. Specifically, 'they pray, shutting themselves in their houses four times a day and four times a night' (western monasticism has a similar pattern of services) with a heavy emphasis on the *pater noster*.[4] Outside the 'monastery', Cosmas reported that 'they go from house to house and eat the goods of others' as well as making regular criticisms of priests, accusing them of drunkenness and robbery. They also attacked the bishops, for not keeping their clergy in order, for not practising self-denial and 'denying us [Bogomil and followers] their prayers'. In other words they still considered themselves part of the Church and considered that orthodox bishops *should* pray for them.[5]

In a way, Bogomil simply extended existing spirituality beyond acceptable limits. Echoes of John of Rila's disdain for secular authority amounted to revolution for Cosmas when extended throughout society:

> They teach their followers not to obey their masters; they scorn the rich, they hate the Tsars, they ridicule their superiors, they reproach the boyars, they believe that God looks with horror on those who labour for the Tsar and advise every serf not to work for their master.[6]

Bogomil was probably doing no more than claiming the right for anyone, even a serf, to lead the contemplative life and not to have perform manual labour. Bogomil stretched this further in the sense that he implied ordinary lay life may not be merely inferior to the spiritual, but actually evil in its preoccupation with the material, explaining this through dualist theology.

The belief that the Devil made the visible things of this world, leaving to God only the heavens and the souls of mankind, is immensely appealing. It explains why the world is the grim place it is and strips away the layers of earthly corruption of our bodies to reveal the angel trapped within. In its acceptance that ordinary believers are prisoners of the Devil's flesh it answers the human dilemma that in earnestly trying to be true to our divine origins by doing good we are, still, irresistibly drawn to sin in this, the Devil's world. Its fascination is probably even stronger in the twenty-first century than it was in the tenth. This can easily lead to it being misread: like most great religions it has ideas that transcend the centuries, but that does not mean it was presented or understood in exactly the same way in each era.

Medieval Christian intellectuals probably found dualism less exotic than do modern western readers. The basic idea had descended from Mani (216–77), a Persian noble; he and his 'Manichees' had competed for converts in the late Roman Empire. One of these had been Augustine of Hippo (356–430) and when he returned to Christianity he set about a rich literature of refutation of the dualists which was enormously influential in later centuries. But in the Balkans dualism was not only a phenomenon of the past. Since the middle of the eighth century a community of Paulicians, dualists from Armenia, at the far edge of Asia Minor, had been settled in Thrace and they were supplemented by a further migration to Philippopolis, the present day Bulgarian city of Plovdiv, around 975. Their value as warriors outweighed Byzantine uneasiness about their religious beliefs.

The concern about dualist heresy was articulated, albeit not very clearly, in a letter from the Patriarch of Constantinople (confusingly also called Cosmas) to Tsar Peter between 933 and 956 which talks of 'a mixture of Manichaeanism and "Paulianism"', evidently reported by the Bulgarian ruler.[7] As far back as 870 an emissary to the Paulicians in Asia Minor had reported that they planned to send missionaries to Bulgaria. At some stage, despite a traditional Paulician reluctance to propagate their faith among other peoples, their exotic beliefs apparently encountered Bulgarian monastic enthusiasm. This would be particularly likely during the reign of Peter as Byzantium deliberately fostered stability on its Balkan frontier by encouraging trade between the empire and the countries north and south of the Danube. The approved routes ran through Philippopolis on the Bulgarian border and Thrace to the west of Constantinople. Bulgarian and Paulician communities would have had ample opportunity to meet even without organised missions.[8]

It is perhaps not surprising that Bogomilism took more than a century to reach Constantinople. Allegations of the heresy entered the range of libels Byzantine churchmen hurled at each other in their acrimonious private quarrels, but the Greek public had not been exposed to the variety of missionaries active in Bulgaria.[9] On the other hand, economic links continued to thrive and the conquest of the Bulgarian state by the Greeks in the early eleventh century may well have increased the undercurrent of internal migration within the empire towards the capital.[10]

It was during the reign of the Emperor Alexius Comnenus (1081–1118) that the best documented case of Byzantine Bogomilism occurred. There are two accounts; one by the chronicler Anna Comnena, the emperor's daughter, the other by Euthymius Zigabenus, his personal theologian. The events described took place in Constantinople between 1097 and 1104, although the suspects may only have met their ends after years of imprisonment.[11] In outline, the Emperor Alexius Comnenus became concerned about heretics in his capital and held a group captive until one of them mentioned Basil, an elderly monkish man who may also have had medical knowledge. Alexius and his brother, Isaac, invited

Basil to expound his teaching to them, while all the time a hidden clerk, perhaps Euthymius himself, made notes. Finally all was revealed and Basil was hauled off to gaol. The emperor then summoned Basil's twelve 'apostles' as well as other followers. After lengthy attempts to find out who of these were the obstinate heretics, Alexius had to resort to the subterfuge of constructing two pyres; one topped by a cross and the other not, with the hope that the truly repentant would choose to die as orthodox Christians. Those that did choose the cross were promptly set free. Even those that did not were not burnt, but had to endure further attempts to convert them by senior churchmen. Many did not survive this persuasion and died rather suspiciously in prison, despite Anna's assurance that 'they were amply supplied with food and clothing'. As for Basil himself, a separate pyre was lit in the Hippodrome and unrepentant to the last, the old man was consumed by the flames.[12]

Most of the features which made these heretics so successful in the West were already in place in the Byzantine metropolis. The appeal was still based on a monastic lifestyle, praying, fasting and dressing in a cloak or cowl. Anna observed that you never saw a lay hairstyle on a Bogomil.[13] The Bogomil leaders wove themselves into the fabric of Constantinople society: Anna referred to the movement's penetration of 'the greatest houses', suggesting a popularity built on household and family. Key to this were the many women who followed Basil, helping him to spread the heresy, according to Anna. Zigabenus noticed the degree of support Basil received from his own family and relations by marriage, many of whom were imprisoned for heresy. Such a structure had taken time to establish; Anna knew that it was a new heresy, but that it predated her father. Zigabenus said that Basil had taught for 40 years and studied for 15, which would mean that he entered Constantinople around 1050.[14]

Much of the Bogomils' appeal was embodied in Basil himself, a tall man with austere features and scraggy beard. When they met, Alexius professed admiration for his life of virtue; to underpin this the Bogomils now had a sophisticated creation myth. Moderate dualism recognises one true God, but two creative forces, good and evil. As such it is easier to reconcile with the monotheistic pronouncements of the Bible. The Bogomils of Constantinople saw Satanael as the first son of God and his steward, who had dared to stir up rebellion among the angels and had been cast down with them as punishment. After creating the world and the body of man Satanael came to a settlement with God that Adam would be filled with life and that his children would at some time take the place of the expelled angels. Satanael went back on his word and copulated with Eve; his fellow former angels, eager to return their descendants to heaven, took the daughters of men as wives. Christ was God's response, a second son, who while never of this world, overcame the Evil One and stripped him of the last sign of his angelic status, reducing his name to Satan. Basil's teaching combined biblical texts with the pre-existing demonology which was a feature of Byzantine religious tradition.[15]

The one aspect of the Byzantine Bogomils which seems very different from later western groups is organisation, but the gulf may be more apparent than real. The Bogomils of Constantinople undoubtedly made a substantial impact. Anna described a 'vast cloud of heretics', Zigabenus, a 'vast sea of impiety', adding that Basil had dragged 'thousands of disciples to the pit of destruction'. There was a two-stage initiation for adherents, both marked by a simple ceremony of the placing of John's gospel on the head, the laying on of hands and the saying of the 'Our Father'. Yet both reports describe an organisational structure quite unable to perform such individual care to a community of thousands. Zigabenus portrayed the heretics as a cult centred around Basil, and Anna referred to Basil having twelve 'apostles', an obviously malicious interpretation to make Basil's relationship with his followers seem a blasphemous imitation of Christ's.

Anna's *Alexiad* as a whole is a very artfully constructed piece, pitching its hero in a series of dramatic individual struggles, designed to show how Alexius was the complete model of an emperor. The battle against Basil was deliberately moved out of chronological sequence to near the end of her account, following his military successes, providing a chance for her to show her father as being equally solicitous for his subjects' spiritual welfare as he was for their physical safety. The overcoming of the cunning enemy within is a climax to the work, so that while Basil was obviously a major figure in the Bogomil organisation, he might not have had the special status accorded him by either Anna or Zigabenus. Moreover, the term 'apostles' ($\alpha\pi o\sigma\tau o\lambda o\iota$) could be used for all manner of disciples including the New Testament's 'sending of the seventy' (Luke 10: 1–12) and even the first bishops, so that when Alexius summoned Basil's 'disciples' 'from all over the land' it may mean that the Bogomil Church was organised on a geographical basis, similar to the later western dualists.[16]

The Bogomils survived Basil's death. Zigabenus was no more than cautiously optimistic, advising readers to,

> take heart for the future. The dragon's head is off . . . we are nourished by the hope that not even the tail will escape the careful concern of the emperor . . . and his zealous search.

In 1107 the emperor ordered specialist preachers to be attached to Constantinople's great cathedral of Saint Sophia to instruct the population in the true faith and to warn them of the dangers of heresy.[17]

Bogomils and Cathars

Whether the Bogomils from the East actually inspired the western Cathar movement is still debated, but there is a good case, given that both Bulgarians and Byzantines described an evangelising religion with dualist doctrine, well able to travel. Certainly, the western Cathars quickly developed the organisational knowledge needed to run a community and provide the sort of complete pastoral care from cradle to grave to gain the support of lay groups. Armed with this they could run autonomous communities with loose ties to each other and capitalise on their preaching and highly visible standard of asceticism.

The evidence of the initial import of Bogomil ideas is circumstantial. A group of heretics at Cologne in 1143 claimed that their heresy had persisted in Greece 'and certain other lands'. Anselm of Alessandria, a thirteenth-century inquisitor more than a century after the event, gave an account of the French going to Constantinople and bringing the heresy back with them.[18] Not surprisingly modern historians have tried to corroborate the tale. There were increasing links between East and West during the eleventh and twelfth centuries made easier by the decline in Saracen raids. Around 1000, Symeon the Armenian completed pilgrimages to Compostella and Rome, and finally retired to a monastery just outside Mantua in north Italy. Another Symeon, born at Syracuse in Sicily and educated in Constantinople, was a monk and pilgrim guide in the Holy Land and on Mount Sinai, before meeting Richard, abbot of the northern French monastery of Saint Vannes who persuaded him to return with him to the West. After many adventures and extensive travels Symeon died in 1035 at Trier on the Moselle.[19] More extensive monastic links existed with Rome and the former Byzantine lands of south Italy, so it is plausible to suggest that the Bogomils came west disguised as monks in the late eleventh century or early twelfth century. Dualism may even have been introduced into the West as a response to the persecution which followed the capture of Basil and his followers.

Monks may also have had an impact in a slightly different context. Traditionally, Byzantine merchants were not renowned for travelling, preferring to allow western merchants to come to Constantinople and other leading towns of the empire, but there is evidence of travelling Greeks: Benjamin of Tudela reported them as one of the many nationalities at Montpellier in 1165, trading from Italian vessels. Byzantine monks during the eleventh century had obtained imperial permits to allow them to trade, often using their own boats. This activity eventually created such unease that it would imply that many monasteries had gone far beyond selling off their own surplus produce and had entered the economy of long distance trade.[20]

In the other direction the economic links were even stronger; besides the well-known Pisan and Venetian tariff privileges in Constantinople from the 1080s onwards, the 1082 imperial edict indicates that many Venetians were active in Byzantine provincial towns by then. The fair of Saint Demetrius in Thessalonika was renowned for its cosmopolitan nature and attracted both Bulgarians and northern Europeans from the early twelfth century. On the Adriatic seaboard, Durazzo provided a meeting place for traders from the western Balkans and businessmen from Venice and Amalfi.[21] Finally, there were diplomatic links, such as the visit of Peter Grossolanus, the archbishop of Milan who travelled to Constantinople with his entourage in 1112 or the further mission from Milan to the Byzantines in 1167, just before the first recorded outbreak of heresy in north Italy.[22] The connections between East and West were constant enough to make Bogomil missions possible almost from the time of their origins in Bulgaria. The key factor in their success or failure was the state of popular religion in the West.

There may have been Bogomil missions to the West as early as 1025. In that year heretics were reported at Monforte near Turin, obsessed with virginity and hinting at a leader across the sea.[23] The 'Manichaeans' of Aquitaine reported a little earlier may have had the same provenance.[24] The most dramatic account of heretics came from Héribert of Périgueux in a source formerly dated to the mid twelfth century, but now also reckoned to have been written in the first third of the eleventh. Héribert commented on a group in Aquitaine, north of the Garonne, which could rapidly educate followers and appealed to nobles as well as monks and clergy. And yet, the alarm having been raised, these movements made little long-term impact. Early Bogomil missionaries may well have miscalculated in that the western laity were still comparatively unreceptive to them for a number of reasons. As was shown in the first chapter, the laity had much less exposure to active religion; there were fewer preachers and very little tradition of wandering holy men until the preaching of reformers in the second half of the century and the recruitment of the First Crusade. However, not surprisingly, the response of western clerics to reports of heretical missionaries from abroad was one of shock and dismay at an unprecedented threat and this is reflected in the sources.[25]

A century later, Bogomil teachings took root successfully in three areas of western Europe where consumers of religious ideas had already been introduced to alternative thinking: Flanders and the Rhineland, southern France and Lombardy. The crucial decade was the 1140s. In the Byzantine Empire there was renewed Bogomil activity. The hysteria which reigned in Constantinople has been compared to McCarthyism and there is no doubt the threat was hugely exaggerated, but there are more sober reports of heresy from old centres such as Philippopolis, and Moglena, between Ohrid and Thessalonika, as well as possible new missions to Thebes (Tevai), in southern Greece.[26] These are contemporary with the first reports of dualist beliefs in the West. The exact nature of the heresy was not at first apparent and it may be that early attempts to introduce dualism in western Europe had only mixed success. The canons of Liège reported a group of heretics from Montwimers in northern France who had fallen into their hands, having been rescued from a crowd wanting to burn them. The heretics had made serious errors in that they had neither succeeded in retaining their secrecy nor managed to convert enough people to prevent them from becoming targets for the mob, yet the canons were still worried. The heresy had 'overflowed' into various regions and its adherents had their own priests and prelates.[27]

The emergency button was pressed in the form of a letter to, inevitably, Bernard of Clairvaux by Eberwin, prior of the abbey of Steinfeld in 1143, concerning the neighbourhood of Cologne. Here there were distinct signs of dualist belief. The heretics rejected milk along with everything else 'born of coition'. Their own food and drink was consecrated, but the Church sacraments were dismissed as 'a sort of shadow, a tradition of men'. They emphasised the contrast between themselves, 'the poor of Christ' and churchmen, even monks and canons regular, who added 'house to house, field to field' for the comfort of themselves in this world. The group had their own bishops and a developed hierarchy of auditors, believers and an elect of those able to baptise. Crucially, they informed Eberwin that their heresy had existed in Greece and other lands since the time of the martyrs. Moreover, the group were professional missionaries, having no fixed house, going from city to city. In Cologne they had fallen out with dissidents who seemed to represent an earlier tradition of anti-clerical beliefs, denying all sacraments except adult baptism and rejecting purgatory and prayers for the dead. The disputes among the two groups had resulted in their discovery by the Church authorities, and a rather suspicious spontaneous burning by 'the people'.[28]

The fertile areas of Flanders continued to provide critics of the Church, but their beliefs are only vaguely decribed. In Arras a group was identified as early as 1153 and were accused of being 'Manichaeans' at the Council of Reims in 1157, but action against them was desultory and three suspects were content to appeal to the pope.[29] A mission to England in 1163 of around 30 German speakers was not only spectacularly unsuccessful, but crushed by the overbearing English government who had the suspects branded, stripped half naked and driven into the freezing winter.[30]

Even having taken into account the bias of clerical chroniclers these early attempts of the heretics to insinuate themselves into northern society look only moderately successful. Dualist beliefs either had to be concealed or were only dimly grasped among more familiar issues as at Cologne. The threat came not from beliefs, but organisations which could provide choice. Characteristic of all these accounts is that they reveal organised spiritual groups operating independently of the Church; a planned mission to England or a bishop and hierarchy in Cologne and Montwimers. Personalities were much less prominent in these movements. They are comparatively well documented because the exile of Pope Alexander III to France in the late 1150s and 1160s meant that northern Europe was under the scrutiny of the papal curia. Further south in the Languedoc area of France and north Italy ecclesiastical authority was shakier and dissidence less well recorded.

Southern France

Bernard of Clairvaux's response to the reports of heresy reaching him in the 1140s was to launch a preaching campaign against the runaway monk, Henry of Le Mans in southern France. It was not unreasonable for the abbot to think Henry was the root of a problem whose threat was more serious in Languedoc than further north. Henry had been preaching there since his escape from Clairvaux, some time after 1135, and had formed an association with Peter of Bruys, a veteran preacher who had begun his career as early as 1112 among the Alpine villages on the trade routes between France and Italy. Peter earned the honour of a refutatory tract from another formidable monk, Peter the Venerable, the abbot of Cluny, and he and Henry had made preaching expeditions as far away as Gascony. The tract itself told of Peter's death and demonstrated the vulnerability of the preacher, particularly far from home. Peter rejected the cross as a Christian symbol since it had been the instrument of Christ's suffering, but when he preached this at Saint-Gilles in Provence where folk made a living from the pilgrims visiting the relics of the saint or preparing to go on to Compostella or Jerusalem, they reacted with fury and Peter was pushed into his own bonfire of crosses.[31]

Henry proved shrewder and the fruit of his long experience was the support of the secular power, namely local knights who could provide protection in the rather anarchic countryside of southern France. They hated clerics and enjoyed Henry's jokes as Bernard found when he

investigated the reasons for Henry's appeal. Bernard realised the importance of pastoral care or rather the lack of it. Due to Henry's influence,
he declared, 'churches are without congregations, congregations are without priests, priests are without proper reverence, and finally Christians
are without Christ'.[32] At first sight the mission was a great success, with
the abbot receiving the adulation reserved for great preachers in
Périgueux, Toulouse and, after initial hostility, Albi. Miracles were performed at his behest and according to some reports the heretic Henry
was apprehended shortly after Bernard's departure.[33]

Bernard was more doubtful; as his biographer Geoffrey of Auxerre
put it:

> We believed that with God's help his [Henry's] evil would soon be stopped.
> A land led astray by so many heretical teachings needed a great deal of preach-
> ing, but the abbot did not think that he could perform such a task, and was
> afraid that it would be a great burden to his brothers.[34]

Bernard had also changed tactics during the course of his tour. His
initial sermons were circulated having been composed just before his
departure and attached to a letter to the count of Toulouse looking for
his support. In these Bernard alternates between use of the gospels and
a fair amount of innuendo about the character of Henry and heretics
in general. The fragment of the sermon against heretics at Albi quoted
by Geoffrey of Auxerre shows Bernard now expounded each point that
the heretic preached and what the true faith said about it. Above all he
acknowledged that his listeners had a free choice.

> I have come to sow, but I find the field already sown with wicked seed. But
> you are a reasonable field: you are, after all, God's field. I will show you both
> seeds, and you can decide which to choose.[35]

Bernard's mission marked a watershed in the response to heresy.
Although he was interested in Henry's fate, he concentrated more on
winning the support of those who had followed the heresy. This tactic
began to expose the extent of the problem; Geoffrey of Auxerre's account reveals a movement which had infected whole villages and was
associated with 'weavers', the mobile industrial workers of Toulouse's
textile industry. In his final letter to the people of Toulouse, after his
return to Clairvaux, Bernard did not mention Henry by name at all.
Instead, he referred to the 'wolves' and 'foxes' that were not yet caught,
their 'word . . . spreading like a canker'.[36]

The assurance and scale of dissent which Saint Bernard found in 1145
suggests that the heretics he was dealing with were Cathars. Early missionaries from the Byzantine Empire or returning westerners would have

needed few texts since they looked mainly to spread ideas by word of mouth and their most important document was the Bible, which was readily available in Latin.[37] A modern observer might have expected rather more reaction to the arrival of a religion proclaiming the existence of two creative forces, but this silence too fits the Bogomil method of conversion. According to Zigabenus:

> In the beginning they teach the newly converted simply, exhorting them to believe in the Father and the Son and the Holy Spirit, to know that Christ was incarnate and gave the sacred gospel to the apostles. They order them to keep the precepts of the gospel and to pray and to fast and keep pure from all uncleanness and live in purity and be long suffering and repent and tell the truth and love one another. In brief, they teach everything worthy, beguiling them with excellent instruction . . .

Dualism may have been known to medieval intellectuals, but it was not at all familiar to the mass of the population. Most evidence shows that the Cathars taught the bare outlines of the dualist creation and then concentrated on their pure life and the two-tier structure of their organisation. Salvation came to those believers (*credentes*) who received initiation from one of the 'good men' (*boni homines*) by means of the *consolamentum* or baptism, closely related to the Bogomils' ceremony and generally administered on the deathbed.[38] This provided a simple, positive appeal beyond the scope of Henry or earlier preachers.

The knights who had laughed at Henry's jokes, or their sons, may well have organised the first recorded confrontation between the new heretics and Catholics at the village of Lombers, south of Albi in 1165. This was a formal debate between the bishop of Lodève, speaking for the bishop of Albi, and an unknown number of 'good men'. Formal assessors were chosen by either side. The audience from both laity and the Church was large and distinguished, including such eminent figures as Raymond V, Count of Toulouse and the archbishop of Narbonne, as well as 'almost the whole' of the populations of Albi and Lombers. The heretics basked in the prestige of the assembled aristocracy and the public nature of the event meant they reached a wider audience than ever. The bishop of Albi's warning to the knights of Lombers at the end of the debate not to support the 'good men' any longer was a futile gesture.

The heretics found support in both town and country. In some ways the distinction is artificial since many influential knights would have property in both and many smaller settlements like Lavaur or Mirepoix had the sort of autonomy enjoyed by larger towns elsewhere. Much has been made of the lack in the south of the close vertical ties of feudal allegiance which dominated northern Europe. Instead, horizontal ties of fellowship were more important, and it was no surprise that the bishop addressed the knights of Lombers as a group or that they should have become the 'good men's' protectors. Inheritance was also different: there was much greater division of patrimonies with the result that a large number of men and women who claimed noble status barely had the resources to maintain it. The new movement may have been useful to such people in that its adherents often organised themselves into small communities such as the two at Villemur on the river Agout, or the house built by Raymond Roger, Count of Foix, carved out of the property of the canons of Saint Antonin at Pamiers: patronage of these communities would have been a cheap investment compared with the cost of a monastic foundation, while also providing a supply of 'good men' to console believers at their death.[39] The nobility provided some prominent heretical women such as the wife and two sisters of the count of Foix or, at a humbler level, poor knights who were forced by poverty to hand over their daughters to be educated and brought up by the heretics.[40]

Many of the early enquiries into heresy focussed on urban dwellers. There was a famous case in Toulouse in 1178 when action was taken against Peire Mauran, a moneylender and member of an influential family that possessed property both inside and outside the town.[41] The bishop of Béziers supplied a more varied picture of urban heresy to the hostile Albigensian crusaders of July 1209. Of a list of more than 200 there is some evidence of support for the heretics among craftsmen, such as five hosiers, two shoemakers, two blacksmiths, two preparers of animal skins and a sheep-shearer; also represented are tradesmen, such as a corn-dealer, a tavern keeper, a mercer and a money-changer as well as four doctors and a noble.[42] In addition, the role of weavers in support-ing heresy is well documented, as Geoffrey of Auxerre suggested, and in Toulouse textiles were such a rapidly expanding industry that the part-ners in the Bazacle water-mills put a barrage across the Garonne in order to increase the flow of water.

Gradually, a dualist doctrine emerged. The group at Lombers had rejected the Old Testament and some of those tried at Toulouse a dec-ade later had allegedly taught that there were two gods, but there is still little evidence that doctrine played a particularly prominent part in the heresy's appeal. A more prominent line of attack was that the heretics were 'good men' as opposed to the wealthy clergy. Attacks on the moral character of priests were characteristic of both the confronta-tions at Lombers and Toulouse. One reason why parish priests may have alienated their flock by, for instance, refusing sacraments until they were paid, may have been that they too were short of money. Protesting against a tax rise from a derisory six shillings a year to a still quite modest 50, the priest of the Dalbade church in Toulouse complained to his monastic patron that his revenues were reduced because of the perverse sect of heretics which abounded in those parts. They were all part of a growing market; the priest also complained that newly built churches in the parish cut into his revenue by attracting people, especially on feast days.[43] The competition meant that clergy with a proven moral lifestyle were at a premium. This probably explains why the ultimate compliment was paid to the two 'heresiarchs' who had testified at Toulouse, Raymond of Baimire and Bernard Raymond; years later, after they had repented, they became canons in the church there.

Both Catholic and heretical preachers laboured under handicaps which meant they were as good as evenly matched. At the time of their conviction Raymond and Bernard had apparently only a reading knowledge of Latin:

> We asked them to defend their faith in Latin, both because we did not know their language well enough, and because the Gospels and the Epistles from which they wanted to support their faith are written in Latin. It became clear that they dared not do this when one of them tried to speak in Latin, so badly that he could hardly string two words together. We were, therefore, forced by their ignorance, absurd though it was, to agree to discuss the sacraments of the Church in the vernacular.[44]

Yet these words of the legate Peter of St Chrysogonus reveal the limitations of orthodox missions, such as that to Toulouse in 1178. Although Peire Maurand had been forced to repent, the preachers could make little impact on the rest of the population if they could not talk confidently to the people in their own language.

Italy

The success of heresy in Italy is little celebrated in comparison with southern France. The Italians were better educated, more prosperous and more used to political autonomy than anywhere else. Heretical movements were absorbed into an already complicated world of competing political allegiances without becoming the defining issue they were north of the Alps. That said, individual preachers and the Cathars were an integral part of the distinctive Italian culture of the twelfth century. The most famous figure was Arnold of Brescia whose spiritual and intellectual authority allowed him briefly to dominate Rome itself. This was the climax of a long career rethinking the role of the Church.

He first emerged as abbot of a college of canons in Brescia in north Italy in the late 1130s, stirring up trouble while the bishop was absent and being expelled for his pains. From there he went to Paris where he taught and was an associate and defender of Peter Abelard, earning him the enmity of Bernard of Clairvaux at the Council of Sens in 1140. He went into exile in Zurich and Bohemia, before being recalled to Rome in 1146 by Pope Eugenius III. If it was a tactic designed to keep Arnold under surveillance it misfired. Allied with prominent noble families Arnold twice managed to expel the pope.[45]

Arnold made the deliberate choice of the lifestyle of a reforming preacher: John of Salisbury described how he had mortified his flesh with fasting and coarse clothing. Even Bernard grudgingly admired 'the man whose life is sweet as honey and whose doctrine is as bitter as poison'.[46] Like Henry, Arnold articulated the desires of communities, the laity of Brescia with their 'itching ears' to hear his views regarding the clergy, the poor students who supported him on Mont Saint Geneviève and the aristocracy of Rome. He flattered the Romans by offering them self-government. Urban lay elites all over Italy demanded this in the form of a commune; Arnold, a true scholar of the twelfth-century Renaissance couched it in the language of antiquity, calling for the senate and equestrian order to be reinstituted. An appeal to so remote a past made even the pope's authority in Rome seem a barbarous innovation. Then, in a letter of 1149, he or a close supporter suggested that the emperor come south and pick the pope. In a later letter, under the pseudonym Wetzel, he suggested that the senate and people of Rome itself might 'make an emperor' and force the Church into a life genuinely poor in spirit and fact. In short the purity of the Church was to be achieved through the laity.[47] Something of Arnold's vision of a reformed Church emerged in his declaration that

> Neither clerics that owned property, nor bishops that had regalia, nor monks with possessions could in any wise be saved.[48]

Only the lower clergy, the humble vicars and chaplains escaped his condemnation, suggesting that they might be the backbone of a Church stripped of wealth and temporal power.

Arnold's position in Rome was politically precarious: the new king of Germany and designated Roman emperor, Frederick Barbarossa, in whom Arnold placed such great hope in his second letter, was now looking for a papal coronation and Arnold was part of the price paid. In 1155, after a week of rioting, Arnold was captured and burnt, as a rebel, not a heretic. According to Otto of Freising his ashes were scattered on the Tiber 'lest his body be venerated by the mad populace'.[49] This assumption that his 'sect' would survive him is not borne out by any evidence except the repeated condemnations of 'Arnoldists' through succeeding decades, perhaps revealing how close to home his ideas had struck.

Arnold prefigured the Cathars in that he led a local movement which had universal pretensions. Further north in Milan, the commercial capital of Italy with a population around 50,000, more preachers were at work sending out a different message, but exploiting a similar situation of a prosperous city in political turmoil. Milan's hardships were more severe than those of Rome. The city had become the victim of Frederick Barbarossa's increasing frustration with his Italian subjects. In 1162 his forces captured and demolished the city. Only the churches were spared and the inhabitants were driven into camps established in the suburbs of the ruined city. One of the worst aspects of the atrocity was that demolition was completed not by Frederick's army, but by volunteers from the surrounding cities.[50]

It was probably during this grim period among the ruins that a group of missionaries began preaching to the Milanese and so came to the attention of the recently appointed Archbishop Galdino. He played an important part in the reconstruction of the city from 1167 and while doing so identified a doctrinal threat which he was to fight until his death in 1176. One of his successes was the conversion of one Bonacursus, who gave an account of the beliefs of the heretics in the 1180s or late 1170s. There was no doubt that they were dualists;

> ... some of them say that God created all the elements, others say that the devil created these elements; but their common opinion is that the devil divided the elements.

Bonacursus termed his former colleagues 'Cathars', picking up a name already used for them in Germany. It was suitably double-edged. Given a classical interpretation it could derive from the Greek for 'the pure', but there was also the more obvious and, for the orthodox, satisfying association with cats and the longstanding belief that heretics performed unspeakable acts with these animals.[51] As far as we know, the Cathars never referred to themselves as other than 'good men' or 'good Christians'.

This early reference to dualism suggests that whereas their northern European and southern French counterparts at this time placed overwhelming emphasis on lifestyle as the foundation of their popular appeal, the Italian heretics from the first were more concerned with matters of doctrine. Bonacursus spent a large part of his tract reinterpreting the Bible; he commented that the Son could not be equal to the Father since he had said 'the Father is greater than I'. Scholarship was mixed with more homely material such as his assertion that dogs are so faithful to man because they were born of the spilt blood of Abel.[52] Only in the final part of the piece did he turn to the customary attacks on the Church: matrimony, Eucharist, baptism with water and oath-taking. Even then there are some distinctive features: in what is to be believed an early draft, Bonacursus abruptly commented that no Jew could be saved and that:

> There are also many among them so stupid as not to believe that the substance of highest divinity is so incomprehensible or uncircumscribed that it cannot be comprehended or circumscribed in any place.[53]

There is the possible implication that at least some of the Cathars had set out on an ambitious intellectual project. At any rate this doctrine-led set of beliefs was echoed by Galdino's response. Like Bernard 30 years before, Galdino saw the problem as one of education and set about instructing people in the fundamentals of the Catholic faith; he died in the pulpit still arguing against the Cathars, using examples taken from the Church fathers and gospels.[54]

As for how the Cathars came to Italy we have to rely on two later writers. The first was an anonymous work, *De Heresi Catharorum*, probably from Milan in the early years of the thirteenth century. Rather than give an explanation of the origins of Catharism, it relates how the Cathars in Italy were first led by Mark, who governed believers across a broad swathe of north Italy in Lombardy, Tuscany and the March of Treviso.[55] A subsequent account came from Anselm of Alessandria, a Dominican inquisitor writing in 1266–7. Influenced by the *De Heresi*, but with access to other sources, Anselm traced the movement improbably back to Mani, but had some knowledge of Byzantine heresy, asserting that it had been brought to the West by French crusaders returning from Constantinople, an attribution which has teased historians ever since. Anselm displayed detailed knowledge when dealing with the arrival of the Cathars in Italy. Specifically, he attributed it to a French notary whose earliest converts were Mark, a gravedigger, John 'the Jew', a weaver and Joseph, a smith. Mark came from the village of Cologno, although he was to found his church in nearby Concorezzo.[56] Anselm correctly states that this was Milanese territory at the time he was writing, but a century earlier it was under the authority of Monza, the ancient capital of Lombardy and dominated by the ancient abbey church of St John. The first Cathars may have emerged as a result of this dispute.

In seeking to escape the influence of its larger parvenu neighbour, Monza and its territories were enthusiastic supporters of Barbarossa in the 1160s and contributed to the demolition squads when he took the city. It was part of Galdino's achievement as archbishop that he brought

Monza to recognise both his own authority and that of Pope Alexander III by the end of the decade.[57] A small part of this process was that Alexander ordered the archbishop of Milan to throw his authority behind the attempts of the church of Monza to collect tithes from the leading citizens of Sesto, a hamlet contiguous to Cologno, Mark's home village. This dispute was a continuation of one which had been going on for 20 years. In 1149 a delegate of the archbishop of Milan had heard a case between the *vicini* (neighbours) of Sesto and the church of Monza, where the *vicini* claimed the right to seek and choose a priest for the churches as they claimed to have done for the previous 40 years. However, they lost the case since the archbishop's representative found it intolerable that laymen should appoint a priest.[58]

Cathar preachers had been able to make inroads into the villages north of Milan because the people there already had a keen interest in pastoral care, having been empowered by the wider disputes on the nature of the priesthood at the beginning of the century. The Church's attempt to restore central control at a time when ecclesiastical authority was weak could only have helped the Cathar preachers to find favour with a spiritually discerning public. It is not surprising then, that the subsequent history of Italian Catharism bore out an identical tension to that within Catholicism. On the one hand the aspiration to uniformity and formal structure, on the other, local diversity and intellectual vigour.

Nicetas's mission

For the Cathars the moment of unity came with the arrival of a Bogomil leader by the name of Niquinta or Nicetas around 1170. His presence in Italy is attested by both the main Italian sources and more uncertainly by a document from southern France. By his authority, Mark the gravedigger became bishop of the Italian Cathars, so establishing an ecclesiastical hierarchy for the group. The mission may also indicate divisions among the Bogomils in the East. As Bonacursus's evidence showed, there were, from early on, two competing doctrines on the nature of creation. Nicetas was from Constantinople, from the 'order of Drugunthia' who were absolute dualists, that is they believed in two equal and opposite forces of God and Satan in the universe; previously the Italians were part of the apparently moderate dualist 'order of Bulgaria', believing that Satan was fundamentally inferior, perhaps a fallen first son of God or corrupt steward of heaven.[59]

These disputes were important, but Nicetas's authority was undermined by the more earthy allegation that the bishop who had consecrated him in the East had been found with a woman, a sin which invalidated not only his own consecrations, but also those of Nicetas. The news was brought by Petracius, another Bogomil, this time based in the heresy's old heartland of Bulgaria. By the time Anselm of Alessandria was writing there were vague allegations that neither Mark nor Nicetas himself had 'come to a good end'. Such charges were, of course, unprovable and fragmentation inevitably followed.

The issues were essentially those that had preoccupied the Church in the eleventh century and echoed the Donatist heresy of the Roman Empire. If the validity of sacraments was to be dependent on the unstained characters of the spiritual elite, then centralised authority would be impossible, because it would be eroded by endless charges of wrongdoing. Catholicism dithered under the influence of some of the reformers, but eventually based spiritual authority on following proper procedure and references to the mysterious choices of the deity for his agents. The Cathars stumbled down the alternative route and found that in the end they needed very little central authority and that they reaped benefits in the confidence the lay community had in its local leaders.

According to all accounts the leading figures in the Italian movement were initially embarrassed by these disputes. Some followers even converted back to Catholicism. The movement sought mediation from a Cathar bishop from northern France, but repeated attempts at reconciliation ended in failure. Yet despite the squabbling reported assiduously by Catholic opponents, the Cathars stabilised into a number of vigorous competing communities, unaffected by the scandals. In doctrinal terms they were split into three, the moderate dualists of Concorezzo, near Milan, with a smaller group becoming known as the Bagnolenses, after their base at Bagnolo, near Mantua. Finally, at Desenzano on Lake Garda were the absolute dualists or Albanenses. Geographically, Cathar communities owing a loose allegiance to one group or another were found throughout north Italy and Tuscany. The movement ultimately grew from the bottom up and its success was to make the misdeeds of its leaders less important than the care taken of ordinary believers.[60]

The same strength appears among the southern French Cathars who had apparently received Nicetas after the Italian leg of his mission. Here the evidence is less certain since it depends on one much-debated document, an account of the so-called Council of Saint Félix de Caraman, east of Toulouse.[61] In the presence of Mark from Lombardy, the Cathar bishop from northern France and a large number of men and women, Nicetas outlined a structure based on a Byzantine model, lightly disguised as the seven churches of Asia from the New Testament. The essence of what he proposed was that the churches were divided by boundaries and that one did not do anything in contradiction of another and so there was peace between them. The southern French took him at his word and instead of one bishop at Albi they created three more at Toulouse, Carcassonne and Agen. These were largely autonomous organisations: their bishops received the *consolamentum* from Nicetas, but they were elected by their own groups and the boundaries of the dioceses were fixed by committees chosen by lay members of each community.

The Cathars were not a universal church that failed, but more a movement which ideally suited the diversity and vitality of the newly empowered lay society. In both Italy and southern France Nicetas acted as a wisdom figure, but the decisions were made by ordinary Cathar believers. Not surprisingly their choices reflected the society around them. The southern French opted for a regional church structure without an overarching authority, while the Italians developed competing local groups with a loose allegiance to a broader ideological alignment. In organisational terms neither was perfect, but it was the first time such a thing had been tried by lay men and women and it was to prove astonishingly durable.

The Waldensians

One Sunday in 1173, Valdes, a merchant of Lyon, joined a crowd of people listening to a street entertainer telling the story of Saint Alexis. Although probably fictitious, the story of Alexis is compelling. A young Roman nobleman is promised to God at birth by his parents. However, lacking any other heirs they break their promise and when he is of age he is married into another aristocratic family. On his wedding night he is reminded of his vocation and escaping from his marriage bed he disappears. He next turns up in Edessa, the present day Urfa in Turkey. Alexis takes to begging on the church steps. A priest, again at divine prompting, recognises his piety and offers him a place in paradise in the shape of the local monastery.

Significantly Alexis rejects the offer and heads back to Rome and the anonymity of the big city. He returns to his father's house, unrecognisable with his unkempt appearance and asks if he can live under the stairs and eat the leftovers from the household's meals (the supposed staircase can still be seen in the church of St Alessio on the Aventine in Rome). This arrangement continues until the voice of God is heard in the Roman forum, announcing to the people that since the city is such a place of sin, He is mindful to destroy it unless one man whose life is truly holy can be found. An urgent search commences for a life of sanctity; suggestions that it might be the pope or one of the clergy are dismissed, the voice warns that time is short. Then a servant remembers the man who lives under the stairs, but Alexis is dying, worn out by a life of travel and destitution. He calls for pen and parchment, writes frenziedly for some hours then dies with the document still in his hand. Led by the servant, a crowd converges on the house while attempts by the household to prise the parchment from the hand of the corpse prove unsuccessful until the pope himself arrives. The pontiff effortlessly takes the document and reads. Alexis's identity is revealed, the remorseful father vows to give his wealth to the poor and the city is saved.[62]

For all its clichés the story's resonances clang down the centuries. There is the whiff of the exotic in the travels to the East, but essentially it is a tale of the city with its alienation, inherent wickedness, corrosive effect on family life and corruption of wealth. The story had already been around for a century, but the Rome described is recognisable in the preaching of Arnold of Brescia and in Lyon it raised issues which struck particularly close to home.[63]

Lyon was a naturally prosperous town. It was built at the confluence of the Saône and Rhône rivers. Goods coming down from northern Europe could continue by river to the Mediterranean or offload for overland transport across the Alps into north Italy. The main beneficiary of this prosperity was the cathedral church of Saint John the Baptist which owned nearly half the town and had its own extensive wharves along the Saône. After the sacking of the cathedral area by the counts of Forez in 1162, the archbishop and chapter fortified it and set about building a new, larger church. A few years later the canons gave up the communal life that had been introduced in the previous century and built their own, fine houses within the Great Cloister, as the ecclesiastical complex came to be known. In the very year of Valdes's conversion experience the archbishop settled the dispute with the count of Forez with a payment of 1100 marks of silver ingots.[64] This would have been physically transferred by escorted wagon or ship. In a relatively small town of 10,000–15,000 people it was colossal, ostentatious wealth. There is little doubt that the town would have been larger had the Church not so dominated economic life. Belatedly, the Rhône was bridged around 1180 to gain a larger share of the increased traffic passing to the east of the town and in 1193 the archbishop gave up many of his rights for a large loan from the business community of the city. Within a generation the centre of economic activity passed to the new suburb on the far side of the Rhône.[65]

Even in the more restricted economy of the 1160s it had sometimes been possible to make money. Valdes had been successful with interests in wine, bread production, property and moneylending. His conversion centred less on the possession of riches than what to do with them. Responsibly, he provided for both his wife and two daughters. He then turned to a quite different project, hiring two local clerics to make translations of parts of the Bible and Church fathers. Valdes paid one of them by handing over one of his commercial bread ovens.[66] The turning point came in 1176. Economic expansion in the twelfth century was punctuated with sharp stinging recessions often due to crop failure. With many urban inhabitants only clinging to existence through begging and casual labour, a comparatively small increase in prices could result in severe hardship. The position would not have been helped by the continuing financial burden of the two major capital projects in the town, the bridge and the cathedral. This is probably what happened in 1176 in the months before the harvest. Between May and August Valdes doled out bread, meat and vegetables daily to all who needed it.[67]

In distributing money to the poor, Valdes spelled out a message for other businessmen. As he cried out, 'No man can serve two masters, God and Mammon', his fellow citizens tried to silence him, but he explained:

> I have acted for both myself and you, for myself, so that from now on they who see me with money may say that I am mad, but I did this for you in part, so that you may learn to put your hope in God and not to trust in riches.

From that August he was commited to a life of austerity, irrespective of the very raw nerves he touched. On the following day he approached a former colleague for a meal and was hastily promised the necessities of life for as long as he lived. Valdes's wife was so shocked that she brought a case to the archbishop's court on the basis that if anyone should support her eccentric husband, it should be her. She won.[68]

By 1177 Valdes had departed as much from the story of Alexis as from his previous life. He had a group of followers and far from hiding away was now preaching and denouncing the sins of himself and others. The development of his ideas marked the flowering of a 'free market' of spiritual choice and a lethal threat to the established Church. Comparisons are often made between Valdes and Francis of Assisi, but there are important differences. Poverty seems less important to Valdes, instead he used his wealth to set up an alternative spiritual programme, translating, preaching and charity for the poor. The comparison seems more appropriate with Valdes's contemporary, Peire Mauran, the patron of Cathars in Toulouse. Both were prominent citizens who had earned their wealth and were now choosing to spend it outside the established religious institutions, in effect privatising religion by setting up secular churches. For the existing Church the problem took on the shape of a dilemma because both Valdes and Peire were moneylenders and, by definition, were beyond the pale of respectable Christian society. For the men themselves the choice may have been simpler since spiritually they had little to lose.

Valdes gradually became more than a local figure. When the long dispute between pope and emperor which had dominated European politics since the 1150s finally ended, Alexander III summoned the Third Lateran Council to Rome in 1179 to confirm his authority. Valdes and his followers appeared before the Council and Alexander publicly embraced Valdes, but gave him only the most limited permission to preach, dependent on being asked by a priest. The papal embrace of a layman as a serious spiritual figure was unprecedented and other clerics attending the Council greeted him with outright hostility. Walter Map, the ecclesiastical and secular civil servant whose criticisms of the Cistercians were mentioned in the previous chapter, also loathed Valdes and his followers. Having been asked by a prelate close to the pope to examine Valdes he revealed him to be embarrassingly ignorant of the technical theology taught in cathedral schools; still Map was honest, or selfish, enough to mention the real reason for his dislike of the 'Waldensians' as he called them:

> They have no fixed habitations. They go about two by two, barefoot clad in woollen garments, owning nothing, holding all things in common like the apostles, naked, following a naked Christ. They are making their first moves now in the humblest manner because they cannot launch an attack. If we admit them, we shall be driven out.[69]

Despite the attacks of Walter Map, Valdes had good reason to be satisfied by the proceedings in Rome. He had avoided condemnation in a climate gradually becoming more intolerant. The Council which had been called to mark the end of the papal schism unknowingly mirrored the divisions of the Italian Cathars by annulling all the ordinations of the unsuccessful papal claimants and consequently all those ordained by their appointees were also deprived of their status. Heresy was also considered, but the Council saw it largely as a problem for southern France and contented itself with a vague condemnation rather than a specific plan of action.[70]

On his way to Rome, Valdes may have been able to make contact with Italian sympathisers. The same chronicle that reported his attendance there also reported the growth of a movement of citizens in Lombard towns in the same year, living at home with their families, but choosing to live a form of religious life. This was more privatisation of religion. The Humiliati, as they were called, avoided lies, oaths and lawsuits and dressed in plain clothing. Moreover, they lived in a world of choices and argued publicly for the Catholic faith against all comers. Like Valdes they received a limited approval from the papacy, but with the proviso that they must hold no more meetings and must not preach. Two or three years earlier, almost certainly with Archbishop Galdino's approval, a more acceptable version of the same group had founded a house at Viboldone, near Milan and not far from the influential Cistercian foundation of Chiaravalle. From somewhere within these groups were to come the Italian branch of the Waldensians, the Poor Lombards.[71] Like the Cathars, the Waldensians had a very loose-knit organisation, shaped mainly by local needs, but with an international dimension.

Valdes, however, was still trying to work within the Church. On his return to Lyon, his promise to the pope was enacted at a council attended by the archbishop and a papal legate. Valdes was compelled to swear to a statement of faith which made it clear he neither endorsed dualism nor any other heresy. A good priest turned bread and wine into the body and blood of Christ no more effectively than a bad one. The whole text was probably supplied to Valdes by the Church authorities, only the concluding section gives some evidence of a negotiated statement; hedged about with reassurances that those with possessions could be saved, Valdes gave this declaration:

> whatever we had we have given to the poor, as the Lord advised, and we have resolved to be poor in such fashion that we shall take no thought for the morrow, nor shall we accept gold or silver, or anything of that sort from anyone beyond food and clothing sufficient for the day. Our resolve is to follow the precepts of the Gospel as commands.[72]

Valdes had moved from his initial philanthropy to a position of complete poverty. The reasons can only be guessed at, but the momentum may not all have come from Valdes's side. A group devoted to near destitution posed no threat to the clergy of Lyon as long as they also did not preach publicly. The Waldensians were in a delicate position; they had to ask permission to preach from individual local priests and then resist the temptation to criticise them when permission was refused. Whatever Valdes had promised, his followers were not so compliant and within a few years there were further complaints about the Waldensians' denunciatory preaching.[73]

Ecclesiastical patience wore thin as the reports of unauthorised religious movements and suspect doctrines multiplied. The death of Alexander III and the accession of Lucius III mellowed papal-imperial relations sufficiently to allow a meeting between the pope and the aged Barbarossa in the north Italian town of Verona in October 1184. The spiritual and temporal heads of Christendom agreed on little else but the need for a crusade to help the deteriorating Christian position in the Holy Land and for action to be taken against heresy at home.

The resulting decree was *Ad abolendam diversarum heresium pravitatem*, '*To abolish the disgrace of different heresies*'. It was an impractical document in that there was little prospect of bishops or their archdeacons making visits to each parish once or twice a year to search for heresies as it recommended. It was also ill-informed, condemning groups indiscriminately; the 'Cathars and Patarines' head the list, Humiliati and Poor of Lyon are taken as interchangeable and the largely imaginary threats from the 'Passagians', 'Josephians' and 'Arnoldists' are tagged on. However, in obtaining the co-operation of the emperor a breakthrough was made in that the secular power accepted the responsibility to aid the Church in uprooting heresy so that, for example, heretical priests could be stripped of their clerical status and handed over to secular authority for punishment. The Cathars were established in Verona and went on with their ceremonies virtually under the noses of such distinguished champions of orthodoxy. Persecution could not possibly succeed unless the laity could be persuaded to accept a dividing line between those groups who were acceptable and those who were not.[74]

This confused and inadequate response by the Church revealed the extent to which the spiritual landscape had changed. In the course of a generation groups which could exist outside the Church threatened to make serious inroads into the monopoly it had enjoyed for hundreds of years. Modern observers have picked up on the doctrine of dualism taught by the Cathars as the most dramatic development of the period. To an extent they are reflecting the perturbation of contemporary observers urgently seeking explanations for lay disaffection – the real change was the growth of confidence among the laity. An increase in wealth, education and spiritual consciousness allowed them to make choices inconceivable to their grandparents, such as adopting movements from the Byzantine Empire or believing that a lay man, like Valdes, might possess the path to salvation.

chapter 4

NAILS TO DRIVE OUT NAILS: THE ALBIGENSIAN CRUSADE, THE FOURTH LATERAN COUNCIL, DOMINIC GUSMAN AND FRANCIS OF ASSISI

Many within the Church were sympathetic to the emphasis placed on preaching by Valdes or the early Humiliati and also wished to improve the quality of pastoral care provided by parish priests. At the same time there was concern about the degree of active participation by the laity in their own salvation and genuine fear of the alternative Church offered by the Cathars. The policies of successive popes in the early thirteenth century reflect this ambivalent attitude, even as they accepted responsibility for co-ordinating the response of the Church to the crisis. Whether organising crusades or educational facilities, they brought unprecedented resources and influence to bear. The problem was that often these were dissipated at local level where there was still a heavy reliance on bishops whose quality varied. In the end the crucial skill demanded of popes was to work with the grain of popular piety. From within the Church, Dominic Gusman evolved an order of anti-heretical preachers, while the laity, represented by a merchant's son from Assisi, set about devising a ministry for themselves which prided itself on its orthodoxy.

There had been no decline in interest in any form of popular spirituality. To say that much religious activity took place outside the Church is literally true since the preaching that continued to draw crowds took place outside in churchyards or in fields. The small religious groups which sprang up in north Italy or which the Cathars had organised in southern France offered a more immediate return for patrons or participants than many larger, more established communities. Above all, in areas where heretical movements had become established there was the excitement of being offered an explicit choice for the first time.

The Albigensian Crusade

The idea that dissident religious movements might be suppressed by force was not a quintessential medieval characteristic and indeed only slowly seeped through the generations brought up on the fruits of the twelfth-century Renaissance and reformers who saw secular influence on spiritual affairs as simony. Yet as Peter of Bruys had found out in Saint Gilles, the laity could violently reject subversive messages, particularly where vested interests were at stake. Sometimes they were encouraged by local ecclesiastical authorities and persistent denunciations of the bishop increased the chances of 'spontaneous' action, such as happened to the unfortunate Ramihrdus at Cambrai in 1076 when bishop's officials locked the suspect in a hut and set fire to it.

In contrast there was the tolerance urged by Wazo, the influential bishop of Liège, in the mid eleventh century, based on the doctrine that it was not man's place to weed out the cockle or weeds from the wheat until the harvest, when the reapers would be angels.[1] Wazo's reasoning was partly humanitarian in that he saw the danger of indiscriminate slaughter which could result, but he also rejected the right of the secular authorities to intervene in spiritual matters, a principle which archbishop Thomas Becket was prepared to die for as late as 1170.

As the Church's engagement in society became more complex, Wazo and Becket looked old-fashioned and naïve. In dealing with problems like heresy, however preferable it was to persuade dissidents back into the bosom of the Church, it did not always work, and since churchmen could not administer punishments endangering life and limb, any coercion had to be applied by the secular authorities. Frederick Barbarossa's swift destruction of Arnold of Brescia, technically for rebellion, ended almost two decades of mischief-making and provided a model for the use of the secular sword at the behest of the guardians of spiritual orthodoxy.

From early on there were those within the Church who thought along similar lines; the canons of Utrecht who reported Tanchelm's preaching to the pope appended helpful quotations from Augustine on the desirability of calling on secular princes to intervene.[2] In doing so they touched upon one of the fundamental relationships in medieval political life, namely that if the established Church legitimised the rule of kings and nobles with divine approval then any attack on the faith also undermined their status. The legislation passed at Verona in 1184 assumed secular rulers would help churchmen seek out heretics on pain of excommunication. Obstinate heretics were to be judged by bishops, and 'left to the secular arm for punishment', both tying in the secular authorities to the process and expressing a willingness to consider life-threatening punishments, including burning, a customary penalty for treason. Unfortunately in southern France in particular the nobles had little power and the bishops were too busy or broke, so the procedures remained a dead letter.[3]

At the accession of the 37-year-old Lothar of Segni as Pope Innocent III in 1198 dualism was well supported and capable of further expansion. The new air of urgency he brought to the problem reflected the seriousness of the situation. He was imaginative enough to try a range of solutions over the following 18 years. From the outset he made it clear that heresy was unacceptable, issuing the decree *Vergentis in senium* (*'Turning to the vexation'*) in 1199 which made the link between heresy and treason explicit by declaring heretics traitors to Jesus Christ. He called on secular rulers to take action against heretics with a clear implication that the death penalty could be employed. Moreover, Innocent added that since treason against the eternal majesty was far worse than against the temporal one, goods could be seized and children disinherited.[4] Once he had obtained maximum room for manoeuvre through this legislation, Innocent showed himself capable of taking a more conciliatory approach and despatched a preaching legation of Cistercians to Languedoc in 1203.

These monk legates faced insuperable problems. The Cathars had put down strong local roots over 50 years, relying on the support of communities and political leaders. Moreover, the sheer numbers of people involved in the heresy meant that a few high-profile preachers could address only a fraction of the potential audience. Innocent had not yet grasped the scale of operation necessary to change the religious culture of an area. Nevertheless, the lack of success caused his patience to wear thin. The preaching campaign had always relied on support from lay rulers and when this was unforthcoming, he excommunicated Raymond VI, Count of Toulouse, in 1207 for his lack of action and contacted Philip Augustus, King of France, as to the possibility of a military campaign against those southern French nobility who favoured heresy. Philip demurred since he had to deal with the threat of John of England who was attempting to recapture Normandy. A military solution still appealed to Innocent. In 1204 the Fourth Crusade had delivered Constantinople into the hands of the West and as Innocent thought, given him the opportunity to reunite Catholicism and Orthodoxy. He was planning a further campaign to recapture Jerusalem which had fallen to Muslim forces in 1187. A crusade against heresy in southern France looked a far easier undertaking than either of these projects. Consequently, when the papal legate and Cistercian preacher Peter of Castelnau was murdered in January 1208 by an official of the count of Toulouse, Innocent saw his opportunity. The crusading bull was issued in March 1208 against the 'Albigensians', another term for the Cathar heretics, and it revealed the muddled thinking which lay behind the campaign.

A crusade was an impressive manifestation of religious enthusiasm in its own right and Innocent had promised the customary reward of remission of sins which would take all those who died on crusade directly to heaven. Yet the objectives of the campaign remained vague; crusaders were to 'work to root out perfidious heresy in whatever way God reveals to you'. Heretics were to be displaced from their lands and replaced with Catholic inhabitants. Above all the huge estates of the count of Toulouse were to be seized 'to drive him to give satisfaction to ourselves and the Church and indeed God'.[5] The trouble was the count of Toulouse had never professed himself to be other than a good Christian and before the crusading army had even set off Raymond VI had resigned himself to penitential scourging and taken the crusading vow himself. The campaign then turned against another less prominent noble, Raymond Roger Trencavel, lord of Albi and Carcassonne. He probably was, in fact, a supporter of heresy, but had not been mentioned before by Innocent.

Having assembled in Lyon in late June 1209 the army first approached the town of Béziers. On 22 July 1209, an ill-advised counter-attack by the townsfolk allowed the crusaders through the gate and the result was a massacre which was to besmirch the reputation of the crusaders for ever. Many inhabitants were killed as they sought safety in a church. The events at Béziers were such a public relations disaster that even sympathetic chroniclers were embarrassed. The apocryphal cry of 'Kill them all, God will know his own,' reveals how a German chronicler saw the attitude of the crusaders. The writer of the verse poem the *Song of the Albigensian Crusade*, compared the mayhem to the Muslim invasions of centuries before:

> They killed the clergy too and the women and the children . . . God, if it be his will, receive their souls in paradise! So terrible a slaughter has not been known or consented to, I think, since the time of the Saracens.[6]

At least the ruthless destruction of the first difficult target made military sense. When the crusaders arrived outside Carcassonne, the town surrendered after only a short resistance and the inhabitants were allowed to leave. Perplexingly, following the slaughter of Christians at Béziers, the proportion of Cathar supporters at Carcassonne were allowed to go free.

With the fall of the town the crusaders had achieved their military goals and so, in conscious imitation of their forebears in Jerusalem a century before, after high Mass had been said in Carcassonne cathedral they elected a leader to consolidate their gains. Significantly, the duke of Burgundy and count of Nevers, the most prominent nobles on the crusade, both refused the honour and in the end the committee of knights and bishops charged with the selection process approached a relatively obscure knight from the Ile de France, Simon de Montfort.

Even at a distance of eight centuries, Simon is an intriguing figure. He had served on the crusade of 1204 and had refused to be diverted to Constantinople, instead serving in the Holy Land. By 1209 as an experienced soldier in his mid-40s, he was courageous, energetic and militarily astute. These qualities were undermined by a political ineptitude which alienated many who were initially impressed. The task he was set was not an easy one: as the winter of 1209 drew on, many crusaders considered their spiritual privileges won and set off home, and those who remained, especially the northern French, found the south deeply hostile, complaining of the wildness of the mountains and the danger lurking in the passes. None of them wanted to be killed in such a place.[7]

So Simon was reduced to 30 knights and a few hundred foot soldiers serving for wages, the number swollen by crusaders in the following summer. Although the first winter was the worst, the pattern was to be repeated throughout the long period of warfare. One inviting solution was to seek allies among the political establishment of Languedoc. There had been initial sympathy for the crusaders' cause. Indeed a 'White Brotherhood' had been recruited even in the Cathar stronghold of Toulouse, but de Montfort steadily alienated potential supporters, mainly by his treatment of the southern French nobility. The captured Raymond Roger Trencavel died in suspicious circumstances a few months after the fall of Carcassonne. At Bram in 1210, over 100 of the garrison were blinded: one man was left with an eye to lead the others to the rebel castle of Cabaret. In the spring of the following year, at the siege of Lavaur, the attackers threw Girauda, the sister of Aimery de Montréal, down a well and stoned her to death, then they hanged her brother and put the other knights to the sword. Through its short-term terror tactics Simon's army sowed the seeds of bitter resistance wherever it went. Having finally broken with Count Raymond VI, de Montfort made an attempt to seize the city of Toulouse in 1211. In a brief and fruitless siege his destruction of vineyards and orchards and slaughter of local farm labourers succeeded only in extinguishing his own support in the city.[8]

Equally alarming were Simon's legislative plans; fiefs and knight service were introduced on the model of northern France and grants to supporters from the north were to be held 'according to the custom and usage of France around Paris'. Local knights who had been heretical believers were obliged to render service as required by de Montfort and his fellow barons.[9] Given this attempt at cultural colonisation it was not surprising that the southern French turned to another outsider for protection, in this case the powerful king on the other side of the Pyrenees, Pedro II of Aragon. Having defeated the Spanish Muslims at Las Navas de Tolosa in 1212 on the Spanish frontier with Islam, Pedro had extensive military experience as well as impeccable orthodox credentials as a fighter for the faith.

Pedro appeared eager to extend his influence north of the Pyrenees and linked up with the count of Toulouse and the count of Foix in the summer of 1213. Most observers forecast that this would be the end of de Montfort's career, but at Muret just outside Toulouse, Simon's boldness was rewarded with a crushing victory, causing the death of Pedro and the flight into exile of Raymond VI and his young son. At the subsequent settlement brokered in Rome by Innocent III at the Lateran Council of 1215, de Montfort finally received the county of Toulouse, Raymond was pensioned off and his lands east of the Rhône kept in trust for his son.

The effect of such a complete victory was to trigger an immediate revolt. After a well-publicised pilgrimage to the shrine of Mark the evangelist at Venice to demonstrate his piety, Raymond rejoined his son and returned to Marseille.[10] They made a good combination and the teenage Raymond increasingly took over his father's position even before his death in 1222. The old man's final years were crowned with triumph. After years of dispute with the city of Toulouse he received an ecstatic welcome on his arrival there in 1217. The following year his old enemy died besieging the city, caught by a rock from a catapult built by the defenders and supplied by the women of the town. Simon's own son, Amaury, carried on the struggle for a few years, but did not have his father's enthusiasm for the task and finally, in early 1224, called a truce.

By then, a new political generation looked at matters rather differently: Innocent III had died in 1216 and his successor Honorius III had turned his attention to the Holy Land, Louis VIII had succeeded Philip Augustus in 1223 and his kingdom had completed the absorption of the lands once ruled by the Angevin kings of England. From a comparatively secure position he viewed the unstable power vacuum in the south of his realm. He bought Amaury's rights from him and prepared to campaign himself. An eventual settlement with Honorius brought him papal blessing and an unprecedented amount of autonomy on what was still technically a papal enterprise. Louis began by crushing Avignon

in Provence and slowly worked his way west. Most of Languedoc surrendered before him and unlike de Montfort, the French crown had the
resources for a prolonged campaign. Although Louis died in November
1226, the struggle was continued by Humbert of Beaujeu, the able military
governor, and by the end of 1228 Raymond was forced to negotiate.
At the resulting Treaty of Meaux or Paris, the price Raymond paid for
recognition as count of Toulouse was the promise of his only child,
Joan, in marriage to Alphonse of Poitiers, the French king's brother. In
addition, he had to seek formal absolution from a papal legate and, most
importantly, to promise to persecute heretics found in his territories.[11]

It is worth asking whether 20 years of warfare had had any effect at all
on heresy in southern France. Despite some mass burnings the Cathar
pastoral structure was left largely unaffected: during the years of crusade
the 'good Christians' simply moved away at the approach of the crusader
army. Moreover, preaching campaigns against heresy became difficult
since the Church became identified with the invaders. The epic poem
the *Song of the Albigensian Crusade* starts by describing the actions of
crusaders, *crozatz*, but later, in the hands of a different author, refers to
them as *li clergue e.ls Frances* ('the clergy and the French'). More than
any other factor the crusade helped create a feeling of regional identity.
As Simon de Montfort tried to recapture Toulouse one defender cried:

> because, by the Holy Virgin in who chastity flourished it's either them or us
> for the land and the county.[12]

Catharism lost what international character it had displayed at Saint
Felix and instead became strongly identified with local communities.

Events at Béziers and Carcassonne proved armies were poor judges of
who was a heretic. When it came to presenting these difficulties, chroniclers put a brave face on the problem and emphasised divine intervention. Peter of les Vaux-de-Cernay recorded that after the siege of Castres
two Cathars, a 'perfected heretic' and his disciple, were led before Simon
de Montfort. The older man was unrepentant, but the younger man
claimed to want to obey the Holy Roman Church in all things. An
argument then broke out among the crusaders about what should be
done with the latter. Simon's judgement was that they should burn him,
along with the confirmed heretic. After all if he was truly penitent the
fire would be expiation of his sins, if he was lying then he was justly
punished. Fortunately on this occasion, God intervened and the truly
repentant man was able to step from the fire burnt only at the tips of his
fingers.[13]

The crusade was the necessary precursor for the extirpation of heresy
in that it changed the political structure of the area and made religious

Orthodoxy a crucial indicator of political reliability for the French kings. Although many southern French nobles were still ready to rebel against the crown, support for heretics was no longer an option. For instance, the notorious Cathar knight, Xacbert de Barberà, found it politic to join James I of Aragon's crusade against Muslim Majorca in 1229.[14] Moreover, the Church was strengthened. By the Treaty of Meaux Raymond was committed to providing funds for specified churches and abbeys in the area and establishing a university at Toulouse to improve the training of clergy.

The Albigensian Crusade is usually represented as a crude attempt at the suppression of heresy or a cynical political exercise in the conquest of southern France. While there are elements of truth in both these analyses, the campaign also formed part of the trend, pioneered by the Cathars themselves, of empowering the laity to make religious judgements. Simon de Montfort could decide who was heretical; the framework for an anti-heretical strategy at the Treaty of Paris 1229 was largely devised by the advisers of King Louis IX. It also marked a realisation about the social networks of heresy; if the crusade was the final punishment for the knights who had laughed at Henry of Le Mans's jokes about the clergy in 1145, then most of the thirteenth century was spent trying to understand and engage them. Once political conditions were safe then designated churchmen could inquire into who supported heresy and how the Cathar organisation functioned, while a wider range of choices in popular religion offered under the Church's auspices could provide competition.

Away from the attempt to uproot the Cathars by force, Innocent introduced a number of other measures which attempted to satisfy the spiritual demands of the laity by providing a similar degree of pastoral care to that given by the heretics. In 1199 the laymen and women who commissioned translations of the Bible in Metz were investigated rather than condemned.[15] His attitude to the atmosphere of spiritual excitement of north Italy was particularly revealing. First of all the Humiliati, condemned in 1184, were recognised once again in 1201, following extended negotiations. This was a recognition of how popular such houses had become within the context of their wider communities. In the intervening period no bishop or civic authority had actually suppressed a house of Humiliati. The pope took the disparate elements of the movement such as married couples living together and communities of women and men and approved the common ideal of a religious life as three integrated orders. But he placed particular emphasis on the clerics involved prescribing 'laws or rules' for the lay members. The Humiliati as a whole were to offer pastoral care for the poor and pilgrims, but were not to undertake work on preaching and penance.[16]

A few years later Innocent struck a huge blow against the Waldensian movement when he readmitted into the Church the influential southern French preacher Durand of Huesca. Having been a learned and capable apologist for the Waldensians and critic of the Cathars, Durand finally offered to convert after he had unsuccessfully debated with Catholics in the late summer of 1207. It took over a year for Innocent for ratify his conversion, but once he had, Durand became an accomplished defender of orthodoxy and wrote two influential attacks on Catharism. He and his followers became known as the Poor Catholics and they too turned their attention to north Italy, where they recruited a further group of disaffected former followers of Valdes, the Reconciled Poor. The career of this latter group reveals a problem with Innocent's policy. Originally devoted to preaching, prayer and, as a subsidiary aim, the conversion of heretics (presumably Cathars), the rule was significantly revised in 1212 with the following words:

> *For since the vast majority of us are clerks* and almost all learned we have decided to concentrate on study, exhortation, doctrine and denunciation against sects of all errors.[17]

So the group made the attack on heresy a priority, but this shift was a result of its changing nature: what had started with its roots in the spiritual community of the laity had become a group of clerical activists. The medieval Church was filled with trained professionals and they tended to take over popular religious movements; like many professionals they also had quite fixed ideas about how things should be done. However original the thinking at the top, introducing change at local level was frustratingly difficult.

The Fourth Lateran Council

One solution to the problem of introducing change was to call together prelates from all over Christendom and explain the papacy's intentions. Innocent's most important legacy was the Fourth Lateran Council of 1215. Proclaimed with over two years notice in 1213, Innocent brought together more than 1200 leading clerics, including abbots of the major monastic houses as well as bishops and archbishops, to an assembly in Rome which lasted for three weeks in November. There had been other councils in the middle ages, but the scale of this gathering was a deliberate attempt to align its legislation with the Church councils of the Roman Empire which had established Christian doctrine.

Historical opinion is divided about the Council. 'A spiritual re-birth will never result from the enforcement of a code of law,' declared one pioneering study of the effects of the Council in England. A more recent work has concluded that 'the legislation of Lateran IV had little appreciable impact on the German church in general, or upon the vast majority of German clerics as individuals'.[18] But consideration of the legislation may be missing the point. In the first place, the Council was a summit conference and important events took place behind the scenes. The anonymous chronicler of the *Song of the Albigensian Crusade*, although an opponent of the crusade, reports delightedly on the personal attention lavished by the pope on Raymond VI and the other southern French nobles in private as he sought a territorial solution to the region's problems. Innocent was involved in the question of who should be emperor and was also trying to mediate between King John of England and his barons.[19]

For many the Council must have been the event of a lifetime. Innocent used all the resonant power of Rome as an apostolic centre, with a host of liturgical feasts appropriate to the city all falling due in November. Saint Peter's and many of the city's churches were redecorated and there was an impressive consecration of Santa Maria in Trastevere on Sunday November 15. Dawn Masses preceded the three main sessions of the Council which reached its climax on St Andrew's Day (November 30) with Innocent ascending a platform for his closing sermon like a great biblical ruler.[20] Innocent also used the impressive communicative arsenal of the Roman curia. The text of his opening sermon was available to those of his hearers who may have missed some of his words in the general hubbub, and each participant was given a copy of the legislation prepared in advance.[21] Everything stressed the pope's power and the centralisation of the Roman Church, because Innocent knew that in fact he ruled over a patchwork of constituencies, where even the most inspired bishop or abbot would come up against entrenched local custom.

Innocent's twin aims for the Council were to reform the Church and lead a united Christendom to recover the Holy Land. He saw the second as a precondition of the first, but he offered delegates corporal, spiritual and eternal rewards. The recovery of Jerusalem was a corporal benefit, the reform of the Church, a spiritual one, but by completion of these they would obtain the third, passing into eternal life.[22] For Innocent the problem and the solution were identical: 'For all the corruption of the people principally stems from the clergy.'[23] Innocent planned to make the delivery of religion more effective through the established infrastructure and he turned to this problem, opening the second session on reform with another sermon. He reminded his distinguished audience that they ought to be plough oxen, useful to the community, as opposed to the rest of society which he compared to asses grazing nearby. In particular, the clergy had to avoid ignorance, especially of divine precepts and the offices in the ecclesiastical sacraments. There was a point to this: 'For the knowledge of the truth in the heart of a priest ought to be manifest.' The manifestation was to be accomplished by prayer; but in conjunction with speaking out, denouncing the sins of the laity, irrespective of the disapproval this might bring or the tithes and offerings which might be lost.[24]

A violent outburst among the delegates concerning the disputed imperial throne then cut short Innocent's speech, but the broad principles found their way into the legislation. In the first place there was machinery for the suppression of heresy. Canon 3 backed the Albigensian Crusade by ordering that secular authorities should be compelled if necessary, to expel heretics from lands subject to their jurisdiction. For the first time it also gave a procedure for how heresy should be investigated, prescribing visits by the bishop or archdeacon to any parish where heresy was suspected, using local reliable lay men as informers.[25] In itself it had little impact, still relying on overworked bishops and leaving unspecified how 'reliable' lay men could be found to denounce their neighbours in heretical areas, but it marked an advance in thinking over *Ad abolendam.*

The bishops and archbishops had already been given a heavy burden by the Council as the primary agents of pastoral care. They were to ensure that priests offered a better service to parishioners, treating them almost as religious consumers. Archbishops were to organise annual provincial councils (canon 6), and arrange that the metropolitan church should have a resident theologian to teach priests. At the diocesan level concessions were made to the cosmopolitan nature of many southern European towns by arranging that if there were peoples of different languages within the same city the bishop might appoint a vicar or deputy to celebrate the appropriate rites (9). Bishops too had to ensure that they had someone to give a rudimentary education in each major church and that he had appropriate financial support (11). There was an explicit recognition of the limitations of prelates when the Council ordered a preacher to be appointed in each diocese,

> who will visit with care the peoples entrusted to them in place of the bishops, since these by themselves are unable to do it and will build them up by word and example. (10)

Importantly Innocent also demanded that these preachers should be able to hear confessions and give penance. Enforcement of this was patchy, but the emergent Franciscan and Dominican friars were to fill the space exactly.

The legislation concerning the conduct of the clergy was to feature in the records of Church courts throughout the century and beyond: although the persistence of cases suggested that clerics never did achieve Innocent's ideal, it is at least clear that there was a realisation of what the ideal was. Priests had to live a chaste life (14), avoiding drunkenness and gambling (15). They were to adopt a modest dress and here Innocent's visual sense came into play; red and green cloth was forbidden as were long sleeves and shoes with embroidery or pointed toes (16). Instead priests should concentrate on regularly celebrating the divine office (17). Further attempts to make the clergy's virtues manifest were contained in the legislation curbing the display of false relics and prescribing the conduct of those sent to preach to collect alms (62). In return Innocent tried to guarantee the priest's livelihood by tackling the thorny question of charging for sacraments. While declaring that marriage and the last rites should be given freely Innocent defended the custom of voluntary offerings to the priest (66). He also closed loopholes to protect the payment of tithes to parish priests (54–6).

In all this Innocent was carrying through his promise in his sermon to make priests worthy of the laity's respect by word and example. There were also indications that Innocent thought about religion from the lay consumer's point of view, for example he relaxed the kinship prohibitions on marriage (50). In addition, he made a concession to the generally prosperous lay men or widows who had joined a religious order or confraternity or who had made property over to one, with the expectation that on their death they would be buried as a member of the order. As it was they could be caught out if the area where they lived was under interdict, as quite often happened, if for instance the religious and secular authorities were in dispute, because normal religious functions such as burial were suspended. Even in these circumstances Canon 57 allowed such interments in an order's churches. The move safeguarded legacies and kept influential supporters happy.

The fact that so many of the ideals expressed in 1215 echoed the pious hopes of Church reformers in the past should not obscure Innocent's achievement in changing the relationship between the priest and people and ensuring that whatever the formal enforcement of the Council's decrees, henceforth some quality control could be enforced by the laity themselves. The one demand made of the laity at Fourth Lateran was that they confess to their own priest and take communion at least once a year at Easter (21). The two events were connected in that confessions were usually heard on Good Friday so that parishioners could take part in the liturgical theatre of Easter Day with a clear conscience.

There is evidence that confession was already popular before it was made compulsory, but inevitably the laity started to equate the efficacy of any penance imposed with the character of the priest imposing it and so they looked to confess and receive penance from the person they knew with the highest spiritual prestige. Innocent had already licensed groups of preachers and his successors were to allow more, so that parish priests quickly had rivals to hear confession. Of course, there was a financial interest in this in that the sacrament was usually accompanied by an offering. Priests seem to have been aware of the threat from the beginning, hence the canon's insistence that only with the permission of the parish priest could the parishioner seek absolution elsewhere. In practice the laity voted with their feet.[26]

Innocent's vision at Fourth Lateran was a carefully limited set of choices in spiritual provision for the laity, overwhelmingly supplied by the existing institutions of the Church with supplementary help from preaching groups. But in admitting that the quality and new duties of the clergy were vital, Innocent and his successors found it difficult to avoid the logic that if other bodies could provide these services more effectively, then they should.

Dominic Gusman

One of those on the fringes of the Council seeking confirmation of the title of his Order of Preachers was Dominic Gusman, then based in Toulouse. Dominic has never had the popular appeal of his charismatic contemporary Francis of Assisi, yet in the context of the fight against heresy the Dominicans were a far more effective force than the unpredictable Franciscan movement and Dominic worked hard and responsibly to ensure that his legacy endured. The Dominicans demonstrated the Church's ability to organise and discipline a European-wide movement to carry out its programme of pastoral care. Such was the Dominican success that its leader's personality became submerged in the character of the movement.

On one level Dominic emerges as accessible and unpretentious. His deathbed confession of being more excited by the conversation of young women than by being talked at by old women is echoed by his cheerful injunction to the nuns of San Sisto in Rome to 'drink up, my daughters' from the miraculously never-ending cup of wine he himself had provided. At the hearings for his canonisation one witness declared that 'he exalted in cheap clothes, though he liked them to be clean'. [27] But there was also an austerity and a belief in discipline; he sometimes had himself beaten with an iron chain and was willing to lock one community of nuns in their own church until they agreed to be transferred to San Sisto.[28]

Born around 1170 in Calaruega in northern Castile, Dominic was a career cleric. He became a canon regular at the cathedral of Osma and as a companion of Diego, the bishop of Osma, became involved in international diplomacy. It was on their return from a visit to the Danish court that, in April 1206, the pair met the despondent Cistercian preaching legation, which Innocent III had commissioned three years before.

Both Dominic and Diego already had an interest in the situation in southern France. On a previous visit Dominic had stayed up all night converting an innkeeper from heresy and now the two secular clerks turned their attention to the monks' preaching campaign. It was Diego who suggested that they 'use a nail to drive out a nail', namely that it was not enough only to win the arguments against heretics, they must emulate their simple lifestyle as well. The Cistercian dignitaries were persuaded to send home all their goods and horses and to continue their preaching on foot armed only with books to confound heretical arguments. Diego and Dominic led the campaign by example and this led to a number of organised debates with both Cathar and Waldensian groups. It was at one of these that the leading Waldensian, Durand of Huesca, agreed to rejoin the Roman Church with his followers.[29]

The debates formalised the idea that the laity had a choice in spiritual matters. The increase in preaching was supported by the production of books and pamphlets. These were symptomatic of the economic strength of the area and the literacy of many of its inhabitants. However, the laity seem to have been genuinely at a loss as to how to evaluate all the instruction lavished upon them. A confrontation was held at Montréal between Cathar and orthodox preachers with three prominent local lay men adjudicating by mutual agreement. Both the heretics and Dominic had produced tracts to state their argument, but after reading them and listening to the preachers the judges could think of no more scientific method of reaching the verdict than by throwing both books on the fire. There are echoes here of the lay crusaders' later inability to tell orthodox from heretical and once again the truth was only revealed by divine intervention. In this case the debate was 'won' by Dominic's book leaping out of the fire no less than three times.[30]

For all the persuasiveness of their preaching, the campaign achieved little. The heretics found plenty of support among the local nobility and arguments often failed to change attitudes.

Once, when he [Diego] had plainly and publicly refuted the heretics' errors and subversion in the presence of many nobles, they laughed at him and defended the heretics who were bringing about their downfall, with sacrilegious excuses. Angrily the bishop lifted his hands to heaven and said, 'Lord, stretch forth your hand and punish them . . . so that vexation might make them understand.'[31]

Jordan of Saxony, one of the first chroniclers of the order, portrays this cry of frustration as a prophecy and justification for the Albigensian Crusade. Diego returned to Spain shortly afterwards and died at the end of that year, 1207. Consequently the mission lost direction. Most of the small group of clergy Diego had brought with him went home. Indeed Dominic may have been among them. Although another report says that he continued to preach and debate, he disappears from the record.[32] The murder of Peter of Castelnau meant that the wider preaching mission was abandoned and Innocent III considered a change in tactics.

Dominic's presence or absence is important. It was one thing to have continued with his preaching despite the crusade, quite another to have only resumed because of it. Certainly his fortunes changed dramatically with its success. From 1211, he received support both from Bishop Fulk of Toulouse and Simon de Montfort. Dominic now had the chance to take on heresy in a wider context. He had already realised that preaching to the laity was not enough unless the Church could provide the sort of social support structures already provided by the heretics. In 1206 or 1207, at Prouille, just a few hundred yards from the Cathar village stronghold of Fanjeaux, he and Diego founded a convent 'to receive noble women who had been entrusted to the heretics to be fed and educated by their parents on account of their own poverty'.[33] This reveals much about both the state of the minor nobility in Languedoc and the social role of religion. The bishop provided the church of Fanjeaux and other properties, giving Dominic both financial support and a role in the structure of the diocese. Simon reinforced his financial position by granting Dominic and his associates the revenues from the fortified village of Casseneuil. In return, Dominic identified closely with the crusaders, witnessing charters redistributing land and presiding over the wedding of Simon's son, Amaury.[34] From then on Dominic's preaching had the threat of force behind it and even the heretics realised that killing him would be counter-productive.[35]

During the next few years Dominic prospered and the number of his followers grew, as they received donations of incomes and churches from de Montfort, Fulk and Peire Selha, a prominent Toulouse businessman. Only in 1215 did the group become an order however, when Dominic received recognition for his band of preachers from Innocent III, adapting the Augustinian rule to evade the ban on new orders imposed by the recent Fourth Lateran Council. To stress their monastic roots they were referred to as 'brothers' (*fratres*), but they were 'friars' not monks, taking vows, but living in the world. Since they wore plain, dark habits they became known as the 'Black Friars'.

It is in the two years between 1215 and 1217 that Dominic's vision of the response to heresy changed. As southern armies closed in on Toulouse in 1217, he announced to his brethren that they were to split up and small parties were sent Madrid, Paris, Rome and Bologna.[36] Two of these destinations were university cities and the Dominican association with learning was strengthened by recruiting among masters and students. This was to be the real success of the order, which for ten years had remained tiny in numerical terms. Many of the preachers from both Paris and Bologna were to preach against heresy in southern France and north Italy. Within a decade the Dominicans were able to take on the heretics on a scale that their founder could only have dreamt of.

Secondly, Dominic became more interested in poverty. Previously he had only insisted on personal poverty for his preachers and the order had grown moderately prosperous. After the Fourth Lateran Council Dominic hardened his position. The rule had already imposed stricter observances on diet, clothing, bedding and fasting, now Dominic proposed that the order would own no property, but still accept revenues to meet their needs. In time he went further, and by 1220 had adopted a position of 'apostolic poverty', renouncing all existing properties and revenues. In this move Dominic may well have been influenced by Francis of Assisi's enthusiasm, although historians within his own order have looked for an independent impetus. In a sense the debate is irrelevant, since any new spiritual movement in the early thirteenth century was obliged to embrace poverty to maintain spiritual credibility. However, for Dominic poverty was always strictly a means to an end. Dominican communities were allowed to own their own churches and though forced to beg for their alms, there was no prohibition on the receipt of money.[37]

Before he died in 1221 Dominic left one more important legacy to his growing order. At the General Chapter at Bologna in 1220 he outlined the structure of Dominican organisation, which was fully articulated by Jordan of Saxony, his successor as Master-General: it can be shown diagrammatically in Figure 4.1.

The structure combined elements from earlier monasticism, notably the Cistercians, with a representative character, which allowed even the ordinary friar to feel that his individual voice could be heard, particularly since few houses consisted of more than 20 friars. The Dominicans were also an efficient organisation. The steering committee of 'diffinitors' allowed day-to-day continuity at provincial level as well as also being a check on the powers of the provincial prior whom they could discipline

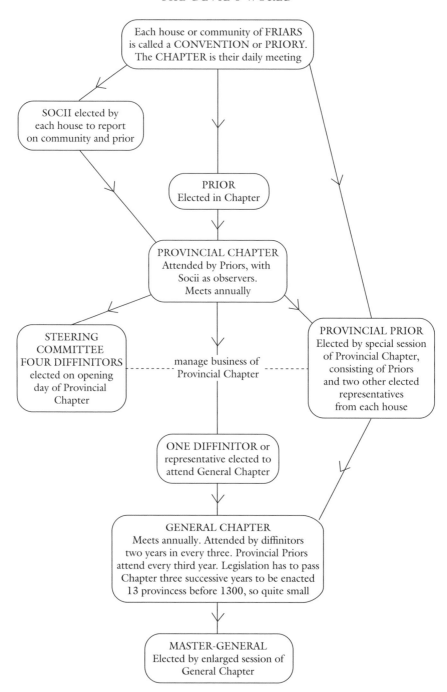

Figure 4.1 Organisational structure of the Preaching Friars

Source: C. H. Lawrence, *The Friars: the impact of the early mendicant movement on western society* (Harlow, 1994), 82–4.

if necessary. The Dominican expansion was rapid, but well directed. At the second General Chapter in Bologna in 1221, five provinces were set up while plans for seven others were also outlined. The battle against heresy was still paramount and preachers could gain comparative experience of their opponents by being sent from one area of Christendom to another. Roland of Cremona was a distinguished university theologian who became a Dominican and preached against Cathars in both north Italy and southern France.[38]

The Dominicans' roots in tradition and their founder's modesty led to some profound differences from their Franciscan contemporaries. Whereas the latter based their existence on the life of one individual which in turn came from his direct revelation from God, the Dominicans laid enormous stress on their order. There is a marked contrast between the importance placed on the published 'Lives' of St Francis and the relatively uncontroversial nature of Jordan of Saxony's *Libellus* on the 'Beginnings of the Order of Preachers'. The title of the latter says much about its author's priorities. Whereas the history of Franciscanism shows a continual tension, sometimes creative, sometimes not, between loyalty to the order and to the vision of its founder, Dominicans were firmly directed towards institutional loyalty to the wider Church.[39]

Dominic was also concerned to protect the individual conscience. Quite directly, the Dominicans maintained that breaking their rules was no sin, merely a contravention against human law. Probably the most famous Dominican of all, Thomas Aquinas (*c.*1225–74) was to state every act of obedience must always be a free, deliberate, rational act. It was less sinful to obey your conscience against the commands of your superior than it was to obey your superior against the commands of your conscience, even if your conscience was in fact wrong.[40] Paradoxically, this fundamental statement of the individual's liberty to make his own moral decisions combined with the emphasis on a collective identity as an order, to produce a fanatically loyal organisation in which the individuals could act with the complete freedom of the justified conscience. When inquisitors to extirpate heresy were being recruited in the 1230s, the Dominicans made ideal candidates.

Francis of Assisi

The most profound sign that religion was now to be organised around the laity's spiritual requirements came from Italy with the growth of the Franciscan movement. Francis of Assisi was a classic rich young man. Once he had decided against going into the family business he had little else to do but decide his spiritual destiny. In a sense it was not surprising that the boy who had never wanted for money turned into the man who claimed he did not need it. His real gift was his own charisma and the ability to suggest to others that they too might have the leisure to undertake their own religious odyssey. This view is clouded by the nature of the historical sources. Accounts written after his death became embroiled in the controversies which overshadowed the movement itself, culminating in the attempt to suppress all other 'Lives' once Bonaventure of Bagnoreggio had produced his definitive version in 1266. Therefore, most of what follows here is based on Thomas of Celano's 'Life' written around 1229, which although concerned with confirming Francis's sanctity, has a relatively uncomplicated agenda and the advantage of being almost contemporary.

Francis was born around 1181 in Assisi in Umbria, the son of a rich cloth merchant, Pietro Bernardone. Although apparently trained in the family business, Francis, unlike Valdes, never had to make money, merely to spend it. Thomas of Celano hints at a wild youth maturing into a young man dreaming of martial glory. For reasons never fully explained, Francis's plans changed. Some sort of crisis began around 1205. After a sales trip to Foligno, Francis tried to donate the entire proceeds to the priest of the decaying church of San Damiano on the outskirts of Assisi. The priest refused it, fearing either that he was being made a fool of, or that Pietro would come looking for his money. The angry merchant did indeed search for his earnings and this began a dispute with his son which was to lead first to imprisonment at home and finally to an extraordinary case in the bishop's court where Pietro tried to get Francis to renounce his inheritance rights. His son obliged by returning everything to his father, including his clothing, leaving him stark naked, covered only by the bishop's mantel.[41]

Despite being given a small church of his own at the 'Portiuncula', a couple of miles from Assisi, by a sympathetic Benedictine monastery, Francis still seems to have been groping for a purpose in life. Only the knowledge of Christ sending out his disciples to preach, supposedly gained from a priest reading the gospels in the Portiuncula, confirmed his vocation. Francis started to preach the virtues of penance, going barefoot dressed in a habit with a cross on, reminiscent of the crusaders.[42] Hundreds of years of hagiography have made him a mythic figure, encapsulated in the Cimabue portrait of 'Il Poverello' in the basilica at Assisi; this is the saint as vagrant, a thin and haggard little man, staring out at the future with luminous eyes. However, the masterpiece was not drawn from life; Cimabue was already recycling a myth received. A probably contemporary picture at Subiaco monastery shows an erect and fine-featured 'Brother Francis' standing confidently, ready to address the viewer.[43] Francis was not illiterate, knowing both French and Latin, but in the main he relied on his excellent memory to absorb and communicate the message of the gospels. His knowledge was reflected in his first 'Rule', which he produced in 1209 and which was cautiously approved by Innocent III. By this time he had converted a small group of followers, mainly from the wealthy youth of Assisi. Francis's obsessions were already in place; despite warning that religion was a matter of interior spirit, much time was spent enjoining the brothers to limit their clothing to two tunics which they could patch, 'to hate their bodies with its vices and sins' and especially not to accept or even touch money.[44]

Francis's charisma brought him the unswerving loyalty of his followers without which the order may well have disintegrated in its chaotic early years. They adopted the title of the 'Lesser Brothers', eventually becoming known as the Grey Friars from their undyed tunics. These brothers said the monastic hours, but their main business was preaching. In a move reminiscent of Dominic, Francis dispersed his small band to various parts of the world in 1217, only to reverse the decision because he desired to see them again. Early missions to Spain, France, Germany and Hungary accomplished little because of a lack of elementary preparation in language instruction: five friars sent to Morocco were killed. Francis himself set off to Egypt in 1219 and secured an interview with the Sultan Al-Kamil, a mission as brave as it was fruitless. Only when projects became better organised were the Franciscans successful. A second mission to Germany in 1221 contained four native speakers, as well as both priests and laymen and letters of recommendation from the pope.[45] From then on the movement achieved startling success. By 1226, the order was divided into twelve provinces; its heartland was still Italy, but it reached England in 1224, and Scotland around 1230.

Francis endlessly sought to broaden the appeal of his religion and succeeded through his extraordinary personality. One of his earliest converts was Clare of Assisi, the 17-year-old daughter of local aristocrats who turned up one night at the Portiuncula in 1211. Francis managed a potentially scandalous situation skilfully, and for a while there seemed a chance that women might be allowed to lead an active religious life in the community. Jacques de Vitry, travelling through Umbria in 1216, reported on the activity of the 'Lesser Sisters', in hospices where they earned a living by the work of their hands. Tantalisingly, he also refers to their 'active life' outside the hospice which perhaps meant tending the sick or the poor. By this time Clare herself had accepted a life of enclosure: placed by Francis next to the church of San Damiano, she and her followers were to follow the Rule of Saint Benedict, and only the insistence on poverty remained of their original Franciscan ideals.

Although Clare received confirmation of this 'privilege' on her deathbed in 1253, it was to extend to her house only. However, other women claimed to be participants in the Franciscan way of life without leaving their homes; 'each of them lived the common life decently, afflicting her body with fasting and prayer'.[46]

Francis also drew up a rule for hermits. His own spiritual career began and ended with long periods alone, and some time between 1217 and 1220 he legislated for small communities of three and four, allowing members to beg for alms and bringing them under the supervision of Franciscan ministers. These communities resemble those organised by the Cathars in southern France and there were probably many like it operating outside any monastic discipline throughout Italy. But it was his preaching that made Francis famous throughout Europe. He spent Christmas 1223 in the little hill village of Greccio. There was still enough of the patrician about Francis to order a supporter to prepare a manger of hay and have ox and ass standing by so that he could enact the memory of Christ's birth. Once the preacher had arrived he put on a stunning performance. In a scene lit with candles and torches, Francis spoke about 'the babe of Bethlehem', pronouncing Bethlehem like a bleating sheep. This may have been the invention of the 'crib'; it certainly showed the unabashed emotionalism of Francis's approach.

> Though he often preached the word of God among thousands of people, he was as confident as if he were speaking with a close friend. He used to view the largest crowd of people as if it were a single person, and he would preach fervently to a single person as if to a large crowd.[47]

The result is recognisable at eight centuries distance:

> . . . people were filled with such grace and devotion that they were trampling each other in their eagerness to see and hear him . . . When he entered a city, clergy rejoiced, bells rang, men exulted, women rejoiced, and children clapped . . . Driven by great faith, people often tore his habit until sometimes he was left almost naked.

Yet Francis continually sought out new audiences. At Bevagna near Assisi he came across a flock of birds whom he instructed to love their Creator before giving them permission to fly off. They responded in much the same way as any other crowd, rejoicing and allowing him to touch their heads and bodies with his tunic. Afterwards, Francis accused himself of negligence for not preaching to them before and from then on was prepared to address all animals, reptiles and even inanimate objects.[48]

With such unorthodox strategies Francis and his followers constantly risked accusations of heresy. The ill-fated mission to Germany in 1217 nearly foundered when the friars replied to the question of whether they were heretics from Lombardy with the only word of German they knew, 'Ja'. Early Franciscans in France were so strongly suspected of heresy that only a sharp letter from Honorius III convinced many bishops to allow them access.[49] Francis himself was protected early on because his family were rich and influential, while the papacy was unwilling to offend the inhabitants of Assisi which lay in a crucial border area of papal influence. As his influence grew Francis took immense care not to offend potential enemies. Thomas of Celano reported that the early Franciscans deliberately chose a priest of dubious reputation to hear their confession so that they could show proper reverence. In the peculiar document Francis drew up in the last years of his life, known as his 'Testament', he once again stressed that he had 'such faith in priests who live according to the rite of the holy Roman Church because of their orders that, were they to persecute me, I would still want to have recourse to them'. More practically, he defused the potential conflict over lay offerings by his decision to live a life of absolute poverty and refusal to accept gifts of cash or land.[50]

Francis also sought protection for his order. Besides humility and simplicity there is a touch of a man well aware of the importance of his work when he went to Rome to seek approval of his rule as early as 1209, just four years after his conversion. He moved rather quicker than Dominic and was more sure-footed than Valdes. Having defused potential jealousies by refusing all papal privileges he then approached the influential cardinal bishop of Sabina to act as his spokesman, thereby ensuring that he would always have someone to put his case at the papal curia. When the bishop died, Cardinal Ugolino, bishop of Ostia, took on the role and was to become almost as important an influence on the order as Francis himself.[51] Francis's lack of organisational ability may have hindered the movement in its early years, but he himself did not hold any office within the order after 1218, when he resigned as Minister General in order to plan his journey to the East. Instead he declared that:

> I firmly wish to obey the general minister of this fraternity and the other guardian whom it pleases him to give me. And I so wish to be a captive in his hands that I cannot go anywhere or do anything beyond obedience and his will, for he is my master.[52]

The 'guardian' referred to was a brother who lived with him and whom he 'obeyed in place of the general minister'. In the long run this was the seed of trouble. Rhetoric apart, Francis had created a double focus for his authority: even before his death there was tension between those who formally acted in the founder's name and those who were witnesses to his example. Francis complicated matters further by intervening himself with letters to the General Chapter and documents such as his 'Testament'.

The effect was mitigated to some extent by Francis's warm relationship with the Church establishment. Francis became a deacon in his early forties and in 1223 he revised his Rule, probably with extensive help from Ugolino. In this document the life of the Friar Minor still consists of preaching, poverty and prayer, but the preaching was now formally subject to the local bishop's permission and no friar could preach without first being examined and approved by the Minister General (Ch. IX). The division of responsibilities regarding prayer reflected a movement increasingly drawing members from those already within holy orders. The priests were to recite the Divine Office, the lay brothers to say multiple 'Our Fathers' (Ch. III). As for poverty, this still held a central place in the Rule where the brothers are described as 'poor in temporal things, but exalted in virtue' (Ch. VI). Because friars could not hold property or income a substantial part of the rest of the Rule wrestled with the consequences. It led to provisions such as that the brothers could ride horseback when 'compelled by obvious need' (Ch. III) and most importantly, that Franciscan officials had the latitude to use 'spiritual friends' to provide for the friars' needs, so long as they did not receive coins or money (Ch. IV).[53]

For all the careful legislation, Francis's example tore holes in rules and located a space where anyone, lay or cleric, could be transformed through personal religious commitment. Something of his magnetic spirituality comes through in the '*Canticle of the Creatures*', composed late in life in his Umbrian dialect. In it Francis praises God through his creation; not only obvious facets like the sun, moon and stars, but fire, 'Beautiful and playful and robust and strong', and death:

> Praised be You, my Lord, through our Sister Bodily Death from whom no one living can escape. Woe to those who die in mortal sin. Blessed are those whom death will find in Your most holy will, for the second death can do them no harm.[54]

The song can be interpreted as a counterblast to the Cathar demonisation of creation. There is also a glimpse into the universality of Francis's vision as 'Brother Sun', 'Sister Moon' and the rest are co-opted as friars. Another clue as to the reasons for the popularity of Francis and his followers is given by the verse in praise of those who 'endure in peace'; composed it is said on the outbreak of a violent dispute between bishop's officials and civic authorities in Assisi. Thomas of Celano also stressed that

Francis made peace between those in conflict.[55] Given that most Italian cities suffered from endemic factional violence the call for reconciliation may have been an important part of the appeal of the early friars.

Above all in the song there is reassurance. Like the Cathars, Francis promised at least an escape from 'second death', the Last Judgement, providing the believer had all in order at the first. This could be arranged through confession and penance as the Fourth Lateran Council ordered. And Francis's guarantees were nigh on unbeatable. His offer to people to lead the life of Christ was seemingly endorsed by Christ himself when Francis received the stigmata, the very wounds of crucifixion, while praying on Mount La Verna, some time in 1225.[56] Whatever the modern observer makes of this phenomenon, in terms of medieval spirituality Francis's wounds were an innovation. They were to recur many times in holy men and women of later centuries, but at the time they were unique, defining and justifying a generation with as striking a sign of divine approval as the success of the First Crusade a century before. Francis was considered as close as was possible to being a living saint and after his death in October 1226, canonisation took place within two years, presided over by Pope Gregory IX, formerly Francis's supporter, Cardinal Ugolino.

Dominic, Francis, the Fourth Lateran Council and the Albigensian Crusade were all 'nails to drive out nails' in their differing attempts to imitate the successful attributes of contemporary heretics, as churchmen understood them. Between them they reproduced the lives of austerity and preaching of the spiritual elite, while attempting to recruit lay defenders of a recognisable faith. At first sight, then, Innocent III's pontificate marks a decisive turning point, a co-ordinated response from the Church. However, it could be argued that it was no such thing. The Albigensian Crusade had proved it was impossible to crush religious movements through military force; the Dominicans showed that the most learned and austere preachers could only persuade a fraction of the population to change their beliefs and the Fourth Lateran Council represented a set of aspirations so ambitious that their dissemination could only draw attention to shortcomings on the ground. As for Francis, he offered a way of life so different from ecclesiastical custom that, although orthodox, it had the potential to bypass the organised Church altogether. Taken as a whole, the policies of the early thirteenth century did not so much defeat heresy as stimulate it. The opening decades of the thirteenth century saw as competitive a battle for souls as at any time before the Reformation.

chapter 5

COMPETING FOR SOULS: FROM THE DEATH OF FRANCIS TO THE FALL OF MONTSÉGUR

The years following the Fourth Lateran Council saw an open competition for souls among religious movements, preaching to and recruiting from a well-informed Christian population who were able to make spiritual choices. After great initial promise it was a period which disappointed many within the Catholic Church. In the early years it seemed as if the Albigensian Crusade had removed the political threat of Catharism, while the arguments produced by heretics would be refuted by careful instruction of the growing number of students at university, many of whom were eager recruits to the new orders of friars. Fourth Lateran was supposed to have spread the message still wider and provided the basics of a spiritual life for every Christian even at parish level. Yet heretical movements proved remarkably resilient. Both the Waldensians and Cathars proved how deeply rooted they were, especially in southern France and northern Italy. Despite some spectacular successes such as the 'Great Alleluia' spiritual revival in Italy of 1233, churchmen became increasingly frustrated with the intractability of these problems, in particular the slowness of the laity to rally to the Church. More disturbingly still for many within the Church, the largest movement of all, the Franciscan friars, began to resemble the heretical organisations, fissured by regional and doctrinal divisions. As time went on even the moderate clerical opinion moved towards discipline and coercion to guide secular society in the right direction.

The Franciscans after Francis

After years of fasting and general abuse of his body, Francis of Assisi died in his mid-forties, on October 3, 1226. His passing was greeted with rejoicing, tinged with only a little sadness, as befitted the departure of a living saint. But writing only two or three years later his biographer Thomas of Celano inserted the following lament:

You know, you truly know, the danger in which you have left them; for it was your blessed presence alone that always mercifully relieved their countless labours and frequent troubles![1]

Francis left a confused legacy. This was literally true from his 'Testament' composed in the last months of his life. He reiterated his exhortations to his followers not to receive churches or have anything built for them unless according to the holy poverty promised in the Rule. Questions remained as to how realistic this instruction could be for a movement now numbering thousands. As the order expanded into less developed areas of Europe such as Poland or those with a very different religious tradition such as the former territories of the Byzantine Empire, the need for churches and dwelling places became acute.

Supplying and organising the friars remained difficult. Their commitment to preaching and, increasingly, to hearing confession, which formed the basis of systematic pastoral care, required the friars to be routinely fed and clothed. From time to time this would necessitate buying goods, thereby violating Francis's horror of contact with money. An organisational framework did exist by 1226, consisting of twelve provinces created by Francis and his advisers, six in Italy, six north of the Alps. Yet unlike their Dominican counterparts the degree to which they represented the ordinary friar was still unclear. Consequently, in May 1230, those behind an attempt to depose the order's elected leader, or Minister General, could turn the reburial of the saint's body in the impressive basilica built for it in Assisi into a chaotic General Chapter of all the friars who happened to be present.

Such incidents raised the issue of how discipline was to be maintained, but here again the founder left little guidance. He conceded that there might be found in the order some who were not reciting even the light burden of religious services as prescribed in the Rule, or even who were not Catholic at all; however, his solution of delivery of the offender in chains to Cardinal Ugolino was hardly practicable.[2] Even the contents of the Rule itself were open to dispute. With dream-like ambiguity, the opening of Francis's Rule for the order stated that:

> The Rule and Life of the Lesser Brothers (*fratres minores*) is this: to observe the Holy Gospel of Our Lord Jesus Christ by living in obedience, without anything of one's own, and in chastity.[3]

Many within the order wondered if that meant that the gospels themselves be considered part of the Rule. Finally, many churchmen were uneasy that such sensitive questions should remain in the hands of lay members of the order, rather than in the hands of trained clerics. Such views were directly opposed to the key point of Francis's vision of a quasi-monastic order which could be joined by untrained lay people, as Francis had been at the beginning.

As early as 1230 Ugolino, a supporter of Francis from the start and now Pope Gregory IX, took a decisive hand in the order's development with the issue of the papal decree of *Quo elongati*.[4] This attempted to resolve a number of important issues. In the first place it reminded the friars that it was only with the consent of brothers and ministers that Francis could legislate and that therefore the order was not bound by its founder's 'Testament'. Gregory also dealt shortly with the status of the gospel in the Rule by deciding that the friars were only bound to observe the gospel's precepts in the same way as any other Christian. One of the reasons Gregory gave for this decision, in flat contradiction of the explicit goal of the life Francis and his early followers had led, was that it was a commitment that the friars had not intended to take on. It showed how much distance had already opened between the leaders of the order and their founder.

Gregory then turned to the delicate issue of handling money. A demand for change is presented as coming from within the order, and Gregory was diplomatic enough to provide alternative solutions to what should be done if the brothers wanted to buy something necessary or make payments for something already purchased. The preferred option was, however, clear. A designated agent should make the purchase from alms deposited with a 'spiritual friend or familiar acquaintance' of the friars: despite the formal language this looks remarkably like the arrangements made for Cathar *perfecti* who held funds through their *depositarii*. Almost as sensitive was the problem of property and here again Gregory provided a brisk solution which severely modified the ideals of the founder. Given that some within the order were claiming that movable property belonged to the order as a whole, Gregory reiterated Francis's precept that the brothers not appropriate anything as their own. Then he subtly undermined the principle by decreeing that:

> the brothers may have the *use* of equipment or books and such other movable property as is permitted, and that the individual brothers could have the use of them at the discretion of general and provincial ministers.

Gregory's distinction between use and ownership released the Franciscan potential for missions to far-off lands and recruitment in the rich cities and centres of learning in western Christendom. Moreover, it is virtually inconceivable that such arrangements did not already exist within the rapidly expanding order. But it was a solution with many weaknesses. To many friars it was an unignorable departure from Francis's ideals. Over time the subtlety of the use-ownership distinction was lost on the

1. Thirteenth-century manuscript illumination of troubadours from Alphonse le Sage's *Las Cantigas*, © Gianni Dagli Orti/CORBIS (IH64074).

2. Castello Scaligero, Sirmione, © K.M. Westermann/CORBIS (WN001950). Last refuge of the Italian Cathars.

4. St. Dominic Sending Forth the Hounds of the Lord, with St. Peter Martyr and St. Thomas Aquinas, *c.*1369 (fresco) by Andrea di Bonaiuto (Andrea da Firenze) (*fl.*1343–77). Santa Maria Novella, Florence, Italy (BAL130097).

3. Plan scénographique de 1550: Archives municipales de Lyon. Sixteenth-century plan of the city of Lyon, showing cathedral, fortified ecclesiastical quarter, and cathedral wharf from the time of Valdes.

5. The staircase under which lived Saint Alexis, the inspiration for Valdes of Lyon. Staircase now in the church of Sant'Alessio, Rome. (Thanks to Helena Bruce.)

6. Italian fresco with early image of Francis of Assisi, © Archivo Iconografico, S.A./CORBIS (CS004509).

7. View of Carcassonne from the west side, state of the fortifications and the city in 1853, illustration from 'Monuments Histori' by Viollet-le-Duc, Eugene Emmanuel (1814–79) (after). Private Collection, Giraudon (XIR217771 #57).

8. St. Francis (fresco) by Cimabue (Cenni di Pepo) (*c*.1240–*c*.1301)
    San Francesco, Assisi, Italy (BEN113975).

9. St. Francis Releases the Heretic, 1297–99 (fresco) by Giotto di Bondone
    (*c*.1266–1337). San Francesco, Upper Church, Assisi, Italy Giraudon
    (XIR63359).

10. Montségur Castle, Languedoc, France (b/w photo) by Simon Marsden (Contemporary Artist). The Marsden Archive, UK (TMA220587).

11. Saint Peter Martyr (oil on panel) by Carpaccio, Vittore (c.1460/5–1523/6). Museo Correr, Venice, Italy (MES97834 #81).

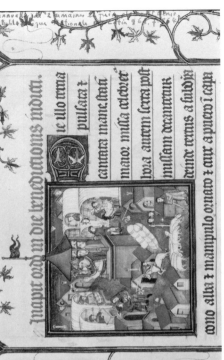

13. Miniature of a bishop blessing the annual fair or market held for two weeks in June on the plains of St. Denis, Bibliotheque Nationale, Paris, France (BAL52371 Lat 962 f.264).

12. Ruined Arena, Verona, © John Heseltine/CORBIS (SL003793).

14. The Porziuncola (Portiuncula), Assisi. First home of the Franciscans. (Thanks to Eva Duve.)

15. Interior view of the church (photo) by Arnolfo di Cambio (*c.*1245–1310). Santa Croce, Florence, Italy (BAT201228 #245).

wider public and even on many within the Church itself; to outsiders the friars eventually became as comfortable as any other order.

Finally, Gregory vastly increased the standing of ordained members of the order by decreeing that as many priests from within the order as necessary be appointed as confessors for the friars in each province. Ordinary friars had a choice of confessing private sins to these confessors or to their ministers or to their 'custodians', officials of the order subordinate to the provincial ministers, if there was one available. The power to hear confession and enforce penance meant that those friars who were ordained tightened their grip on Francis's unreliable lay membership.

The fear of allowing the laity a spiritual role seemed to be borne out by the career of Brother Elias, a long-time companion of Francis and a trusted deputy. Elected Minister General in 1232, he was accused of gross personal extravagance. Moreover, the great church he designed in Assisi for the body of the founder inevitably excited unease that Francis would not have approved of such ostentation.[5] It is difficult not to have sympathy with Elias in that he was faced with many of the tough decisions hitherto avoided by the followers of the saint. He had secured Francis's body, and the magnificence of his building served as both pilgrimage centre and headquarters for the order. The translation of Francis's prestige into stone was as good an insurance as any that his teachings could not be forgotten or condemned in any change of fashion. Elias also increased the number of provinces and appointed lay members of the order to head them, as no doubt Francis would have wished. In his personal conduct he realised that he was not a saint and could not live as one. As the head of a major international order he would not be taken seriously by monarchs and prelates if he appeared on foot and dressed in rags. Besides, he was not a young man and suffered ill health. Consequently, he acquired horses, a retinue and ate well. Under his tutelage the order prospered and expanded. But Elias had made powerful enemies. The Franciscans had been successful in attracting idealistic scholars in the universities and recent recruits from Paris such as Alexander of Hales and John of La Rochelle launched attacks on him in the late 1230s, so that by 1239 tension had reached such a pitch that a General Chapter was summoned in Rome by Gregory IX himself.

Elias made a robust defence of his lifestyle and stated that it had been the chapter's wish that, if his illness required it, he could have a horse and 'eat gold' if necessary. Another academic, Haymo of Faversham, replied tartly that the brothers may have wanted him to eat gold, but not to possess a treasury; neither were the two expensive thoroughbreds Elias had acquired what was envisaged when the brothers said he might have a horse. Amid loud complaints from Elias and his supporters that these were lies, the Minister General was deposed.

The chapter has been presented as the triumph of priests and intellectuals over simple laymen and there is something to this, but it illustrated some of the conflicts within a cosmopolitan international order. Elias's opponents were almost all northern Europeans brought up in a tradition of centralised government and aware of the need for an independent Church administration to ward off encroachment from the state. By contrast, the early Franciscans had been organised informally because in Italy they could generally rely on the favour of the local secular power; only as they moved into other areas, especially in their missionary work, could no such support be guaranteed. The close relationship with the papacy which developed under Gregory IX gave the Franciscans the backing of the best organised and most influential power in Europe (contemporaries were not to know that it was already past its zenith). In return, Franciscans were employed in a broader strategy to make the Church more attractive to the laity.

With Pope Gregory himself present, even the Franciscans were biddable and they elected as Elias's successor Albert of Pisa, the provincial minister of England, an associate of Francis, and also a priest. It was a major step in the 'sacerdotalisation' of the movement, but may not have been unwelcome at the time. Albert said Mass and then spoke to the large group of friars who had assembled to hear the outcome of the chapter.

> You've just heard the first Mass said in this order by a Minister General. Now with the blessing of Jesus Christ, go to your houses.[6]

He masked an undertone that the reliable clerics were now in charge with a sincere attempt to achieve reconciliation and closure of a painful episode. Elias continued to carp at his demotion, but strained the loyalty of most of his supporters by joining the affluent court of Gregory's bitter enemy, the Emperor Frederick II. There he propounded the virtues of Church poverty without a trace of irony, until his death in 1253.

Albert's rule was short: he died in 1240 and was replaced by Haymo of Faversham, who had never met Francis. He saw the sad end to Elias's career as a way of liberating the order from the grip of its founder and introduced reforms, overtly copied from Dominican practice. The powers of the Minister General were curtailed and instead a more democratic structure established. Provincial ministers were to be elected by Provincial Chapters with *custodes* and guardians to be appointed by the Provincial Minister after consultation with the Provincial Chapter. A chapter of elected diffinitors was to meet during the two years there was no General Chapter. This may have proved rather too democratic since there is only one recorded meeting of such a body at Montpellier in 1241. Haymo also looked at the recruitment strategy of the movement; while the life of poverty had only ever appealed to the well-off and assorted academics, Haymo now institutionalised this by decreeing:

> We order that no-one be received into the order unless he is competently instructed in grammar or logic, or a layman whose entry into the order would be a celebrated and famous example for the clergy and people.[7]

Besides Elias, there was already some dissent against the direction the order was taking. To the north-east of Assisi in the hills of the area known as the Marches of Ancona, there were groups of friars insisting on living a life close to that of Francis, while several of the saint's companions, notably Brother Leo, his confessor and secretary, had retired into grumpy exile to observe developments.

There is an ambivalence about the events of the early 1240s. They made Francis literally inimitable and in doing so missed the opportunity of opening access for all to the life of Christ and his apostles. But in closing this door they opened many others, offering the pastoral care which had become so important in the late twelfth and early thirteenth century. The order was permitted to hear confessions of those who attended sermons in 1237 and was allowed to bury lay people who requested it within their walls in 1250.[8] The 'betrayal' of Francis's original ideals gave the order its real strength, flexibility. Franciscans became missionaries to the East and to the newly conquered Greek Orthodox Lands of the Latin Empire, they became schoolmen in the emerging universities throughout Europe. They also became bishops, supervising pastoral care, and yet they retained their primary role of wandering preachers.

The Franciscans also brought Church influence to bear on the growing number of lay religious movements which were springing up in the mid thirteenth century to demonstrate that the laity were not prepared to wait for the Church to offer routes to salvation, but could take their own. To the long-established lay confraternities, often linked to a church, were added organisations which offered the chance for lay people to live a life as close to the monastic as possible. In Italy many were gathered in the legitimised Humiliati movement. In the north of Europe they became known as Beguines and were established in the urban environment of the Low Countries and northern France as well as cities in Germany such as Cologne. Many of the participants were women, but there were male and mixed communities, including married couples and even whole families.[9]

There were, in addition, lay believers, inspired by Francis himself, who continued to live at home and pursue their working lives. Like monks they fasted, abstained from meat four days a week and observed chastity. Those who were literate said the monastic hours or Psalms, those who were not recited *Pater Nosters*. They met at regular intervals to attend Mass and hear preaching, being particularly touched by Francis's emphasis on penance to save their souls from the sins they had committed. There is no evidence that Francis specifically created a Third or Tertiary Rule for such people, but sources from the early 1240s start to link him with these groups, suggesting that the friars were drawn in. An anonymous writer from Perugia described the problem. Having set up houses for widows, spinsters and virgins seeking salvation, the friars faced an appeal from married men:

> 'We have wives who will not permit us to send them away. [!] Teach us, therefore, how to take this route safely.' The brothers founded an order for them, called the Order of Penitents, and had it approved by the Supreme Pontiff.

There was encouragement from the papacy for both Dominicans and Franciscans to take responsibility for these 'Tertiaries' as they became known.[10] Whatever doubts some churchmen may have had about the friars they showed an ability to reach a wider public and regulate the explosion of religious activity which was taking place.

The Cathars

The real impact of Dominic and Francis was that they made it once again fashionable to be orthodox. Francis may have led the life of someone who 30 years before would have been considered a heretic, but he insisted on absolute obedience to the Church and to the papacy in particular. The Dominicans offered a dynamic intellectual alternative to heresy and moreover offered a career structure to bright young students and academics whereby they could use their skills, keep their principles and yet advance up the career ladder.

The Cathars in southern France shared in some of the intellectual advances of the period, driven no doubt by the keen competition for new recruits, but they were stronger at providing the low-level pastoral care so much in demand in the early thirteenth century. People wanted two things from religious movements, first, men and women whose lives they could respect and, secondly, some sort of assurance as to their own salvation. At its height the Cathar movement delivered both with efficiency and conviction. There were appropriate 'good Christians' to perform the vital *consolamentum* ceremony on the deathbed of a believer to secure the soul's place in heaven and in the meantime the 'good men' preached, blessed and gave advice and help.[11]

Conditions for the heretics were growing harder. One area of activity for the eager recruits for the Dominican friars in particular was the inquisitions which were organised against the Cathars in the 1230s and these, despite pauses and setbacks, became gradually more professional and wide-ranging by the early 1240s. Cathar 'good men' proved difficult to catch, but the sect was vulnerable because of the crucial importance of the presence at a believer's deathbed of the 'good man' or *perfectus*, as the inquisitors termed him. Through him, with the help of prayers and a copy of a gospel or New Testament placed on the head, the believer gained admission to the 'Church of God'. This Cathar *consolamentum* combined mechanistic ritual and a profound spiritual experience. While the adherence to exact formulae conveyed security of salvation to the believer, the ceremony was also usually the culmination of a lifetime's relationship with the Cathars in which there were responsibilities on both sides. When the *perfecti* arrived they had to ask about the attitude of the believer to the Cathar Church and indeed whether he was in debt to the Cathars, in which case it must be paid promptly if possible. In life, the responsibilities of the laity to the *perfecti* were not onerous, they had to greet them respectfully, with a bow and a request to be blessed.[12] They had to provide meals, accommodation and occasionally a guide as they moved in pairs around the region. Raymond Carabassa and his companion stayed with a woman of Bram in Languedoc for four months in 1242, paying for their food. Two years later as he once again moved from village to village Raymond was given freshly baked bread and produce from a believer's vineyard. Other gifts to *perfecti* included fish, nuts, leeks, beans and strawberries.[13]

Much of this pattern of unexpected guests for dinner, and lodgers staying for periods of one night to months on end, is part of the system of reciprocal favours recognisable to anyone who has lived in remote communities or a student house. It is a kind of 'goodwill economy' which forms and binds communities. Other factors could also open the door and may have determined the extent of hospitality; *perfecti* were well aware of family connections such as when Lombarda of Villepinte stayed for three weeks in Fanjeaux in the home of her son-in-law's brother. Family ties succeeded where bribery failed in releasing *perfecti* captured at Mirepoix in 1243 because one of the 'good men' was the uncle of his captor. Lordship was also important; the Niort family protected heretics in the 1220s and 1230s in their lands south of Carcassonne.[14]

It was in death that believers paid their dues to the Cathar Church. In return for the *consolamentum* the *perfecti* expected a bequest. Esclarmonde, wife of Lord Assaut, left the heretics a tunic, 22 pence, an embroidered linen cloth, a gold coin, a winnowing fan and a cloak. Two *perfecti* had to be fetched to her as she lay ill in a cowshed. Often the gifts were more portable such as cash or horses, although in the years before the Albigensian Crusade, even land was given. While the Cathars stressed that the believer should not be turned away if unable to pay, the lay consensus was that it was appropriate for *perfecti* to receive something for their efforts, so that after an unnamed sick woman had been consoled on her deathbed in Moissac, two *saumatae* of wine were collected from a number of people for the 'good men'.[15]

Such arrangements required the *perfecti* to command widespread respect, for not only did the believers themselves have to have faith in the heretics, but their relatives had also to have at least enough regard for the heretics to hand over the bequest: it is here that the ties of blood and time paid their dividend or, as one knight put it:

> 'We cannot [expel them and hunt them down] we were raised with them, we have relatives among them and we see them living lives of honour.'

The 'good men' never forgot that believers had a choice. In towns like Gourdon and Montauban, north of Toulouse, where there were Waldensians and Cathars, several believers gave money and food to both, despite their mutual antagonism. There was a practical element to visiting heretics. The Waldensians developed a speciality in medical care, relying both on their technical knowledge and their high spiritual prestige to bring about a cure. The laity clearly understood that there were differences between the two groups as formal disputes between them were common events, such as the one G. Ricart escorted the Cathar 'good men' to one Easter Day. These were semi-public affairs taking place in people's homes.[16]

Inquisition penances from the early 1240s reveal a world where previously people had made day-by-day decisions about which religious group to patronise. Sometimes there were family influences. One witness listened to Waldensian preaching, but gave more practical support to a group of Cathars, taking them from Toulouse to Montauban, because one of them was his sister. He respected them enough to make them a gift.[17] There are hints that some people were working out their own individual theological views: a man disputed with the Cathars about the creation, another received a Cathar 'good man' into his home only to tell him he preferred the Waldensians, yet another declared to the inquisitors his disbelief in all the Church's sacraments, and that it was a sin to swear, kill or lie with one's wife. He thought that only in the Cathar Church were all saved. Most were not so exclusive: there were plenty of lay people ready to share their table with both groups and declare them to be 'good men'.[18]

Local ties often counted for more than wider allegiances. One known Cathar supporter from Castelnaudary, far from home on business in Narbonne, lay dying, so his companion fetched two local *perfecti*. Because the man could not be sure of these spiritual figures as he could of his local ones from Toulouse, he instead asked for the Cistercian monks of Boulbonne Abbey close to where he was born and so committed his body into their hands.[19]

Given the movement's dependence on deathbed bequests, it is not surprising that so much effort went into gaining popular respect. The *perfecti* took on a range of pastoral responsibilities. Preaching and debating were important. According to one believer, speaking was one of the manifestations of the divine within corrupt human flesh:

> Lucifer had made Man and God said that he would make him speak. But Lucifer answered that he could not and so then God breathed into the bones of Man and Man spoke.[20]

The Cathars seem to have been largely successful in imparting the basic doctrine of dualism, of creation being an unending war between God and the Devil, with the Devil responsible for the corrupt, visible things of this world, although whether evil was an independent force or originally part of the creation of a beneficent God was left uncertain. There were also the inevitable attacks on the Church, with marriage, baptism and the Eucharist receiving regular mockery, as well as the idea of the literal resurrection of bodies. Preaching and disputing with opponents from the Dominicans and Waldensians continued despite the deteriorating security situation until around 1230. After then such confrontations became more risky. A Cathar *perfectus* around 1241 was willing to visit the home of a Waldensian supporter to argue his case, but it was dangerous and unlikely to bring tangible benefits to the movement.[21]

'Good men' often shared meals with believers and this was an important part of their contact. There was some ceremony to it with *perfecti* often blessing bread and then distributing it. The obvious parallels with communion or the Eucharist should be treated with caution. The bread was as important as the ceremony and could be kept. Bread baked by a *perfecta* on Christmas Day 1242 was carried to a household and then blessed by two 'good men', but more often the household provided its own bread. In a similar fashion, people brought loaves of bread for Francis and there was a competitive aspect to the phenomenon.

> The perversity of heretics was shamed, the faith of the Church was extolled and, as believers rejoiced, heretics hid . . . [short paragraph praising Francis's

devotion to the Church] . . . The people used to bring him loaves of bread to bless, which they kept for a long time, and, on tasting them, they were cured of various diseases.

In neither case is it clear what the bread was actually for. An Italian treatise on heretics, written in the late 1230s and attributed to the Franciscan James Capelli, attempted to analyse this difficult area.

Some of them say that the purpose of the act is to ward off contamination from partaking of food, for they believe foods to be evil . . . Certain others, however, say that this is done only in commemoration of the death of Christ.

Both the Cathars and Francis were trying to satisfy the laity's appetite for a graspable holiness. The Church eventually provided bread blessed by the priest for the laity, outside of the Mass. 'Parishioners should find blessed bread (*panem benedictum*) with candles on any Sunday in every Christian church in the world', declared the reforming bishop of Salisbury in 1256.[22]

In the days before persecution the Cathars looked after both the living and the dead. Through their network of local deacons acting within bishoprics, they could confer the *consolamentum* on dying believers and could then bury them in Cathar cemeteries. Rather than being exclusively a badge of allegiance, these most likely flourished in competition with crowded local Catholic churchyards. Several Cathar believers still found their way into consecrated ground. Even more valuable to the heretics were the houses of Cathar men and women throughout Languedoc. These communities were small and informal: they took in children, especially young girls and women, particularly widows. There was little indication of permanence and indeed individuals seem to have been able to leave as their life circumstances changed.[23] There are similarities with communities in Italy, such as the Humiliati. The loss of these institutions which cemented Catharism into the social fabric was a major effect of the Albigensian Crusade and forced the heretics to rethink their relationship with believers.

In the 1220s and 1230s there were still options open: Paubert Sicart rented land to some Cathar *perfectae* not far from Montauban, his wife received presents of wine. A community of 'good men' established a weaving workshop at Cordes around 1225. These were the pathetic remnants of a once considerable Cathar infrastructure:

They used to have fields, vineyards and their own houses, workshops, oxen, asses, mules and horses, as well as gold and silver and many earthly possessions in this world. They laboured day and night and they were great businessmen for earthly money.

wrote their old adversary, Durand of Huesca, in the early 1220s, simultaneously gloating over the fall in Cathar fortunes and sneering at the hypocrisy of a group who professed to despise the things of this world.[24] In truth, the Cathars faced a serious problem, for they were now more dependent than ever on lay supporters' goodwill and yet had far fewer resources with which to maintain it.

One solution to these losses was to fall back on the one major fixed asset which remained, the small castle of Montségur. This lay in the foothills of the Pyrenees, remote enough to be difficult to besiege, but still close enough to the road and river network for most of Languedoc to remain relatively accessible. The castle had been renovated just before the Albigensian Crusade and belonged to Raymond of Pereille, a minor noble and Cathar sympathiser. Having already served as a refuge in the early days of the crusade, the fortress's role was consciously enhanced around 1232 by the veteran Cathar bishop of Toulouse, Guilhabert de Castres. As the decade wore on and inquisitors were introduced into southern France the castle became the home of most of the Cathar hierarchy, with both Guilhabert and, after his death around 1240, his successor, Bertrand Marty, staying there. *Perfecti* were able to use it as a base so that the Cathar network of pastoral care proved stubbornly durable. As for the castle, it became a religious community, a site of pilgrimage, a place for believers to die, and a chance to meet relatives who were *perfecti*.[25] It also became a workshop and financial centre.

In 1244 Peire-Roger de Mirepoix took 50 doublets made in the castle, possibly by the *perfecti* themselves. A market emerged there where people came from the surrounding villages to sell foodstuffs to the heretics. The Cathars may well also have banked savings; one long-time supporter made discreet enquiries after the fall of the castle about what had become of the 300 *solidi* he had deposited with the heretics there. Such a move should not surprise us; there is evidence that the Templars performed similar functions in their castles.[26] Nor was it the only benefit the *perfecti* could provide, in that there are records of them lending small sums of money to supporters, but this would be nowhere near as lucrative as acting as a *depositarius* for the heretics: collecting money left to the heretics and storing it until required. The heretics commonly dispensed their favour as 'little gifts', shirts and shoes for a scribe, a cap for a barber in return for shaving them and sharing a jug of wine.[27]

These profits lie in the shadowy area between a market and a goodwill economy. No transaction was without its spiritual dimension. When Peire de Corneliano and his uncle undertook to guide seven 'good men' from the citadel at Roquafort to the church at Crassenx, a fee of ten *solidi* was agreed, but the heretics refused, or were unable to pay, so

Peire ceased to even greet Cathars for the next 34 years. Peire's extreme reaction may indicate a deep sense of betrayal. One function of the Cathars was as a religious confraternity, an essential part of which was to provide a network of trust and credit in the wider market.[28]

On the other side of the Alps there are signs of similar arrangements as far as can be gathered from the sparse surviving inquisitorial documents from Orvieto. Heretics are given hospitality and in return, preach, bless bread and give little gifts.[29] However, in many towns the Cathars were still able to preach openly. With more competing religious groups in the Italian context, all living similar lifestyles, ideology was more important to the Italian Cathars in their attempts to establish a distinctive identity. Writing in the early 1240s, from Saint Albans in England, Matthew Paris made slightly nervous fun of a common Catholic paranoia. He gave an unlikely account of a cleric, 'Yves of Narbonne', in the service of the archbishop of Bordeaux who is falsely accused of heresy, and so naturally runs off and pretends to actually join the 'Patarines', or Cathars. In fact, the 'letter' is an indictment of towns and regions who were supporting the Emperor Frederick II in his struggle with the papacy and therefore the writer feels little constraint in his description of the decadence just below the surface.

The fugitive makes his way to Como in north Italy, then Milan, from where he proceeds along the Po valley. The heretics he has fallen in with are, of course, hypocrites, but Yves gets to munch pastries, cherries and other delicious food as well as drinking the superb Patarine wine. During this period he is told that the heretics send capable students from Lombard and Tuscan towns to the University of Paris to be instructed in theology and merchants to the fairs of Champagne where they might get the chance to subvert wealthy patrons who shared their table. Yves turns from this tale of decadence to describe the blood-curdling invasion of eastern Europe by the Mongols, but his description may hold some truth: Italian Catharism produced a series of smart, colourful characters who could take on Catholic opponents and attract the support of lay patrons.[30]

The Italian Cathars were divided into at least three groups after the disputes of the twelfth century; those of Concorezzo who embraced moderate dualism, the Albanenses who put forward the absolute dualist doctrine of two gods, and finally the Bagnolenses, divided between a majority who agreed with the Concorezzans and others who were still in sympathy with the Albanenses. What is known about the history of the Italian Cathars at this point comes from a series of widely disseminated disputes within the Concorezzans and Albanenses. As seen in the cases of Peter Abelard and the Franciscans, such quarrels need not necessarily be detrimental to popularity. A series of inquisitorial writers, Moneta of

Cremona (1241), Raynerius Saccone (1250), a former *perfectus*, and Anselm of Alessandria (1266–7) all felt obliged to record the arguments in their accounts, while refutations also came from lay writers such as Salvo Burci in Piacenza in 1235 and the enigmatic 'Giorgio' who probably wrote in Lombardy in the 1240s.

The dominant figure for almost half a century was Nazario, bishop of the Concorrezzans. He continued the link with the Bogomils early in his career when he travelled to Bulgaria in the 1190s to be taught by the bishop and his deputy, or 'elder son' as he was termed. He re-emerged around 1200 and back in Italy swiftly rose to be first elder son and then bishop himself. He survived a challenge from a younger rival before achieving venerable old age, dying in the early 1250s.[31] His career was mirrored by Belesmanza who was bishop of the Albanenses in the early decades of the thirteenth century before being challenged by the young scholar, John of Lugio, around 1230.[32]

Their disputes were surrounded by texts: the *Secret Book* or *Questions of John* came with Nazario from Bulgaria. It offers the comforting picture of ourselves as descended from angels, and that though trapped in the clay bodies made by Satan, we might yet become angels again. Both moderate and absolute dualists could make use of the other Bogomil text which came from the Balkans at this period. This was the *Vision of Isaiah* which revealed, 'the great battle of Satan and his might opposing the loyal followers of God, and one surpassed the other in envy. For just as it is on earth, so also it is in the firmament.' To these were added home-grown productions such as John of Lugio's *Book of the Two Principles* and the work of Desiderio, the younger rival of Nazario, which was read by Thomas Aquinas.[33]

These texts are not in the same class as those produced by the great scholars of the mendicant orders, with whom they conspicuously fail to engage; even the most impressive, John of Lugio's *Two Principles*, struggles to maintain its coherence at times. However, as a marketing ploy to attract the clever, rich sons of merchants, also pursued by the friars, they were pitched exactly right. Although heretic teachers were recorded in Orvieto, the main Cathar intellectual developments occurred in the north-east of Italy which, besides Bologna, had no less than five universities in Piacenza, Vercelli, Vicenza, Reggio and Padua.[34] Such institutions were not great seats of learning, indeed some only led an intermittent existence, but they were hungry for both students and teachers and they were certainly places where Cathars could recruit and *perfecti* could gain an elementary training in the scholastic method used by their opponents. The area had extensive economic links, with both northern Europe, and with Greek and Slavonic culture through Venice and Adriatic ports, such as Dubrovnik and Durazzo. The market in learning which had bred Abelard was still in existence in north Italy and there were still posts in civic administrations for graduates to go to, whatever their religious beliefs.

The Cathars also had their own schools. There are shadowy references to them at Verona and Milan in the years around 1200, and more certainly at Gattedo, the castle near Milan, belonging to Robert Paeta, a minor noble, who had erected small houses within the castle walls where 'schools of perversity' had taken place, run by heretic masters and prelates. Nazario had taught there and was buried within its walls, according to a document of Innocent IV in 1254 which demanded his exhumation and the destruction of the castle.[35]

For the Italian Cathars, then, learning was important. It allowed them to compete with the Dominican and Franciscan friars. Latin texts could filter down to wider communities through preaching in the vernacular. All this time the Italian Cathars, too, had systems of bishops and local deacons to provide pastoral care and the *consolamentum*. Yet in spite of this many Catholic writers were confident of the Cathars' decline. Salvo Burci reported in 1235 that the scandal of disunity had brought many believers back to the Roman Church, while Raynerius Saccone, reviewing the situation in southern France and the former Byzantine Empire as well as Italy, declared in 1250:

> O reader, you can safely say that in the whole world there are not as many as four thousand Cathars [i.e. *perfecti*] of both sexes.

This may not have been as reassuring as it sounds. Salvo is probably reciting old gossip of the original schism in the Cathar Church over 50 years before. Raynerius's description of animosity between the Concorezzenses and Albanenses resembles the tensions between orders within the Church; otherwise mutual recognition among Cathar groups reveals a movement relatively at ease with itself.

The numerical evidence is more intriguing. In so far as medieval numbers can be trusted at all, Raynerius's own figure of 1500 Concorezzenses throughout Lombardy is certainly comparable to the Franciscan Thomas of Eccleston's boast in the mid 1250s that in England (and Scotland) the Franciscans had 1242 friars in 49 places. Therefore, unwittingly, Raynerius may in fact be demonstrating that the Cathars of Concorezzo had more than adequate resources.[36] Leaders of all religious movements in the thirteenth century were aware of the importance of being part of the wider networks of society. Dominic, when he sent his followers to the university cities of Paris and Bologna, ensured that they would come into contact with a vast transient academic population, thus disseminating Dominican ideals throughout Europe. On arriving in England in the late summer of 1224 the small party of Franciscans established communities in the cosmopolitan centres of London and Oxford within weeks and achieved a similar effect. The Cathars of north-east Italy were able to spread their doctrines easily, even though they had few active 'good men'. The description of them attributed to the Franciscan James Capelli, notes the simplicity of the Cathar Church structure, and stresses the importance of the travelling bishop and his two 'sons'. Whereas the early Cathars may have been trying to establish a geographical network on the lines of a parish system, it was now realised to be unnecessary. Instead, the crucial role for the local deacons was to run hostels where visitors to the town could be housed. The Cathars may not have been winning the competition for souls in thirteenth-century Italy, but they were comfortably holding their own.[37]

Southern France too had forged a Cathar movement with its own distinctive character. The growth in learning penetrated to a lesser extent and differences in doctrine never became the defining issue they did in Italy. An anonymous account of Cathar beliefs appeared in the early years of the thirteenth century. This described, from the Catholic point of view, a heresy which is still absolute dualist, although it briefly recounts a variation which talked of only one God. However, the theology is distinctive to Languedoc; among the Evil God's first creations is a 'bee eater' (*serena*), a colourful, small bird mainly found in Iberia and southern France, accompanied by a lion, an eagle and a 'spirit'. The Cathar heaven described is a cheerful, if masculine, paradise of eating, drinking and hunting; '. . . everyone there will have a wife, and sometimes a mistress'.[38]

The acknowledgement of both moderate and absolute dualists persisted in accounts of Catharism in southern France and there is evidence that here too the standard of learning was improving. The *Vision of Isaiah* is actually recorded in Languedoc before Italy and its influence can still be seen on local heretics in the fourteenth century. Durand of Huesca, writing in the early 1220s, made excerpts of a recent Cathar tract to which he replied. The description of heaven now relies, rather conventionally, on biblical quotations and deductions from them. Not only did Durand evidently face a formidable opponent, but he made references to disputes in the Carcassonne, Albi and Toulouse dioceses of the Cathars which reflected those of the 'Greek', 'Bulgar' and '*Drogoveti*' dualists in the East. Taken with rumours of a Cathar 'pope' from the east coast of the Adriatic appointing a representative in southern France, there may have been some continuation of contact with Bogomil movements in the former Byzantine Empire.[39]

Pressures exerted on the heretics by the Albigensian crusaders may well have arrested the movement's intellectual development since no later comparable sources are found. Education remained important to the southern French Cathars on a more pragmatic than academic basis. Copies of the New Testament in the vernacular were in circulation and it or a copy of John's gospel was used in the *consolamentum* which in turn was inscribed in Cathar service books. Some works obviously did seek to persuade. In 1244 the noblewoman or *Domina*, Finas, recalled how 30 years earlier she had read heretical books in order to make up her own mind about the beliefs of the Cathars. It is worth remembering that there was a lively market in books in the early thirteenth century, so that possession of them was as much a sign of a material consumer choice as a spiritual one. Often oral and written culture overlapped as 'good men' or 'good women' explained a text read aloud by themselves or someone else to an audience.[40]

The Cathar community in Languedoc had different strengths from that in Italy. One of the most well-informed observers of the heretics was Peter of les Vaux-de-Cernay writing in the early years of the Albigensian Crusade. He paid little attention to Cathar doctrine and attributed the success of the heretics in southern France to their attacks on the Catholic Church. He also recorded in some detail the lives of the 'good men' or *perfecti*; their clothing, diet and hierarchy and then added unflattering stories of their relations with the dying.[41] Without realising it his mockery reveals one of the Cathars' great strengths. He recalled an occasion when there was a dispute over the consoling of an unconscious man. Instead of taking their dispute to a religious leader, as the Italian Cathars might have done, the heretics turned to a sympathetic local knight, Bertrand de Saissac, to make a decision. To a monk, asking a layman to judge such issues was simply ridiculous, but for the Cathars it made good sense: Bertrand was both a respected local figure and had the secular authority to enforce his judgement. His ruling was pragmatic: '. . . as to this man, I will support the position and declare him to be saved. However, my judgement is that all others who shall have failed to recite the Lord's Prayer in their final moments are damned.'[42]

A close relationship with the local nobility allowed the Cathars to maintain a balance between independence and remaining in touch with key supporters. When the boundaries of the Cathar bishoprics set up at the Council of Saint Felix were disputed in 1226, the Council of Pieusse created the diocese of Razès. The new bishop was consecrated by the Cathar bishop of Toulouse with a lay knight, Guilhem de Villeneuve, 'assisting' at the ceremony. The link between secular and religious was completed by Guilhem's wife who was a *perfecta*.[43] As in Italy, Cathar bishops and their supporters became more important in the 1230s when it became difficult to support *perfecti* in local deaconries. However, in both regions, the loss could be sustained as the Cathars realised that their Church could be run by a network of relatively few highly connected individuals. The migration to Montségur in the 1230s not only included bishops and deacons, but also messengers (*nuntii*) to run errands and guide the Cathar prelates.[44]

The southern French Cathars' vulnerability sprang from the same source as their strength; such a close relationship with the local nobility meant that their fortunes rose and fell together. The failure of a badly organised revolt by Raymond Trencavel in 1240, followed by the defeat of a much more ambitious campaign by Raymond VII of Toulouse in the summer of 1242, dispirited opponents of royal intervention and Catholicism alike. Montségur's beacon of spirituality attracted unwelcome attention and systematic inquisitions into heresy in 1241 and early 1242 also started to take effect. Consequently, on the night of May 28, 1242 a party of armed men from Montségur rode 50 miles from the castle to the village of Avignonet and slaughtered the inquisitors and churchmen who were staying there. In the aftermath of the summer's revolt, this apparently spontaneous and short-sighted action, born of frustration, made Montségur look like the home of both religious heresy and treason against the French crown. Appropriately, an army was raised the following year by a partnership of the royal seneschal of Carcassonne in conjunction with the archbishop of Narbonne and bishop of Albi.[45]

After a long siege the castle fell in March 1244. Right to the end Catharism kept its close relation of spiritual and material exchanges of goodwill. The Cathar bishop of Toulouse, Bertrand Marty, besides preaching, distributed salt, pepper and olive oil to the soldiers. Other 'good Christians' of both sexes gave cash, shoes, clothing and purses. In return some of the lay defenders received the *consolamentum*. Whether 200 really burnt in the field below, the *prat dels crematz*, as Guilhem de Puylaurens claimed, will probably never be known, but the persistence of the legend with its apocalyptic associations shows that popular imagination had no difficulty in recognising a historical turning point. Nor will we probably ever learn the nature of the Cathar 'treasure' removed down the mountainside just before the surrender. A quantity of gold and silver had been removed the previous Christmas and, given the Cathar dependence on supporters' legacies and soft loans, it could have been the account books. As we have seen, these would have been as spiritually significant to the movement as some of the more romantic options considered by later writers.[46]

The Waldensians

The Waldensians in the thirteenth century followed a now familiar pattern. They competed with other apostolic groups to provide pastoral care alongside the pursuit of learning to help preaching. They were less successful than the Cathars or Franciscans, but the highly publicised arguments among them disguised a loose confederation of groups who claimed a common ancestor and were extremely effective in the spiritual markets in which they moved, mainly Italy and France, although there may have been a nascent group in Germany. Little is known about Valdes or his followers after their condemnation in 1184, but the 'Poor of Lyon' appear in Piacenza in the 1190s preaching and also hearing confessions, according to the bishop. The diversion of funds away from established institutions is confirmed by the allegation that they said no one could be saved unless they took up their habit or became their 'maintainer' or 'friend'.[47]

There are reports of a division within the movement by 1205 with the emergence of the 'Poor Lombards', as opposed to the 'Poor of Lyon', but this was not a simple geographical split since there were people from north of the Alps or 'ultramontanes' as they were termed, among the Poor Lombards. The defection of Durand of Huesca described in the previous chapter was a further blow. He took with him a group of followers to become known as the Poor Catholics and began recruiting in Italy. There had been an interest in education among the Italian Waldensians since the commune of Milan had given them a field in which to build a school, later destroyed by the archbishop. Durand, who sought to revive this Waldensian tradition in a Catholic context, asked for permission to rebuild it for the new converts. Later reports from the 1230s also single out Milan as a centre of specifically Waldensian learning, the first fruit of which apparently came in the conference organised at the north Italian town of Bergamo in May 1218 to reconcile the two parties.[48]

By this time Valdes was dead and the leadership of the Poor Lombards had also changed. It was a measure of the confidence of the Italian group that they had reconciliation proposals prepared. There are parallels here with Fourth Lateran, which had attempted to clarify various issues within the Catholic Church two and a half years earlier, as well as with the disastrous attempts at reunion by the various groups of Italian Cathars. The Waldensians learnt from both. Their conference was carefully arranged so that most of the issues were settled by lower-profile meetings between the two parties. Clearly, they also had scribes on hand to transmit the results of the conference to other Waldesian communities. The Bergamo assembly was intended to reach a final agreement and so delegations of six on each side arrived to negotiate the more difficult problems.

The unfortunate failure of the conference meant that the scribes were instead set to work producing a lengthy justification of the Poor Lombard position in a letter to a third group of Waldensians, possibly German.[49] Like the Franciscans, the Waldensians were faced with the problem of how the movement should be organised when the founder had stepped down. Two rather different cultures were springing up. North of the Alps the French suggested a pragmatic holding operation on the fringes of the Church, accepting the validity of Catholic priests. Their admiration for Valdes was unbounded, but they were willing to compromise on his insistence that there should be no other head for themselves or the Italians, even after his death, by allowing provosts, rectors and ministers to be chosen by both sides to guide the movement (chapters 4 and 5). The Italians were more ambitious. Valdes had never approved of the communities of people attached to them who had continued to work for a living. Now, the Italians wanted recognition for them and to be able to ordain their own ministers (chapter 6). One of their delegates, 'Brother Thomas', even wanted every member of the Waldensian congregation to give up their right (*ius*) to rule themselves, just as they had once theoretically given the right to Valdes, so that a powerful successor, or *pontifex*, could be created.[50] Even most of his fellow Poor Lombards were unwilling to go that far (chapter 10), but the negotiations make clear that the Lombards were well on their way to setting up their own Church.

Surprisingly, both sides managed to compromise on these and other issues. The conference failed when it came to discuss whether Valdes was in paradise and the administration of the sacrament of bread. One of the French delegates stood up, declaring that, 'we say that Valdes is in God's paradise', adding that if the Italians could not say the same there could be no peace between them. Clearly emotions were running high in response to the measured statement from the Italians that Valdes may be in paradise if he had made amends for all his sins and offences before his death (chapter 15). There may, however, be an issue here which was to become all too familiar to Franciscans after the death of their founder. The Poor Lombards may not have held any personal mistrust of Valdes, but they did not want to be bound by his authority and the reason for this became clear when the next subject came up, the Eucharist. With a battery of authorities from the scriptures and Church fathers the Italians established their position that only a priest free from sin and therefore from their own ordination could administer a valid sacrament. Their admission that this was a change to their previous position only demonstrated their newfound confidence and depth of learning (chapters 16, 20–5).

The conference should not be seen totally as a battle between 'know-alls' and country bumpkins. The Poor of Lyon did not have the intellectual firepower of the Lombards; significantly they relied on a treatise from Verona to support many of their points. Moreover, if the Lombard writer is to be trusted they were divided as to what they actually did believe concerning the Eucharist. French arguments instead centred on the relationship between priest and people. The Poor of Lyon restricted the right to baptise to priests and then declared simply,

> . . . we believe . . . that the bread and wine become the body and blood of the Lord if a priest ordained in the Roman Church has received and blessed it . . . whether righteous or unrighteous, so long as the congregation of the baptised upholds him in his office (chapter 22).

This is the end position of the French Waldensians. The priest holds his position by ordination it is true, but also by the confidence of the community whom he serves. To bind those ties tighter still, it is envisaged that that congregation will be those that he or one of his colleagues has baptised himself. With this formulation the Poor of Lyon did not need to strike out on their own, because they could seek out sympathetic priests to form discrete communities.

As with the Cathars, the Waldensians proved adept at finding a place in the communities of southern France. There is a tantalising echo from the early 1220s of clerks and Waldensians singing and reading together in church in Avignonet, of all places, where the inquisitors were to be slaughtered 20 years later. More often they were found on the edge of the regions of Cathar influence, such as the Quercy area where they acted as medical practitioners, applying ointment for eye ailments, dispensing herbs and binding wounds. In addition, they persisted in their heartland around Lyon and the Rhône and Saône valleys offering forthright, if not very coherent, critiques of Church doctrine.[51] As for their Italian counterparts they became radicalised, rejecting not only sacraments, but also the justice of 'kings, princes and potentates'. They were still present in Salvo Burci's Piacenza in the mid 1230s and Raynerius Saccone wrote about them in his round-up of heretics in 1250. The latter noted their divisions and alleged that the Poor of Lyon allowed both lay men and women to consecrate the host, which may show that they too were in effect establishing their own Church.[52]

If the Cathars and friars acted like supermarkets of pastoral care the followers of Valdes were more like corner shops. As the thirteenth century wore on they diverged in their beliefs and methods of pastoral care, sharing little more than a respect for a common founder. Yet they were still quite capable of instilling profound faith and loyalty. One mother and daughter earned the respect of the inquisitor Stephen Bourbon through their doctrinal argument, though it led them both to the stake.[53]

The growing diversity of beliefs and religious groups in the early thirteenth century was symptomatic of a ferocious market for salvation. The mission articulated at Fourth Lateran to involve the laity was unexpectedly accomplished with large numbers listening to preachers and passionate debates over doctrine and lifestyle. However, the result was more confusion than conformity and the papacy found itself forced to turn to the one group which had retained its cohesion in the difficult years after 1215.

The Dominicans

For the Church, the Dominicans were the success story of the period. They grew steadily, consolidating in depth by setting up rather larger convents than the Franciscans. From about 20 houses at Dominic's death they had almost 100 by 1234 scattered across Europe, with the most influential located in educational centres such as Oxford, Paris and Bologna.[54] It is worth remembering that the Dominicans were a later phenomenon than the Franciscans whose founder quickly moved from being locally to universally revered. Dominic, stuck in inhospitable Languedoc, only became well known in the last four or five years of his life. The Dominican expansion came in the 1220s and enthusiasm reached a peak in the mid 1230s with the canonisation of the saint.

Such tensions as were present in the order were held in check by organisational clarity of vision. Jordan of Saxony, Dominic's elected successor, proved an able Master General. In his letter to the brothers of the province of Lombardy in 1233 he may have grumbled about friars unwilling to embrace poverty, arguing about small things which were not worth the trouble, lecturers (*lectores*) who did not deliver and students who did not settle to study, yet his tone is one of unfulfilled potential rather than despair. They could do better and help even more people to eternal life. Sometimes this confidence could go too far. The General Chapters of 1240 and 1246 had to forbid friars from attacking prelates and other individuals in their preaching. Compared with the Franciscans and other religious groups, the discipline held. By medieval standards the Dominicans exercised a kind of 'democratic centralism' which made it difficult for dissident views to gain a hearing, and backed it up with coercion in the shape of the prison, which the General Chapter ordered to be built for 'apostates and unquiet brothers' in 1240.[55]

At times, being a Dominican must have been intoxicating: in the late 1220s they were asked by Gregory IX to reform some established monasteries; in the early 1230s the first three Dominican bishops were appointed and their posts reveal the respect for the order held by the pope.[56] The first was Raymond of Le Fauga, appointed to the heretical stronghold of Toulouse, the second was John the Teuton, the new bishop of Bosnia with a further mandate to suppress heresy and try and negotiate papal supremacy in a formerly Orthodox area. Thirdly, Clement of Dunblane was sent to the western highlands of Scotland to rebuild his ruined cathedral there and preach in Gaelic.

The friars' entry into the ecclesiastical hierarchy was not accomplished without disquiet on both sides, but positions of responsibility offered opportunities to disseminate Dominican ideals and besides there was no sign that it had diminished their spiritual appeal. In fact, for a moment in 1233 popular preaching by one Dominican turned into real political power. A series of natural disasters in the early 1230s strained the social fabric of the north Italian towns. A flooding of the Po which caused chaos in 1230 was followed two years later by an infestation of locusts and grasshoppers which ruined the harvest. The following spring, when prices would have been at their highest and the poor risked starvation, was a fruitful time for a preaching campaign which started with an eccentric 'freelance' preacher in Parma who blew on a horn, led children through the streets and sang psalms and praises to the Virgin in the local dialect. Very soon the 'professional' preachers from the Franciscan and Dominican orders moved in and achieved overwhelming success that summer. The response went well beyond popular piety. All over north-east Italy individual preachers were called upon to mediate between warring factions and even revise civic statutes. The Dominicans and Franciscans benefited greatly from being able to launch a co-ordinated campaign, one aspect of which was a series of carefully orchestrated 'miraculous' visions one preacher had of another preaching in a different city at the same time. The appearances by a number of charismatic individuals all preaching reconciliation on an organised basis probably made impact enough. As evening drew in and the time for the sermon approached, the shops closed and the crowd assembled carrying tree branches and lighted candles. As they waited they sang 'Alleluia', which gave its name to the revival.[57]

The most prominent preacher was a Dominican, John of Vicenza, and his biography is a familiar one. He was born in the north-eastern town of Vicenza in 1200, the son of a lawyer who was well off rather than rich. Sent to study nearby at the fledgling 'university' of Padua, in many ways John was typical of those who were educated, young and enthusiastic enough to take part in the heretical and orthodox movements on offer at the time. John just happened to hear Dominic preach in Padua in 1217 and so joined the Black Friars.

In 1233 he began preaching in Bologna and by August he had the city and most of north-east Italy outside Venice at his command. By the end of that month he was 'rector' of Verona and preaching to vast crowds from a specially constructed wooden platform. The Alleluia's wave of enthusiasm which had swept John to power then disappeared as quickly as it had begun. One by one the peace agreements unravelled. Within days John found himself stranded and powerless. The preachers could not enforce their will, only articulate the unconscious desires of their listeners, and as the weeks passed many of them were seen to be favouring one faction or another. Yet the short period in power demonstrated what could be achieved when a member of the new spiritual elite had the machinery of the secular power at his disposal. John was prepared to use physical force to back his moral authority. He presided over the burning of 60 men and women from the 'better families' of Verona as heretics, because they would not take oaths accepting him as peacemaker. Discussion has centred on whether these were 'real' or 'political' heretics, but it should be clear that at this stage it made no difference; those who were not with John were against him, he was a man intending literally to change the world.[58]

The generation which grew up in the 1220s and 1230s experienced some of the most spiritually exciting years in European history. The competing visions of Christianity in the early years of the century had matured and new movements and institutions offered opportunities of participation as never before. Yet diversity was not celebrated and a generation on from the Fourth Lateran Council it had become clear how ephemeral were preaching campaigns like the Alleluia, how difficult it was to reform local clergy and above all the impossibility of removing heresy either by persuasion or force. The most successful of the preaching movements of the early thirteenth century had been the Dominicans and they had also been the most methodical. Their pastoral care to the laity had always included a fair degree of discipline and it was their methods which influenced the establishment of formal inquiries or 'inquisitions' in the areas where the Cathars and Waldensians were still strong.

chapter 6

RESTRICTING CHOICE:
THE INQUISITION AND THE
DECLINE OF THE CATHARS

The same year as John of Vicenza was presiding over the burning of heretics in Verona, Conrad of Marburg, a secular priest, was putting dissenters to death in Rhineland and Robert 'le Bougre', a former Cathar turned Dominican friar, was being encouraged to continue burning folk on the borders between France and Germany. Technically these were different operations, since the last two were inquisitors, specifically designated by Pope Gregory IX to investigate heresy, but in practice the episodes were similar and reflect a growing impatience among churchmen with the spiritual marketplace which had emerged in the early thirteenth century. Only later, after this approach had encountered repeated failure, did a more considered strategy emerge, relying on systematic gathering of information and the imposition of a range of punishments. The 'ad hoc' inquisitions became a recognised institution and their accumulated records slowly buried the remaining Cathars.

Roots of the Inquisition

The Albigensian Crusade revealed an influential body within the Church unafraid to use physical force to extirpate the threat of heresy. Yet the shortcomings of such an approach were obvious, not least because as at Béziers, the faithful died with the heretics. The Fourth Lateran Council concentrated on identifying individual heretics, but did not provide an answer as to how heretical communities might be broken down. Movements on the scale of the Cathars and Waldensians had not been encountered by the Church in hundreds of years, so it was perhaps natural for contemporaries to turn for advice to the thinkers who had led the fight against heresy in the Roman Empire.

The early Church was wary of persecution, being all too aware of its own persecuted status under many of the pagan emperors, and mindful of Christ's pronouncement that those who were persecuted for his sake were blessed. However, at the end of the fourth century it was threatened from within by the dissenting sect of 'Donatists' who prefigured some of the heretics of the Middle Ages by suggesting that the validity of the sacraments depended on the moral state of the celebrant. In their eagerness to establish the doctrinal unity of the newly Christianised Roman Empire, writers struggled to think of ways to bring over recalcitrant congregations once the preferred procedure of persuasion and reconciliation had failed. In his sermons Augustine of Hippo considered the problem of how the flock might be saved from bad pastors. In a vivid image he answered the protest that it was hard to pick the grape among the thorns:

> If you hunger and have nowhere else to take from, carefully put in your hand, so that you are not scratched by the thorns, namely that you do not imitate the deeds of evil men, and pick one hanging between the thorns, but born of the vine. To you will come the nourishment of the bunch. The torment of the fire is saved for the thorns.[1]

Having acknowledged the delicacy of the operation he then called upon bishops to be good shepherds and feed their sheep with discipline to lead them from the clouds and rain of error. That this discipline might sometimes be harsh was implied in his comparison of heretics with sick horses and mules cured through 'medicinal pains and tribulations' despite their biting and kicking those who seek to help them.[2]

Augustine was less help when it came to what practical remedies might be applied or to who might carry them out. The veterinary analogy was addressed to an imperial official, but the lines between bishops and secular authorities were becoming blurred. Later readers were entitled to think that the will of the great spiritual thinker might be embodied in contemporary Roman legal thought and the eager canon law graduates of Bologna and elsewhere trawled ancient imperial legislation for relevant ideas. They found their forebears full of suggestions for the punishment of the unrepentant dissident of which more later, but there was little on how obstinately heretical communities might be discouraged. Fining supporters of heresy, as the imperial code suggested, looked too much like tolerance and taxation; even Augustine had ignored it. Exile of key heretical figures raised the obvious question of where the heretics were then going to go. The only Roman penalty which tapped into the pool of supporters of heresy was the confiscation of family property of a convicted heretic. This was a draconian step, even more so in the clan-oriented Middle Ages. It could only take place where the heretics were a defined minority, otherwise the effectiveness of its crude collective responsibility would be obliterated by the creation of regiments of people with literally nothing to lose. As for who should identify the heretics, the imperial legislation said nothing; it was the responsibility of local officials to take action.[3]

Thirteenth-century popes did have an answer to this last problem. In the search for reform of the Church, Innocent III and his successors had innovated by introducing a procedure 'through inquiry', *per inquisitionem*, whereby a designated official could begin action against an individual on the slimmest of evidence of rumour or reputation. Initially used against fornicating priests and corrupt abbots, Gregory IX was to combine it with the long-established papal policy of designating specific preachers in heretical areas. In the febrile atmosphere of the 1230s Augustine's warning about the thorns was lost as Catholic preachers finally saw a means to gather grapes by the bunch.[4]

It is generally agreed that the first inquisitor was Conrad of Marburg. He had once been confessor to the saintly Elizabeth of Hungary and received a papal commission to preach against heresy in 1227, which in 1231 was extended to include the imposition of penalties and the involvement of local secular authorities, if necessary. Since churchmen could not spill blood or take lives, the 'secular arm' was formally in charge of the burning of heretics. Like John of Vicenza, Conrad commanded a popular following and destroying heresy was only part of his programme; he interfered in the formal visitations of clergy and nuns, attempting to force them into leading lives of strict observance. Although he was not a friar himself Conrad was aided on his travels by local Dominican communities, and acquired two assistants, a Dominican friar named Conrad Tors and a lay man called John. Conrad's tactics were ruthless; those accused had to confess themselves guilty and have their heads shaved. Those who denied their crime were burnt. Conrad's violent approach finally lost the support of the archbishops of Trier and Mainz when he accused Count Henry II of Sayn of heresy and, without protection, he was murdered at the end of July 1233. His two assistants also seem to have met violent ends shortly after.[5]

Robert 'le Bougre's' career was similarly dramatic. He had started in Milan around 1215 where he fell in with a Cathar woman and had risen to become an important *perfectus*. His fashionably abusive nickname punned on the eastern origins of the Cathars while suggesting equally exotic practices in his private life. At some point Robert reconverted into the Dominicans and along with two other Black Friars started preaching against heretics in Burgundy in October 1232. In the following spring, just as the Great Alleluia was getting under way in Italy, he received permission from Gregory IX to begin investigating heresy in La Charité-sur-Loire, in the Nivernais region of central France. Robert claimed dramatic results. People came forward spontaneously wearing chains or wooden collars as a mark of penance and willing to denounce partners and children.[6] His persuasive powers were particularly effective with women. To encourage enthusiasm Robert usually burnt the recalcitrant. In the confusion, several bishops were afraid of having their jurisdiction usurped and petitioned to have him stopped. The pope duly obliged in 1234, but felt it necessary to allow the inquisitor to resume the following year.

Robert continued his activity throughout the 1230s and finished the decade with the burning of over 180 heretics at Mont Aimé in Champagne in May 1239.[7] This was a large assembly attended by the king of Navarre, the count of Champagne and sixteen bishops, and yet Robert is almost unheard of afterwards. Chroniclers agree that he was disgraced and imprisoned, but also hint that this was not the end of the story. Robert was henceforth an ambivalent figure, a man of past glory with a fatally flawed character. The Dominican chronicler Gerard de Fracheto has him leaving the Dominicans, wandering through two other orders before finally joining the Cistercians at Clairvaux. After being received with great honour, here too he was disgraced 'and was reduced to a vile position in that monastery'.[8]

John, Conrad and Robert have more in common than is generally recognised. The parallels between Robert and John are particularly striking, both from the schools of north Italy, charismatic, but spiritually restless. At their peak both had the moral authority to interfere in secular politics, Robert being asked to mediate between France and England by Gregory IX. Both too had enemies within the Church; Alberic of Trois Fontaines described Robert quite gratuitously as, 'a man who seemed of great religion, but was not really'. All three faced resentment from various bishops. This was not surprising since they were taking over an aspect of their job. In canon three of the Fourth Lateran Council it had been bishops who had been charged with inquiring into suspect parishes and there obtaining the testimony of two or three honest men as to who in the area might be a heretic. As to why they never fulfilled this function it is now becoming clear that bishops at this time were men under pressure. Their chapters demanded an administrator who could stand up for the rights of the see, the papacy and public opinion were looking for someone interested in issues of pastoral care.[9] There were often also delicate issues of local politics to consider. But Fourth Lateran also stated that such investigations could be undertaken by any 'honest, suitable persons', and since this was a matter concerning preaching and pastoral care, the Dominicans with their almost revolutionary zeal seemed ideally suited to the role.

The 'dogs of the lord' (*domini canes*) always had the disciplined excitement of the hunt about them, but when required to make an *inquisitio* (the word just means 'inquiry') preaching was an important component, as Gregory IX's early appointments make clear.[10] Consequently, not only Dominicans were made inquisitors, Franciscans and bishops were also sometimes considered suitable. However, the Dominicans fitted perfectly because the papacy was looking for the spiritual excitement of the Alleluia, combined with a rigorous approach. It was no coincidence that the great preacher John of Vicenza surfaced after years of obscurity, as inquisitor for Lombardy in 1247. Innocent IV granted a 20-day indulgence to all who attended his sermons.

The real test for the inquisitors was in Languedoc. Bishop Fulk of Toulouse had been too poor and embattled to carry out Fourth Lateran's decree so the Dominicans had already been taking action against suspected heretics as the chronicle of a local Black Friar, Guilhem Pelhisson, made clear. Roland of Cremona, the Dominican academic, led a party of friars and clerics to dig up and burn the body of a man who had been made a canon of St Sernin at his death as well as receiving the Cathar *consolamentum*. When a leading Waldensian died, the friars were able to raze his house to the ground, exhume his body from the cemetery and drag it through the town before burning it. Even though the royal victory over the count of Toulouse gave them considerable scope for action it is conspicuous that the friars were not yet tackling living heretics. A further step was taken at a council at Toulouse in 1229 which strengthened the investigative procedure outlined at Fourth Lateran.

> We decree . . . that the archbishops and bishops shall swear in one priest, and two or three laymen of good reputation, or more if they think fit, in every parish, both within cities and outside, who shall diligently, faithfully and frequently seek out the heretics in those parishes by searching all houses and subterranean chambers which lie under any suspicion. And investigating any additions or constructions joined to the roofs themselves, or any other kind of hiding places, all of which we order to be destroyed.[11]

In other words, organised tribunals were now authorised to patrol suspected villages searching outhouse, cellars and roofspace. Again the lack of evidence of such inquiries actually taking place probably explains why, in April 1233, Gregory issued documents creating inquisitors in southern France, still emphasising preaching and offering such men as an adjunct to activity by bishops.[12] The first inquisitors were Peire Selha, the former supporter and early companion of Dominic and Guilhem Arnaud, later to find martyrdom at Avignonet. The new inquisitors were seen as a communal Dominican effort, particularly as the new bishop of

Toulouse, Raymond Le Fauga, was himself a Black Friar. They also had the support of Durand of Saint Ybars, the lay consul of Toulouse who was keen to obtain wealth confiscated from heretics, having lent large sums to Count Raymond VII. With this apparently formidable combination, the inquisitors swung into action.

The initial Dominican emphasis was on burning heretics alive and dead. Along with burning, property was confiscated so that families were ruined. One alleged heretic died desperately professing his loyalty to the Roman faith, while an old woman dying was manipulated into confession by the bishop, who had her burnt on her bed. Such actions aroused popular indignation, but the friars seemed heedless of the consequences; the inquisitor, Arnaud Catalan, attempting to enforce another posthumous burning in Albi in 1234, barely escaped with his life. Inquisitions in Carcassonne and Narbonne were halted for fear of unrest. The crisis in Toulouse came in 1235 after Guilhem Arnaud had cited twelve leading citizens. He was promptly driven out of the city and retreated to Carcassonne. He ordered further citations, but the local clergy were too afraid to deliver them after they were threatened with death. So Guilhem turned to his Dominican colleagues and the prior explained the ideal opportunity for martyrdom that delivering the summonses would offer; the whole community volunteered.[13] In fact, all the delivery of the citations achieved was such an explosion of popular anger that the entire convent was expelled and the Inquisition suspended by the town authorities. Although the inquisitors resumed in late 1236, their activities were halted once again in 1238, when Raymond VII appealed to the pope.[14]

Burning as a punishment for heresy

In both instances above the inquisitors learnt the importance of co-operation with the lay power. Secular rulers may have been opposed to heresy, but they disliked disorder more. Royal officials prevented Guilhem Arnaud burning members of the Niort family in Carcassonne, 'because they thought a war would result'. This may also explain the decline of Robert and why the death of Conrad went unlamented. While the secular authorities could not support heresy and indeed carried out burnings, they were still uneasy at the hysteria generated by anti-heretical measures in the 1230s.

This is not to say that the threat of sending heretics to the stake did not continue to be an integral part of the inquisitors' activities. It had been a traditional penalty for the obstinate heretic since at least the eleventh century and it remained a deeply symbolic example of the co-operation of Church and State, reflected in the intellectual processes behind it. In *Vergentis in senium* issued in 1199, Innocent III, a student of Roman law, not only excommunicated heretics, but classed heresy as treason, since the heretic offended God and Christ, the lord of all, and was therefore guilty of *lèse majesté*. Various penalties then followed from such a serious offence, such as the confiscation of goods and the disinheriting of children. This was also Innocent's way of reminding secular rulers that although the official Church sanctioned their position with divine blessing there was no reason why an alternative religious movement should. In their own legislation, secular rulers took the hint. The Emperor Frederick II referred to heresy as being a crime against the State as much as against the Church, and in legislation from the late 1230s prescribed the penalty of 'consignment to the judgement of the flames'.[15] Burning was a Roman penalty for treason, but treason of a very particular kind, namely the forging of imperial coins. This connection of burning with counterfeiting coins was, as it were, common currency in the thirteenth century and when the Dominican Thomas Aquinas was writing his *Summa Theologica* around 1270 he picked up the analogy in considering the question of whether heretics should be tolerated:

> On their own side there is the sin whereby they deserve not only to be separated from the Church by excommunication, but also to be severed from the world by death. For it is a much graver matter to corrupt the faith which quickens the soul, than to forge money, which supports temporal life. Wherefore if forgers of money and other evil-doers are forthwith condemned to death by the secular authority, much more reason is there for heretics, as soon as they are convicted of heresy, to be not only excommunicated, but even put to death.[16]

The problem with coinage was that in the thirteenth century throughout most of Europe it was nothing like so simple as 'forged' or 'genuine'; commercial transactions could take place in coinage bearing the head of any ruler, provided people were willing to accept the coin at face value, or recognise its intrinsic worth. For Aquinas the provision of different spiritual coinage was an anathema, for the spiritual currency must never resemble the chaos of the physical one, and therefore in comparing the heretic to the forger of money, for whom the penalty was death by burning, he advocated restriction of spiritual choice in the strongest possible terms.

More pragmatic reasons dictated how often the punishment was employed. In contrast to the excesses of the 1230s, between 1249 and 1257 inquisitors in southern France only handed over 21 heretics to the secular arm. The famous inquisitor Bernard Gui, who as a character in the film and the novel *The Name of the Rose*, provides the looming menace of 'the Inquisition', burnt just 41 people in his 15-year career at the end of the century. Too much should not be made of this change of policy. Just as Béziers convinced many that open resistance to the Albigensian Crusade was useless, so the initial wave of inquisitorial burnings meant that the number of openly obstinate heretics declined markedly in subsequent years. Terror sometimes brought results. Catharism in northern France and Germany seems not to have recovered from the respective attacks of Robert and Conrad. Even in areas where it persisted there was the continued intimidatory effect of seeing friends and public figures consigned to the flames every few months. The message got through beyond even the dreams of the trained Dominican communicators and the program is still running. All subsequent generations have assumed that heretics were burnt by 'the Inquisition', which is exactly what you were meant to think.

Penance and procedure

The resumption of inquisitorial operations after the revolt of 1240 saw a change of policy. A Franciscan friar was added to the team in a conscious move to make it look less severe.[17] Even when Guilhem Arnaut and the Franciscan Stephen of Saint Thibéry were murdered at Avignonet in 1242 there was little change in inquisitorial tactics. Instead of travelling round the countryside, hearings were held in central places and between May 1245 and August 1246 almost 5500 witnesses were interviewed from the area of the Lauragais around Toulouse. It was these inquisitions of the 1240s combined with military operations which fatally damaged organised heresy in Languedoc.

Inquisitors were now starting to compare notes and pay more attention to procedure. Raymond de Peñafort, a former Dominican Minister General, produced a guide for the inquisitors of Aragon in 1242 and three years later a similar document was produced in Narbonne.[18] The arrival of the manuals marked the implementation of a more subtle strategy. The process started with a general sermon being preached followed by a summons issued through the parish priest for all the parishioners to appear before the inquisitors to answer for their acts. In return, these voluntary penitents would receive milder penances. The procedure also tackled the difficult problem of the insincere or vague confession. To be believed would-be penitents had to take an oath to tell the truth about themselves and others, living and dead, in the matter of heresy. Moreover, they had to swear to pursue and seize heretics themselves or aid the Church or secular authority.

Interrogation began with the question of whether the witness had seen any heretics, where and when, how often and with whom. From this fairly innocuous opportunity for the witness to confess some involvement with heresy the inquisitor then assessed the extent of their participation, whether they had listened to the heretics' preaching, whether they had helped them by giving them lodging or conducting them from place to place. He was also interested in whether witnesses had eaten or drunk with heretics, particularly if there had been any ceremonial aspect to the meal, such as the eating of bread blessed by the *perfecti*. Finally, the inquisitor worked at determining the witness's role in the structure of the heretical sect, whether they had had the *consolamentum* ceremony or as the inquisitors put it, 'received the [kiss of] Peace' from the Cathars, in which case they would have been *perfecti*.[19] What they were not particularly interested in was the nature of people's beliefs. Instead they set out to map heresy, both physically in the sense that records were filed not by name but by village, and socially, in that they wanted to know who had been involved in any gathering, who might provide hospitality or act as a contact to fetch the 'good men' for the dying. Quite consciously the inquisitors shifted from the pursuit of major heretical figures to the disruption of the informal networks the Cathars had set up. The inquisitors then summoned those who had been mentioned and had not come forward or those who perhaps had been less than frank about their involvement. The questioning began again.

When the interrogation process had finished the inquisitors took stock in their capacity as heretic hunters, friars, and confessors. A further assembly was called and the penances read out for those who had confessed, starting with the least severe and finishing with those who were to be 'released to the secular arm' for burning. The penances reflected the twin aims of the inquisitors, they wanted to both mark out and exclude the former heretic from the wider Christian community and at the same time provide a route for the penitent to gain readmittance to that community. They were designed to force the believer to choose: not to complete a penance was taken as a conscious relapse into heresy and made the perpetrator liable to be handed over to the secular arm.

The result was that victims had to display their new allegiance in one or more of a variety of ways. They were allowed to become consumers of religion again, only in the most restricted sense. They were packed off on pilgrimages, either to nearby shrines or more distant venues such as Canterbury or Compostella in Spain. Often they had a timetable of when the journey should have been completed and had to produce letters from priests at the shrine to prove that they had been there. The pilgrimage sites themselves were loaded with significance, usually of those making the right choices, such as the shrine of Saint Martial at Limoges who, having killed a number of pagan priests, had then brought them back to life and converted them. Saint Leonard at Noblat became popular in the twelfth century after his powers to liberate from jails became known.

There is some evidence from the penances handed out at Gourdon in Quercy in 1241 that pilgrimage was considered a suitable penance for women. Over 90 per cent of women penitents from there were sentenced to pilgrimages as opposed to 54 per cent of men. For men, pilgrimage could be combined with crusade and many of fighting age were packed off to defend the ailing Latin Empire of Constantinople. But the feeling grew that pilgrimage allowed penitents too much latitude. There was for instance the chance that Cathar penitents on the Rome or Compostella route could find other heretical communities. Worries were expressed in 1243–4 that 'through the perfidy [of penitents on crusade] the dam of faith might be breached'. The route to Constantinople went through Bosnia and Bulgaria, still recognised as Bogomil strongholds. Pilgrimage remained as an inquisition penance, but it declined in importance.[20]

An obvious way of linking penitents with orthodox religion was through enforced acts of charity such as the financial support of paupers or even occasionally subsidising the Church through the support of priests. These penances were considered particularly suitable for those who had been financial backers of heresy. A man who had looked after Cathar funds had to provide financial support for a pauper for life as one of a number of penances. A woman who had given shelter to a Waldensian and bread, wine and nuts to the Cathars now had to support a poor person for a year, as well as embarking on a number of pilgrimages. There was an unmistakable link between this penance and ill-gotten gains, for instance through moneylending.[21] Pons de Capdenier, a rich but devout merchant, a benefactor of the friars, made the following stipulation in his will:

> I order and desire that one pauper may hold and remain in my houses and that pauper may have his necessities from the incomes and profits which may pertain and ought to pertain to my houses and this is always and forever for the love of God and the redemption of my soul.[22]

A Cathar woman who had received a loan from the heretics, possibly at preferential rates, had to support a pauper for a year. The monetary penance also struggled to find favour, despite being recommended at the Council of Béziers in 1246 as a way of raising funds for prisons and inquisitors' expenses. It was too ambivalent, given that Cathars also believed in charity, and above all, it was too private. The Church had to be seen to be victorious.[23]

The two penances which inquisitors eventually favoured were imprisonment and cross-wearing. The latter may well have originated with Dominic himself. Some time between 1206 and 1212, he and his companions distributed penances to a number of supporters of heresy in the Lauragais area near Toulouse. The one we know most about was Pons Roger, a former Cathar *perfectus* who was given a penance which balanced humiliation with respect for his previous way of life. Pons was ritually flogged, as he was led, clad only in breeches, from the entrance to the village to the church by a priest on three Sundays or feast days. But the rest of the regime imposed by Dominic emphasised his reabsorption into the orthodox community. Pons was to fast rigorously, except the festivals of Easter Day, Whit Sunday and Christmas Day when he was to eat meat, 'in denial of his old error'. He was to say ten *Pater Nosters* (Our Fathers) seven times a day and 20 in the middle of the night. He was to attend Mass daily and the afternoon service of vespers on feast days. He was even to wear 'religious clothing', probably the same black habit he wore as a Cathar, with the significant addition of small crosses on each breast. The obvious parallels here with signs of persecution (such as the yellow roundels which Fourth Lateran ordered the Jews to wear) should not preclude the possibility that in this early period Dominic may even have thought to confer a degree of spiritual status on such penitents, since there are records from the late twelfth century of pilgrims, crusaders, Templars and Hospitallers wearing crosses.[24]

These symbols were transformed in the world of the 1240s when inquisitors held the power of life and death. By 1246 people had to be forbidden from ridiculing or doing business with cross-wearers. In 1241 Dominic's former companion, Peire Selha, ordered over one-third of penitents to wear crosses, generally for between one and three years. Wearers had difficulty in finding work, but it was not possible just to discard these stigma since the combination of public opinion and the written records of the inquisitors now preserved the names of transgressors. While victims could flee to a place where they were unknown, it would mean taking the huge step of abandoning their former life, thereby achieving a similar isolation to what the inquisitors intended anyway.[25] In delineating who had made their choice and then had renounced it the inquisitors gradually made the laity in southern France more wary of choice itself.

Cross-wearing became effective on the back of the expansion of imprisonment and this was the inquisitors' major innovation. Previously imprisonment had been used to contain and not to punish. Its place in the English legal system, for instance, was as a holding tank for suspected criminals until the arrival of the visiting justice. Punishment was usually physical: exile, mutilation or death. On the other hand, the inquisitors borrowed from monastic tradition requiring that a monk be kept from both the common table and services if he had committed severe offences. It was a punishment aimed at the 'contumacious', those who had obstinately refused to admit their offence and it was also to ensure the safety of the community. The Dominican thinker Raymond de Peñafort explained in his instructions to Aragonese inquisitors in 1242 that *perfecti* who had renounced heresy and then gone back to their old beliefs should have their excommunication lifted if they once again repented of their error. However, they should serve their penance shut up in perpetual prison, 'in order that they may save their souls there and that they may not otherwise corrupt others'.[26]

The penitential aspect of prison therefore was designed to correct those whose penance was suspect, the punitive to keep them from spreading their beliefs within the community. The impressive theory was confronted by a less accommodating reality on the ground. In 1237 the inquisitors conceded that a prison for penitents had yet to be built in Toulouse although they did obtain the use of the bishop's prison there. In Carcassonne where the king's prison was available for inquisitors, confidence was undermined by the escape of nearly 20 inmates in the late 1230s. In the early 1240s, penitents had to donate building materials such as sand and cement, but even in 1243–4 the Council of Narbonne decreed that sentences could be deferred since there was still not enough stone and cement for prisons. The decisive period came in the wake of the fall of Montségur. In 1246 the inquisitors bought a house near the church of Saint Sernin and Louis IX put the royal prisons in Béziers at the inquisitors' disposal in addition to those at Carcassonne for the inquisitors' use. In the same year, to pay for the construction of more jails, fines for minor offences of heresy were reintroduced. From then on, the inquisitors had a presence in the centre of most major towns, somewhere to hear informers, keep prisoners and store their all-important records.[27]

The Inquisition at Toulouse in 1245–6 also showed an impressive level of co-operation among the clerics themselves. The idea of 'the Church' in opposition to heresy had rarely had any concrete substance in the past, but the two Dominican inquisitors worked with parish priests who accompanied witnesses from their own village. The Benedictine monastery supplied both a venue and its prior, who often asked questions as a 'de facto' inquisitor. The rest of the Toulouse Dominican community was still also involved, with the chronicler Guilhem Pelhisson taking part and a large number of canons and lesser clergy taking down or witnessing confessions.[28] Moreover, it was the Church backed by royal authority, as the lines between civil and ecclesiastical government were deliberately blurred by the use of royal prisons for inquisitors and of civic notaries to act as scribes for the Inquisition.

Once the punishment of imprisoment was available its use rapidly increased. Only about ten per cent of those given penances in 1245–6 were imprisoned, then one of the inquisitors at Toulouse condemned 192 more to incarceration between 1246 and 1248. The sentence of perpetual imprisonment was usually at the inquisitor's pleasure. As was explained to the inmates in the prison chapel at Carcassonne by an inquisitor in 1279, additional penalties could be avoided if they would only add to their confessions. In fact, many of those condemned reappeared in society within two or three years, retaining their status as former heretics and therefore still under suspicion. Whatever the physical conditions, inmates emerged impoverished from prolonged periods in jail because imprisonment was accompanied by confiscation of goods mainly to reimburse the secular power for expenses incurred. Prisoners still remained responsible for the cost of their upkeep, however, and this could entail a further sale of assets or incurring debts. Some hardships could be ameliorated by corruption and in 1282 the inquisitor of Carcassonne had to forbid his prison guardian from eating, gambling and exchanging gifts with prisoners, as well as lending them money.[29]

The examples of striking abuses such as the jailer's wife giving a set of internal keys to a prisoner so that he could visit any cell are balanced by the undoubted harshness of the general regime. In 1285–6 the town consuls complained of conditions in the Carcassonne jail: small, dark and airless cells where prisoners could not tell day from night, other cells where prisoners were kept in shackles and slept on the ground, defecating and urinating on themselves since they were unable to move. This severe punishment, the *murus strictus*, was only given to a small minority of convicted heretics, but was used routinely for those who had not confessed. As a result they could languish for years without sentence as happened to some unfortunate citizens of Albi arrested in an Inquisition sweep of 1299–1300. Papal letters of 1310 and 1313 urged an immediate conclusion to the process, but there is no evidence of their release. For most prisoners, sentenced to the more lenient *murus largus* and able to wander freely within the jail, imprisonment was tedious rather than oppressive. There was no segregation of prisoners and to break the monotony, visitors were permitted.[30]

The making of an institution

The acquisition of buildings in southern France marked an important stage in the development of an *esprit de corps* among inquisitors there. In Italy Peter of Verona, or Peter Martyr, as he is sometimes termed, the first inquisitor to be canonised, also raised the status of the heresy hunters. By the end of the 1250s the inquisitors were also bound together by their own literature on how to conduct themselves and their own private understanding of the opaque papal legislation allowing them to use torture. It is still too early to talk of 'the Inquisition', but not of inquisitors as a group set apart with their own traditions and developing ideology.

From a modern perspective the definitive artefacts of the inquisitors were their registers which were both records of the depositions of witnesses, and the confessions of penitents. They were a major innovation in the 'technology of power' and where they have survived they have proved an irresistible fascination for those interested in the history of heresy. The laity also recognised their significance. The killers at Avignonet were careful to steal the registers belonging to Guilhem Arnaud in the naïve belief that this theft and the cutting out of the inquisitor's tongue would be enough to restore matters to how they were before the inquisitors came. For the Inquisitors the work was closely related to their own activities within the competitive arena of towns. Moneta of Cremona insisted on the duty of the shepherd to drive the wolf from his flock; in other words the Inquisition grew out of pastoral care and the dividing line between preaching campaigns and Inquisition was sometimes blurred.[31]

Instructions had been issued to Dominicans to help local bishops throughout the 1230s and in 1239 a formal Inquisition was attempted in Orvieto, north of Rome. As in Toulouse, it was paralysed by local politics and ended in an attack on the Dominican convent. More successful from the Orthodox point of view were the events in Florence where in 1244 the Dominican inquisitor Ruggero Calcagni was aided by the charismatic preacher Peter of Verona, who founded confraternities such as the Society of the Virgin and the Society of the Faith. Peter was a familiar type from north-east Italy, born in Verona in 1205, and raised in a Cathar family, he was sent to study in Bologna, only to be converted by Dominic at the age of 15. Besides being a persuasive preacher and a major figure in the intellectual battle against the Cathars, he also realised the value of less conventional tactics. Confraternities were familiar in Italian towns as a means of harnessing lay religious enthusiasm. Members could live a semi-monastic life; praying, fasting, and attending

Mass and confession. They often had charitable goals such as the distribution of food to the poor and many included the disavowal of heresy in their statutes. Peter innovated by making such organisations paramilitary; they disrupted Cathar preaching and beat up supporters. A series of street fights in August 1245 made up the battle against heresy in Florence and, as so often, ended in defeat for the inquisitors and the Dominican convent coming under threat. Violence was usually symptomatic of inquisitorial failure. The power of written records depended on support for the inquisitors from the secular authorities and in most Italian cities, as in Florence, this was still lukewarm or non-existent.[32]

The remainder of Peter's career further highlights the frustration which militant orthodox preachers like himself must have felt. He returned to being a conventional Dominican prior, but served in tough cities known as heretical strongholds, such as Piacenza and Como. Pope Innocent IV invited him to go to Cremona in 1251. Perhaps thinking of his exploits in Florence, he left Peter's exact role deliberately ambiguous, merely stating that he and his companion, 'go personally to Cremona . . . and to extirpate the deformity of heresy from the city itself and the surrounding district, carefully and effectively'.[33] The word *inquisitio* was not used, but Peter had the scope to perform any action necessary. However, he had little time to undertake the mission before he was formally appointed an inquisitor for Lombardy, based in Milan. He had been active in his new post only a few months when he was ambushed and murdered by Cathar supporters on the road from Como to Milan on April 6, 1252. Despite his energy and undoubted ability Peter achieved little because at best he had only the toleration of secular rulers. Over the following two decades this situation was to change. The death of the Emperor Frederick II in 1250 was the start of a steep decline in imperial fortunes which was to leave the papacy as the dominant political power in Italy and able to exert pressure on local rulers to be more zealous in defending the faith.

In this campaign Peter proved far more influential in death than in life. Since he was already a well-known personality before becoming an inquisitor and had not held the post for long enough to become unpopular, he proved better martyrdom material than other victims such as Guilhem Arnaut or Conrad of Marburg. He was canonised the following year and his depiction in the habit of a Dominican friar, his head split open with a cleaver, became a popular image in later medieval churches. His cult showed how far the propaganda war against heresy had progressed. Almost a century before, Archbishop Galdino died in his Milanese pulpit, still preaching against heresy and fulfilling his public office, yet he remained an obscure figure outside the city. The legends which surrounded Peter's death circulated throughout Christendom and emphasised his role as a good Christian; his dying words were supposedly those of Stephen, the first apostle to be martyred, 'Lord do not hold this sin against them.' A more far-fetched tale has Peter, unable to speak, making one last use of his education to write in his own blood, '*Credo in Deum*' ('I believe in God'), the opening words of the basic statement of Christian beliefs, the Apostles' Creed.

Peter's canonisation sanctified the role of the inquisitor. His cult, based on the Dominican priory in Milan, combined with political changes in the city to turn it from a centre of heresy to a bulwark against it. In the popular imagination, through Peter, the inquisitor could now be depicted as protecting communities against false prophets leading the laity to damnation. There was an also an ideological message. Francis and Dominic had offered a strategy to fight heresy mainly through attractive alternatives. By making Peter a saint, Innocent signalled a shift in emphasis and endorsed Peter's tactics of targeted violence and the extirpation of heresy by any means possible.

Torture

The association of the Inquisition with torture really belongs to the sixteenth century, with its specialist paraphernalia and cast of sadists, but the first steps were taken by inquisitors of the mid thirteenth century in an effort to obtain confessions of heresy. Surprisingly, although violence was common enough in medieval society, it was a new and double-edged weapon as part of a judicial investigation. The first record of its employment was in the towns of north-east Italy, such as Vercelli and Verona, where suspects were tortured in the secular courts to obtain evidence when all other means had failed. The frequency with which it is mentioned suggests that it had a measure of support from those who had to fight against crime and disorder. Jurists, however, saw the potential dangers and the Vercelli statutes of 1241 restricted its use to known criminals, thieves or men of ill-fame. Bolognese statutes made it very difficult for any citizen of the city to be tortured, in other words exempting the rich. There was further suspicion north of the Alps; Louis IX of France in 1254 deliberately addressed the issue by forbidding the torture of 'honest people of good reputations, even if they are poor'.[34]

Within the Church, canon lawyers were interested in the new technique because it promised convictions in difficult cases like clerical immorality or heresy where eyewitnesses were rare; it also had the spiritual value of nudging the suspect to acknowledgement of his sins through confession. There was also a deterrent value. One writer even went so far as to suggest that the judge should torture a person of bad reputation as a matter of course in order to show what happened to evildoers and incidentally pick up information about other crimes. The obvious objection, pointed out as early as the 1220s, was that confessions under torture could be simply lies told from fear of pain, while some who were guilty could remain silent even in agony. For all that, it seemed to work, provided safeguards were in place, such as requiring confessions to be repeated well away from the scene of the torture. The most common complaint about torture in statutes was that civic officials tended to overuse it.[35]

In the circumstances, inquisitors could not ignore such a powerful weapon, but they were comparatively slow to deploy it. It was difficult enough to convince public opinion that those with bad reputations should include heretics. As we have seen, the hostility felt by many communities to the persecution of religious allegiance led to a number of inquiries ending in riot. Only the shock felt at Peter's assassination allowed Innocent IV to publish *Ad extirpanda* in May 1252. In addition to demanding once again that *podestàs*, communes and other city governments take action against heretics, article 35 of the decree emphasised that heretics were just as bad as other criminals; they were 'robbers and killers of souls, thieves of God's sacraments and the Christian faith'; as such, rulers had to compel captured heretics to confess and accuse others by any means short of damage to limbs and the danger of death. This has usually been interpreted as a licence for secular officials to use torture to obtain confessions from suspects identified by inquisitors or bishops. Yet the issue remains obscure. Four years later Pope Alexander IV allowed friars to absolve one another in cases where they might have incurred a sentence of excommunication through human fragility and when, by the nature of their office as inquisitors, they could not go to their own priors. The text is short, uneasy and evasive; it makes no mention of what the offences that need to be forgiven might be. It also does not explain why the performance of the office of inquisitor made it impossible to be absolved by the convent prior in the usual way: was it because of the nature of the offence or simply because the inquisitors might be far away from home?[36]

According to Bernard Gui's extensive manual for inquisitors, written in the early 1320s, inquisitors recognised torture as one of the ways in which confessions could be extracted from suspects. However, they had much greater expertise in the use of imprisonment about which manuals discoursed at length, weighing up the effectiveness of solitary confinement, food deprivation and shackles. Torture they scarcely mentioned. It is reasonable to ask whether inquisitors needed the more dramatic formal infliction of physical pain or whether their imprisonment techniques amounted to tortures in themselves. In Vienna in the mid thirteenth century, statutes forbade torture by hunger, thirst and chains, suggesting that such a blurring of distinctions did take place. Inquisitors were well aware of the psychological potential of imprisonment; Bernard Gui talked about the advisability of keeping heretics separate from one another so that they could not talk, and how a particularly obstinate suspect confessed all after nearly two years of lonely imprisonment punctuated by repeated interrogation. This was not new knowledge; an anonymous treatise of at least 40 years before recommended that those who would not confess should be imprisoned, deprived of visitors, fed false tales of other witnesses testifying against them and encouraged to confess by Inquisition agents feigning pity.[37]

By comparison the physical tortures available to inquisitors were crude. They did not mention any in their own writings, but contemporary legal sources suggest that suspects could be beaten or they could have their hands tied behind their back and the other end of the rope thrown over a beam in the roof. The victim was then raised slowly into the air putting progressively greater strain on the arms and back, until confession was forthcoming. The inquisitors' silence is almost matched by the lack of complaints from suspects. When rumours swept Carcassonne that witnesses were being constrained to make depositions, it was denied by the witnesses themselves in the presence of an audience of 'religious men'; instead they stated that they had confessed 'for the salvation of their souls and the defence of the Christian faith'. This may not be a disingenuous reading of the sources because 'constraints' did not include prolonged detention which was already being used in the 1250s. This had the advantage of not compromising the inquisitors' spiritual aim of replicating the suspect's spontaneous choice of heresy in the past with an equally spontaneous choice of confession and repentance. Legally too, torture was unnecessary: confession may have been the 'queen of proofs' in the thirteenth century, but a conviction could be obtained on the evidence of two eyewitnesses. The volumes and volumes of Inquisition records asking witnesses who was present when the heretics ate, preached or administered the *consolamentum* ensured that when the inquisitors failed to obtain a confession they could at least secure a conviction.[38]

The inquisitors and the decline of Catharism

The pressure exerted on organised heresy increased over time. Peire de Beauvilla, a young man recently married who had taken part in the massacre of inquisitors at Avignonet in 1242, was finally apprehended after 35 years on the run. The resulting testimony is one of the most substantial on record: staunch Cathar as he had been since childhood, Peire may well have felt that he had little to lose by confessing since the movement he described had largely disappeared. Peire's story is of initial Cathar resilience finally undermined by dwindling resources and growing hostility from secular authorities.

In the immediate aftermath of the massacre, it had evidently been too dangerous for Peire to return home so he made for the alpine border town of Cuneo, west of Genoa. At first sight Italy may have seemed an unusual destination for flight from Languedoc, but there were good cultural and economic reasons to attract migrants from southern France. As the most advanced economy in Europe fortunes could be made there. Notarial records from Genoa show southern French merchants trading there from around the mid 1220s. Troubadours such as Elias Cairel, Guilhem de la Tor and Guilhem Figueira found employment in Italy while patrons such as William IV of Montferrat and Emperor Frederick II encouraged writers in Provençal. Individual enterprise was matched by the ambitious towns on the southern French coast. Narbonne concluded trade treaties with both the Pisans and the Genoese in 1224 and Montpellier renewed existing trade treaties with the two Italian cities the following year.[39]

When the inquisitors started to disrupt the lives of the Cathars and their supporters in Languedoc, Peire de Beauvilla and other fugitives could blend into an established community. Cuneo provided a meeting point for immigrants and exiles. It stood on the route of the two newly opened Larche and Tende passes from Provence as well as the long-established Mont Cenis pass, and it was easily accessible from Genoa. Having supported himself peddling cloth, Peire arrived there in 1242 via Genoa, and found fugitives from southern France and two Cathar *perfecti* working in a workshop making leather straps. The journey was simple enough to allow Peire to return home regularly throughout the 1240s to see his wife and family in Languedoc.

During the following decade Peire moved his family into Lombardy. In the 1250s and early 1260s they lived in or visited various towns such as Pavia, Piacenza, Cremona and Alessandria. They kept in touch with the southern French Cathars in exile, because the community of family and people from the same region was the pillar of a family business. Peire's cousin, a *perfectus* by the name of Stephan Donat, was now based in Lombardy and he provided not only a house for the family, but 100 pounds of capital for a moneylending enterprise. This prospered, despite the ill-fated involvement of Peire's son who took away a large part of the capital and wasted it. Peire did most of the travelling, but divided the profits equally with Stephan.

There were plenty of people requiring Peire's services; the southern French Cathar hierarchy were now based in north Italy, having come under increasing pressure from inquisitors after the accession in 1249 of the king's brother, Alphonse of Poitiers as the new count of Toulouse. In 1252 Peire witnessed two believers becoming *perfecti* in Pavia and also reported the presence there of the Cathar bishop of Toulouse. He claimed to have seen no less than eleven named *perfecti* in Cremona two or three years later and gave the names of nine more seen in Piacenza around 1257.[40]

The 'good men' needed to remain in close proximity to their supporters. Peire de Belstar, active in Pavia around 1252, later went back to Languedoc to organise the passage to Italy of a group of local women who wanted to receive the *consolamentum*. An associate in Italy, Raymond de Manso, returned to become Cathar deacon of Vielmorès in 1257. Messengers were required to make the frequent journeys between southern France and Lombardy, but discreetly. One Cathar exile in Cremona persuaded a messenger to take goods to his father in Toulouse, but if he were questioned to say that they had met in Provence.[41] The movement of goods and people required money: Stephan Donat and his companion were asked to bank 100 pounds for a woman who planned to make the journey from Languedoc to Italy around 1255. *Perfecti* themselves relied on the goodwill of believers to finance travel. After one visit to Languedoc in 1268 the *perfectus*, Guilhem Raffard, got into an unseemly row with a noblewoman who would not, or could not, pay for his return trip to Lombardy. Such disputes did little for the Cathars' reputation and there is a hint that the strain may have been becoming too much even for their formidable powers of organisation. The woman who sent money to Stephan Donat never did make the journey, but redirected it to her mother who was already a *perfecta* in Italy. Another woman showed splendidly 'mix and match' unfulfilled spiritual yearnings when she commented that had she the money 'she would like to go on pilgrimage and so would like to go to the good men, namely the heretics in Lombardy'.[42]

The last flowering of Catharism in Italy needed both economic and political help. During the wars between the so-called 'Ghibelline' towns who supported the Emperor Frederick II and the 'Guelf' towns professing loyalty to the pope, people with unorthodox religious views were useful. Particularly for the Ghibellines, they emphasised a measure of choice in religion, building on the tradition of Arnold of Brescia that the Church could be organised differently, with greater emphasis on poverty and a more decisive role for the laity and the secular power. In the 1240s Frederick himself harboured the renegade Franciscan, Brother Elias, one of the Church's fiercest critics. While it was not quite respectable to support movements such as the Cathars, Frederick made little effort to enforce his own legislation against heresy and several of his most prominent supporters were reputed to have heretical sympathies.

Gradually, tolerance of religious dissent became untenable. This was partly due to the preaching and propaganda of leading friars such as Peter of Verona or Anthony of Padua and partly due to the changing political situation within Italy. Frederick's death in 1250 did not lead to the demise of the Ghibellines, the word was after all just a label, but it did become difficult for rulers to deny the papacy's legal authority. Any potential opponent of the pope as a political figure therefore became obliged to demonstrate satisfactorily orthodox religious credentials. The first victim of this syndrome was Ezzelino da Romano, the most powerful Ghibelline ruler after the death of Frederick II. He was a ruthless opponent of the papacy with little regard for the rights of the Church and his territories centred on north-east Italy, where Catharism was strong, but there is no evidence of any interest in heresy. The accusation from the pope that he had allowed his lands to become a refuge for heretics in 1246 was the thirteenth-century equivalent of allegedly harbouring terrorists and there was no satisfactory way of avoiding the charge without verification by papally appointed inquisitors. Ezzelino refused and paid a political price for a political stance. A 'crusade' was organised against him in 1255, which eventually defeated him shortly before his death in 1259.[43]

One of Ezzelino's opponents in that war, his one-time ally Oberto Pallavicini, is an altogether more intriguing figure. Originally a rural noble in north Italy, Pallavicini had risen to become an important ally of Frederick II in his extensive struggle with the papacy and its allies in the Lombard towns. In the years after Frederick's death he acquired control of a number of towns in north Italy, sometimes claiming a formal title such as 'perpetual *podestà*' and sometimes content to rule through nominees. By 1253 he controlled Cremona, Piacenza and Pavia and as early as 1254 an ally was accused of heretical sympathies on account of associating with him. In December 1260 Pope Alexander IV issued a bull against Oberto which showed a fair degree of accurate intelligence and made more specific allegations against him than had ever been made against Ezzelino. Alexander alleged that because of Oberto's sympathies heretics came to his lands to sow their heresies from Lombardy and also from Provence and the Toulouse region. He went on to accuse Oberto of having in his household one Berengar, who had been condemned previously for heresy, but who was now protected by the Italian magnate. It was true that there were Cathars among the southern French migrants to north Italy and it is possible that this is Berengar de Jouarres, a knight from Homps near Carcassonne and a Cathar supporter who had been reported to the Inquisition in southern France as having been in Cremona between 1252 and 1255.[44]

Pallavicini knew that to maintain his position in the faction-ridden world of Italian civic politics he had to keep powerful economic interests happy. During the 1250s he made trade agreements with cities which lay outside his direct control. He worked first to secure a supply of goods from Genoa by guaranteeing, in June 1253, the commune of Cremona's help in cases of non-payment for goods bought in the port by Cremonese merchants. The following year an agreement was concluded with Montpellier. This applied to all the towns under Pallavicini's control and refers to the difficulties caused by 'the discord of men and the evil of the time', especially for 'merchants wishing to travel through different parts of the world and especially through Lombardy, who are frequently attacked on the pretext of any reason'.

The treaty laid toll rates for merchants crossing Oberto's lands in Lombardy. In return he promised safe conduct and compensation for anyone robbed, except in cases of debt. The tolls were to be paid by the bundle or bale although the merchants themselves, their horses and servants were exempt. Moreover, the merchant on foot, travelling through Pallavicini's territories with simply a bundle of goods on his back, paid nothing. Remembering Peire de Beauvilla's early career selling cloth this would have allowed fugitives from southern France to move around with the minimum of attention from the authorities. For Montpellier merchants and those who wanted access to Italian markets it extended the town's longstanding relationship with Genoa to the hinterland of the Po valley. Pallavicini also gave his blessing to the treaty of monetary union among Lombard cities concluded in May 1254, his dominance of the area supplying the necessary injection of political will.[45] Once again the context of heresy was of close economic links. Piacenza, where Peire de Beauvilla operated as a moneylender, was a banking centre and by the end of the 1240s two of the leading Genoese banks were run by native Piacenzans; one of these, Guglielmo Leccacorvo and company, also had strong links with Cuneo, the transit town in the Alps on the route from southern France to Italy.[46]

It is quite possible that in this context Pallavicini may have welcomed contacts with Cathars, particularly from Languedoc, as the pope had alleged. He had created a cosmopolitan trading area which was a home to Cathar communities in a context where southern French culture and troubadours were still fashionable. Moreover, Oberto was faced with evidence of God's disfavour with the Roman Church. Louis IX of France's crusade ended in disaster in the summer of 1250 with the king's capture and an enormous ransom demanded by the sultan of Egypt. This was not just a symbolic disaster; several Lombard banks including that of Leccacorvo failed having made large loans to crusaders. Oberto's enthusiasm to build trading links in the early 1250s may well have been a response to adversity brought on by an ill-conceived religious enterprise. Whatever Oberto's feelings, he was concerned to keep papal influence in his territories to a minimum and this attitude helped his lands to become a haven for heresy. In Cremona a dispute with the papacy about the appointment of the bishop meant that the town was without episcopal jurisdiction from 1248. Consequently, there was no ecclesiastical support in the town for campaigns against heresy like the one suggested to Peter of Verona by Innocent IV in 1251.

Eventually, even Pallavicini fell victim to a changing political culture which brought religious conformity in its wake. The invasion of Italy in 1265 by Charles of Anjou, the brother of the French king, provided just such a transformation. He had been called in by the pope to establish control over southern Italy, the kingdom of Sicily, where Manfred the illegitimate son of Frederick II had become king. The progress of Charles of Anjou's army destabilised Italian politics as it made its way over the Alps and down through Lombardy and with it arrived a different conception of heresy from that of Italian secular rulers. Coming from a French context, for Charles the idea that heresy was a form of treason was not a vague concept, but a central belief. As in Languedoc, the loyalty of local secular authorities could only be proved by vigorous action against heresy. This belief was bolstered by two French popes, Urban IV (1261–4) and Clement IV (1265–8), the second of whom, Gui Fouçois, was himself from Saint-Gilles in the south and a former bureaucrat of Alphonse of Poitiers. Following Charles's decisive victory over Manfred at the battle of Benevento in February 1266, Ghibelline towns rapidly changed allegiance: Cremona reconciled itself with the pope and as proof of its sincerity invited in the inquisitors in June 1266. Piacenza followed suit and that summer held a solemn ceremony, supposedly at the instigation of some of the citizens and the new consuls. Papal legates said Mass over the relics of St Justina with the service attended by no less than 60 nobles who swore perpetual peace among themselves.

And then the legates together with the preaching brothers [Dominicans] who had been deputed to that office by the lord pope, captured and burnt many heretics in the city of Piacenza and in the city of Cremona and they sent many of the Provençal tongue to 'Provence' [the Italian term for southern France in general] loaded in chains.[47]

This was not quite the end of the Ghibelline cause, since Frederick's grandson, Conradin, marched south in 1268, but his supporters could not afford to be accused of heresy and there was no relaxation of attitudes.

Religious culture was also changing. In the wake of the Guelf triumph, the friars were creating institutionalised versions of the great lay movements of 30 years before; a 'Consortium of Faith and Peace' was set up in both Cremona and Piacenza. Members had to hunt down heretics, keep their city obedient to the pope and Roman Church and prevent disturbances to the peace of the city by those opposed to the current settlement. There was also a real attempt to draw a line under a previous era with the Consortia's declared intention to prevent any new 'consortia, societies or associations', not under their own control. Lay choice was restricted in other ways as well; although there were annually elected officials for the Consortia, elections were to take place with the consent, and in the presence of, the prior of the local Dominicans and Franciscan custodian of the city. The advice and agreement of the friars were required on all major issues.[48]

These sort of measures, giving a strong lay body of support to assist inquisitors, seem to have been decisive; the last great account of Italian Catharism was written by the inquisitor Anselm of Alessandria during the upheavals of 1266 and the years following. He records Cathar bishoprics in north Italy, but the characters are mostly shadowy, appearing in no other source, while his classic account of the entry of a Cathar into a strange house shows a group suspicious and on the defensive.

> When any Cathar or a believer of any sect enters a strange house of any Cathars, especially if he does not know who are the Cathars among those he encounters there, he says, "*Bessea trona*! Can we do something for our betterment?" Or he may say, "Is there a crooked stick here?" Then if there is anyone there who is not of their belief and of whom they are suspicious, the elder answers, "Be seated." By this the newcomer understands that there is someone there whom they fear.[49]

Most of the refugees from Languedoc also found that it was time to leave. Their flight may have been hastened by the resentment developing against all the French caused by Charles of Anjou's insertion of his own officials in positions of power. In Pavia in 1271 a group of Frenchmen were attacked while making their way back from the papal curia. The crowd then went on to storm the local Dominican convent which they suspected may have been harbouring more French, perhaps revealing that many saw the friars as much occupiers as the French.[50]

In the final years of crisis the Cathar community may have recovered a little of the cosmopolitan nature of its early years. Between 1265 and 1275 Peire de Beauvilla met southern French 'good men' ministering to Italian believers in the port city of Genoa. A more substantial gathering of southern French and Italian Cathars came together in the tiny fortified fishing village of Sirmione, on the shores of Lake Garda. The importance to the Cathars of the towns of north-east Italy lasted until the end of the movement. Sirmione was near Desenzano, the home of the Albanenses sect, but probably had closer links with the heretics of neighbouring Verona. As might be expected, that city had a long record of Ghibelline sympathies and refusal of any papal Inquisition and consequently, in the late 1260s, it was placed under interdict for its support of Conradin's failed bid to dislodge Charles of Anjou. At the same time as being cast into political isolation, Verona attracted a variety of immigrants. A southern French community can be discerned there in the 1250s, probably working in the town's leather and cloth industries, but any Cathars among them would probably have been forced to flee when anti-heresy legislation was applied in 1270 in an attempt to get the interdict lifted.[51]

The southern French witness Guilhem Raffard recalled being consoled in Sirmione in the presence of three Cathar bishops, Bernard Oliba of Toulouse, Guillaume Pierre, bishop of the heretics of France, and an unknown bishop of the heretics of Lombardy. Admittedly, there is the air of a court in exile about these proceedings, but southern French witnesses talk of a community of some 15 *perfecti* from their own country as well as referring to 'many other heretics of Lombardy staying there'.[52] Sirmione was important enough to attract the attention of Mastino della Scala, the ruler of Verona, together with his Franciscan bishop and inquisitor, Fra Timidio, and their expedition succeeded in capturing the village in November 1276. The resultant haul of between 166 and 200 heretics were not burnt immediately, pending negotiations with the papacy. Their final execution in February 1278 provided one more grisly spectacle for Verona's old Roman arena and a suitably fiery end for organised Catharism in Italy. It also illustrated the new political domin-ance of orthodoxy, with the interdict duly being lifted in October of the same year as this display of anti-heretical zeal. The Church's organ-isation of repression now had the same impressive reach across Christen-dom once enjoyed by the heretics. In 1279 Pope Nicholas III received a request from two Languedocian inquisitors for the transfer of a group of southern French heretics who had recently been captured and im-prisoned in the diocese of Verona.[53]

The inquisitors triumphed because, aided by a gradual decline in political options for the elite, they succeeded in destroying Catharism as a credible choice for consumers of religion much lower down the social scale. At their most generous the inquisitors offered career opportunities for Cathar *perfecti* who defected and there is a steady stream of men who rose high in the Church despite a heretical past. A less elevated tactic was the amelioration of penalties in return for spying. Inquisitors were not afraid to invest time and trouble in such cases. The believer Amblard Vassall was arrested in his native Languedoc in 1266 and taken to Lombardy, where he was released on condition he would betray Cathars to the Church authorities. The scheme in this case failed because Amblard's former colleagues were suspicious of his inquisitorial contacts, but the inquisitors did develop a reasonable intelligence network. This paid dividends when an attempt by southern French Cathars to set up a Montségur-style redoubt in south Italy in 1264–5 was snuffed out almost immediately after letters were sent to Manfred of Sicily requesting the heretics' arrest. The messenger was Sicard Lunel, another former *perfectus* who had found long-term employment with the inquisitors.[54]

The inquisitors' greatest achievement was that they changed the idea of consumption of religion. Previously, support for heretical groups had been a soft choice for both *perfecti* and believers. For the latter, as has been shown, one religious group was as good as another, depending mainly on the lifestyles of its individual representatives. On the other hand, those who were actively involved in a religious movement relied on a 'goodwill economy', where shelter and support were exchanged for spiritual benefits and occasionally soft loans. A constant inquisitorial presence made both sides look at the price. Guilhem Prunel, a *perfectus* active in southern France in the 1270s before fleeing to Italy, speculated aloud how wealthy an ailing supporter was and targeted a rich man with a beautiful house who had been generous in the past. A man consoled at Sirmione noted that for performing the ceremony the Cathar bishop, Bernard Oliba, demanded and took a sum which was almost all his money.[55]

The laity also started to take a more objective view of their spiritual contacts. There are cases in the 1260s where hospitality is refused to the *perfecti*. Others watched the infrastructure of their movement crumble before them. Guilhem Raffard described his return to Languedoc, travelling from Pavia to Genoa among merchants, being passed round supporters and relatives in Languedoc before wandering the county of Toulouse as a beggar to avoid detection. This was less of a disguise than falling on hard times, since Raffard had set out as a merchant. Eventually Guilhem was taken in by an old woman who sheltered him for two years.[56]

Returning Cathar believers found life very uncomfortable indeed given that an investigation by an inquisitor could lead not only to a personal penance, but also the confiscation of a family's goods. One was bribed to return to Lombardy. Peire de Beauvilla describes his homecoming vividly after 35 years on the run. He turned first to his family and on his arrival went to the house of a cousin who led him to the house of his daughter, Ermengarde. She 'received him with joy and fear', but nevertheless embraced him and kissed him as her father. Various other relatives visited, curious to ask after uncles in Lombardy, but frightened enough to need comforting by the old fugitive. In particular, Peire's son-in-law Paul, who had married Ermengarde while he had been absent, was afraid. He asked the older man if he was a heretic. Peire replied that he was, but tried to reassure Paul, saying that he wanted only to meet up with his sons and arrange to stay with friends. A meeting was arranged with his sons and brother, but before it could take place he was arrested in the house of Paul and Ermengarde. Suspicion points to Paul as the informant.[57]

If having the heretics around was too great a price to pay then the alternative rendered the movement, quite literally, worthless. This is surely what one witness was driving at when he declared that:

> The good men were valuable and this land is worth much less since they dared not remain in it.

This was an educative process; the same analysis which forced the laity to look at the value of Catharism could be applied to other movements.[58]

chapter 7

THE DECLINE OF THE HOLY MEN: 1244–1300

In the second half of the thirteenth century popular religion was shaped by three important developments. In the first place there was less room for heretical movements since the laity were far better policed by inquisitors. Secondly, this did not mean there was any less variety in religious beliefs or fewer charismatic preachers, only that they were, or claimed to be, part of one of the existing orders, usually the Franciscans. The internal disputes among the Friars Minor are often recognisable as modified versions of tensions among previous generations of Cathars and Waldensians and although both these sects still existed, the intellectual energy of writers now focussed on disputes within the Church. Finally, faced with the shrill disputes on their behalf, lay men and women began to reshape the Church in their own image. By now their experience as consumers of religion allowed comparisons to be made of which movement best suited their taste. Moreover, there were far more opportunities to customise and participate in the religious life at local level. Given the uncertainty of who was holy and who was not, they turned their backs on spiritual elites, heretical and orthodox alike.

The struggle for orthodoxy:
the Franciscans before 1274

The clearest example of the rejection of holy men was the Franciscan movement. By the end of the thirteenth century, if not discredited, it had lost the privileged status in the popular imagination bequeathed by its founder. To be fair, a reaction against the friars or a decline in their popularity was not unforeseeable and Francis had taken steps against such an eventuality. He had taken out two insurance policies when he founded the Friars Minor. In the first place he sought to minimise resentment from secular clergy by making his order a community of beggars offering no threat to the revenues of parish priests. He had also aligned his followers with the papacy as the most powerful institution in the western world and this seemed to guarantee both protection against potential enemies in Church and State and a disciplinary body of last resort in case trouble arose from within the order itself. The second half of the thirteenth century saw the unravelling of both these policies because of the decline of the papacy.

The high point of papal political influence on secular politics came in 1266 when the French prince Charles of Anjou was installed in southern Italy with the backing of the pope. Charles proved to be every bit as independent-minded as the previous rulers of south Italy, but held undue influence over the papacy due to his proximity to Rome and the fact that he was a papal nominee. Successive pontiffs were distracted from more spiritual concerns by Italian politics. The situation was not helped by development of an extensive management machine dedicated to the running of the Church. As management often does, it appropriated more and more decisions to the centre, so that whereas the papacy of the early twelfth century had fought for free elections to major ecclesiastical posts, that of the late thirteenth century increased its power of patronage over appointments at all levels through so-called 'papal provisions'. There frequently amounted to the promotion of papal relatives or the building up of national groups in the college of cardinals. The combination of factional fighting and squabbles between French and Italian cardinals led to the greatest problem of all for the papacy as an institution. Between 1267 and 1297 there were no less than eleven popes; for six and a half years there was no reigning pontiff at all, sometimes for a year or more at a time. Not surprisingly, there was little continuity of leadership for the Church and the lack of it exposed the inability of the Franciscans to solve their own problems.[1]

The foremost of these difficulties was familiar to the followers of Valdes and also to the early Cathars, namely, what was the authority of founders and early leaders. The Franciscans had a General Chapter to elect Ministers General, but their legitimacy depended on how they measured up to a perceived vision of the founder. This vision changed with time. As more reminiscences of the saint were collected, the role of poverty became more prominent and by the end of the century the character of Francis himself underwent a change, becoming gloomier and more prone to prophesy tribulations for the order. The movement was therefore broadly divided between those who saw a changing order maintaining Francis as a guiding spirit and others who regarded him as a role model for friars, if not humanity itself.[2]

In the 1240s this could be a creative tension. The organisational ability of a Minister General like Crescentius of Iesi enabled necessary investment in bricks and mortar for the burgeoning order and over 100 schemes for the extension and rebuilding of Franciscan premises were approved, despite grumbles from the more zealous brothers. It was evidence of a shift in opinion that John of Parma was elected Minister General in 1247. Learned, devoted to poverty, wearing only a habit of rough cloth, he traipsed everywhere on foot and was given to arriving unannounced at friaries the length and breadth of Christendom. Yet even John's resemblance to the order's founder could not save him from embarrassment. When the saintly King Louis of France attended the Provincial Chapter held in 1248 at Sens, the king and his entourage sat down with the friars for a feast at royal expense. Louis was a great supporter of the friars and sensitively arranged that the meal should have no meat, but it was still a major display of tasty consumables. To begin with there were cherries and fine French wine, reminiscent of Yves of Narbonne's contemporary account of Cathar extravagance. This was just the beginning; along with the finest white bread, the apogee of medieval consumer well-being, the friars were served:

> Fresh beans cooked in milk, fish, crabs, eel-cakes, rice in almond milk and grated cinnamon, roasted eel in splendid sauce, cakes, cheese and fruit in abundance.

This was clearly a very special occasion (the menu was remembered 40 years later!) and John distanced himself from the proceedings by eating at a separate table, but there is no doubt that though the feast was an honour the friars could not refuse, it was awkward for the zealous, and all too easily enjoyed by the rest.[3]

Yet it was a different manifestation of the founder's ghost which was to sink John. The friars were jealously regarded by the secular clergy and nowhere more so than in the university cities where they had both numbers and influence. John's protégé, Gerard of Borgo San Donino, an Italian living in Paris, published a work in 1254 entitled *An Introduction to the Eternal Gospel*. From the start of the order many Franciscans had thought they were fulfilling a vital preparatory role for the second coming of Christ. Now Gerard incorporated this millenarian tradition to announce a new age of preparation for the event, to begin just six years later in 1260 and to be proclaimed by the Franciscans. Many other component bodies of the Church were outraged and the work was condemned in October 1255 with the author kept in chains for the remainder of his life with neither books nor company.[4] Remembering Francis's own impeccable doctrinal orthodoxy and emphasis on co-operation with existing orders and secular clergy, John felt his position undermined and he resigned in February 1257.

The influence behind Gerard was the twelfth-century monk and thinker, Joachim of Fiore, and it was his apocalypticism which further marked out elements of the Franciscans from the rest of the Church. It was not quite the equivalent of the Cathar teaching that salvation could only be found within their ranks, but the interest in the special Franciscan role in the second coming raised the stakes to cosmic significance. Joachim had been a Cistercian monk in Calabria and gained a reputation as a holy man who wrote apocalyptic visions, before dying in 1202. One of his most striking was that there were to be two new orders of spiritual men leading Christendom from one status to the next. These were radically to alter the conventional monastic ideal by becoming inter-mediaries between the life of contemplation and the active life of the secular priest. The parallels between this idea and the two new orders of friars were obvious; moreover, there was a clear implication in Joachim's writings that the new phase of history that the orders were to ushered by the orders was only a prelude to the end of history itself, which was not far off.[5] Joachim's views interested elements right across the Franciscans. While there was nothing unorthodox about the ideas in themselves, taken in conjunction with an extreme emphasis on poverty they could mark out some of the Franciscans as a movement almost separate from the Church. The combination inspired some and made enemies of others. Hugh of Digne, prior of Hyères in Provence and a former provincial minister, was a resonant figure in the Franciscan movement of the 1240s and early 1250s as a scholar in his own right, a friend of John of Parma and a great preacher. Under the protection of Innocent IV he famously admonished the papal court for its sloth and luxury, accusing the cardinals of delighting only in their 'little lap dogs and rings and sleek horses and . . . kinsmen'.[6]

Hugh was careful to restate the order's anti-heretical mission and rejected the false austerity of Catharism. For him the perfect life of poverty was not something which could endure for ever, instead it made sense within a Joachite framework of the friars ushering in a new era. His teaching struck a chord with lay people of every status. Notaries, judges, physicians and learned men would gather in Hugh's chambers. Outside their convent, the friars at Hyères also encouraged,

> a large number of men and women doing penance for their sins, even though they live in their own homes and wear secular dress.[7]

For Hugh or John of Parma, Joachim's ideas were powerful enough to make sense of poverty and united enough shades of Franciscan opinion to even reach outside the order, but in less subtle hands they became a disruptive social force.

Joachim had supposedly placed the end of the world at 1260 and when that year finally arrived, such was the influence of the prophet that groups of 'Flagellants' formed among the laity, parading half naked through the streets and whipping themselves in penance for their sins. The origins of this movement in Perugia, not far from Assisi, point to a strong Franciscan involvement, yet it spread way beyond them, reaching northern Europe the following year. As in the 'Alleluia' of 1233, there was also a political and economic agenda as the penitents sought to bring peace between the warring factions in Italian towns and demanded the return of 'ill-gotten gains', a customary euphemism for an attack on moneylenders. As with the Peace movement of earlier centuries, the apocalyptic tone should not conceal the earthly benefits which penance was expected to deliver.

The short-lived Flagellant movement proved the first of a number of embarrassing fellow travellers claiming inspiration from the Franciscans, some of which emerged as heretical movements beyond the Church's control. In the charged year of 1260 or shortly after, one Gerard Segarelli, a native of Parma, applied to join his local Franciscan house and was refused, probably because the socially superior friars, now mostly ordained clerks, regarded him as 'of base family, an illiterate layman, ignorant and foolish'. Nevertheless Segarelli's inspiration from Francis was sincere and having meditated for days in the Franciscan church over a painted lamp cover depicting the apostles, he sold his house and scattered the money in the town square. Segarelli attracted the same kind of people as himself; small farmers selling their fields and vineyards, turning to preaching and living off alms. They termed themselves 'Apostles' or 'Apostolic Brethren' and tried to involve senior local churchmen as patrons for the group, as Francis had done. The world of the 1260s had become more suspicious and all overtures were refused. The movement gained adherents in several Italian cities before lapsing into chaos with different factions of 'Apostles' fighting in the streets and a bizarre attempt to kidnap the founder by some of his own followers.[8] Such movements placed the Friars Minor in a dilemma; the more conservative mood among churchmen demanded that the order distanced itself from such movements as Segarelli's, yet in doing so they risked turning their backs on the spiritual hunger for involvement in religion which Francis had so dramatically acknowledged and on which they still relied.

The original Franciscans had also benefited from finding the secular Church in crisis due to the rise of organised heresy. By 1260, the secular clergy had recovered a little of their poise. They turned their attention to bodies within the Church which might be threatening the time-hallowed structures of parish and bishop and in the universities they found champions who identified the orders of friars as the problem. In doing so they outlined a new, less-demanding religion which increasingly marginalised austere spiritual elites. In 1256 William of Saint Amour, a Burgundian secular clerk in Paris, published *On the Perils of the most Recent Times* in which he attacked the friars' pastoral work, claimed back the apostolic succession for parish priests and then criticised mendicancy, the way in which the friars begged for their necessities of life. In William's opinion the friars should work for a living. The friars were still influential enough to have the recalcitrant William packed off into exile. Almost at once Gerard of Abbeville, archdeacon of Ponthieu and Cambrai in the modern border area between France and Belgium, began work on the two books which comprise *Against the enemy of Christian Perfection*, and having written them, waited until the outbreak of further disagreements between the secular masters and friars at Paris in 1269 before releasing his work in late summer.

The spiritual ideals of the friars were recruiting talented masters and students and the jealousy of the secular masters still owes something to Walter Map's century-old assessment of the Waldensians that if admitted they would eventually drive out ordinary clerics. Gerard's contribution was to reassert a spirituality for secular clerks, less austere, comfortable even, but useful to the Church and dealing with lay concerns, such as poverty and diet. Gerard first attacked the hypocrisy of the friars over the former, which depended on all their possessions technically belonging to the pope which he then let them make use of. How could they be said to have the *use* of food without ownership, if they then ate it? Food was important to Gerard; he devoted a quarter of the first part of *Against the enemy* to the subject and attacked the friars' diet and fasts almost as much as poverty. It was illogical to him that the friars ate fish yet would not eat meat, would drink water, but not wine or cider (a nice touch this from the cider-producing area of northern France). The crucial point for Gerard is from Luke (10:7), that followers of Christ should eat whatever is provided, even if the food was pleasant and a form of flesh. Gerard mischievously borrows from Augustine when he says: 'Who would not rather prefer eating fish in the manner of the Lord, than lentils in the manner of Esau or barley like mares?' Christ had performed miracles to serve fish to 5000 whereas Esau's hunger for a mess of lentil pottage cost him his birthright (Genesis 25: 26–34).

Besides an enthusiasm for food, Gerard brought many of the arguments over the apostolic life full circle. The friars had evolved partly in response to the lifestyle of heretics and Gerard now took Augustine's arguments against the ancient Manichaean dualists and applied them to the Franciscans and Dominicans; he implied a resemblance to heresy and undercut the idea of a spiritual elite leading a distinctive life. The main point was taken from Augustine's great work, *The City of God*:

> It is a matter of no moment . . . whether he who adopts the faith that brings men to God, adopts it in one dress and manner of life or another, so long only as he lives in conformity with the commandments of God.

In other words there was choice of clothing and diet for Christians.[9]

Consumption without guilt also applied to the second book of the work where he argues against the friars for a wealthy Church:

> Blush in shame, therefore, and understand that allowing God's benefits or opportunities to be dispensed in common; does not at all detract from [Christian] perfection; for, according to the Apostle [Paul], piety which best bestows perfection, has the promise of life both now and in the future, abounding here in spiritual goods and having a sufficiency of temporal ones.

Citing Jerome, 'wealth does not hinder a rich man [from salvation] if he uses it well', Gerard stressed the Church's charitable obligations to widows and orphans, as well as arguing that rich individuals may also have an abundance of virtue. Various wealthy figures from the Old Testament are then quoted, such as Abraham, Joseph and David. Gerard is on thinner ice with the New Testament, but is safer employing the examples of the Roman Emperor Constantine and the English Saints Edmund and Edward the Confessor. The reference to the Confessor was particularly pertinent because in the year *Contra adversarium* appeared, Henry III of England unveiled an elaborate new tomb for the saint in Westminster Abbey, the religious house to which Edward had been a lavish benefactor.[10] Gerard drove his point home by quoting Augustine to the effect that a sacred place such as a church building should be sufficiently endowed and that an impoverished Church dishonoured God and cooled popular devotion.[11]

These attacks wounded the Dominicans rather less than the Franciscans in as much as the Black Friars never had any problem with beautiful churches and were already displaying their versatility in a variety of roles within the Church hierarchy. In contrast, the Friars Minor still staked much on poverty and austerity. Since both literally and metaphorically it required a saint to lead the Franciscans, the order was fortunate in identifying a suitable candidate, one Bonaventure of Bagnoreggio, a doctor's son from near Orvieto who combined intellectual strength with a modest lifestyle and formidable powers of organisation. By the time of Gerard's attacks he had already stamped his authority on the movement. He had reaffirmed poverty at a General Chapter at Narbonne in 1260, compiled a new biography of Francis and when it was published in 1266 ordered the destruction of all previous versions of the saint's life. In this last exercise in medieval censorship, to the eternal regret of historians, he was largely successful.

Bonaventure was sensitive to charges that, like heretics, the Franciscans undermined the Church's existing structures. He refuted Gerard with his *Apologia Pauperum* or '*Defence of the Poor*' in 1269. The friars' work was to help priests: in instructing in the faith they were builders, in warning against imminent dangers they were watchmen, and so on. As regards food and drink, did not the *Ordinary Gloss* on the Bible, a key text in medieval university education, quote the Venerable Bede to the effect that, 'it is fitting that the cup selected for heavenly grace [the friar] be free of any worldly stimulant', therefore no wine or any other strong drink? The friars were anchorites living on bread, legumes and vegetables, spiced only with salt. Unfortunately Bonaventure knew that many within his order would not recognise this diet and in defending them he found himself agreeing with Gerard. After an uncomfortable discussion of Esau and his lentil pottage, he declared that:

> It is clear that we are free to use delicate food in the proper circumstances of time and place without incurring any sin.

Finally he reaches back to Pope Gregory the Great's defence that, 'it is not the food, but the appetite that may be vicious'. Similarly, in dealing with wealth, Bonaventure defended Franciscan poverty, while conceding the right of those who have money to make charitable use of it. The Franciscans' special status helped those who helped them, 'He who receives a just man . . . shall receive a just man's reward,' to quote Matthew's gospel (10:41). Bonaventure was halfway to admitting that it was not whether you had wealth or not, it was what you did with it that was important.[12]

Even if Bonaventure could win disputes within the Church, the changes in religious culture they implied were already making life uncomfortable for the Franciscans. Segarelli's modest success took place against a background of what might be termed 'friar fatigue'. The 'Friars of the Sack' were a perfectly legitimate order founded in Provence in the 1250s and dedicated to penance and poverty, symbolised by the mantle of sack cloth which they wore over their habits. When they entered the north Italian town of Modena, the Franciscan chronicler Salimbene quoted a wealthy female supporter of the Franciscans:

> In truth, Brothers, I say to you that we already had so many sacks and scrips emptying our barns that we had no need of these Brothers of the Sack.[13]

In 1261 the Knights of the Blessed Virgin Mary were formed by a Bolognese noble and his companions. The order followed the mendicant pattern in that there were to be two sections, one allowing lay men to live in the world and the other comprising clergy living under a rule. They had a specifically anti-heretical mission to fight for the defence of the Catholic faith and the liberty of the Church if threatened, and also to provide a peacekeeping force where town communes were split by faction. Yet from the start they had a mixed reputation; they seemed to parody the mendicant ideal in that they were funded by exemption from civic taxation, so they genuinely had no thought for the morrow. Consequently, as a result of their high living they were mockingly known as the 'frati godenti', the cheery brothers. For the furious Salimbene they were a threat to other orders and moreover, 'I do not see what use they can be to the Church of God – save perhaps to save their own souls.' Unfortunately, this was an argument which could be used just as forcefully against the Franciscans themselves.[14]

The Franciscans after 1274: the path to heresy

When the Church had met at the Lateran Council in 1215 the problem had been the clergy, when it met at Lyon in 1274 the problem was the laity and the 'bad customs' which had 'crept over' them. Along with organising yet another crusade and healing the breach with the Greek Church, legislation for the Council was derived from a series of reports commissioned from leading Church figures. One of the most influential came from Humbert of Romans, the Dominican Master General and noted preacher in his own right. Having rightly pointed out the increasing dangers to the crusader states from the Saracens, Humbert had little to say about heresy other than noting the latent threat from those 'now in hiding, who once thieved openly from the Church'. So he concentrated on the Church's relations with the laity, proposing fewer feast days so that the poor could work to feed themselves, confronting the old problem that divine services usually had to be paid for and recognising 'friar fatigue' through a proposal to reduce the number of mendicants and reform the *quaestuarii*, the friars charged with collecting alms from the laity. Humbert also returned to the issue which had irritated the townsfolk of Lyon a century earlier, in Valdes's time, namely that communities of clerks such as cathedral chapters were too ostentatious in their pomp and prodigality. According to Humbert, the Church could also put on a better show by adopting features of the friars' services. Singing could be taught better in all churches, and Mass might be said and heard better if it was shortened. In other words the Church was starting to define itself by the need to appeal to consumers.

In terms of how such changes might be carried out, Humbert's analysis demonstrated why the Church was always vulnerable to dissident movements which could organise effectively at local level. Beyond fulminating against ignorant or absent priests Humbert had little idea of how to make the local clergy more receptive to the needs of their parishioners. The legislation of the Council was feebler still. The main cause of absenteeism in parishes was pluralism, that of priests holding multiple offices, but the Council only legislated that in such cases someone should be responsible for care of souls. Such a deputy or vicar was often underqualified and, because the parish revenues were being creamed off by the absentee incumbent, almost inevitably underpaid. A few of the smaller orders were gradually suppressed, including the unfortunate Friars of the Sack. The Council was a monument to disappointed ambition on all counts; the healing of the schism proved ephemeral and the planned crusade never took place.[15]

Nevertheless, Humbert was right to place his emphasis on how lay men and women related to the friars and secular clergy rather than on shadowy heretical movements in the background. Over the next 20 years serious dissent came chiefly from within the Church itself and the Franciscans in particular. Bonaventure was not able to guide the Franciscan movement any further. He attended the Council, preached at the solemn Mass of reconciliation with the Greeks and then died, so was buried at Lyon. The Council's legacy was taken up by his former student, Peire John Olivi from southern France, who emphasised the lay perception of the friars. He argued that 'the majority of men' would find a profession of poverty ridiculous if it then allowed luxurious use of goods. This was an implicit criticism of the comfortable conditions enjoyed by many within his own order and Olivi proposed a sensitive solution, not objecting to a convent keeping small quantities of beans or olive oil, or an individual enjoying a meal of good bread, chicken and white wine if offered it on the road, but he did draw the line at stockpiles of wine and wheat. All the while his Joachite apocalypticism reminded his audience that this deprivation was only a temporary state.[16]

It was a sign of the times that Olivi had a chequered career; he was smart enough to survive a condemnation of his writings in 1283 and yet within a year of his death in 1298 his books were being burnt at General Chapter. The fact that they were was probably due to the emergence in the same period of distinctive Spirituals or *zelanti* in the Franciscan heartland in the marches of Ancona, in Tuscany and south of Rimini as well as on the coast of notoriously heretical Languedoc. They took a far harder and more dogmatic line on poverty. Ragged and hungry, they lived in remote caves from which they emerged to preach imminent doom for urban populations. They represented a small but essential part of late thirteenth-century spirituality and picked up urban converts such as Jacopone da Todi, a prosperous notary in Bologna who joined the Franciscans in middle age in 1278. Like Francis he wrote poetry in vernacular Italian, and his *The Pain of Living* described mental stress and physical fatigue in a surprisingly modern way:

> *Exhausted I throw myself on my bed*
> *Aching for rest;*
> *And then of a sudden*
> *My cares begin to whirl about me,*
> *Robbing me of sleep*
>
> *At daybreak the wheel starts to turn again*
> *The pressure mounts*
> *I never seem to do*
> *What I've set out to do*
> *And by nightfall I get the usual recompense.*[17]

To be a Spiritual, then, was not just a condemnation of urban sins, or even material affluence, it was an introspective rebellion reasserting the self against the pressures of contemporary existence. When briefly allowed to form their own order in 1294, the radicalism of the Spirituals' leaders such as Peter of Macerata was unleashed. He called himself Brother Liberato, literally true since he had been let out of jail, spiritually also in that he promised the sort of spiritual freedom enjoyed by Francis himself. However, there was the abiding suspicion that he and his supporters considered themselves freed from the traditional obediences of a friar in favour of their own personal revelation of the divine. With arguments over doctrine and authority, the Franciscans now resembled the Waldensian and Cathar heretics they had largely replaced and the surprise was not that the Spirituals were declared heretics, but that it took so long.

After repeated attempts to discipline the order and reduce its influence by restricting Franciscan rights to preach and hear confessions, it was left to Pope John XXII (1316–34) to offer radical solutions. In three pieces of legislation he transformed the status of the Franciscans. As he explained to them, above chastity and poverty, 'the greatest good of all is obedience if it is strictly kept'. After consultation with all parties including the Spirituals, he issued *Quorundam exigit* in October 1317, regularising the storage by individual convents of stores of food for several months rather than relying on day-to-day charity. By doing so, he changed the terms of debate. Previous relaxation of the Franciscan lifestyle had been couched in terms of justifying why the founder's rule had to be modified, the onus was now on the Spirituals to comply with whatever the current authorities decided. In December 1322 John renounced the fiction of papal ownership of the friars' property in the bull *Ad conditorem*. The Franciscans now owned property whether they liked it or not. It only remained to sanctify ownership itself and this was done by the bull *Cum inter nonnullos* in November 1323. Accepting the logic that even Christ and the apostles had owned the clothes they stood up in, then owner-ship in itself was no sin and to suggest as much tantamount to heresy. It was the legislation of 1317 which inspired the most obstinate opposition, and in the southern French port of Marseille 25 friars defied it, were duly brought before an inquisitor, himself a Franciscan, and asked to recant. All but five complied, of which one was condemned to perpetual imprisonment and the remaining four were burnt on May 7, 1318.[18]

The story of the Franciscans redefined heresy in that the radical Spirituals deliberately marginalised themselves. The Cathars, Waldensians and even the original Franciscans had ambitions to set up separate Churches or achieve the radical reform of the existing one; the Spirituals with their obsession with poverty and personal revelation prided them-selves on their minority status. They created only opposition groups and colourful anti-heroes. Ironically, in doing so they became one of the range of options in the spiritual marketplace they so despised. Looking forward to the heresies of the fourteenth century, they all carried the Franciscan Spiritual imprint – the Fraticelli in Italy, the Beguines of southern France and the so-called Brethren of the Free Spirit of Germany and Bohemia. They were always there and they were extraordinarily difficult to eradicate, but they were by definition self-limiting.

The laity's reaction to the friars' turmoil was relatively muted. It is fair to say that many were not bothered. Crowds still flocked to the ostenta-tiously large Franciscan church of Santa Croce built in Florence in 1294, providing as it did a large open space for preaching by merging aisle and nave with a minimum of visual interference. At the same time the church's dimensions allowed key patrons of the mendicants, such as the banking families of the Bardi, Peruzzi and Alberti, to establish beautifully decorated mortuary chapels unobtrusively within its walls. By this means the friars could pray for souls in purgatory, provide a conduit for excessive business profits and take on a pastoral role to the population at large.[19]

Religious choices, c.1300

Men and women in 1300 had many more means of relating to religion than their forebears a century earlier. They could dedicate a proportion of their lives to it through a panoply of lay orders, guilds, and pilgrimage sites; they could be instructed through reading, university study or being harangued at sermons; and if they could not spare the time for active involvement with the Church they could at least partake of its benefits through the purchase of indulgences or prayers for their souls. Relations between clergy and laity were as complex as ever, and society still agonised over the character of priests, but the idea of the Church being replaced by an alternative organisation had become obsolete.

A century or more of relatively uninterrupted economic growth meant that by 1300 the material world was in a better position to compete with religion for people's time and money. Edging down Cheapside in London involved running the gauntlet of some 4000 enterprises, all eager for sales. And it was a truly international economy; one prosperous late thirteenth-century merchant in Southampton bought decorated jugs from south-west France, a sheath of Spanish leather, ate imported figs and grapes and kept a small African monkey as an exotic pet. Even those of modest means had choices to make; as well as wine shops and alehouses depending on where you were in Europe, most towns had now at least one cookshop offering fast foods to tempt those on their way home from work.[20]

As well as a more varied diet, there was more to wear. The cloth trade reached new heights of competitive efficiency in the years around 1300. Over half the cloth sold at Orvieto in central Italy in 1299 was not made in nearby Florence, but imported from northern Europe. This was not luxury material; some of it was bought by aristocratic households for the clothing of servants and children. For the cheapest import, a plain white cloth from Caen in Normandy, transport added only $7\frac{1}{2}$ to $8\frac{4}{5}$ per cent to the initial cost and it could be finished and dyed in Florence and still compete on price with most of the local products. In the last years of the thirteenth century the former Cathar strongholds of southern France – Toulouse, Carcassonne and Narbonne – became associated with the export of cheap cloth to Italy and Spain, through so-called 'village cloths' usually made in the surrounding countryside at a heavy discount relative to urban workshops.[21]

It was not just that cheap cloth came from all over, but that the good stuff was available to people of relatively modest means. In the small towns of Provence, most of the customers for the better quality col-oured cloth from Ypres and Châlons in the north were notaries, doctors, merchants and clerics. Needless to say the rest was bought by the per-petually impecunious southern French nobility. They would have been among those who benefited from the growth of local credit which helped lubricate the sophisticated economy of the late thirteenth century. Much attention has been paid to the bill of exchange; loans disguised as currency transactions which allowed long-distance trade to take place without the need of transporting large amounts of currency. Possibly more important were small-scale facilities, local guilds of merchants who operated informal credit and loan facilities and the pawnbroker who provided cash and took possessions as security. Above all there were the network of small-scale banking facilities run by Italians, indiscriminately termed 'Lombards', in the smaller towns of the 'big banana' trade axis. Operating over a radius of about ten miles in the closing decades of the century, they replaced the Jews as primary moneylenders and also inherited their mantle of popular loathing. All these relied on a certain degree of discrimination on the part of their customers and in turn they kept the mechanism by which economic choices could be made running smoothly in difficult times.[22]

For this was a world on the edge of the abyss. The steady growth in population in Europe was levelling off at the end of the thirteenth century. The reason for the expansion's end is as elusive as why it began, but a deterioration in climate may be to blame. Grim weather brought about the severe European famine of 1315–17 which, more than the terrible plague of 1348–51, marked the end of an economic era. The rains of those years revealed underlying economic weaknesses. There is debate over whether the 60 million people in Europe could still be fed from the continent's soil. Even in an advanced area such as north Italy, the country may have been 'under-developed', its towns suffering from 'an in-built tendency to outgrow resources'. Quite apart from this brutal hypothesis, there were other problems; the wealth-enhancing supplies of silver dug out of the mountains of Germany and Bohemia were gradually giving out while the increasingly efficient taxation of communities for warfare by late medieval governments may also have slowed economic activity.[23] Because most of these troubles were still in the future in 1300 a mood of optimism persisted despite the problems; the city authorities of Lucca and Bologna announced ambitious plans for the expansion of their city walls on the assumption that not only would they have the population to fill the new boundaries, but that they would generate the wealth needed to build and maintain the fortifications. In the short term at least, difficulties may have been compensated for by human resourcefulness.

The idea of a Church which dispensed salvation through a clerical elite was also breaking down. Long-term factors favoured the growing influence of the laity. The increase in the Church's scale of operation and the recognition of a potentially lucrative career structure led to an increase in the number of men in some type of holy orders. By 1300 it has been estimated that one in twenty of the population in towns was a cleric. But this did not mean that there were jobs for them all within the Church and the increasing number of low paid posts involving pastoral care, or 'cure of souls' as it is picturesquely known, was a direct function of this glut of clergy. In these circumstances the influence of the laity was hard to resist. They created posts which reflected their tastes, particularly through guilds or fraternities, sworn assemblies of men and women, often from the more prosperous section of the community. They were a form of organisation as natural to the period as the committee is to ours, and in the thirteenth century their numbers increased and they took on more explicitly religious tasks.[24]

One example was the demanding fraternity of the Blessed Virgin at Perugia whose regulations were set down in 1312: its members were to meet every Sunday at the local Dominican church, where they were each to purchase a candle and listen to a sermon. Then the men were to process through the church, its cloister and, finally, the town, all the while singing Lauds in response to the chanters at the head of the procession. The women had the rather less exciting task of staying in the church with their candles. The Dominican friars were heavily involved in the guild and one can see an extension to the laity of the order's own sense of drama and love of processions. Marching through the streets in best clothes (no doubt taking full advantage of the range of cloth on offer in central Italy), clutching candles and chanting a monastic service was a sure sign of belonging, whether the elite was social or spiritual. Money was required at every turn; two pence to buy the candle, a monthly gift to finance a Mass to the Virgin and an expected gift in the last will and testament. In addition, many confraternities demanded their members' presence at a periodic feast for which a contribution was also expected. Despite these expenses, many members may still have seen participation as an economic benefit. Quite apart from the informal social contacts with potential customers, suppliers and trading partners, the guild's financial demands may have acted as a basic credit-rating mechanism, weeding out the less solvent.

But even the most hard-headed businessman or woman received other benefits from membership. The social gatherings helped foster mutual trust and friendship in the volatile world of the medieval town and both were as necessary in death as in life. Medieval purgatory was a time of intense physical pain to atone for sins committed in this life. Intercessory prayers, by well-wishers among the living could, however, shorten the experience. The fraternity members of St Katharine in Norwich in 1307 had not only to provide a Mass and candles for dead members but also, if they had sufficient education, to join in the communal parts of the

Mass, or to say 20 Our Fathers and the prayer to the Virgin for the soul of the deceased if they were not. The Perugia fraternity contented itself with ensuring that there was a Mass for dead members said on the first Monday of every month and that the fraternity was represented by someone carrying one of its torches at a member's burial.[25] There was also spiritual help for the living; on the first Wednesday of every month a Mass was said to the blessed Virgin Mary specifically for the living members of the fraternity. All were obliged to attend sermons, say confession four times a year, receive communion at Christmas and Easter and honour all four feasts of the blessed Virgin Mary, fasting on the eve of each if they could.

Within living memory Perugia had been the home of the Flagellant movement and its proximity to Assisi meant there was still a presence of Franciscan Spirituals, yet by providing such a complete environment for lay spiritual fulfilment the fraternity showed that it was possible to remain active in society and be a good Christian, undercutting the role of established heretical groups. The alliance of Dominican friars and enthusiastic laity delivered a popular product of certified orthodoxy. Many fraternities were established specifically to defeat heresy and the guild of the Virgin in Perugia nodded in this direction by honouring Peter Martyr, the tireless Dominican fighter against the Cathars, with an annual candle on his feast day. The round of Masses, processions and confession soothed the troubled consciences which had been so fertile for heretical ideas in the past. The difficulty of over-large profits that had so troubled Valdes and Francis was solved by standardised almsgiving for the foundation of hospitals or relief of the poor or destitute members, so that they too had a vested interest in the guild's prosperity. The difficult theology of whether the sacraments were valid if administered by a corrupt priest was neatly bypassed because the members of the guild themselves hired the priest to say Mass and hear confessions. Even a dying member could be reassured that the Masses said for his soul would be said by a priest to his taste, because the people making that choice would, as far as the laws of admission to the guild could manage, be forever people exactly like him or herself.

While to some extent confraternities were a symptom of the Church's efforts to reach out to the lay people, by this time they were predominantly enabling the laity to exercise greater influence over the Church. At its most basic it was the decision of the men of Louvres, north of Paris, to form a confraternity to rebuild their church and pay its debts, from which it is easy to see how the laity might start to influence worship. The chamberlains of Perugia's guild confidently organised nightly Lauds of the Blessed Virgin Mary sung in the Dominican church, 'along with other services they think best, with the end in mind of best causing our devotion to the Virgin to grow and increase'. No doubt the Black Friars advised, but ultimately the cult of the Virgin lay in the hands of the consumer.[26]

Other lay tastes affected Church ceremonial. As has been seen, from Perugia to Norwich the laity liked lights; the candles looked good, had an elemental spiritual significance and they helped the congregation see what was going on, especially at the climax of the Mass. According to the members' own account, the guild of St Katherine at Norwich began in 1307 when certain parishioners of the church and others devoted to God wanted to honour St Katherine, the Virgin, the Holy Trinity and to 'continue the increase of light in the said church'. The increase of light in churches in general seems to have started around the middle of the thirteenth century. Louis IX was an enthusiastic proponent, placing between four and eight candles on the altar for Mass in the royal chapel depending on the solemnity of the feast, and cramming on twelve on the days when the court commemorated his father and mother or the more distinguished of his predecessors. The papal court increased the number of candles on the altar during Mass at around the same time, going against quite recent recommendations of austerity in the matter by Innocent III who had a maximum of two. In Perugia the Mass for dead guild members was said, 'with wax candles burning throughout the choir'.[27]

Whereas once churchmen had feared that organised heresies would subvert the Church, now the danger was that lay enthusiasm for private guilds would end up bypassing the parish system and this was true particularly in Italy where urban parish churches were taken over by immigrants from a single place or members of a particular trade or fraternity. In some places, particularly in Germany and Italy, this took the form of parishioners once again having the right to present the name of their chosen priest to the bishop, a move which was fiercely resisted elsewhere.[28]

During the thirteenth century many large ecclesiastical institutions consolidated their rights over a parish by 'appropriating' it, appointing themselves as rector and then installing a 'vicar' or substitute priest, usually on a small fraction of the income. As early as 1215 the reformers at the Fourth Lateran Council had expressed dissatisfaction at this and sought to ensure that the priest received an adequate income from the tithes. This had some impact and there are a smattering of examples of priests taking their patrons to court to obtain a fairer share of the parish income. In the most interesting cases the parishioners themselves became involved. The majority were disputes over who should be responsible for the upkeep of the fabric of the local church, but this could easily lead on to other matters. In 1262 the abbey of le Val Benoît in Flanders gained a judgement from the dean of Maastricht that it was only necessary for the abbey to provide a small bell in the parish church of Simplevelt, such as could be heard outside the churchyard; if the parishioners wanted a bigger bell such as could be heard throughout the parish they could pay for it themselves. The social significance of the bell that both summoned folk to services and regulated the working day led to several leading parishioners attempting to have the judgement overturned at a council in Maastricht in 1282. They argued from the principle that those who received tithes had responsibilities, so consequently the rest of the parishioners' wish list for their church came tumbling out. They wanted a decent-sized bell and they wanted an ornamented altar (almost certainly candles), singing (for which a Mass book with music was to be provided) and stained glass in two of the church windows. Not unreasonably, they also wanted to stay dry, so they asked that the abbey repair the roof between the choir and the tower. The parishioners won on all counts. As the growth of the fraternities show, had they lost they may well have gone ahead and organised the church to their taste anyway; moreover, they may well have had the wholehearted support of their priest.[29]

In the years since 1100 the laity had also had an influence on the prestige of sacraments. As has been seen in the activity of the guilds, the Eucharist or Mass was central to the lay experience of Catholicism. Although people never tasted the wine which was Christ's blood and only had the bread of the Host two or three times a year, there was no doubting their enthusiasm to witness the event; the demand for candles was at least partly so that the laity in the nave could see the priest elevating the Host. Perhaps the long hours of instruction from friar preachers had its effect here because there is quantifiable evidence that the Church had seen off some of its adversaries. While there were still those who declared before inquisitors that even if Christ's body was as big as a mountain it surely would have been eaten by now, they were outnumbered by the burgeoning new cult of *Corpus Christi*, the body of Christ, with the consecrated wafer from the Eucharist being venerated in midsummer processions all over Europe.[30]

As for the other sacraments, infant baptism had at last been accepted and was almost universally performed, whereas there was still little interest in confirmation which required the presence of a bishop.[31] Such a state of affairs may well have suited the busy episcopacy. Bishops were more assiduous about insisting that lay couples went through the sacrament of marriage, laying down penalties for those living in sin and demanding that local priests make sure couples got married. There were still doubts about the sacramental nature of licensing sex: Olivi and other dissident friars raised the case in learned institutions and were probably aware that their point of view was shared by many local clergy who may not have followed the theological arguments, but saw the difficulties of interfering in their poorer parishioners' informal living arrangements or the complex transfers of property which were at the heart of the marriage alliances of the better off. Only in Italy where the lay power often wanted marriages solemnised publicly for the sake of legal clarity did the Church receive the backing of the civic power in forbidding concubinage and cohabitation.[32]

If churchmen were uneasy about marriage, the laity were ambivalent about the sacrament of penance. In one sense it was easy; Fourth Lateran had stated that everyone had to confess at least once a year to their parish priest otherwise they would be debarred from the mandatory Easter communion. Although the penance that followed from confession entailed time and expense, more were put off by the toe-curling embarrassment of revealing sins to the local priest in private. The Church tacitly admitted the problem in the second half of the thirteenth century by licensing wandering friars to hear confessions. The Franciscan Humile of Milan was invited to preach and hear confessions in the mountains of central Italy. There he met a woman who had been raped while walking alone. When she tried to confess this 'sin' to a local priest he took her weeping behind the altar and also forced her to have sex; the same happened with a second and third priest. Only Humile the friar gave her absolution. The story is from Salimbene and carries his usual lurid trademark, yet the unreliability of local priests in sensitive situations was widely acknowledged. The Dominican preacher Humbert of Romans urged friars to go to less populous places, not just the towns and cities, even though friars moving into a parish often triggered resentment from local clergy. One solution was that fraternities could address lay reticence to confess by hiring a suitable priest to hear the confessions of all the members and give appropriate penances.[33]

Such a move may explain the impression given by the evidence that penance became mainly a sacrament for the better off, despite the earlier assiduous attempts to promote it for all. There was an emphasis on getting heads of households, male and female, to confess, and although in Orléans in 1314 it was decreed that they were responsible for making their servants and children attend also, it was more in hope than expectation.[34] The same pattern can be seen with the deathbed sacrament of extreme unction or anointing of the sick and the final confession and communion. More assiduous priests carried out the duty to the extent that many resented the friars 'muscling in', but the likelihood of receiving a cleric of any kind at the bedside increased greatly with wealth and social prominence.[35]

Pilgrimage and heresy

For many people one way out of the embarrassment of the business of penance and confession was to undertake a pilgrimage. By 1300 the numbers making religious journeys had vastly increased since two centuries before and had become an enormous activity for many churches and communities. More than any other devotion pilgrimage symbolised religion's new status as a consumer good. Since 1100 the proportion of the sick looking for cures and the pilgrims on the road as punishment for crime had declined and the vast majority of pilgrims were healthy, reasonably law-abiding and looking for spiritual benefits. These had been formalised as 'indulgences'; attendance at a certain shrine earned the remission of a certain amount of the penance due after death for sins committed in life provided, of course, that the pilgrim was truly contrite and had confessed.

Typically indulgences were given in 40-day packages and only God and the believer knew whether or not they had been earned. Popular demand for something more tangible at a shrine inspired a thriving trade in pilgrimage badges for sale at the sites. These were generally images or symbols of the shrine, manufactured in tin, lead or even silver and gold; a scallop shell from Compostella could be worn on the hat, an image of the Madonna with Christ sitting on her knee from Le Puy could be pinned to the bag or 'scrip' that every pilgrim carried. Pilgrimage created profound spiritual resonances from a very simple recipe. By simply putting one foot in front of the other the devotee gained quantifiable benefits in eternity in terms of periods of penance reduced. On earth, the badges and other souvenirs had the healing powers of the saint, particularly if they had been physically pressed against the shrine; the badge also provided proof of pilgrimage which could obtain entry into the local branch of that saint's guild when the pilgrim returned home.[36]

Such manifestations of a successful popular religion did much to undermine the mass appeal of alternative belief systems such as Catharism. The number of shrines multiplied in the thirteenth century so that although some fell out of favour, the total number of pilgrims increased and those involved in servicing the needs of pilgrims, providing food and accommodation, selling badges, staffs, scrips and shoes, also rose correspondingly. In 1300 Pope Boniface VIII took advantage of the turn of the century to proclaim a 'Jubilee' in Rome itself, contributing to the inflation in the value of indulgences by promising pilgrims 'full forgiveness of their sins' and quietly reducing the qualifying hurdle to those 'having confessed or being about to'. It was wildly popular; as the crowds increased near the close of the year just before Christmas, one pilgrim reported being nearly trampled to death on a number of occasions, while at the basilica of Saint Paul two churchmen stood at the altar, literally raking in the pilgrims' offerings day and night.[37]

New pilgrimage sites were still being created despite the fierce competition and high stakes involved. Once shrines were established they stood or fell by their appeal to the laity: neighbouring clerics were only too aware that existing pilgrimage sites and religious institutions were fighting for the same limited patronage. Consequently, this was an area particularly closely policed and under such inspection plenty of unorthodox beliefs were exposed. In Milan, Guglielma, a noblewoman of holy character, after originally associating with the Humiliati, late in life turned to the Cistercian house of Chiaravalle until her death in 1281. There is the air almost of being 'headhunted' in that the monks provided her with a house in the city for the last years of her life, dressed her in a Cistercian habit on her death and prepared a tomb for her near the abbey a few miles from the city. The monks encouraged pilgrims and meetings of those who had known her and the cult was looking at a promising source of offerings. However, the Cistercians had already provoked local animosities to the extent that the body required an armed escort for the transfer to Chiaravalle and three years later, a group of Guglielma's 'followers' were arrested by Dominican inquisitors.[38] In a city the size of Milan it cannot have been unusual to find eccentric religious beliefs and those propounded to the inquisitors were original, to say the least. Their devotees, a group of mainly lay men and women, proposed among other things that Guglielma was the incarnation of the Holy Spirit and that their leader Manfreda was her vicar on earth, a legitimate alternative to the existing Pope Boniface VIII. What was very difficult to prove was that Guglielma herself was culpable and the game was given away by the inquisitors who frequently referred to Guglielma as *sancta* in their own questions.[39] Nevertheless, after a protracted halt in proceedings her body was burnt with a few of the leaders of her cult in 1300.

Even more remarkable was the case of Armanno Punzilupo who had died in Ferrara in December 1269, revered for his spirituality and austere way of life. He was buried in the cathedral and his tomb became a centre of miracles which were investigated with a view to canonisation. Here too the attention paid to the tomb raised intense jealousy, this time of the local Dominicans, who stood to lose considerable revenue from the revival in popularity of the cathedral. Moreover, in 1254 a Dominican inquisitor had heard Punzilupo's confession of heresy. This was never denied by the cathedral clergy who claimed that he had subsequently led a blameless life, protesting his innocence as late as 1300. The exact details of Punzilupo's 1254 conviction were not made clear, other than that he had greeted two heretics and ridiculed priests for thinking that God could be kept in a casket, a reference to the Eucharistic wafer. The second inquiry was to last more than a decade and was to end in 1301 with the burning of Punzilupo's bones and their disposal in the river.

A group of informers were assembled, known as the *cazzagazzari* or 'Cathar hunters', and these included at least one Inquisition spy from the former Italian Cathar stronghold of Sirmione. There was enough inconsistency in their testimony to make it clear that something very peculiar was going on. Some claimed that Punzilupo was a member of the Bagnolenses sect of the Cathars, another had him recommending the Poor of Lyon. There was also disagreement over whether Punzilupo was a 'clothed heretic' or *perfectus*, or whether he was merely one of their supporters. Faced with evidence of Punzilupo's good works, the inquisitors were reduced to fabricating evidence that the miracles were 'faked' and that those who flocked to the tomb were heretics. One witness claimed that Punzilupo had told him that he carried a cross and professed devotion to the Roman Church in order that his heresy might not be discovered. There was also an important shift in approach by inquisitors going on here. Earlier depositions, such as those from southern France, had concentrated on uncovering heretical speech. Actions with conformity to orthodoxy had passed largely unquestioned. In Armanno Punzilupo's case the inquisitors sought to show that an outwardly devout life was only there to mask the inner heretic. Obviously, once such an assumption was made there could be no escape for the accused.[40]

There was more to these cases than casual corruption and they belong outside the chapters on organised heresy. They illustrated the dilemma faced by those who sought to direct lay religion. Having quite effectively destroyed the organised heresies of the mid thirteenth century they faced a laity of sophisticated consumers who tended to select their own method of religious participation with little reference to doctrinal labels. The clarity of opposition to the Church had disappeared and consequently the atmosphere tended to grow more oppressive as its victory proved more difficult to police than its defeat.

In summary the world of 1300 was that of late medieval Catholicism, a vibrant show of marketable religion from austere mystics to lay communities of men and women of varying degrees of spiritual commitment, to the most unthinking mechanical devotion of the indulgence received by a holidaying pilgrim. It was probably unrecognisable to Francis of Assisi and anathema to the heretical leaders of the twelfth century, but it did have enormous vitality and flexibility. It had seen off its opponents and was still doing good business two centuries later when Luther was to call for its reformation. This is not to say that there were not still alternatives outside the Church; Cathars, Waldensians and the more extreme followers of Saint Francis had also learnt to adapt and they flourished in the cracks of orthodoxy, but their existence was literally marginal in remote mountainous settlements far from influence, where they were relentlessly pursued by inquisitors.

chapter 8

WOMEN AND HERESY

From 1100 to 1300 the religious status of women changed at a faster rate than ever before or, arguably, since. In 1100 the only overt way a woman could express her spirituality was by entering a nunnery, an institution dominated by the daughters of the aristocracy. Theologians warned of the dangers of women in religion. Yet the examples of Clare of Assisi and the Humiliati in chapter 4 demonstrate the rapid change taking place and in the twelfth and thirteenth centuries women came to play an important role in both heretical and orthodox religious movements, as patrons, participants or active supporters. Throughout the remainder of the thirteenth century religious women frequently remained the subject of suspicion and the intriguing possibility remains that they turned away from established religion and embraced heresy because they found a more satisfying spiritual role there.

Women started from a weak position. Twelfth-century writers emphasised the broad streak of misogyny expressed by the Church fathers of the late Roman Empire, with the views of Jerome picked up by Abelard and Walter Map, among others.[1] The defining issue for such writers was the superiority of virginity for women over the married state. There are clear echoes here of the contemporary conflict among male clerics over whether the more spiritual life was withdrawal from the world or fruitful engagement with it. As it became clear that this debate was ending in an emphasis on life outside the cloister, it is tempting to conclude that the stridency of contemporary writers was a reaction to the evidence of their own eyes as women too took a more active part in the religious life of society.

The most traditional role was as patrons and there was an increase in the number of monastic communities founded in the twelfth century. However, such ventures were expensive, and the trend was to found smaller, more informal communities. Within the Church this led to the growth of movements such as the Augustinian canons, clergy living under a rule. These more economical foundations may have been especially attractive to female patrons and in southern France where aristocratic ambitions were severely cramped by modest means, something of the same feeling could well account for the close association of Cathar communities with prominent local noblewomen. Blanca of Laurac, besides becoming a *perfecta* herself, set up a community of Cathar women in the early thirteenth century and facilitated religious discussion. She organised public debates between Cathars and Catholics led by Dominic's patron, Diego of Osma, at Montréal in 1207 and the following year between leading Cathars and Waldensians.[2]

Sometimes the mechanics of patronage were less obvious: Diana d'Andolo, a young noblewoman of Bologna who had fallen under the spell of the early Dominicans, persuaded her grandfather to sell land to the order, thus allowing the friars to set up their first church and cloister in the heart of the university district in 1219. Her 'price' would seem to have been the establishment of a house of Dominican nuns in Bologna and perhaps a rather higher profile for female spirituality in the order than Dominic or his successors had initially planned. Such a pattern of 'behind the scenes' influence cannot have been uncommon in the thirteenth century even if most aristocratic women lacked Diana's consummate skill in manipulating patriarchal figures.[3]

Women could also make their religious preferences clear after their deaths. From the bequests which have survived, women were more generous than men, prepared to give away a greater proportion of their wealth to charitable causes. Medieval Italy's literate society has allowed modern analysis of the dying wishes of even relatively modest testators from several towns. Over the course of two centuries the nature of pious bequests changed quite markedly as has been outlined in chapter 2, nevertheless women displayed distinctive characteristics to their giving. Many hospitals were founded and grew up in the twelfth century, and as time went on a growing proportion of the offerings to them came from women. Such institutions provided care in old age and undoubtedly for some women the promise of such a bequest was a shrewd investment for their own widowhood. Beyond worldly considerations, donors shared founders' sentiments that offerings were for 'honour of God and the use of the poor'. Significantly, women donors directed their generosity to their own choice of religious institution and these were often staffed by other women.

Possibly it was because their own role in worship was so limited that women who invested in Masses for the soul wanted close control over who they were for and who might say them. As time went on such prayers for the dead came to occupy an increasingly large part of the laity's charitable effort and women's in particular. By using their bequests and instructing a priest to deliver their prayers to God, women honed their skills as consumers. In one sense they were conservative in that they were less willing than men to explore new forms of social piety such as dowries for poor girls; however, their interest in new orders and institutions demonstrated that they judged the characters of contemporary individuals and communities rather than relying on tradition to guide them.

As long as women had a certain amount of wealth they were not without influence. For the modern observer, noting their presence within heretical movements, the crucial question is to what extent the lack of a sacramental role in contemporary Catholicism led to a sense of exclusion. It is naïve to think of a 'women's movement' of the Middle Ages, but there is evidence that women favoured forms of religion which involved other women. Their presence in hospitals has already been noted, and even more striking was the degree to which Genoese women were willing to give to new nunneries founded in the early thirteenth century at a time when lay interest in monasticism, as a whole, was falling. The trend was not confined to Genoa; all over north and central Italy bequests to nuns rose steadily until the beginning of the fourteenth century. Women were also happy to look beyond established religious communities; even in the charged atmosphere of Toulouse around 1200, they made bequests to *reclusanie*, small groups of women or even individuals who lived in stalls or sheds on bridges, or near town gates and churches. Such women were a staple of religious life in Italian towns also.[4]

It is not surprising therefore that some women made choices which lay outside the boundaries of orthodoxy. Just occasionally the process behind such choices can be seen. In the southern French town of Montauban, around 1208, Austorgue de la Mothe advised her two little girls that the 'good Christians' (Cathars) could save souls better than the clerks of the Church of Rome, the bishop of Cahors or the canons of Montauban. If this statement to inquisitorial interrogators can be taken at face value it offers an important clue to the Cathars' success: the Roman Church is atomised to a distant bishop and the local canons with whom the 'good Christians' compete, although Austorgue is aware that in making such choices she is also rejecting the Roman Church as a whole. Shortly afterwards the mother and her daughters became *perfectae*. Their new status allowed them to do more than their Catholic counterparts. Arnaude de la Mothe, one of Austorgue's daughters, recalls preaching many times to mixed audiences as a young woman in the early 1220s. Yet there were limits to women's spiritual influence even among the Cathars; no woman became a Cathar bishop and examples of women performing the *consolamentum* are rare. In Italy there is even less trace of women taking responsibility within the Cathar organisation. Raynerius Saccone was careful to state that there were 'four thousand Cathars of both sexes', but the *consolamentum* was only performed by Cathar women 'in case of need'.[5]

Perhaps taking on a sacramental or preaching role was less important than that Catharism allowed women to gather and live a religious life in public. A full generation before the first appearance of *reclusanie* or the expansion of nunneries, the picture of female Cathar life is of numerous small communities. Even if the Dominican Jordan of Saxony's assessment was correct, that they were places where the local minor nobility sent their daughters to be educated and brought up for lack of anything better, they were influential and independent, eventually mirrored in the Catholic Church by the Beguines in northern Europe and the Humiliati in Italy. There may have been a distinctive pastoral role for *perfectae* without the performance of any sacrament. When Fabrissa de Marlac lay dying around 1240, she was consoled by two male *perfecti* who left immediately after the ceremony, so that her last hours were shared by two female *perfectae* who 'served and guarded her'. In a similar case from 1235 the *perfectae* Arnaude de la Mothe and her companion were rewarded by the dying woman with a tunic and money nearly as generously as the men who had consoled her.[6]

The role of Cathar women persisted as times got harder in the 1240s and 1250s. Peire de Belstar, himself a *perfectus* in exile, took the risk of returning to the southern French village of Verdun to organise a party of five women willing to make the arduous and expensive journey over to Lombardy to receive the *consolamentum* among the southern French communities in exile. There was probably a living to be made in the textile towns of Pavia or Cremona and the exiles evidently did not feel complete without their houses of Cathar *perfectae*. The women themselves were probably less conspicuous in an urban context, particularly in Lombardy where communities of Humiliati or even less formal houses of religious women were not uncommon.[7]

Other movements of the early thirteenth century allowed women to play a role complementing the sacramental role of men. In northern European towns such as Antwerp, Magdeburg and Liège women collected around one charismatic individual or came together to form religious communities. They were termed 'Beguines', probably derived from the *Albigenses* or Cathars, known in the south of France. The derivation, if correct, shines a light into the collective consciousness of the thirteenth-century laity. Since these women were resolutely orthodox, *Beguines* describes a way of life rather than any affiliation.[8] They were to become renowned for their extensive buildings and the mystical writings of such as Marie of Oignies, Mechtild of Magdeburg and Hadewijch (perhaps of Antwerp). But in the thirteenth century the buildings did not yet exist and most women never did become mystics. Instead communities concentrated on prayers for themselves and their families, funding candles and getting a priest in to say Mass.[9] Not surprisingly, they became articulate critics of the priesthood, administering an ostentatious rebuke to a cleric they considered unworthy of hearing their confessions and seeking out other sources of pastoral provision, such as the local Dominican convent. Writing in the second half of the thirteenth century, Mechtild of Magdeburg is blood-curdling about the fate of the souls of corrupt priests in general. They float in boiling metal, only to be extracted by the metal claws of demonic fishermen, who boil and eat them before vomiting them back into the pool. However, the fate of the local canons in Magdeburg is dealt with through a more constructive, homely metaphor:

> God calls the cathedral canons billy goats because their flesh stinks of lust in eternal truth before His Holy Trinity. The skin of a billy goat is noble and this is true of their authority and possessions. But when this skin is removed at death they lose all their nobility. And our Lord was asked how these goats might become lambs. Our Lord spoke thus: "If they eat the fodder that Canon Dietrich puts in their trough, that is, holy penance and sincere advice in confession, they shall become . . . lambs."[10]

Mechtild threw her influence behind local reformers' moves to keep the cathedral clergy up to the mark through offering them the sort of pastoral care approved by Fourth Lateran.

In southern Europe women probably found their most active role in the Waldensians. Geoffrey of Auxerre was a veteran commentator on heresy who, as a young Cistercian, had reported on Bernard's campaign against Henry of Le Mans. As an old man around 1180 he described two women who had been disciplined by the bishop of Clermont for preaching within the diocese. It is tempting to link these with the followers of Valdes, fanning out from Lyon, some 80 miles to the east. Some time later the women upbraided the bishop for forcing them to renounce their sect with threats and arguments. Geoffrey is shocked and, having compared them to Jezebel, calls the women 'prostitute preachers'. Geoffrey has learnt his old master's skill in sexual innuendo and certainly implies the women were not chaste, but he was also a product of the twelfth-century renaissance and the charges may be more than mere allegations of pollution. The biblical Jezebel's crime was that she was a patron of the heathen religion of Baal by protecting and supporting his prophets. Together with her husband Ahab, she corrupted Israel with an alternative religion. More specifically still, when Ahab coveted the vineyard of one Naboth, Jezebel arranged for Naboth to be falsely accused of blasphemy and stoned to death. Geoffrey may have seen similarities with the situation in Clermont; the vineyard was a common metaphor for the Christian community and Naboth represented the bishop. The contemporary account of the Third Lateran Council by Walter Map had already articulated the career clerics' fear that Valdes's eventual aim was that they should be driven out. As for the allegation of prostitution, the women were probably guilty in the sense that after their preaching they accepted money or offerings in kind from their audiences as did most male wandering preachers.[11]

Evidence suggests that Catholic fears were not misplaced. Although heavily outnumbered by the Cathar presence, Waldensian activists of both sexes were patronised by women according to Inquisition penances from the early 1240s. At Beaucaire, Bernard Fabrissa rented a house on behalf of two Waldensian women. Such women preached, generally in informal surroundings, advising followers, teaching them not to lie or swear oaths, or expounding such subjects as the Lord's Passion. The evidence of the rented house connects with other contemporary accounts, suggesting small communities of Waldensian women, much concerned with prayer. Moreover, from these records, it was lay women who mainly noticed such Waldensian holy women, so that it would appear that the movement had a gender-specific appeal.[12]

Orthodox writers of the thirteenth century struggled to acknowledge the possibility of preaching women. The Cistercian monk Bernard of Fontcaude felt it necessary to refute at some length Waldensian claims that women could preach and, in the 1260s, the Franciscan Eustace of Arras conceded that in theory at least, women might be able to preach and cited the precedents of Saint Catherine and Mary Magdalene, the original preacher prostitute. This all suggests that while women were not allowed to preach the question was kept under review; in a similar fashion to the discussion of the status of lay preaching.[13]

Nevertheless, within the Catholic Church women rarely got more than the chance to talk informally to small groups of other women, and they were further hampered by their exclusion from education. The rise of the universities severely restricted women's access to more advanced learning and while this was not an absolute block to commenting on the scriptures it was a severe obstacle in the competitive preaching world of the thirteenth century. There is evidence that the heretics were able to redress the balance a little; the daughters of the nobility educated in Cathar communities have already been mentioned.[14] Almost a century later the author of the *De Vita et actibus*, describing the Waldensians, refers to learning sessions after prayers where 'men and women who want to learn scripture, receive a reading from their doctors' which was 'received and repeated many times'. This may be more than basic Bible study in that the terms *doctores* and *lectio* ('reading') would be most familiar to those in higher education. There is also a case of a heretical woman teaching. Under interrogation in southern France in 1319, the Waldensian John de Vienne recalled how, about two years before, Jacoba, a Waldensian woman of around 40 who lived near a joiner's workshop in Avignon and 'knew how to read', taught him the articles of faith, the seven sacraments and a view of Church organisation which restricted the sacrament of ordination to just three levels – deacon, priest and bishop. Again, this may be more advanced than it might seem at first sight. John had already received an education in the vernacular from a man in Toulouse ten years before and these more technical points from Jacoba may have been his advanced training as an activist in the group. The significance of 'knowing how to read' may be that she knew Latin. The question begged is from where did Jacoba receive *her* learning. There is no great history of Waldensian activity in Avignon, but when Jacoba was in her early twenties the town had become home to the papal court. One possibility is that Jacoba had received her education from a Catholic cleric; one can only speculate as to the circumstances in which she might then turn to an anti-clerical cell of heretics in early middle age.[15]

The learned older woman is a recurring theme in accounts of heresy. At Reims in the late 1170s a so-called *erroris magistra* (mistress of error) humiliated her clerical interrogators with a display of knowledge of both New and Old Testaments. She went on to escape her captors by jumping out of the window, allegedly assisted by demons and a ball of thread: such an outlandish even by medieval standards probably conceals a more embarrassing truth such as that she was liberated by the crowds assembled to see her burn. Reims was also a clerical city and it may be that the woman already had her education in the scriptures before joining the heretical group, usually identified as the Cathars. These older women steeped in arcane learning may foreshadow the accusations of witchcraft trials in later centuries. On the other hand, the widow of independent means was even acknowledged by contemporaries as one of the strongest types of women in society at this time. In mid thirteenth-century Toulouse, university jurists considered the theoretical question of whether a widow was more fit to educate her children than the tutor assigned by her deceased husband. After thinking the unthinkable, they found in favour of the tutor.[16]

Most women lacked the means to become patrons and the zeal to become holy women. Instead, their invaluable contribution to religious life came through their control of the household economy, with innumerable meals cooked, food given and shelter provided for the charismatic male preachers who roamed Europe. Perhaps the most undervalued were the so-called 'concubines' of priests; as early as the tenth century Italian priests protested against attempts to impose a life of celibacy on them because 'unless they were maintained by the hands of their women they would succumb to hunger and nakedness'. The persistence of the phenomenon of the 'married' priest suggests that there must have been something in it for the woman involved, perhaps an enhanced economic and social status and more contact with the world beyond family, not dissimilar to the lay religious women's communities of the thirteenth century.[17] Women were no less crucial for the Cathar *perfecti* persecuted by inquisitors. The woman of Bram who accommodated two 'good men' for four months has already been mentioned, but most favours for heretics were less spectacular; a bed for the night, some shopping when they were wary of going out and numberless meals. In return these women supporters had their bread blessed, were preached to, and of course, eventually received the *consolamentum* which would allow them to take their place in heaven. The Cathar *perfecti* seem to have realised how crucial their female supporters were and occasionally supplemented spiritual rewards with little gifts of their own, items useful to the domestic economy such as cloth, pins or clothing.[18]

The description of the Waldensians in the *De vita et actibus* pays a backhanded tribute to the importance of women to the group. After both men and women have finished their prayers and their study session 'they do what they want, and the women prepare the food'. The unequal division of labour was sweetened by gifts from the preachers to homes who received them. These were aimed at the women of the household:

> At different times they also make visits into the houses of believers in this way, and in many places the heretics bring trinkets for their children and families, namely belts, knives, needleboxes and needles.

Perhaps the balance was redressed later in life; elsewhere, the *De Vita* refers to houses of old Waldensian women served by younger, more active heretics.[19]

Clare of Montefalco and the growth of intolerance

In the last quarter of the thirteenth century there is an appreciable change in attitude from the ecclesiastical hierarchy. It was alleged at the Council of Lyon in 1274 that ignorant Beguines were reading and explaining biblical texts. William of Saint Amour used the same arguments as he had against his old enemy, the friars, and alleged that the poverty of the Beguines was a sham and their begging an excuse to skive off productive work. As with men's movements, the trend was to restrict the laity's choice of religious expression. In 1298, Boniface VIII ordered that all religious women must live in perpetual enclosure, specifically barring as 'dangerous and abominable' visits to the homes of secular people or visits by outsiders to the nunnery. This was more than an attack on mobility, as an enclosed religious house was forced to live off endowments of land because, from behind high walls, begging for alms was impossible.[20]

Until such legislation curbed the formation of new female religious movements there were still opportunities for women to participate in orthodox spiritual life surprisingly similar to the Cathars and Waldensians. Attached to Clare of Assisi's order, the Poor Clares were *serviziali* or lay sisters. They lived in the convent, but were allowed to come and go, receiving gifts and under instructions from Clare, 'to praise God when they saw beautiful trees, flowers and bushes; and, likewise always to praise Him for and in all things when they saw all peoples and creatures'. The rule prescribed for the Poor Clares by Pope Innocent IV barely mentions them, but it is clear that Clare herself had a more exalted view of them as the public female face of the order.[21]

Outside the established orders female spiritual figures still thrived, but in restricted circumstances. Many claimed personal contact with the godhead, but since this was dangerous ground they were usually legitimated by a male confessor or scribe belonging to an established order, often the Dominicans. In the later part of the century there were mutual benefits from such an arrangement; in return for the spiritual kudos received by the flagging mendicant movement in mediating these visionaries, the women themselves were protected against accusations of heresy. Those involved were adept at making the difficult choices necessary in the religious scene of the late thirteenth century.[22]

One such was Clare of Montefalco who lived the life of an enclosed nun and died in 1308, whereupon the symbols of Christ's Passion were found etched on her heart. The local civic ruler and the bishop took an interest and commissioned a *Vita* or spiritual biography of the holy woman; a little later, her companions were interviewed with a view to her eventual canonisation. The proceedings showed the difficulties a group of spiritual women had in establishing themselves. Clare and her sister had founded the community around 1281 and had withstood fierce opposition from surrounding monastic institutions, including insults, stones thrown at the house and physical violence. The displeasure of Clare's rivals was not wholly irrational in that in the famine year of 1283 the nunnery was in competition for alms with three other local religious houses. Consumer choice was a matter of life or death for the new community and enclosed or not the nuns went out and begged for survival.[23]

In late thirteenth-century Italy the minefield of heresy had to be negotiated. Clare was confident that the Dominican preacher Egidio of Spoleto was a 'man of good spirit' before she had met him, but was forthright against the Spiritual Franciscan Bentivenga da Gubbio later arrested for heresy. In the proceedings of canonisation one of her companions recalled frequent warnings:

> Quite often she had heard Clare preaching about persons who would come to the monastery in order to spread poison under the guise of sanctity but with a false heart. People of this ilk afterward did come to the monastery. Before they came, she warned the women to beware and not to speak to them unless she were present, fearing for them as for her flock. Clare told the sisters that those brethren and false religious would at first speak with subtlety about the spirit so that they might afterward more easily achieve their false purpose.[24]

Clare singled out 'some Fraticelli and Franciscans' for special suspicion. Her position was bolstered by her connections. The valley of Spoleto lay to the north of Rome and represented the limit of the papacy's political influence as a secular power, so relations with individual towns had to be handled with extreme care. Clare had the support of her local bishop and of the duke of Spoleto, moreover she had friends at the papal curia itself in the Colonna and Orsini families. Despite all these and a burgeoning local cult, the medieval process of canonisation petered out and Clare had to wait over five centuries before her sanctity was confirmed. The papacy's move to Avignon distracted the attention of the curia and allowed Clare's enemies to be heard: one claimed that her Franciscan chaplain had died while imprisoned for heresy. Above all, the idea of a saintly woman who had been outside the cloister was too dangerous. While she lived, Clare was safe, and her local popularity meant that the cult could not be suppressed, but she suffered from the collective loss of nerve about authorising new forms of sanctity.[25]

Insofar as they lived without an allegiance to an order and were in a position to make informed judgements on those who did, Clare and her followers were typical of the form of religion on offer around 1300. Her community sought support from influential supporters in the locality and relied on the willingness of the local community to endorse the lifestyle of the nuns with alms. In return, Clare was willing to admit to the cloister lepers to be kissed and babies to be cured and in death to leave a set of incorruptible relics which are still earning income for the citizens of Montefalco to this day.

The twelfth and thirteenth centuries saw women subvert their inferior theological position through clever exploitation of the choices they were offered around 1200. Through their patronage new religious orders both orthodox and heretical were able to spread. When women participated in religious movements, because they had little place in formal hierarchies, orthodox and heretical alike steered towards pastoral care and a close relationship with the laity. As supporters they encouraged that tendency and with their hospitality and control over the household economy they underpinned informal movements. To stress the reciprocal nature of these relationships is not for one moment to undermine the genuineness of religious feeling involved. Even saints knew the score. The other Clare, of Assisi, was said to have declared to her sisters when an invading army was near, 'we have received much wealth from this city and it has ordered that we must pray to God to guard the city'.[26] The choices were well defined and local, but with a wider context which most women were aware of. Women's standing was curtailed by inquisitorial restriction of religious choice in the later thirteenth century; the repression of heretical movements also made it more difficult for them to play a meaningful role within Catholicism. The result was to force women into becoming either even more demanding consumers of religion, as we have seen in our review of religion around 1300, or to become the hidden backbone of the revived heresies of the 1290s and early fourteenth century which are the subject of the final chapter.

chapter 9

'JUST AS THERE ARE 72 TONGUES . . .': THE DECLINE OF ORGANISED HERESY

The organised heresies of the twelfth century continued to exist into the fourteenth. Indeed the decades either side of 1300 even saw a small revival of both Cathars and Waldensians, as well as the last eruption of popular religious fervour in the name of Francis of Assisi led by Fra Dolcino. In one sense the reasons for the popularity of heretical movements did not change in nearly 200 years; they offered an alternative to local ecclesiastical institutions and they knew their communities well enough to build up reservoirs of loyalty among supporters. In another way the heretics of 1300 were often rather different from their predecessors, relying more on books to gain converts, discussing religion at dinner parties and tending to offer a belief system which might run alongside membership of the established Church as much as an alternative to it.

What had also changed was the degree of policing of the laity concerning their religious beliefs. Whereas in the twelfth century heretics were routinely released to disappear into the population, by the fourteenth inquisitors were specialised, trained officials in touch with one another and aware to an almost paranoid degree of the ability of small movements to spread like disease through the population. Such repressive skills were necessary because the 1290s witnessed a series of events which placed the papacy in its gravest crisis since clashes with secular rulers over simony nearly two centuries before. While most believers in Europe were more worried about the conduct of their local churchmen, rumours of scandal at the top always raised doubts over whether popes really were the successors of the apostles. Given the delicate political balance in Italy, this could sometimes prove decisive. In 1294, after a vacancy of over two years, the cardinals elected an 85-year-old hermit monk as Pope Celestine V; in the few months he ruled he seemed to offer a whole new era for groups like the Spiritual Franciscans, before he was persuaded to abdicate by Cardinal Benedetto Caetani, who ten days later emerged as Pope Boniface VIII.

The papal abdication was profoundly destabilising and Boniface's reputation grew still murkier when Celestine died in captivity in May 1296. A more politically astute pontiff might have built as wide an alliance of friends as possible, but Boniface commenced two fatal quarrels with the rival Colonna family in Rome and the ruthless king of France, Philip IV. In reversing Celestine's encouragement of the Franciscan Spirituals he ensured hostility from that quarter, too.[1]

Fra Dolcino

The career of Fra Dolcino in the early years of the fourteenth century shows how much had changed in the previous 200 years. Although he and his followers are usually associated with apocalyptic dreams and poverty to the point of destitution, there is more than a hint of similarity to preachers such as Henry of Le Mans and Tanchelm from the early twelfth century in the calls for reform of the Church. Only when the Dolcinians faced persecution did they become the violent fanatics who became so notorious. Similarly, most supporters of Fra Dolcino were quite unremarkable and accepted him as part of the spectrum of spiritual expression which surrounded them.

Dolcino was the bastard son of a priest from Novara, west of Milan, who inherited Gerard Segarelli's followers. The last years of Segarelli are little known. Having apparently escaped from benign episcopal detention in Parma, he was condemned by both Honorius IV in 1286 and Nicholas IV in 1290, before being imprisoned once again in 1294. The moves against him were brought under the Fourth Lateran legislation forbidding unauthorised orders, but the truth was probably that Segarelli and his followers posed an all too credible alternative to the bickerings within the Franciscan movement as tensions increased. On July 18, 1300 he was burnt at the stake at Parma. After Segarelli's long eclipse it is unclear how many followers persisted in their allegiance and it may be that in effect Dolcino elegantly created a movement of which he could claim that Segarelli had been the founder.

Within a month of Segarelli's death Dolcino had issued a letter proclaiming himself head of the movement and issuing a personal view of Church history and the future.[2] He emphasised his own importance and the gravity of the times with apocalyptic imagery and Joachite schemes of the past and future. The use of these themes, familiar to Spiritual Franciscans and sympathetic laity, also represented a shrewd political strategy to build as wide a community as possible for the 'Apostles'.

Dolcino adapted Joachim's view of Church history and added to it. For him too the Church was moving into a new era; however, unlike the mendicants it began not with Francis and Dominic, but with Segarelli 40 years later. The two saints and their benighted followers were therefore consigned to history. Besides Dolcino and his followers, the future belonged to Frederick of Sicily (1295–1337), who would become emperor. There would also be a new pope to be elected by God rather than the cardinals and by this means the Church would be reunited. Even this was not so incredible. Dolcino spoke approvingly of Celestine V and contemporaries were swift to notice that at the end of the 1290s, Frederick of Sicily was interested in religious reform despite ruling a kingdom which was under papal interdict.[3] More frightening was the attribution to Dolcino of a willingness to reform the Church, if necessary through violent elimination of clerks and monks unless they converted to the new order. The psychological resonance of the illegitimate child wreaking vengeance on his father's caste is too obvious to ignore, but the threat is vague and there is no evidence of it being carried out by Dolcino or any of his followers at this stage.[4] Even a sensational source, the anonymous *History of Fra Dolcino, the heresiarch*, written after his death, has him reflecting rather modestly that his followers would perhaps go to paradise, but at least purgatory.[5] They, in turn, saw him in exalted company, but not necessarily apocalyptic. Rolandino de Ollis, a close associate, preached that just as God had renewed the world through the water of the Flood, the law of Moses and Christ so now he ought to renew the world and the Church through the so-called Apostles.[6] Indeed Dolcino's first letter could be read as a manifesto for reform of the Church by means of the Ghibelline opponents of the pope.

The Apostles called themselves *minimi*, or 'least'; it was at once a sideswipe at their Franciscan predecessors who termed themselves the 'lesser brothers' or *fratres minores* and an appropriation of their tradition. They recited the Lord's Prayer, the Hail Mary and the Creed and wandered through villages chanting, 'Do penance for the kingdom of heaven is at hand.' As far as was possible they ate in the street or in public, leaving what they could not eat so that they demonstrated their modest appetites. Nevertheless, they attracted offerings and, according to an account of the 1320s, were apparently prepared to receive tithes. Dolcino even attracted a rich patron in the diocese of Novara who provided sanctuary when the preacher began to be persecuted.[7]

Supporters of the Apostles were dedicated to the life. In December 1303, a follower at Bologna was facing severe punishment since he had already confessed once and had then abandoned his penance. With nothing to lose he described how they lived:

Praying, contemplating the lives and passions of the saints and when it is necessary to eat, begging and seeking alms and the basics of life. The role of the said apostles is to conserve their poverty, to sell everything and give it to the poor. They are not to have or possess goods of their own.[8]

The witness, however, does not go on to condemn the Roman Church out of hand, indeed he thinks it a good thing, but he comments that he did not feel that 'pastors' of the Church could understand the sayings of the prophets and the Apocalypse unless God had revealed it to them, which he had to Dolcino.[9] A similar sentiment was expressed by a woman who had heard Rolandino de Ollis preach. And Rolandino himself in September 1304 was not above directly confronting a priest and asking what he thought of the Apostles since people said they were heretics. The priest's reply is revealing, particularly in the light of Dolcino's threats: 'I don't want to judge, but I believe that you (*pl.*) are good rather than bad.'[10] A lengthy discussion then ensued with help of a Bible which the priest had brought along.

The impression from these admittedly partisan sources is that religious excitement did not blind either clerks or laity from making informed decisions on the merit or otherwise of the movement. Salvetto Petriçoli consulted a local friend in orders as to whether his apostolic visitors were good or bad men in 1303, and after talking to them the friend concluded that they were bad. However, Salvetto relied on his own judgement and ignored the advice to capture them.[11] He must have been quite experienced in making his own mind up about such matters as in any diocese there were a number of religious persons and institutions with varying degrees of permanence and useful connections with the Church. On his way to see Dolcino, Rolandino stayed with a hermit woman in the diocese of Modena. On his return journey his hosts included an abbot, two sisters 'who stayed in a sort of hermitage' and a sympathetic priest.[12]

In a second letter of December 1303, Dolcino outlined a further programme centring on the extraordinary events of that year. The dispute between Boniface VIII and Philip IV of France concluded in September with an armed band sent by the French king breaking into the papal lodgings at Anagni, striking the pope and holding him prisoner. They were forced to release Boniface after a brief captivity, only for him to die the following month in Rome. So at the time of Dolcino's letter Boniface had been dead a matter of weeks; while many felt that the usurper pope had got his just deserts, even conservative observers felt that the physical attack on the successor of Saint Peter and the Vicar of Christ marked a cataclysmic decline in the office. Dolcino seized the opportunity to revise his predictions and exploit the confusion. He still saw Frederick as the great reformer and specified 1304 and 1305 as the years in which 'cardinals, monks, nuns, friars and all clerks would be laid desolate'. He also revealed a little more about the shadowy organisation behind him. Although Dolcino mainly operated between Vercelli and Novara, west of Milan, some of his immediate followers, men such as Longino da Bergamo and Valderico da Brescia, came from the towns of north-east Italy, now familiar as centres of dissent and suggesting the possibility of contact with older heretical teachings. The list was headed by 'sister Margarita most dear of all to him'. This was Margarita di Trento, from the mountains north of Lake Garda, perhaps Dolcino's lover, and undoubtedly a spiritual figure in her own right. It was not unreasonable to see Dolcino as a major threat. He claimed around 100 followers, with a further 4000 throughout Italy. This may have been exaggerated, but an inquisitor would need no reminder that it was comparable to earlier movements, not least the early friars themselves. At least one contemporary agreed as to his importance; Dante Alighieri reserved a place in hell for Dolcino while he was still at large. He was to be alongside Mohammed, that other great 'sower of scandal and schism' and his punishment was to be continually cleft in two from chin to anus.[13]

By the time of his final draft of the *Inferno*, Dante probably knew that Dolcino's fate had been scarcely less horrible. In 1304 Dolcino and followers fled to the diocese of Vercelli and were given hospitality by the villagers of Serravalle who were later punished by inquisitors for their generosity. Such reliance on the local communities makes what follows rather suspect. According to the *History*, the group began to live as brigands. They operated from remote bases in the mountains and fell upon local villages and travellers in the passes, making profitable business out of ransoming prisoners.[14] Other accounts say that Dolcino was preaching an extreme form of freedom of choice:

> . . . anyone of whatever rank or order, be he of the monastic or the secular clergy, may lawfully and at his pleasure transfer to their life, condition, or order; that a man without his wife's consent, or a wife without her husband's, may give up the the matrimonial state to enter their order.[15]

Whatever the truth of the matter, and there may well have been a third letter which explained Dolcino's actions, but has not come down to us, Pope Clement V organised military action against the Dolcinians giving a full crusading indulgence to participants. After a gruelling campaign in the mountains in winter, Dolcino was captured just before Easter 1307 and he and Margarita were ritually torn to pieces, after which their bodies were burnt.[16]

By the end of his career Dolcino does seem to have been preaching millenarianism with a genuine expectation of the imminent arrival of the Antichrist, but he was more than a discredited prophet of doom. His followers stayed loyal after his death, to the extent that Bernard Gui devoted a substantial part of his *Manual for Inquisitors* to how suspected 'Pseudo-Apostles' should be treated in the early 1320s. Even at the distance of 25 years Boninsegna of Arco could recall Dolcino as a good man who spoke beautiful words, and who would explain about the gospels and the things which would happen in the future from the Bible he possessed.[17]

Dolcino cleverly blended old appeal with new; to the old paradigm of the charismatic preacher with an agenda for reform and the lifestyle of austerity he added the sketch of a new one. With the help of the growth of literacy and purchasing power within society, the spiritual figure, safe in his mountain retreat, could communicate his appeal via letter and word of mouth. Dolcino had his own copy of the Bible so, unlike Valdes, he required no intermediary between himself and the word of God, and he also flattered his supporters that they could do the same. Whatever proclamations he might have made as his opponents closed in, Dolcino was not really an apocalyptic figure. He was rooted in the world, commenting freely on Italian politics and what might happen in the future. He seems not to have induced a fear of the end of the world, but a desire to challenge the local priest on doctrine with the help of the Bible. This kept his message alive so that he still had admirers 25 years after his death throughout north Italy, in southern France and even Spain.

The Waldensians

Chapter 5 compared Waldensians to the corner shops of heresy, sup-plying their customers with a basket of basic spiritual goods, varied to take account of local tastes. As such they proved remarkably successful and were the only religious grouping outside the Church to last until the Reformation and beyond. The variations in taste make it easier to talk about the history of 'Waldensianisms' after the middle of the thirteenth century. One road which came to a rapid dead end was the Waldensian path to mysticism. In his activity around Lyon in the 1240s, the inquisitor Stephen of Bourbon found traces of the union with God which some Franciscans were starting to explore. When preaching in Valence, on the Rhône, a Catholic informant said that he had heard the doctrine that 'the soul of every good man is in very truth the Holy Spirit, who is God and that a good man so long as he remains good, has no soul other than the Holy Spirit, or God'. Stephen returned to these beliefs, this time using evidence he had gained as an inquisitor.

> I have heard in the confessions of a large number of their leading members – that any good man is the son of God just as Christ is. And in the same way, they say of Him that He had no other soul but God, or the Holy Spirit, who is God . . .

But if some erstwhile followers of Valdes were then leaning towards antinomianism, the idea that inner grace or presence of God dispenses the believer from the normal rules of religion, the idea did not spread.[18] Even in Stephen's experience most believers did not reach such elevated levels. Their rather old-fashioned ideas were still elegantly expressed as in their three-fold division of ordination. Those who were ordained by man but not God were priests of poor character, those who were ordained by God but not by man included Waldensian laymen and even women who might take the sacraments. The pinnacle of the hierarchy was still reserved for those who were priests of good character, ordained by both God and man. There were also still Waldensians around Montauban, north of the main Cathar strongholds in southern France, although their influence was weakened by two major Inquisitions in the 1240s.[19]

From his vantage point in north Italy a generation later, the inquisitor Anselm of Alessandria also acknowledged the presence of Poor Lombards and the Poor of Lyon, as he termed them. Although they still had their historic disagreements, summarised in chapter 5, the issues highlighted reveal the influence of contemporary Franciscanism. According to Anselm, the Poor of Lyon or Ultramontane:

> . . . does not work for himself or anyone else for a price, neither does he spend nor save anything. He is sandaled and wears his clerical status on top of his shoes, or footwear cut away at the top; and he does not save coins, but his companion does it for him, nor does he keep any food from day to day and he carries only one tunic.

To the issue of work is added that of what clothing they should wear, whether to handle money and of living strictly for the day by not saving food.[20]

Anselm said that according to information given to inquisitors in Genoa the Poor Lombards had indeed formed their own Church led by 'Bishop' Andrew Gruara. More surprisingly, according to other informants, the Poor of Lyon also had their own bishop, although Anselm's description of their Mass still assumes that there may be an ordained Catholic priest among them and they believed a sinful priest might still administer extreme unction. From this it would appear that some

Ultramontanes were moving towards a sacrament whose validity depended on the good character of the person administering it, but they were not there yet. North of the Alps an anonymous contemporary of Anselm's, the secular priest or possibly Dominican author known as the 'Passau Anonymous', described a community along the Austrian Danube, which probably extended into Bohemia and included adherents of both the Lombard and Lyonist traditions. However, both had been adapted to meet local needs; men, women and children were allowed to preach and the nub of the group was the ten 'schools' where formal instruction in scripture was given. They had a strong missionary impulse and it is tempting to think that one of the attractions of the schools might have been to equip students in the skills of literacy needed to escape to the urban centres of Germany and Italy. The acknowledgement that adherents could choose the form of religion they followed was tempered by the doctrine that to attend any other church would be adultery. To some extent this policy must have worked since 'Waldensian' heretics in Lower Austria were still being investigated in the early decades of the fourteenth century.[21]

Nothing more is known about Waldensian groups until the 1290s. The obvious interpretation may be the right one. They offered little threat and their numbers had become insignificant. The evidence from the 1250s and 1260s shows interests coinciding with those of the Franciscans and it is quite possible that some were subsumed into the Spirituals or even the followers of Segarelli. As ever, we are dependent on the writings of inquisitors, but after Anselm ceased to supplement his initial notes some time in the early 1270s we have virtually nothing until the end of the century when inquisitorial action revealed witnesses who were prepared to talk about what was happening in the years immediately before.

There were also still Waldensians active in north Italy. The expense accounts of the Dominican inquisitor Lanfranco da Bergamo give them nothing like the prominence of the Cathars he hunted relentlessly from his base in Pavia, but there were a handful of Waldensians, Poor Lombards and Poor of Lyon, as he termed them fairly indiscriminately. In August 1294, 35 pounds were confiscated from a Pavia resident who had received that sum from a female heretic of the Poor of Lyon. Lanfranco took another seven pounds from James, a mason from Lumello, condemned for being a member of the Poor Lombards. These were substantial sums and point to some reasonably prosperous support for Waldensian communities. The information may well have come from Peter of Martinengo, described as 'of the sect of the Poor of Lyon' who went to the stake in Pavia for his beliefs. Half burnt, he then abjured and so was dragged into the inquisitor's house where he lingered for more than three weeks before death put an end to his suffering. Further arrests were made on the strength of the dying man's confession.[22]

A more substantial Waldensian presence emerged in southern France and one which served a very particular community. In the 1280s immigrants from Burgundy had entered the region to the west of Toulouse as well as the little town of Alzon between Millau and Montpellier, probably attracted by the thriving textile industry. They were joined by fugitives fleeing the inquisition of 1290–5 conducted in the area around the old Waldensian home of Lyon. By the time inquisitors started to take an interest in 1310 a whole generation had grown up in their new homes, well aware of their distinctiveness and served by a heterogeneous leadership of *maiores* or 'brothers' from Burgundy, Provence, the Toulousain and even northern France. In addition to the usual declarations that the 'brothers' were good men, keeping to the way of God and the apostles, one witness bluntly stated that they were in opposition to the clerks and monks.[23]

The irony was that aspects of their spirituality would have delighted those behind the reforms of Fourth Lateran. The 'brothers' taught the gospels and the letters of the apostles, while believers' most important contact with them was confession, with accompanying penance and absolution. The ceremony had something of a rite of reaffirmation, generally only performed on an individual once every four or five years. More routinely, the *maiores* knelt with the family on the bench from the meal table and led them in prayer. To this cosy core of domestic religion, however, was added a general condemnation of Catholic belief in purgatory with the dead going straight to paradise or hell: there was a touch of dualism in the belief that this life was itself a penance, a purgatory for sins. Both believers and preachers seemed unaware of their Waldensian heritage and were only identified as such by the inquisitors. There was still room for a renegade priest in their ranks, but on the whole they had turned their back on Catholicism. As with the southern French Cathars who fled to Lombardy in the 1240s and 1250s the presence of their own distinctive 'good men' cemented a community in a foreign land, the degree of respect given to them marked a personal choice.[24]

More representative of a native French tradition of Waldensian thought were the group picked up by the inquisitor Jacques Fournier in Pamiers on the fringes of the Pyrenees around 1319. They too had left home, but were from the Occitan-speaking areas south of Lyon, particularly Vienne. They called themselves the 'Poor of Christ' and while they did not reject sacraments from a Catholic priest, they had their own hierarchy of deacons, priests and a *maioralis*, all ceremonially ordained. The chief witness was one Raymond de Sainte-Foy, who had come to Pamiers via Vienne, Avignon and Montpellier, among other places. In the last he attended the schools of theology, run by the Franciscans. This must have been in the late 1290s or early 1300s when pressure on the Franciscans increased, so the experience may have been a formative one. Certainly he took no tithes himself because of his desire for poverty. Instead, a small group of followers supported him by spinning and 'other business'. Other influences included the *maioralis*, John of Lorraine and Michel the Italian, giving an air of cosmopolitan contacts from one end of Christendom to the other. The truth may have been rather less exciting; there are few local followers recorded and although Fournier interviewed Raymond in great detail, his immediate associates are dismissed in a few pages. Given that the modern edition of Fournier's inquisition runs to three volumes, he seems to have found Raymond intriguing, but of little consequence.[25]

Nevertheless, the picture of religion offered is an appealing one; there is a hint of wealthy support when another witness recalled meeting Raymond in Montpellier in the house with the red bars on the window. In Toulouse, in a house near the huge monastery of Saint Sernin, they listened to John of Lorraine reading to them from a vernacular book of the gospels after dinner. Raymond himself explained that although he thought it better the scriptures were recited in Latin, he used Occitan since he was talking to a mixed audience, some of whom did not know Latin. One feature all the witnesses of the Poor of Christ agreed on was that it was wrong to swear an oath and it is this which links them to the Waldensian tradition. Fournier was also unyielding; however Raymond might frame an acceptance of the Roman Church, the inquisitor was taking no chances so Raymond died at the stake.[26]

It is possible that the various groups from the Waldensian tradition were in some loose contact with one another. Certainly it was an abiding inquisitorial belief. In a piece now redated to around 1300 and thought to be written in southern France, an anonymous inquisitor reported that the heretics held an annual council or General Chapter around Lent, mostly in Lombardy, but sometimes in Provence or elsewhere. Attendance was by all leaders of heretical 'houses', but it was not a large gathering with, for example, three or four coming from 'Alamannia', the German-speaking areas north of the Alps. Within the analogy of a self-governing family, there is some pooling of alms and money given by friends and believers, the largest contribution also coming from 'Alamannia'. Ordinations of senior figures took place here and pairs of 'visitors' were chosen to minister to friends and believers. This rather more formal structure would certainly fit with Raymond's testimony of 1319 and the idea is reprised in Bernard Gui's great treatise of the years before 1324. He adds the detail that the delegates pose as merchants and meet in a house leased long before by one of their believers.

There may be a degree of circularity in this, which fed an established paranoia, but not all is fantasy; a fragment of corroborative evidence can be added from Lanfranco da Bergamo's expense accounts. In Vercelli, on the route from Italy to France, Lanfranco confiscated the enormous sum of 100 pounds from one Olderato da Monza as a consequence of the condemnation of his late sister, Contessa. This may have been linked to the capture in the town of one Tebaldo 'de biserzio', from whom Lanfranco also gained 17 pounds. Tebaldo abjured and taking one of the Inquisition spies with him, promised to find the 'Waldensian pope' and deliver twelve other heretics into the inquisitor's custody. The area was one into which the inquisitor could not go because of warfare and Tebaldo disappeared from the record. An overzealous and greedy inquisitor could possibly have been outwitted here and there is no other mention of a *papa* as such, but the 'papal' role is not so far from the *maior* referred to by Bernard Gui and easily confused with the *maioralis* of Raymond de Sainte-Foy. Moreover, assuming three or four delegates from Burgundy and Provence respectively to match the German contribution and there would be a discreet gathering of around twelve, a number of suitable apostolic significance. The large amounts of money confiscated may have been outgoing or incoming contributions to the council. There is, of course, nothing more satisfying than a good conspiracy theory and the case is far from proven, but when the comparison is made with the Cathars, a little central direction could go a remarkably long way.[27]

The Waldensians had been a threat to the Church because they offered a prospect of what the Church might look like run by the laity. Consequently they were remarkably adaptable and could reflect the spiritual issues of the time, unencumbered by excess baggage of doctrine or history. While the disagreements at the Bergamo conference of 1218 may have been learned and profound, by the end of the century there was little trace of them remaining. Believers wanted to confess and be saved and they shaped an organisation which could help them do this. What marginalised Waldensian groups, besides sporadic persecution, was that in most places a parallel process was under way in the Catholic Church. Waldensians persisted generally in inaccessible mountainous areas where they represented sturdy resistance to interfering city folk, or to cack-handed attempts to replace one language with another. So they survived in Bohemia, parts of Germany and the high Alps, relying mainly on oral culture and constantly changing to offer an alternative choice. In most places they were eventually subsumed by the followers of Jan Hus in the early fifteenth century, or by those of Luther and Calvin a century later. In the southern Alps they did the subsuming, and emerged as the standard-bearers of Protestantism in modern Italy.

The Cathars

The Cathars were far better than the Waldensians at maintaining a sense of identity and they paid for it accordingly. For Italy, the inquisitor Anselm of Alessandria compiled a list of Cathar bishops, perhaps as late as 1275. This monument to the Cathars' obstinate desire to organise lent an air of order to near chaos. Anselm had to amend his original list of the Albanenses, since the bishop had died and his deputy or 'elder son' had converted, and the deacon of Brescia had been burnt. The Church of Concorezzo was more settled, although it was far smaller than that of the Albanenses. It was based almost entirely in Cremona, Piacenza, Alessandria and Brescia, and was run by inhabitants of those towns. Of the hierarchy of the Bagnolenses Anselm gives no word.[28] There is no doubt that Italian Catharism was fatally weakened by the fall of Sirmione in 1276 and by the systematic imposition of inquisitors which followed the triumph of the Guelph party in many Italian towns, but the very completeness of this victory led to a certain complacency which allowed the Cathars to persist, if not to prosper.

Anselm was apparently the last Italian inquisitor to bother compiling notes on heretical opponents. Instead some of his colleagues fabricated heresy, to the point where it could be called a protection racket. There is evidence that a small group of Franciscan friars in north-east Italy in the Veneto and the Trevisan March made great profits in the 1280s and 1290s from spurious charges of heresy, often levelled against the dead or those foolish enough to be disrespectful to inquisitors.[29] Corrupt or not, Pope Boniface's shortage of money in his early years combined with his grandiose plans to restore the political hegemony of the see of Peter, put pressure on inquisitors to deliver more heretics and confiscations. We have some expenditure and income accounts from Lanfranco da Bergamo, the Dominican inquisitor based in Pavia in the 1290s. In June 1295 he was 'audited' by a papal official and had to pay 108 florins to the pope's bankers in Milan. If Lanfranco's bookkeeping was even approximately accurate, this was so far in excess of any profit he was returning that it resembles a tax demand. Certainly it had a stimulating effect on the inquisitor who increased his 'productivity' from just 19 places visited in 1294, to 29 in 1295 and 37 in 1296 when he was 'audited' again in October. This time the inquisitor looks to have assembled a considerable income, although the sum he was relieved of was far less.[30]

After the first audit Lanfranco was rather less scrupulous in his convictions in his urgent need to raise cash. He raised over 100 pounds from the Baralioni family of Pavia on the strength of their late father's heresy. Contessa de Monza, the late sister of Olderato de Monza, a resident of Vercelli, was condemned for heresy and her brother fined 100 pounds. By the end of the year Olderato was dead and the inquisitor was able to sell off his house and two other of his properties for a further 85 pounds once expenses and exchange fees had been deducted. Indeed, selling and renting out the properties of convicted heretics became one of Lanfranco's most lucrative sidelines.[31]

Lanfranco's world is a contradictory one. At first sight it was one of a growing institution facing an ever-diminishing threat. Having acquired a house for the inquisitors to which he added a prison and stabling for horses, Lanfranco ordered parchment and writing materials to record the office's privileges and 'consultations'.[32] He kept a community of sad spies, such as Helena, the one-time Cathar who, as the record states, had done much for the Inquisition, because of which she was now poor and had to have her rent paid.[33] All this was mainly paid for from the goods of long-dead heretics, extracted from their children. On closer inspection Lanfranco was an inquisitor still on the track of an active enemy. There was nothing corrupt or complacent about the operation in 1293 to capture the Milanese heretic William who was living in Parenzo, now Porec in Croatia, a small port on the Capo d'Istria under Venetian control. First, a spy was hired to locate William, then Lanfranco made the journey. Once there, a kind of posse was recruited from local Franciscans to aid the inquisitor in his capture and then the party of two inquisitors, their attendants and the prisoner made the long journey back to Milan where William was burnt.[34]

These contradictions are explained as much by the inquisitors' position as by what had happened to the Cathar heresy; the former had premises to maintain, staff to pay and the leaders of the local commune to impress; they needed a steady source of income. The old structures of the latter had decayed in Italy and even the obstinate communities of southern French Cathars in exile had largely evaporated. Evidence from this time casts light on the fate of one of the influential Cathar Oliba brothers. Some time after June 1295 Lanfranco seized a house in Pavia, which was owned by Peire, a 'scholar' from Provence, but was rented by the wife of Peire Oliba. This seems to have been the remnants of a household recorded as being in Pavia as far back as the 1260s when Peire Oliba and his brother Bernard, the last Cathar bishop of Toulouse, had shared a house with Peire's wife and one Peire Bonum, another *perfectus* who may have been the Provençal 'scholar'. In the later record there is no sign of Peire Oliba, who must be assumed captive or dead and no further news of his by now aged wife after the inquisitor seized the house. An entry shortly after in the same document makes it clear that Peire the scholar had now died and the inquisitor sold the house. The laconic entries suggest a tidying up of business rather than a major coup.[35]

Back in southern France, a different generation started to take an interest in Cathar beliefs. The most extensive revival was based around the Autier family. Peire was a middle-aged lawyer from Ax (modern Ax-les-Thermes) in the foothills of the Pyrenees. Everything suggests that there was no longer a surviving local oral tradition; instead Peire was converted while reading an unknown heretical book. To pursue his interest in the sect further he was forced to travel to the long-established transit town and traditional Cathar refuge of Cuneo in the Italian Alps which he reached some time in 1296 and where he was joined by his brother and illegitimate son. After time in Cuneo and the spa town of Acqui Terme three pairs of 'good men' became active in Languedoc. Within a year of their arrival in November or December 1299, Peire had established himself in Toulouse and the *perfecti* had met some of the local nobility in the Sabarthès. Political events were in Peire's favour. The dispute between Philip IV of France and Pope Boniface VIII caused a suspension of inquisitorial activity between 1291 and 1297 and at a popular level Boniface's treatment of his predecessor caused widespread suspicion. A brief reconciliation between the pope and French king allowed inquisitors to act in Carcassonne in 1297 and two years later at Albi, but further tensions from 1301 gave the Cathars some respite. Only after Boniface's death and the papal court's subsequent move to Avignon in 1305 were friendly relations resumed and the inquisitors could set to work in the region with renewed vigour.[36]

In this brief time and with the slenderest resources – there does not seem to have ever been more than 16 *perfecti* – the Autiers built a movement that was to survive for 30 years and was only extirpated by one of the most exhaustive of all medieval Inquisitions. Making no attempt to rebuild the hierarchy and territorial structure of the former Cathar Church, Autier's group contained some talented preachers who explained a new version of Cathar doctrine, mitigating the starkness of this world being the creation of an evil god with an emphasis on metempsychosis, the transmigration of souls through people and animals until they were in the body of a consoled believer. When such a believer died the soul went to paradise so quickly it could pierce a brick wall.

To suit a new age, Autier offered a material return to believers who supported himself and his companions in their attempt to follow 'the way of God and the apostles'. While they fasted extensively and avoided fat, eggs and cheese at all times, believers were assured of salvation in the next world, as well as an abundance of wealth and everything good and useful to them in this.[37]

Such promises were accompanied by a streak of ruthlessness. Always clandestine, Autier's Cathars ensured loyalty through family contacts and were quite capable of murdering potential informers. They also adapted and extended the *endura* for believers, a fast until death after the *consolamentum* had been applied. It had not been unknown in Cathar circles previously and it did resolve the difficult dilemma for the believer who, having in all good faith thought that death was near, then recovered and found him or herself with the unwanted status of 'good Christian'. However, it must have occurred to the Autiers that the fast ensured not only the soul's salvation, but also its owner's silence in any subsequent investigation by inquisitors. Finally, Autier never confused austerity with poverty; he and his followers ensured funding through the pragmatic doctrine that almsgiving could not help the believer, unless it was made to the 'Church of God', namely themselves.[38]

In the end, Autier's Cathars faced impossible odds. In terms of theology the laity's agenda was more than ever set by the Roman Church. Cathar preachers' attacks on marriage, infant baptism and prayers for the dead only emphasised how much these features had become part of the laity's everyday experience since they were first criticised in the twelfth century. The lengthy and repeated denunciation by the heretics of the 'delusion and scandal' of the Eucharist highlighted how central it was for most of the audience. A much better show was now on offer in church than when the first Cathars preached and it was almost an admission of defeat that the Autiers accused churchmen of deceiving the people by singing during Mass. Logistically, the need for secrecy limited the number of converts the heretics could make and the pressure increased in 1300 when inquisitors began to show an interest in their Italian refuge at Cuneo, the overland terminus for fugitives from southern France, as well as Genoa, the main seaport. Spies were regularly sent to both places to gather information and in late 1302 these were successful in delivering native Italian supporters or southern French in exile. However, the most potent danger to the leadership was betrayal by their compatriots in southern France and following the appointment of a new inquisitor, Bernard Gui, at Toulouse in 1308 all of the main players fell into Inquisition hands during the course of the following year.[39]

Nevertheless, Peire Autier did provide a modernised version of Catharism which enjoyed some success, in contrast with the confusion which surrounded the short-lived revival further north in Albi. There the motivation was partly political. Bernard de Castanet, the bishop of Albi, dominated town politics and was heavily committed to the building of the expensive fortress cathedral of Saint Cecilia which still glowers over the town today. Local lawyers and royal officials comprised the natural opposition to episcopal domination and some of them may have flirted with heresy, giving it a decidedly 'middle class' feel. Two young citizens, a retailer and a lawyer, paid a courier to cross the Alps in search of a *perfectus* in 1296. He visited Genoa and the thermal springs at Acqui. While there he met another man sent to look for a *perfectus* by an older supporter from Albi. In turn they met two southern French migrants who took them to the village of Visone where there existed three or four huts on the hillside housing a community of heretics. The party returned to Albi with Guglielmo Pagani, a Lombard 'good men'.

This snapshot of Cathars in the mountains suggests a quasi-monastic group and the contrast with the society to which Guglielmo was introduced in Albi may explain what followed. He was entertained for dinner on the Sunday evening. It proved somewhat embarrassing for the hosts: they had forgotten the dietary requirements of the *perfectus* and offered him chicken and then cheese before sending out for fish. The Lombard experiment was not repeated and local Cathars subsequently relied on two older *perfecti* in the area.[40]

This situation presented problems of its own; visits were sporadic and the suspicion is that the qualities of the veteran *perfecti*, Raymond Desiderii and Raymond del Boc, did not quite the match the expectations of their educated younger supporters. On their return to the region after many years the 'good men' speculated gloomily on the chances of receiving money due to them from long-dead adherents of the sect. Younger believers had to be taught the basic Cathar greeting ceremony. Still, the position was not hopeless: while many of the new supporters were making a conscious choice to listen to the Cathars, family ties still counted for something and the *perfecti* were still able to find hospitality from the grown-up children of former supporters, such as Pons Philippus of Lautrec, with whom they shared plaice, nuts, and a bottle of wine. The welcome could, however, be a little grudging when the *perfecti* reminded their host of old family debts.[41] The Cathars' return did not escape the attention of the bishop of Albi; arrests were made in late 1299 and 1300 and there were at least two burnings. Most of the group were simply left to rot in the Inquisition jail at Carcassonne despite attempts to obtain royal or papal intervention.

The problems facing the Cathar revival were obvious. It was difficult to provide systematic pastoral care, especially the all-important *consolamentum* for the dying, due to the lack of a territorial network of Cathar *perfecti* such as had existed before the Albigensian Crusade. Despite the common links with Lombardy there is no sign the Autiers and Albi heretics knew of each other's existence. In the straitened circumstances in which they found themselves, however, this may have been an advantage; Peire Autier's followers were able to persist in their devotion because he had in effect created a number of independent cells, so the last of the *perfecti*, the disreputable Guilhem Bélibaste, could survive in the remote villages of the Pyrenees for a further twelve years after escaping from prison in 1309 until he was lured into a trap in 1321. At the same time the heretics took advantage of the more integrated economy and society of the fourteenth century in which they could travel comparatively conveniently. The professor of medicine at Montpellier from 1290 to 1314 was from Brescia, and when the consuls of Albi asked four jurists of Toulouse whether they were entitled to a town hall, one turned out to be from Piacenza and another from Bologna. It was perfectly possible, therefore, for the Autier brothers to obtain a set of Parma knives and pass themselves off as pedlars.[42]

Renewed persecution of heresy in central Italy in the 1290s revealed the persistence of Catharism among the moderately prosperous there also. Attention centred on one Bonigrino da Verona, a resident of Bologna who had served several times as a representative of the tanners, grocers, purse makers, usurers and other small businessmen who made up the *popolo* of the Italian city. Bonigrino was a streetwise supporter who shows that in the 1270s and 1280s at least it was still possible to play the system and get away with it. He had first come into contact with Cathars on the shores of Lake Garda, the home of the absolute dualist Albanenses, and had attracted sporadic Inquisition attention since 1273. There were three subsequent appearances before inquisitors in the 1270s and 1280s; he was fined, but did not pay; sentenced to cross-wearing, he quietly removed them. He lied a lot; never more so than when he promised in 1283 to 'return to the unity of the Church with good heart and unfeigned faith'. Summoned again in 1296 he was asked whether he wanted to persist in his errors and face death, to which he answered he did and wanted to die for his faith.[43]

Bonigrino's straightforward acceptance of his situation lent an unusual frankness to the discussions with his interrogators. His views did not fit easily into the doctrinal schemes maintained by any of the three groups of Italian Cathars earlier in the century. He believed in one God, but declared loudly that the Devil had created snakes, dragons and scorpions and the like. Asked if the Roman Church was the head of Christianity and if the pope was head of the Church, he replied that 'they were as long as they followed Christ's orders and were good men'. He even allowed that priests who were 'boni homines' or good men and in a state of penitence might sacrifice the body of Christ by saying Mass. All this may have been mere evasion or redolent with private meanings lost to both us and the interrogators in the way that a child has a private truth. Certainly, the exchange that followed on who made the human body was childish, as witness and inquisitor chased each other back to Adam and Eve. However, just before it Bonigrino came out with a sentence so unusual for the middle ages, it still has the power to startle:

Dixit quod sicut sunt LXXII lingue, ita sunt LXXII fides. [Literally, *He said that just as there are 72 tongues, so there are 72 faiths.*]

The statement was not questioned, suggesting it was not an area into which the inquisitor wanted to follow and the obvious reading is that Bonigrino was mocking the Church's attempts to enforce doctrinal unity. Even modern scholarship has not deadened Bonigrino's laughter; the statement that the world had 72 languages was a contemporary commonplace. Since European medieval scholarship had only identified two or three alternative religions to Christianity, 'creeds', in the sense of subdivisions of Christianity, is perhaps a better translation than 'faiths'.[44]

Bonigrino may also have been implying something more. An informed man like Bonigrino would have had at least the rudimentary knowledge of a second language, Latin, and in a university city like Bologna he would hardly have been able to avoid it. The issue of when it was appropriate to use Latin or the vernacular, the spoken language, was one which was starting to concern both Church and secular government. Boniface VIII's letters concerning peace between England and France in 1299 had been read to the English parliament in both Latin and 'the native tongue'. Bonigrino's contemporary Dante Alighieri was to ponder the question at length in his *De vulgari eloquentia* written three or four years after Bonigrino's interrogation. Dante makes a conscious decision to use 'the more noble language, the vernacular', but the significance is that use of language is a choice and the poet drew particular attention to Bologna, both as a place whose borrowing from the surrounding areas created a beautiful speech and as being remarkable for the variation of speech within its boundaries, perhaps a reference to the cosmopolitan nature of the city's student population. Bonigrino himself would also have known the northern dialect of his native Verona. What he drew attention to was not just the sheer number of faiths or creeds, but their nature, to be used in appropriate situations in all or in part, just as he was doing in his conversation with his interrogator. Bonigrino was offering to die for his beliefs, but they were ones which every individual chose for themselves. Small wonder, then, that the inquisitor avoided the issue.[45]

The subsequent burning of Bonigrino, the bones of his deceased wife Rosafiore and their companion, Bompietro, caused a riot. The crowd murmured at the pointless burning of the dead and then were enraged when Bompietro repented at the stake, asked for communion and was refused. Order was finally restored and some 300 people were subsequently summoned to explain themselves. During interrogations which stretched over the next few years, the inquisitors trawled a rich shoal of dissatisfaction at their actions, and some of the variety of belief which Bonigrino had warned of. A few witnesses appear to have been Cathars, some claiming allegiance to the Bagnolenses, one of the old established groups of Italian dualists. Bompietro had already put such statements into perspective by indicating that he did not distinguish between the various heretical sects and beliefs, but believed that the heretics were 'better men' and that in their faith lay salvation. Certainly, the Cathar believers were a cosmopolitan community. Of just under 100 who had some allegiance to the sect, the largest part came from the north-east: Ferrara, Mantua, Verona were all towns on the route back to Lake Garda. There were half a dozen from the old Lombard stronghold of Cremona and more had travelled north from Tuscany. They seem to have migrated mainly for economic reasons, seeing that the fear of persecution was by then more or less universal in Italy. When matters of faith were referred to they mainly spoke of old leaders and better times but, as with the southern French exiles a generation earlier, their shared religion helped them establish a sense of community in a cosmopolitan city. Only around 20 came from Bologna itself and in contrast to previous generations had made no inroads into the university, having recruited just four *perfecti* from the city in 30 years.[46]

The striking feature of this and other actions against Catharism in the fourteenth century is the massive overreaction in proportion to the heretics rather modest achievements. The last *perfectus* of the Autiers' mission, Guilhem Bélibaste, was burnt in the spring of 1321, and by then he served a small community of remote shepherds quite literally on the margins of society in the Pyrenees. Yet the early fourteenth-century Inquisition brought together in southern France the most formidable battery of intellectual and organisational ability ever assembled against heresy; Bernard Gui, historian and author of the definitive manual for inquisitors, *The Practice of Inquisition*, Jacques Fournier, the future Pope Benedict XII, Bernard de Castanet, a future cardinal, and Geoffroy d'Ablis, theologian and author of an influential commentary on Peter Lombard's *Sentences*. The new proximity of the papal court at Avignon undoubtedly brought the heretics of southern France to wider attention once more, but the response may be a sign of a deeper understanding among inquisitors of how heresy spread. In 1304 the renegade Franciscan friar Bernard Délicieux declared that all the south was clear of heresy except for Carcassonne, Albi and Cordes and even then there were less than 50 heretics. He went on to allege that inquisitors made up others.[47] This may have been true, in that inquisitors could be corrupt or overzealous, but Bernard and subsequent observers may have missed the point; it was not numbers that counted. Bernard Gui described the paralysis when Boniface and Philip IV were in dispute:

> During this persecuting of inquisitors and disruption of the Office, many *perfecti* met and started to multiply, (and heresies to swarm) and they contaminated people in the dioceses of Pamiers, of Carcassonne and of Toulouse and the Albigeois region, as was manifest subsequently from the legitimate investigation and arrest of these *perfecti* and of their believers: *from such seeds they produced the fruit.*

From the familiar pest and disease metaphors, Bernard proceeds to a second stage of exponential growth of heresy which must be stopped before it can propagate. The inquisitors finally understood heretical networks. Even the arrest and burning of the Autiers brought no let up of pressure. Francis da Paucapalea, the inquisitor for lower Lombardy, made his way to the general council of Vienne in 1311 especially to discuss the deceased Guilhem Autier and the Waldensians of the French Alps.[48]

As for the Cathars, individuals found sanctuaries in Aragon and Sicily and perhaps Corsica. There were shadowy communities in the mountains of Lombardy and Piedmont and persistent rumours from the huge area of southern Hungary, Slovenia and northern Croatia, known then as Sclavonia. They knew the game was up; 'see how God's sheep are scattered', commented one supporter after one fruitless search for *perfecti*. The last heretics were isolated: in 1307 the inquisitor Francis da Paucapalea put in a claim for horses:

> Without these an inquisition cannot easily be carried out in parts of Piedmont since the Cathars and Waldensians live in very distant and dangerous places.[49]

It is not possible to say precisely who the last Cathars were, or when they might have died out, only that they were rather less suited to this marginal existence than their Waldensian counterparts. Whereas Waldensian communities persisted with only occasional visits from their 'good men' the Cathars had to be present at the death of a believer.

Moreover, even in its simplest form, dualism as a belief system was decisively different enough as to require constant reinforcement in the minds of adherents. Finally there are signs, even during the revival of the 1290s, that Catharism had become a generational creed and the movement may have died with them as the fourteenth century wore on. Alternatively the Cathars may have gradually lost their identity until they were indistinguishable from the Alpine Waldensians.

It would have just been possible for someone listening to the first Wyclifite preachers at St Paul's Cross in London in the 1380s to have been present at the burning of Guilhem Bélibaste some 60 years before, an elderly Gascon wine merchant, perhaps. And yet if there were such a figure able to have made the comparison, he or she kept silent, perhaps judging it unwise to venture into such matters. The disappearance of the Cathars in western Europe was so total that the hunt for their legacy has carried on ever since. Dualism has been seen as the precursor of witchcraft; after all it is a short step from acknowledging the Devil as the creator of this world to worshipping him as such. Yet if this study has shown one thing it is that doctrine was not so very important. The Cathars wore their view of the theoretical universe as a badge of recognition; attempts to explore its theological implications and ramifications led only to dispute and fragmentation. Of far greater significance was the Cathar blueprint for a holy man or woman for the laity, poor yet articulate, moral yet tolerant of believers' failings. This was the figure which was copied by the Waldensians and the friars and reinvented again and again in the subsequent centuries. The Cathars also explored how a Church might be organised, starting with grandiose titles and councils in imitation of contemporary Catholicism and finishing with a far more modern-looking structure of cells of believers, given pastoral care by a respected local 'good man'. Our Gascon merchant would have certainly recognised that influence in the earnest little groups of Lollards in London and the Midlands and their sympathetic priests.

In the days of 'the monopoly', life (and death) was easy for the laity, functions of the physical body barely noted by a clerical elite absorbed in collective imprecations to the Almighty. It was agreed by all that few were saved, but that it was important to avoid the distractions of the world. Then the Cathars appeared offering, by means of a simple ceremony, safe passage to heaven, fashioned for each individual and validated by the lives of those who administered it. These were not distant monks or drunken priests, but people the believer knew and respected. The stimulus given to popular religion eventually crowded out the heretics. By the time the Cathars departed there were, within the Church itself, competing institutions, wandering preachers and different ways of religious life, perhaps not surprisingly perceived as 72 creeds. Every town was a crowded spiritual marketplace displaying everything from gaudy excess to flesh-wasting asceticism. It foreshadowed the modern age in that plenty is on offer, but we evaluate it ourselves and sometimes it seems that choosing our path to salvation is the biggest distraction of all. In this sense it was, and is, the Devil's world.

NOTES

Introduction

1. Richard Tomkins, 'Christ replaces Coke as the focus of youthful longing', *Financial Times*, 30 July 2004, 12, reproduced with permission.

2. For the middle ages such a connection between spiritual and economic values is certainly implicit in Richard Southern's description of the medieval Church in the West as 'the most elaborate and thoroughly integrated system of religious thought and practice the world has ever known', *Western Society and the Church in the Middle Ages* (London, 1970), 15, or Lester K. Little's tracing of the 'correlations' between 'monetary economy, urban society and a spirituality founded upon poverty' in his *Religious Poverty and the Profit Economy in Medieval Europe* (London, 1978), xi.

3. Material on consumers in history: G. McCracken, 'Fashion versus patina', *Culture and Consumption. New approaches to the Symbolic Character of Consumer Goods and Activities* (Bloomington, Indiana, 1988). Economic explanations: H. Perkin, *The Origins of Modern English Society* (London, 1968), esp. 96–7. N. McKendrick, J. Brewer and J. H. Plumb, *The Birth of a Consumer Society: the commercialization of eighteenth-century England* (London, 1982). The consumer as Romantic: C. Campbell, *The Romantic Ethic and the Spirit of Modern Consumerism* (Oxford, 1987). Overview in P. Corrigan, *The Sociology of Consumption* (London, 1997), 1–16. As political movement: M. Hilton, *Consumerism in 20th-century Britain* (Cambridge, 2003). Warnings against inappropriate historical usage: A. McCants, 'Meeting needs and suppressing desires: consumer choice models and historical data', *Journal of Interdisciplinary History*, 26 (1995).

4. Leisure in the Middle Ages: E. Leroy Ladurie, *Montaillou: village occitan de 1294 à 1324* (Paris, 1975), 389–400, cited in J.-L. Marfany's contribution to the debate on 'The invention of Leisure in early modern Europe', *Past and Present*, 156 (August, 1997), but the extent to which religion was a pursuit of the Middle Ages gets lost in this debate. In Pamiers the church choir was a major social forum and a friar in Montaillou was invited to begin a secular feast by singing the *Ave Maria*. J. Hatcher, 'Labour, Leisure and economic thought before the nineteenth century, *Past and Present*, 160 (August, 1998), 77–83. Glaber, see Ch. 1; quotation from *No Washing Machines Then: Braughing People Remember*, eds V. High and M. Nokes (Ware, 2004), 87–8. L. Taylor, *Soldiers of Christ: preaching in late medieval and Reformation France* (Oxford, 1992), 28–36.

5. Campbell, C. op. cit., 74–5.

6. Bernard of Clairvaux, *Letters*, 2nd edn, trans. B. Scott James (Stroud, 1998), no. 391. See below chapter 5 n. 35 for Cathar heaven.

7. G. Dickson, 'Revivalism as a medieval religious genre', *Journal of Ecclesiastical History*, 51 (2000), 482–5, 494–5. N. Cohn, *The Pursuit of the Millennium*, 2nd edn (London, 1970), 128–31 presents an older view.

8. L. K. Little, op. cit., see above n. 2; R. I. Moore, *The First European Revolution, c.970–1215* (Oxford, 2000).

Chapter 1

1. N. Tanner (ed.), *Decrees of the ecumenical councils* (London, 1990), 31; P. Brown, *The Rise of Western Christendom*, 2nd edn (Oxford, 2003), 161, 449–51; D. Ganz, 'The debate on predestination', *Charles the Bald: court and kingdom*, eds M. T. Gibson and J. L. Nelson, 2nd edn (Aldershot, 1990), 283–302.

2. C. Morris, *The Papal Monarchy: the Western Church from 1050 to 1250* (Oxford, 1989), 64–8.

3. For simony, Acts 8: 9–24; nicolaitism, *New Catholic Encyclopedia* (Washington, 1967), vol. 10, 459.

4. H. E. J. Cowdrey, 'Archbishop Aribert II of Milan', *History*, 51 (1966), 4; R. I. Moore, 'Family, community and cult on the eve of the Gregorian Reform', *TRHS*, 30 (1980), 62.

5. Gregory VII, *Epistolae Vagantes*, ed. and trans. H. E. J. Cowdrey (Oxford, 1972), 19.

6. Registrum, Lib. iii, No. 10a and 'Contra illos' Lib. viii, No. 21, trans. in *Readings in European History*, 2 vols, ed. J. H. Robinson (Boston, Mass. 1904–18) i, 282 and 284.

7. D. L. D'Avray, *The preaching of the friars: sermons diffused from Paris before 1300* (Oxford, 1985), 18–21.

8. The linking of the movement with a sudden collapse of authority is associated with Georges Duby outlined in his *Les Trois Ordres ou l'imaginaire du féodalisme* (Paris, 1978); the millenarian aspects of the movement were explored in R. Head and R. Landes (eds), *The Peace of God: social violence and religious response around the year 1000* (Ithaca, 1992) especially in Landes's own article 'Between aristocracy and heresy: popular participation in the Limousin Peace of God, 994–1003', 184–218. R. I. Moore has made many comments on the Peace movement, but in his *First European Revolution, c.970–1215* (Oxford, 2000) he stressed its importance in the redistribution of power over the next two centuries (8–9). A sceptical tone as to both the movement's importance and its apocalyptic nature was given by D. Barthélemy's *La mutation de l'an mil: a-t-elle eu lieu?* (Paris, 1997), 300–61 and his article 'La paix de Dieu dans son contexte (989–1041)', *Cahiers de civilisation médiévale*, 40 (1997), 3–36. Many of my comments are drawn from these.

9. See A. G. Remensnyder, 'Pollution, purity and peace: an aspect of social reform between the late tenth century and 1076' in Head and Landes, op. cit., 283–7.

10. Rodulfus Glaber, *Opera*, ed. and trans. J. France, N. Bulst and P. Reynolds (Oxford, 1989), 194–7.

11. *Gesta Francorum*, ed. Hill, Book 2, ch. viii: Baudri of Dol and Guibert of Nogent for preaching. See also P. J. Cole, *Preaching of the Crusade to the Holy Land, 1095–1270* (Cambridge, Mass., 1991), 5–37.

12. D. C. Munro, *Translations and Reprints from the Original Sources of European History*, vol. 1, no. 4, ed. D. C. Munro (Philadelphia, 1896), 8. 'Letters of the

Crusaders' from 'Annales Sancti Disibodi', ed. G. Waitz in MGH *SS* vol. 17 (Hanover, 1861), 17.

13. J. L. Cate, 'The Crusade of 1101' in *A History of the Crusades*, ed. K. M. Setton, 5 vols (Pennsylvania, 1958), vol. 1, 346–9, 366.

14. C. E. Boyd, *Tithes and Parishes in Medieval Italy: the historical roots of a modern problem* (Ithaca, N.Y., 1952), 99–100.

15. G. Constable, 'Resistance to Tithes in the Middle Ages' in *JEH*, 13 (1962), 179.

16. John of Salisbury, *Letters*, eds W. J. Millor, S. J. and H. E. Butler and C. N. L. Brooke, 2 vols (London and Oxford, 1955–79), 5–6. Cited by E. Mason, 'The role of the English parishioner, 1100–1500' in *JEH*, 27 (1976), 19–20.

17. C. N. L. Brooke, 'The missionary at home: the Church in the towns, 1000–1500' in *Studies in Church History*, 6; *The Mission of the Church and the propagation of the faith*, ed. G. J. Cuming (Cambridge, 1970), 66, 69–70.

18. Morris, op. cit., 295, J. Becquet, 'La paroisse en France aux XIe et XIIe siècle' in *Atti della sesta settimana internazionale di studio, Milano, 1–7 settembre, 1974: Le istituzioni eclesiastiche della "societas christiana" dei secoli xi–xii: diocesi, pievi e parrochie* (Milan, 1976), 202–3, J. H. Mundy, 'The Parishes of Toulouse from 1150 to 1250' in *Traditio*, 46 (1991), 172–4, S. Reynolds, *Kingdoms and Communities in western Europe, 900–1300* (Oxford, 1984), 93–4.

19. *Histoire de Carcassonne*, eds J. Guilaine and D. Fabre (Toulouse, 1990), 67–9, 73–4.

20. Carcassonne, *PL* 151, col. 418, cited in Becquet, op. cit., 204. Cahors, *PL* 151, cols 424–5.

21. Boyd, op. cit., 158–9 and n. 9.

22. Reynolds (1984), op. cit., 93–4, Boyd, op. cit., 145. See also J. W. Brown, *The Dominican church of Santa Maria Novella at Florence* (Edinburgh, 1902).

23. Brooke, 'Religious sentiment and church design in the later middle ages' in *Medieval Church and Society* (London, 1971), 163–7, Morris, op. cit., 298–9.

24. J. D. C. Fisher, *Christian Initiation: baptism in the medieval West: a study in the disntegration of the primitive rite of Initiation* (London, 1965), 102–4 and 109–10.

25. Brooke, op. cit., 73. In Milan communion of infants may well have continued into the fifteenth century (Fisher, op. cit., 106).

26. Rupert of Deutz, 'De Divinis Officiis', *PL* 170, col. 112 for worries about infant deaths and damnation. In addition to Fisher, outlines of the development of baptism are given by J. Dellany in the *Dictionnaire de Théologie Catholique*, t. 2 (Paris, 1932), 250–96 and by P. Torquebiau in *Dictionnaire de Droit Canonique*, t. 2 (Paris, 1937) esp. 275–6.

27. A. Angenendt, *Geschichte der Religiosität im Mittelalter* (Darmstadt, 1997), 469.

28. L. L. Mitchell, 'Confirmation' in *DMA*, 535–6.

29. Morris, op. cit., 381. P. F. Palmer, ed. *Sources of Christian Theology*: vol. 2 *Sacraments and forgiveness* (Westminster, Maryland, 1959), 296–8.

30. A. Murray, 'Confession before 1215' in *TRHS*, 6th series, vol. 3 (1993), 73–4, 79.

31. C. N. L. Brooke, *The Medieval Idea of Marriage* (Oxford, 1989), 126–43.

32. M. Searle and K. W. Stevenson, *Documents of the Marriage Liturgy* (Collegeville, Minnesota, 1992), 12–13, 148–54, 115–16.

33. R. I. Moore, 'Family, community and cult on the eve of the Gregorian reform' in *TRHS*, 30 (1980), 63; Boyd, op. cit., (quoting Gratian), 139–40.

34. Becquet, op. cit., 212; M. Chibnall, 'Monks and pastoral work: a problem in Anglo-Norman history' in *JEH*, 18 (1967), 171.

35. Glaber, op. cit., 86–7.

36. N. Housley, 'Pilgrimage' in *DMA*, vol. 9, 654–61. S. Runciman, 'The pilgrimages to Palestine before 1095' in Setton (ed.), (1958) op. cit., vol. 1, 68–78.

37. D. Carrasco, 'Those who go on a sacred journey: the shapes and diversity of pilgrimages' in *Concilium*, 4 (1996), 13–14.

38. Carrasco, ibid., 20–1.

39. Housley, op. cit., 656, 659. E. Cohen ' "*In haec signa*": pilgrim-badge trade in southern France' in *Journal of Medieval History*, 2 (1976), 194, 196–7.

40. Cohen, op. cit., 194–5; D. Webb, *Pilgrims and Pilgrimage in the medieval West* (London, 2001), 46. Cf. St Æbbe's shrines at Coldingham in R. Bartlett (ed.), *The Miracles of St Æbbe of Coldingham and St Margaret of Scotland* (Oxford, 2003). For Glasgow see the 'Life of St Kentigern' by Joceline of Furness, ed. A. P. Forbes in *The Historians of Scotland*, vol. 5 (Edinburgh, 1874).

41. R. Landes, *Relics, apocalypse and the deceits of history* (Cambridge, Mass., 1995), 58–63.

42. Landes, ibid., 237–46, 255. The monks' greed is cited, 64, n. 62. Cf. Moore, (1980) op. cit., 52 and the same author's 'Literacy and the making of heresy, 1000–1150' in Biller and Hudson, 27–8.

43. L. C. Bethmann (ed.), 'Chronicon S. Andreae Castri Cameracesii', lib. 3 in *MGH SS*, vol. 17, 540, trans. in Moore, *The Birth of Popular Heresy* (London, 1975), 24–6.

44. C. Dereine, 'Les prédicateurs "apostoliques" dans les diocèses de Thérouanne, Tournai, et Cambrai-Arras durant les années 1075–1125' in *Analecta Praemonstratensia*, 59 (1983), 173–5.

45. Dereine, ibid., 175–8, 185–6.

46. Dereine, ibid., 182–5.

47. D. Nicholas, *Medieval Flanders* (Harlow, 1992), 58–9, 91.

48. *Codex Udalrici* in *Monumenta Bambergiensis*, 296–300, ed. P. Jaffé (Berlin, 1869) trans. WEH, 96–100 and Moore, op. cit., 29–31. Also two versions of the *Vita Norberti*, ed. R. Wilmans in *MGH SS* XII, 690–1, partly trans. in Moore, op. cit., 31–2 and a section in *Sigiberti Gemblacensis chronographia: Continuatio Praemonstratensis*, ed. L. C. Bethmann in *MGH SS* VI, 449, trans. in WEH, 100–1.

49. *Actus pontificum Cenomannis in urbe degentium*, eds G. Busson and A. Ledru (Le Mans, 1901), 407–15, trans. in WEH, 108–14.

50. Moore, op. cit., 38.

51. *Gesta Treverorum: additamentum et continuatio prima* 20, ed. G. Waitz in *MGH SS*, 8, 193, trans. in WEH, 105–7.

52. *Vita Norberti* in Moore, op. cit., 31–2 and WEH, 673, n. 12.

53. *Bulletino dell'Istituto storico Italiano*, 65 ed. R. Manselli (1953), 36–62, trans. Moore, op. cit., 46–60.

Chapter 2

1. S. Packard, *Twelfth Century Europe; an Interpretive Essay* (Amherst, 1973), 20.

2. P. Spufford, *Money and its use in medieval Europe* (Cambridge, 1988), 95–6, 109–11.

3. G. W. Grantham, 'Espace priviligiés: productivité agraire et zones d'approvisionnement des villes dans l'Europe pré-industrielle' in *Annales*, 52 (1997), 695–725. Grantham's mathematical model suggests that a town of 50 000 could be fed from a radius of 36.8 km, assuming a yield of eight hectolitres per hectare. The soils of Flanders produced 35 per hectare, 702.

4. N. J. G. Pounds, *An economic history of medieval Europe*, 2nd edn (Harlow, 1994), 101–2.

5. Charter of Lorris, trans. in D. Herlihy, *Medieval Culture and Society* (New York, 1968), 177–80.

6. B. Geremek, 'The Marginal Man' in J. Le Goff (ed.), *The Medieval World* (London, 1990), 365–6.

7. C. Dyer, *Standards of Living in the Middle Ages* (Cambridge, 1989), 199.

8. D. F. Harrison, 'Bridges and economic development, 1300–1800' in *Economic History Review*, 45 (1992), 240–61; J. Masschaele, 'Transport costs in medieval England' in *Economic History Review*, 46 (1993), 266–79; M. Cook, *Medieval Bridges* (Princes Risborough, 1998). For European evidence see below n. 15.

9. R. S. Lopez and I. W. Raymond (eds.), *Medieval Trade in the Mediterranean World* (New York, 1955), 109–14, 352n. C. Dyer, 'The consumer and the market in the late middle ages' in *Economic History Review*, 42 (1989), 310.

10. Dyer, (1989) op. cit., 62–3.

11. The one anomaly here is Venice, which was undoubtedly rich, though lying outside the 'banana', but since most of its trade originated from or was destined for the 'banana', it is less of an exception than it first appears.

12. Runciman, *CEHE*, vol. 3, 146, Pounds, op. cit., 365–8.

13. J. E. Tyler, *The Alpine Passes* (Oxford, 1930), 8, 18, 163. Y. Renouard, 'Les voies de communication entre France et le Piémont au moyen âge' in *Bullettino storico Biblio-Grafico Subalpino*, vol. 61 (1963), 233–56.

14. R. S. Lopez, *CEHE*, vol. 3, 374, I. H. Ringel, 'Der Septimer. Zur verkehrsgerechten Erschliessung einer Passstrasse im Mittelalter' in *Die Erschliessung des Alpenraums für den Verkehr* (Bolzano, 1996), 269.

15. *The Itinerary of Benjamin of Tudela*, ed. and trans. M. N. Adler (London, 1907), 3–5. See also A. Roach, 'The Relationship of the Italian and Southern French Cathars, 1170–1320' (unpublished Oxford D.Phil. thesis, 1990), 62–95, for much of what follows, although I have modified my views.

16. C. Devic and J. Vaissète, *Histoire Générale de Languedoc*, ed. A. Molinier *et al.* (Toulouse, 1886–7), vol. 6, cols 14–17, 263–6.

17. A. Dupont, *Les Relations commerciales entre les Cités maritimes de Languedoc et les Cités méditerranéennes d'Espagne et d'Italie du Xème au XIIème siècles* (Nîmes, 1942), 122–3, K. L. Reyerson, *Business, Banking and Finance in medieval Montpellier* (Toronto, 1985), 11, Pounds, op. cit., 368.

18. *Notai Liguri del secolo XII: (4) Oberto da Mercato*, ed. M. Chiaudano (Genoa, 1940), 130–1, 40–1, respectively.

19. J. Combes, 'Les foires en Languedoc au moyen age' in *Annales ESC*, vol. 13 (1958), 233–4.

20. P. Wolff, 'Les luttes sociales dans les villes du Midi français XIII^c–XV^c siècles' in *Annales ESC*, 2 (1947), 444; J. C. Russell, *Medieval Regions and their Cities* (Newton Abbott, 1972), 156, 68–70.

21. J. H. Mundy, *The Repression of Catharism at Toulouse: the Royal diploma of 1279* (Toronto, 1985), 13–17: Devic and Vaissète, op. cit. vol. 8, cols 364–5, 439–40, vol. 6, cols 380–1. Combes, op. cit., 247.

22. Combes, op. cit., 235–6.

23. Moore, *The First European Revolution, c.970–1215* (Oxford, 2000), 105–6.

24. Herlihy, 'Treasure hoards in the Italian economy' in *Economic History Review*, 10 (1957), 1–14; Fulbert, letter 113 to Hildegarius, *PL* 141, cols 261–2.

25. C. H. Lawrence, *Medieval Monasticism: forms of religions life in Western Europe in the Middle Ages*, 2nd edn (London, 1989), 108, J. F. Benton (ed.), *Self and Society in Medieval France: the memoirs of abbot Guibert of Nogent* (Toronto, 1970), 60–3.

26. B. Scott James (ed.), *The Letters of St Bernard of Clairvaux*, 2nd edn (Stroud, 1998) no. 118.

27. Bernard, *Letters*, Scott James (ed.), no. 137.

28. P. Zerbi, 'I rapporti di S. Bernardo di Chiaravalle con i vescovi e le diocesi d'Italia' in *Vescovi e diocesi in Italia nel medioevo (sec IX–XIII)*, Atti del II convegno di storia della chiesa in Italia (Roma, 5–9 sett, 1961), (Padova, 1964), 219–315, esp. 257–8.

29. D. S. Buczek, '"Pro defendendis ordinis": the French Cistercians and their enemies' in *Studies in Medieval Cistercian History presented to J. F. O'Sullivan*, Cistercian Studies Series, 13 (Shannon, IR, 1971), 88–109. Walter Map, *De Nugis Curialium*, eds M. R. James, C. N. L. Brooke, R. A. B. Mynors (Oxford, 1983), 73–113.

30. Figures calculated from Table 3 in D. Herlihy, 'Church Property on the European Continent, 701–1200' in *Speculum*, 36 (1961), 105.

31. Guillaume de Puylaurens, *Chronique*, ed. J. Duvernoy (Paris, 1976), 40–5.

32. C. Lansing, *Power and Purity: Cathar heresy in medieval Italy* (Oxford, 1998), 27–8.

33. S. Bonde, *Fortress Churches of Languedoc* (Cambridge, 1994), 66–94.

34. J. H. Mundy, 'Charity and social work in Toulouse, 1100–1250' in *Traditio*, 22 (1966), 236–7, 208 n. 14.

35. Roach, op. cit., 101–2. Tentative estimates, based on *vidas*. See below notes 43 and 44.

36. John of Salisbury, *Policraticus*, ed. and trans. M. F. Markland (New York, 1979), 10–12.

37. L. Paterson, *The World of the Troubadours* (Cambridge, 1993), 114–15.

38. Paterson, ibid., 113.

39. For a detailed version of this and what follows, see Roach, op. cit., 96–128.

40. Paterson, op. cit., 99.

41. Roach, op. cit., 97–8.

42. J. Boutière and A. H. Schutz, *Biographies des Troubadours* (Paris, 1964), 560–1, 351–5 respectively.

43. *The Poems of the troubadour Raimbaut de Vaqueiras*, ed. J. Linskill (The Hague, 1964), 31, 108–16 and see J. Longnon, 'Les troubadours à la cour de Boniface de Montferrat et en Orient', *Revue de Synthèse*, 23 (1948), 45–60.

44. The seven who left for Italy besides Aimeric were Folquet de Romans, Guilhem Augier Novella, Albertet (de Sisteron), Peirol, Elias Cairel, Guilhem de la Tor, Guilhem Figueira. See Roach, op. cit., 109 for details of patrons and references.

45. Boutière and Schutz, op. cit., 425–31 and *The Poems of Aimeric de Péguilhan*, eds W. P. Shepard and F. M. Chambers (Evanston, Illinois, 1950), 8–19.

46. Boutière and Schutz, op. cit., 250–1.

47. W. Burgwinkle, *Love for Sale: Materialist Readings of the Troubadour Razo Corpus* (New York, 1997), 121–4. For the theory that the two 'Ucs' are one and the same see ibid., 136.

48. F. Zufferey, 'Un document relatif à Uc de Saint Circ à la Bibliothèque Capitulaire de Trevise' in *Cultura Néolatina*, 24 (1974), 9–14.

49. Burgwinkle, op. cit., 46 and *Annali genovesi di Cafaro e suoi continuatori*, ed. C. Imperiale, vol. 3 (Rome, 1923), 26.

50. Notably D. de Rougemont, *L'amour et l'occident*, 2nd edn (Paris, 1956), 68–76, trans. as *Passion and Society* (London, 1956) and R. S. Briffault, *Les Troubadours* (Paris, 1945) trans. (New York, 1965), 147–57.

51. 'Un sirventes novel vueill comensar' in R. Lavaud (ed.), *Poésies complètes du trobadour Peire Cardenal* (Toulouse, 1957), no. 36, 222–7.

52. The three most likely candidates are: Aimeric de Péguilhan, see n. 47 above, Uc de Saint Circ, whose conviction for usury came with an injunction to pay as much for his usury as for heresy, and Peire Cardenal, whose use of Cathar vocabulary and discussion of theological issues was quite daring, without displaying any heretical commitment. See Roach, op. cit., 119–20, 116–17 respectively.

53. J. Sumption, *The Albigensian Crusade* (London, 1978), 59–60, Boutière and Schutz, op. cit., 32–3.

54. Peire Vidal, *Poesie*, ed. D'A. S. Avalle, 2 vols (Milan, Naples, 1960), vol. 1, 95–6, *Estat ai gran sazo*.

55. R. Harvey, 'Courtly culture in medieval Occitania' in S. Gaunt and S. Kay, *The Troubadours: an Introduction* (Cambridge, 1999), 20, Peter of les Vaux-de-Cernay, *History of the Albigensian Crusade*, trans. W. A. and M. D. Sibly (Woodbridge, 1998), 13, G & L, vol. 1, 16.

56. Roach, op. cit., 120, 171–2.

57. R. W. Southern, *Scholastic Humanism and the Unification of Europe*: vol. 1 *Foundations* (Oxford, 1995), 142–3.

58. Hugh of St Victor, *Didascalicon*, trans. J. Taylor (New York, 1961), 62, 74–9. R. N. Swanson, *The Twelfth-century Renaissance* (Manchester, 1999), 29.

59. John of Salisbury, *Metalogicon*, trans. D. D. McGarry (Berkeley, 1962), 98.

60. Southern, op. cit., 267–9.

61. Abelard, *Sic et Non*, eds B. Boyer and R. McKeon (Chicago, 1976), 101.

62. M. T. Clanchy, *Abelard: a medieval life* (Oxford, 1997), 304–6, *The Letters of Abelard and Heloise*, trans. B. Radice (London, 1974), 78.

63. Scott James (ed.), op. cit., no. 244 and cf. no. 249 and 327–8.

64. Abelard, *Ethics* (29), (44), trans. P. V. Spade, *Peter Abelard: Ethical Writings* (Indianapolis, 1995).

65. D. Luscombe, *The School of Peter Abelard* (Cambridge, 1969), 136–7, *De Heresi Catharorum* and Ermengaud of Béziers, WEH, 167 and 233, respectively.

66. Radice (trans.), op. cit., 115.

67. Luscombe, op. cit., 62–4.

68. A. Hunt, 'Abelardian ethics and Béroul's *Tristan*' in *Romania*, 98 (1977), 501–39, esp. 506. D. Luscombe, *Peter Abelard's 'Ethics'* (Oxford, 1971), 40 (my translation). Béroul, *The Romance of Tristan*, trans. A. S. Fedrick (London, 1970).

69. *Sancti Bernardi Opera*, VIII, eds J. Leclerq and H. Rochais (Rome, 1977), Letter 190, esp. 18 and 24–5.

70. Review of sources in J. M. M. H. Thijssen, 'Master Amalric and the Amalricians: inquisitorial procedure and the suppression of heresy at the University of Paris', *Speculum*, 71 (1996), 43–65, esp. 46.

71. Caesarius of Heisterbach, *Dialogus miraculorum*, WEH, 259–63.

72. Sources used here besides Caesarius: the Chronicle of Guillaume le Breton in *Société de l'histoire de France*, vol. 210, ed. H. F. Delaborde (Paris, 1882), 230–3; *Chronicon universale anonymi Laudunensis*, ed. G. Waitz, in *MGH Scriptores* (26), 454; the Lord's Prayer is translated in WEH, 731 n. 19. The Melrose Chronicle is cited in G. Dickson, 'The burning of the Amalricians' in *JEH*, 40 (1989), 350 n. 11.

73. Thijssen, op. cit., 43.

74. Caesarius, op. cit., 259.

75. Amiens incident in *Chronicon . . . Laudunensis*, 454. The fragmentary text of interrogations is given in Thijssen, op. cit., 57–8; 'usque ad V annos omnes homines erunt spirituales' in *Contra Amaurianos*, ed. C. Baeumker (Münster, 1926), 51.

Chapter 3

1. D. Obolensky, *The Byzantine Commonwealth* (London, 1971), 217.

2. Obolensky, ibid., 103–4. M. Angold, *Church and Society in Byzantium under the Comneni* (Cambridge, 1995), 170–1. J. Shepard, 'Bulgaria: the other Balkan "empire"' in *New Cambridge Medieval History*, vol. 3, *c.900–1024*, ed. T. Reuter (Cambridge, 1999), 569–79.

3. R. Morris, *Monks and laymen in Byzantium, 843–1118* (Cambridge, 1995), 25–6, 116–17. J. V. A. Fine, *The Early Medieval Balkans* (Ann Arbor, Michigan, 1983), 169.

4. J. and B. Hamilton, *Christian Dualist Heresies in the Byzantine World, c.650–c.1405* (Manchester, 1998), 116–17, 130. An attempt to redate Cosmas's account to the thirteenth century has largely been rejected. See M. Dando, 'Peut-on avancer de 240 ans la date de composition du traité de Cosmas le prêtre contre les Bogomiles?' in *Cahiers d'études cathares*, 34 (1983), 3–25.

5. Hamilton, op. cit., 132, 129, 121–2 respectively.

6. Hamilton, op. cit., 132.

7. Hamilton, op. cit., 98–102 and Intro., 25.

8. Peter of Sicily in Hamilton, op. cit., 67. P. Stephenson, *Byzantium's Balkan Frontier* (Cambridge, 2000), 47.

9. Hamilton, op. cit., 148–9. The pit under the altar for the priest's bodily functions seems unlikely, but the allegation that the heretics had built a church complete with paintings and icons is even more incredible, given our state of knowledge of dualist heresy in both East and West.

10. Stephenson, op. cit., 87–8. Some historians doubt the connection with Bulgarian heresy; see M. Angold, *Church and Society in Byzantium under the Comneni, 1081–1261* (Cambridge, 1995), 476, and E. Hösch, 'Kritische Anmerkungen zum gegenwärtigen Stand der Bogomilenforschung' in *Kulturelle Traditionen in Bulgarien: Bericht uber das Kolloquium der Südosteuropa-Kommission 16–18 Juni. 1987*, eds R. Lauer and P. Schreiner (Göttingen, 1989), 103–15. M. G. Pegg, *The Corruption of Angels: the great inquisition of 1245–46* (Princeton, 2001), shares their opinion (15–16) and has a useful round-up of bibliographic material, 144–6.

11. P. Magdalino, 'The Pen of the Aunt: Echoes of the mid-Twelfth Century in the *Alexiad*' in T. Gouma-Peterson (ed.), *Anna Komnene and her Times* (New York, 2000), 34–5.

12. Anna Comnena, *Alexiad*, trans. E. R. A. Sewter (London, 1969), 497–504 and Hamilton, op. cit., 175–80.

13. Hamilton, op. cit., Zigabenus, 191, 193–4; Anna Comnena, op. cit., 175.

14. Hamilton, op. cit., 175, 178, 179 (Anna): 193, 203 (Zigabenus).

15. Hamilton, op. cit., 183–7, esp. 185 for Zigabenus's implicit acceptance of demons.

16. Magdalino, op. cit., *passim*.

17. Hamilton, op. cit., 203–4, Angold, op. cit., 487.

18. WEH, 132, 168. *PL*, vol. 182, col. 180 and see below n. 35.

19. J. Ebersolt, *Orient et Occident: Récherches sur les influences Byzantines et orientales en France avant et pendant les croisades* (Paris, 1954), 53–5 and *Acta sanctorum ordinis S. Benedicti: saeculum VI*, pt. 1 (Paris, 1701), 153–60 and 371–6.

20. Benjamin, *The Itinerary of Benjamin of Tudela*, ed. and trans. M. N. Adler (London, 1907), 3–5, M. Hendy, '"Byzantium, 1081–1204": the economy revisited, twenty years on' in his *Economy, Fiscal administration and coinage of Byzantium*, III (Northampton, 1989), 22, A. Harvey, *Economic Expansion in the Byzantine Empire: 900–1200* (Cambridge, 1989), 238–9.

21. M. Angold, *The Byzantine Empire, 1025–1204* (Harlow, 1984), 250. A. Ducellier, 'L'Albanie entre Orient et Occident aux Xie et XIIe siècles: aspects politiques et économiques' in *Cahiers de Civilisation Médiévale*, 19 (1976), 4–5. See also B. Primov, 'The spread and influence of Bogomilism in Europe' in *Byzantino Bulgarica*, 6 (1980), 325.

22. K. Ciggaar, *Western travellers to Constantinople: the West and Byzantium, 962–1204: cultural and political relations* (Leiden, 1996), 275.

23. WEH, 86–9.

24. WEH, 74–6.

25. WEH, 139, *PL*, vol. 181, cols 1721–2 and *Annales Monastici*, vol. 1, ed. H. R. Luard (London, 1864), 15. See also G. Lobrichon, 'The chiaroscuro of heresy: early eleventh century Aquitaine as seen from Auxerre' in R. Head and R.

Landes (eds), *The Peace of God: social violence and religious response around the year 1000* (Ithaca, 1992), 80–103 and C. Taylor, 'The letter of Héribert of Périgord as a source for dualist heresy in the society of early eleventh-century Aquitaine' in *Journal of Medieval History*, 26 (2000), 313–49. Moore's *'manichaeus ex machina'* (Head and Landes, op. cit., 324, n. 41) may well have been present, but flopped.

26. Hamilton, op. cit., 227–9 (Nicholas of Methone?), 225–7 (Life of Hilarion of Moglena) and Intro., 41–2. By analogy there may well have been some real heretics in Constantinople, just as there were some genuine Communists in 1950s America. Anna's emphasis on Alexius's cool, rational approach would have contrasted with the hysteria which seems to have seized Manuel's court. See Magdalino, op. cit., 15, 35–6.

27. WEH, 140–1, E. Martène & U. Durond (eds.) *Veterum scriptorum et monumentorum . . . amplissima collectio* 9 vols (Paris, 1724–33), I, 776–8.

28. WEH, 127–31, *PL*, 182, col. 677 and see R. I. Moore, *Origins of European Dissent* (London, 1978), 168–72.

29. R. I. Moore, *The Birth of Popular Heresy* (London, 1975), 80–2.

30. WEH, 245–7, William of Newburgh, *Historia Rerum Anglicanum*, ed. R. Howlett, 4 vols (London, 1884–9), I, 131–4. Other refs Ralph of Coggeshall, WEH, 252, *Chronicon Anglicanum*, ed. J. Stevenson (London, 1875), 122; Annals of Tewkesbury in *Annales Monastia*, ed. H. R. Luard (London, 1864), I, 49.

31. Peter the Venerable's tract in *PL* 189, cols 719–850, prefatory letter trans. in Moore, op. cit., 60–2.

32. B. Scott James (ed.), *The Letters of St Bernard of Clairvaux*, 2nd edn (Stroud, 1998), 388–9 and Sermon 65 on the *Song of Songs* translated in WEH, 132–8.

33. Geoffrey of Auxerre, *Vita Prima*, *PL* 185, cols 410–13, trans. in Moore, op. cit., 41–5.

34. Moore, op. cit., 43.

35. Moore, op. cit., 45–6.

36. Scott James, op. cit., 389–91 (Letter 318).

37. Hamilton, op. cit., 194 and see B. Hamilton, 'Wisdom from the East: the reception by the Cathars of Eastern dualist texts' in Biller and Hudson, 38–42.

38. Barber, *Cathars*, 79–80.

39. Barber, op. cit., 41 and 51.

40. Jordan of Saxony, *On the beginnings of the Order of Preachers*, ed. S. Tugwell (Dublin, 1982), 7.

41. There are three accounts of the mission to Toulouse of 1178: Roger of Hoveden, *Chronica*, ed. W. Stubbs, Rolls Series 51 (1868–71), ii, 150–5, trans. WEH, 194–200; Peter of St Chrysogonus (Pavia), *PL* 199, cols 1119–24, trans. Moore, op. cit., 113–16; Henry of Clairvaux, *PL* 204, cols 235–40, trans. Moore, op. cit., 116–22.

42. Barber, op. cit., 65–6.

43. J. H. Mundy, 'Parishes' in *Traditio* (1991), 183, 202–3.

44. Moore, op. cit., 114, *PL* 199, col. 1121.

45. John of Salisbury, *Historia Pontificalis*, ed. and trans. M. Chibnall (London, 1956), 63–5. Otto of Freising, *Deeds of Frederick Barbarossa*, trans. C. C. Mierow (New

York, 1953), 142–4, also in WEH, 148–50. Still valuable is G. W. Greenaway, *Arnold of Brescia* (Cambridge, 1931).

46. Scott James, op. cit., 331 (Letter 251).

47. Moore, op. cit., 68–71, P. Jaffé (ed.), *Bibliotheca Rerum Germanicarum*, I (Berlin, 1864), 335–6, 539–43.

48. Otto of Freising in WEH, 149.

49. WEH, 150.

50. P. Jones, *The Italian City-State, 500–1300* (Oxford, 1997), 337–9.

51. M. Lambert, *The Cathars* (Oxford, 1998), 43–4; WEH, 170–3; *PL* 204, 775–7.

52. WEH, 696, n. 6. Disputed, but, since loyalty is a virtue, the sense must surely be that dogs are sprung from the blood of the murdered, innocent brother.

53. WEH, 697.

54. *AASS*, eds G. Henschenio and D. Papebrochio (Paris, Rome, 1866), 20 April, 590–1.

55. A. Dondaine, 'La hiérarchie cathare en Italie, I: Le "De Heresi Catharorum in Lombardia"' in *AFP*, 19 (1949), 306–12, reprinted in his *Les hérésies et l'Inquisition, XIIe–XIIIe siècles*, III (Aldershot, 1990), WEH, 160–7.

56. A. Dondaine, 'La hiérarchie cathare en Italie, II: Le "Tractatus de hereticis" d'Anselme d'Alexandrie, O. P. III: Catalogue de la hiérarchie cathare d'Italie' in *AFP*, 20 (1950), 308–24, reprinted in his *Les hérésies et l'Inquisition* IV, trans. in WEH, 168–70.

57. G. Barni, 'Dall'eta comunale all'eta Sforzesca' in *Storia di Monza e della Brianza*, eds A. Bosisio and G. Vismara, 4 vols, I (Milan, 1973), 198–201.

58. A-F. Frisi, *Memorie storiche di Monza e su corte*, 4 vols, II (Milan, 1794), 67 and 57–8 respectively.

59. B. Hamilton, 'The Origins of the Dualist Church of Drugunthia' in *Eastern Churches Review*, 6 (1974), 115–24 and see discussion in Barber, op. cit., 7, n. 3.

60. For the embarrassment see Salvo Burci, in Ilarino da Milano, 'Il "Liber supra stella" del Piacentino Salvo Burci contro i catari e altre correnti ereticali' in *Aevum*, 19 (1945), 309, WEH, 270: location of Cathar groups, Raynerius Saccone, 'Summa', in A. Dondaine (ed.), *Liber de duobus principiis* (Rome, 1939), 70, WEH, 337.

61. The document was first published by G. Besse in his *Histoire des ducs, marquis et comtes de Narbonne* (Paris, 1660), 483–6, from a manuscript which has never been found. A strong case was made for its authenticity by B. Hamilton in 'The Cathar council of Saint Félix reconsidered' in *Archivum Fratrum Praedicatorum*, 48 (1978), 23–53, but Besse was a notorious forger of sources and the reader notes with unease his effortless reproductions of documents dating back to Carolingion times. Nevertheless, if Besse did fake the document then it is certainly one of his better efforts. There is nothing else quite like it, orthodox or heretical. The most valuable section of Hamilton's article is the breaking down of the Council into three component parts which suggests that even if the published document was a product of Besse's imagination, he was working from documented information which was not. For further discussion see Barber, op. cit., 7, n. 3. The text is published in the Hamilton article and there is a partial translation in J. and B. Hamilton, op. cit., 250–2. Pegg, op. cit., thinks it a thirteenth-century forgery, 146.

62. *La Vie de Saint Alexis*, ed. M. Perugi (Geneva, 2000), trans. N. V. Durling in T. Head (ed.), *Medieval Hagiography* (New York, 2001), 321–40.

63. E. Cameron, *Waldenses: rejections of Holy Church in medieval Europe* (Oxford, 2000), 13, dismisses the story as a *topos* found in many saints' lives (see the example of Aibert of Crespin in ch. 1 above), but no one, not even his own followers, considered Valdes a saint and the story appears in a hostile source. It would coincide with the contemporary fashion for street minstrels. See above ch. 2, 21.

64. N. Reveyron, *Primatial Church of Saint John the Baptist* (Lyon, 1997), 7–8; P. Spufford, *Money and its use in medieval Europe* (Cambridge, 1988), 213.

65. *Histoire de Lyon*, eds A. Pelletier and J. Rossiaud, 2 vols, I (Le Coteau, 1990), 319–21, L. K. Little, *Religious Poverty and the Profit Economy in Medieval Europe* (London, 1978), 120–1.

66. A. Patschovsky, 'The literacy of Waldensianism from Valdes to *c*.1400' in Biller and Hudson, 115.

67. The two main sources for Valdes's conversion are the *Chronicon universale anonymi Laudunensis* in *MGH SS*, XXVI, 447–9 and Richard of Poitiers, *Vita Alexandri Papae III* in G. Gonnet (ed.), *Enchiridion Fontium Valdensium* (Torre Pellice, 1958), 164–6.

68. *Chronicon universale*, 448, trans. WEH, 201–2. For the idea that the archbishop may well have sympathised with Valdes, see M. Rubellin, 'Au temps où Valdès n'était pas hérétique: hypothèses sur le rôle de Valdès à Lyon (1170–83)' in M. Zerner (ed.), *Inventer l'hérésie?* (Nice, 1998), 209–12.

69. WEH, 203–4. There is supporting evidence for Map's point of view from Geoffrey of Auxerre in Gonnet, op. cit., 46–8.

70. Gonnet, op. cit., 29–30.

71. *Chronicon universale*, 449–50. F. Andrews, *The Early Humiliati* (Cambridge, 1999), 38–42, 44–7.

72. WEH, 204–8, A. Dondaine, 'Aux origines du Valdéisme: une profession de foi de Valdès' in *AFP*, 16 (1946), 231–2.

73. *Chronicon universale*, 449.

74. Gonnet, op. cit., 50–3.

Chapter 4

1. *Herigeri et Anselmi Gesta episcoporum Leodensium*, II, 62–4 in *MGH SS* VIII, 226–8 trans. in WEH, 89–93.

2. WEH, 100: see above ch. 1, n. 48.

3. Gonnet, *Enchiridion*, 50–3.

4. Text in *Die Register Innocenz' III. 2. Pontifikatsjahr, 1199/1200 Texte*, ed. O. Hageneder *et al.*, (Rome, Vienna, 1979), 3–5. See also M. Bévenot, 'The Inquisition and its antecedents, III' in *Heythrop Journal*, 8 (1967), 63–5.

5. Peter of les Vaux-de-Cernay, *History of the Albigensian Crusade*, trans. W. A. and M. D. Sibly (Woodbridge, 1998), 36–8.

6. Caesarius of Heisterbach, *Dialogus miraculorum*, book v, ch. 21 and see Barber, *Cathars*, 211, n. 20. William of Tudela and Anon, *Chanson de la*

Croisade Albigeoise, ed. H. Gougaud (Paris, 1989), laisse 21, 64, trans. as *Song of the Cathar wars*, trans. J. Shirley (Aldershot, 1996), 21.

7. Ibid., laisse 36, 82, *Song*, 27.

8. Bram, Peter of les Vaux-de-Cernay, *History*, 78–9; G & L, 148–9; Lavaur, Gougaud (ed.), op. cit., laisses 67–71, 118–26, *Song*, 41–3; Toulouse, Gougaud (ed.), op. cit., laisses 787–93, 134–40, *Song*, 45–7.

9. Statutes of Pamiers, *Histoire Générale de Longuedoc*, eds C. Devic and J. Vaissète, plus tard E. Roschach and A. Molinier *et al.*, 16 vols (Toulouse, 1872–1904), reiussued (Osnabruck, 1973), vol. 8, cols 630, 634, trans. in Peter of les Vaux-de-Cernay *History*, Appendix H, 325, 329.

10. Gougaud (ed.), op. cit., laisse 151, 238, *Song*, 82.

11. J. Sumption, *The Albigensian Crusade* (London, 1978), 218–24.

12. Gougaud (ed.), op. cit., laisse 204, 484–5 (my translation). See A. Roach, 'Occitania past and present: southern consciousness in medieval and modern French politics' in *History Workshop Journal*, 43 (1997), 1–22, M. Barber, 'The Albigensian crusades: wars like any other?' in *Dei gesta per francos. Studies in honour of Jean Richard*, eds M. Balard, B. Z. Kedar and J. Riley-Smith (Aldershot, 2001), 54.

13. G & L, vol. 1, 117–18, trans. Peter of les Vaux-de-Cernay, *Chronicle*, 62–3.

14. J. Costa i Roca, *Xacbert de Barberà: lion de combat, 1185–1275* (Perpinyà/Perpignan, 1989), 51. Cf. A. Peal, 'Olivier de Termes and the Occitan nobility in the thirteenth century' in *Reading Medieval Studies*, 12 (1986), 109–30.

15. M. Lambert, *Medieval Heresy: popular movements from the Gregorian Reform to the Reformation*, 2nd edn (Oxford, 1992), 73.

16. F. Andrews, *The Early Humiliati* (Cambridge, 1999), 69–72.

17. E. Cameron, *Waldenses: rejections of Holy Church in medieval Europe* (Oxford, 2000), 50–7: 1210 rule in Gonnet, op. cit., 136–40, 1212 revision in *PL*, 216, cols 648–50, esp. 648D. My emphasis.

18. M. Gibbs and J. Lang, *Bishops and Reform, 1215–1272* (Oxford, 1934), 179; P. B. Pixton, *The German Episcopacy and the implementation of the decrees of the Fourth Lateran Council, 1216–45: Watchmen on the Tower* (Leiden, 1995), 464.

19. Gougaud (ed.), op. cit., laisse 143, 214–16, *Song*, 72–3.

20. B. Bolton, 'A show with a meaning: Innocent III's approach to the Fourth Lateran Council, 1215' in *Medieval History 1, Bangor: Headstart History, 1991*, 53–67 and also in her *Innocent III: Studies on Papal authority and pastoral care*, XI (Aldershot, 1995).

21. Pixton, op. cit., 193.

22. *PL*, 217, col. 675.

23. *PL*, 217, cols 678–80.

24. *PL*, 217, cols 679–84.

25. *Decrees of the Ecumenical Councils*, ed. N. P. Tanner (Georgetown, 1990), 233–6.

26. Ibid., ch. 1, n. 30.

27. Jordan of Saxony, *Libellus de Principiis Ordinis Praedicatorum*, ed. H. Scheeben in *MOPH*, 16 (Rome, 1935), no. 92, trans. as *On the Beginnings of the Order of Preachers*, by S. Tugwell (Dublin, 1982). *Miracles of St Dominic by the Bl. Cecilia*, ed. A. Walz in *APF*, 37 (1967), 30–1, trans. in S. Tugwell (ed.), *Early*

Dominicans: selected writings (Mahwah, NJ, 1982), 391–2. Canonisation proceedings, Tugwell, ibid., 75.

28. Tugwell, ibid., 73, Walz, *AFP* (37), 43 and see M.-H. Vicaire, *Histoire de saint Dominique*, 2 vols, II (Paris, 1982), 271–4.

29. Jordan, op. cit., no. 20. For Durand, see Guillaume de Puylaurens, *Chronique*, 55.

30. Jordan, op. cit., nos 24–5, Peter of les Vaux-de-Cernay, *Chronicle*, 20, Guillaume de Puylaurens, *Chronique*, ed. J. Duvernoy (Paris, 1976), 56–9 and see Vicaire, op. cit., vol. 1, 218–19. Only Jordan has the miracle, but all sources agree on the lay adjudicators' indecision.

31. Jordan, op. cit., no. 33.

32. Jordan states that he stayed (*Libellus* nos 31 and 33), but there is no other record of him over that period, and there is a strong possibility that a subprior would return to his diocese for the election of a new bishop. My thanks to Dr Simon Tugwell for pointing this out.

33. Jordan, op. cit., no. 27.

34. Peter of les Vaux-de-Cernay, *History*, Appendix, 297 and *Monumenta Diplomatica S. Dominici*, ed. V. Koudelka, *MOPH*, 25 (Rome, 1966), 22–3.

35. Jordan, op. cit., no. 34.

36. Jordan, op. cit., no. 47ff.

37. R. F. Bennett, *The Early Dominicans* (Cambridge, 1937), 39–51 still seems convincing, but see Tugwell, op. cit., 112, n. 80, Vicaire, op. cit., vol. 1, 349–50, vol. 2, 176–8, W. Hinnebusch, *History of the Dominican Order* (New York, 1965), 154–7.

38. W. L. Wakefield, *Heresy, Crusade and Inquisition in Southern France*, 1100–1250 (London, 1974), 229 n. 20, 139, 192, n. 4.

39. Although the confession that he enjoyed the conversation of young women was suppressed in 1242 for the next seven centuries. Hinnebusch, op. cit., 118, n. 191.

40. Bennett, op. cit., 169.

41. Thomas of Celano, 'Vita Prima', ch. 6, 290, trans. as 'Life' in *FAED*, vol. 1, 182–96.

42. Ibid., 295–7, *FAED*, vol. 1, 201–2.

43. The image concurs with the physical description given by Thomas of Celano, ibid., 358–9, *FAED*, vol. 1, 253; see also E. Duffy, 'Finding St Francis: early images, early lives', in P. Biller and A. J. Minnis (eds) *Medieval Theology and the Natural Body* (York, 1997), 193–236.

44. 'Regula non bullata', ibid., 186–7, 'Earlier Rule' in *FAED*, vol. 1, 64–5, 69–70 and 79.

45. C. H. Lawrence, *The Friars: the impact of the early mendicant movement on western society* (Harlow, 1994), 43–4, 47.

46. Lawrence, op. cit., 41–2, Jacques de Vitry in *FAED*, vol. 1, 579, Franciscan women in 'Compilatio Assisiensis', *Fontes*, 1581: 'Assisi Compilation', *FAED*, vol. 2, 177.

47. Thomas of Celano, 'Vita', *Fontes*, Greccio, 359–62, preaching, 348: 'Life', *FAED*, vol. 1, 254–7 and 244–5 respectively.

48. Thomas of Celano, 'Vita', *Fontes*, crowd hysteria, 337–8, birds, 333–4, 'Life', *FAED*, vol. 1, 236–8 and 234 respectively.

49. Germany, J. B. Freed, *The Friars and German society in the Thirteenth Century* (Cambridge, MA, 1977), 26; France, Jordan of Giano and Honorius's letter, *FAED*, vol. 1, 559–60.

50. Thomas of Celano, 'Vita', *Fontes*, 320: 'Life', *FAED*, vol. 1, 223. 'Testamentum', *Fontes*, 227: 'Testament', *FAED*, vol. 1, 125.

51. Thomas of Celano, 'Vita', *Fontes*, 305–7, 348–50: 'Life', *FAED*, vol. 1, 210–12, 245–6.

52. 'Testamentum', *Fontes*, 230: 'Testament', *FAED*, vol. 1, 126.

53. Thomas of Celano, 'Vita', 'Regula Bullata', *Fontes*, 361, 171–81: 'Life', 'Later Rule', *FAED*, vol. 1, 256, 99–106 respectively.

54. 'Canticum fratris solis', *Fontes*, 39–40: 'Canticle', *FAED*, vol. 1, 113–14.

55. Thomas of Celano, 'Vita', *Fontes*, 376: 'Life', *FAED*, vol. 1, 269.

56. Thomas of Celano, 'Vita', *Fontes*, 369–71: 'Life', *FAED*, vol. 1, 263–4.

Chapter 5

1. Thomas of Celano, 'Vita', *Fontes*, 389: 'Life', *FAED*, vol. 1, 279.

2. 'Testamentum', *Fontes*, 230–1: 'Testament', *FAED*, vol. 1, 126–7.

3. 'Regula Bullata', *Fontes*, 171–2: 'Later Rule', *FAED*, vol. 1, 100.

4. *FAED*, vol. 1, 570–5.

5. M. Robson, *St Francis of Assisi* (London, 1997), 269, notes how little record we have of contemporary criticism of the new basilica.

6. J. R. H. Moorman, *A History of the Franciscan Order from its origins to the year 1517* (Oxford, 1968), 96–104, Thomas 'of Eccleston', *Tractatus de Adventu Fratrum Minorum in Angliam*, ed. A. G. Little (Manchester, 1951), 67–9, G. Merlo, 'Storia di frate Francesco e dell'ordine dei Minori' in *Francesco d'Assisi e il primo secolo di storia francescana*, ed. M. P. Alberzoni *et al.* (Torino, 1997), 22.

7. Moorman, op. cit., 100, Merlo, op. cit., 23.

8. F. Andrews, *The Early Humiliati* (Cambridge, 1999), 222.

9. Andrews, op. cit., 192–8, C. Morris, *The Papal Monarchy: the Western Church from 1050 to 1250* (Oxford, 1989), 468–70.

10. C. H. Lawrence, *The Friars: the impact of the early mendicant movement* (Harlow, 1994), 112–16; G. Casagrande, 'Un ordine per I laici. Penitenza e Penitenti nel Duecento' in Alberzoni *et al.*, op. cit., 237–47; 'Anonymi Perusini', *Fontes*, 1345: 'The Anonymous of Perugia' in *FAED*, vol. 2, 54–5, cf. 'Legenda trium sociorum', *Fontes*, 1432–3: 'Legend of the Three Companions', *FAED*, vol. 2, 103.

11. For much of what follows see A. Roach, 'The Cathar Economy', *Reading Medieval Studies*, 12 (1986), 51–71, although my views have changed somewhat; see Further Reading.

12. 'Provençal ritual' in WEH, 492, L. Clédat (ed.) *Le Nouveau Testament traduit au XIIIe siècle en langue Provençale scrivi d'un rituel cathare* (Paris, 1887), xxii–xxvi; M. G. Pegg, *The Corruption of Angels: the great inquisition of 1245–46* (Princeton, 2001), 93–4.

13. Doat MS 21:189r, 202r, 220r; 22:14v, 55v.

14. M. Lambert, *The Cathars* (Oxford, 1998), 148: Doat MS 22:194r–5r: W. L. Wakefield, 'The family of Niort in the Albigensian Crusade and before the Inquisition' in *Names*, 18 (1970), 97–117, 286–303.

15. Doat MS 21:293v.
16. For Waldensian medical knowledge, e.g. Doat MS 21:201v, 232v–33r, 233v–34r, and see P. Biller, '*Curate infirmos*: the medieval Waldensian practice of medicine' in *The Church and Healing*, ed. W. J. Sheils (Oxford, 1982), reprinted in his *The Waldenses, 1170–1530* (Aldershot, 2001), 49–67. Easter Day debate Doat MS 21:208v, others Doat MS 21:196–7, 232–33, 250v.
17. Doat MS 21:242, Geralda de Biele was in a similar situation with a Cathar sister and niece, 21:250r.
18. Creation, Doat MS 21:263; preferring Waldensians, 21:201; views on sacraments, etc. 21:217; approval of both groups, 21:232, 208, 204, 241–2, etc. Some of the evidence in ns. 16–18 is printed in H. C. Lea, *A History of the Medieval Inquisition in the Middle Ages*, 3 vols (London, 1888), vol. 2, Appendix.
19. Guillaume de Puylaurens, *Chronique*, ed. J. Duvernoy (Paris, 1976), 55–6, Doat MS 21:187v, 241v *et al.*, Pegg, op. cit., 112 respectively.
20. Doat MS 25:38v–39r.
21. Barber, *Cathars*, 96–7, Doat MS, 21:203v.
22. Barber, op. cit., 79: Pegg, op. cit., 116–17: Thomas of Celano, 'Vita', *Fontes*, 338: 'Life', *FAED*, vol. 1, 238: James Capelli (attrib.), in *Disputationes nonnullae adversus haereticos*, ed. D. Bazzocchi (Bologna, 1920), CL, trans. in WEH, 305, F. E. Brightman, *The English Rite*, 2 vols, 2nd edn, vol. 2 (London, 1921), 1044.
23. Cemeteries: Guillaume de Puylaurens, op. cit., 30: Cathar houses, Barber, op. cit., 35, 40, 75: Pegg, op. cit., 118–19.
24. Doat MS 21:321r: Doat MS 24:137r: Durand of Huesca, *Une Somme anti-cathare: le 'Liber contra Manicheos'*, ed. C. Thouzellier (Louvain, 1964), 120–1.
25. Lambert, op. cit., 140–1, cf. Pegg, op. cit., 102–3.
26. Doat MS 24:173v, 22:153r, and cf. M. Barber, *The New Knighthood* (Cambridge, 1994), 267–8.
27. Loans: Doat MS 21:188r, 201v, 239r, 246r, 23:166r, 183v–4r, 24:265r, 282v. *Depositarii* 21:144r–5v, 189r–v, 208v, 198r–v: *munuscula*, etc. 21:187v–88r, 205v–6r, 197r.
28. Doat MS 24:22v–23r and cf. G. Rosser, 'Crafts, guilds and the negotiation of work' in *Past and Present*, 154 (1997), 3–31.
29. Mariano D'Alatri, *L'Inquisizione Francescana nell'Italia centrale del Duecento* (Rome, 1996), 176, 210–17. See also C. Lansing, *Power and Purity: Cathar heresy in medieval Italy* (Oxford, 1998), 66–7.
30. 'Yves of Narbonne', in Matthew Paris, *Chronica Maiora* (7 vols) ed. H. R. Luard (Rolls Series, LVII, London, 1872–83) vol. 4, 270–7, WEH, 185–7, but see J. Duvernoy, *Le catharisme: II L'Histoire* (Toulouse, 1979), 184–5. I translate 'rabiolae' as 'pastries' rather than 'raisins' or 'rissoles' (WEH, 702, n. 5). Alfred Hoare's Italian dictionary (Cambridge, 1915) has 'rabiolae', 'some kind of sweetmeat' as the 'base Latin' source, later than the fifth century, for the modern Italian 'raviolo'. This is a very rare word for most of Paris's readers, who would probably only know it in its Latin context, but given that Yves is in Italy then something like 'ravioli' with a cheese or sweet filling would not be unlikely. The accusation that the heretics ate meat would be too good for Yves to miss, yet he makes nothing of it, so I rule out meat-filled pasta.

31. Nazario appears in the accounts of Raynerius Saccone, *Summa de Catharis et Pauperibus de Lugduno*, ed. A. Dondaine in *Un Traité néo-manichéen* (Rome, 1939), 76–7, Anselm of Alessandria, ed. A. Dondaine, 'La Hiérarchie cathare en Italie, I: Le Heresi Cathororum in Lombardia' in *AFP*, 19 (1949), 307–8 and Moneta of Cremona, *Adversus Catharos et Valdenses*, ed. T. Ricchini (Rome, 1743), 248. See also WEH, 344, 362–3, 752 n. 10 respectively. See also for the discussion that follows, Biller & Hudson, esp. articles by Hamilton and Paolini.

32. Dondaine (1939), op. cit., 70–1, *WEH*, 337.

33. *Secret* in WEH, 458–65, *Vision*, 449–56, esp. 450, *Book of Two Principles*, 515–91. See also Biller and Hudson, op. cit., 56, n. 89 and 101.

34. H. Rashdall, *The Universities of Europe in the Middle Ages*, eds. E. M. Powicke and A. B. Emden, 3 vols, vol. 2 (Oxford, 1936), 1–37 and see map from *Grosser Atlas zur Weltgeschichte*, H-E. Stier *et al.* (Munich 1990), 23. The leading dualist master in Orvieto was a Lombard, C. Lansing, *Power and Purity: Cathar heresy in medieval Italy* (Oxford, 1998), 31.

35. T. Ripoll, *Bullarium Ordinis Fratrum Praedicatorum*, vol. 1 (Rome, 1729), 254.

36. Salvo Burci in WEH, 270, Raynerius *WEH*, 337. Thomas 'of Eccleston', Little, op. cit., 11.

37. This implies that the religious movements of the thirteenth century were 'scale-free' networks and that from 1250 contemporaries were starting to be aware of it. See P. Ormerod and A. P. Roach, 'The medieval Inquisition: scale-free networks and the suppression of heresy' in *Physica A*, 339 (2004), 645–52. For an overview of the subject see A.-L. Barabási and E. Bonabeau's article in *Scientific American*, vol. 288, no. 5 (2003), 50–9. Capelli, WEH, 302–3 and the unreliable extracts printed in I. V. Döllinger, *Beitrage zur Sektengeschichte des Mittelalters*, 2 vols, vol. 2 (Munich, 1890), 278–9.

38. A. Dondaine, 'Durand de Huesca et la polémique anti-cathare' in *AFP*, 24 (1959), 268–70, WEH, 231–3. Bee eater: scientific name *merops apiaster*, C. H. and K. Fry, *Kingfishers, Bee Eaters and Rollers* (Princeton, 2000), 154.

39. B. Hamilton, 'Wisdom from the East: the reception by the Cathars of Eastern dualist texts' in Biller & Hudson, 52–3, Durand of Huesca, *Une somme anti-cathare: Le 'Liber contra manichaeos'*, ed. C. Thouzellier (Louvain, 1964), 138–9, 210–11, Hamilton, op. cit., 263–4.

40. Doat MS 22:67r–v. And see P. Biller, 'The Cathars of Languedoc and written materials' in Biller & Hudson, op. cit., 75–7.

41. G & L, vol. 1, 7–20; *History*, Peter of les Vaux-de-Cernay, 9–15.

42. G & L, ibid. 16, Peter of les Vaux-de-Cernay, ibid., 13.

43. Doat MS 23:270r.

44. Doat MS 22:233r–235v, 24:54r.

45. W. L. Wakefield, *Heresy, Crusade and Inquisition* (Berkeley, 1974), 169–73.

46. Doat MS 24:179r–80r, Guillaume de Puylaurens, *Chronique*, 186, Doat MS 24:171v. M. Baigent, R. Leigh, H. Lincoln, *The Holy Blood and the Holy Grail* (London, 1982), 49–58, most famously advanced the case for Cathar possession of the Holy Grail, without a shred of evidence.

47. E. Cameron, *Waldenses: rejections of Holy Church in medieval Europe* (Oxford, 2000), is sceptical about an early presence in Germany, 98. For Piacenza see Dondaine, op. cit., 273–4.

48. WEH, 715, n. 7 and Stephen of Bourbon in *Quellen zur Geschichte der Waldenser*, eds A. Patschovsky and K.-V. Selge (Gütersloher, 1973), 47.

49. After the proceedings of the Cathars at Saint Félix, this is probably the second most awkward document of medieval heresy. While its authenticity has not been questioned there are a number of variant readings leading to confusion. Should, for instance, 'massarius of Verona' be treated as a proper name or an absconded 'treasurer'? More worryingly, why does the writer repeatedly call the 'carta' quoted by the French, false, while incorporating its text into the agreement? Clearly there is more to be discovered here. I have used the edition in Patschovsky and Selge, op. cit., 20–43. See also WEH, 278–89.

50. Described as 'perverse Doctor of the Lombards', according to Moneta of Cremona, op. cit., 403.

51. Pegg, op. cit., 187, n. 4, P. Biller, '*Curate infirmos*: the medieval Waldensian practice of medicine' in *The Church and Healing*, ed. W. J. Sheils (Oxford, 1982), 61–3, Stephen of Bourbon, WEH, 346–51.

52. Salvo Burci, WEH, 272–3 ed. Ilarino du Milano, *Aevum*, 19 (1945), 317; Raynerius, WEH, 345–6.

53. Cameron, op. cit., 73–4.

54. Morris, op. cit., 458.

55. Jordan's letter translated in S. Tugwell OP, *Early Dominicans: selected writings* (New York, 1982), 122–5: preaching restrictions, A. Thompson, *Revival Preachers and Politics in Thirteenth Century Italy* (Oxford, 1992), 103: prison, R. B. Pugh, *Imprisonment in medieval England* (Cambridge, 1968), 376–7.

56. Gerard de Frachet, *Lives of the Brethren*, trans. P. Conway (London, 1955), 124.

57. Thompson, op. cit., 29–79 is the main source of information on the 'Alleluia'.

58. Parisio of Cerea, *Annales Veronenses*, ed. P. Jaffé, *MGH SS*, 19 (Hanover, 1866), 8 and see Thompson, op. cit., 71.

Chapter 6

1. *De Civitate Dei*, ed. J. E. C. Welldon, 2 vols, 2 (London, 1924), 396; Bk. 18, ch. 54: *Sermones*, ed. C. Lambot, *Corpus christianorum: series Latina*, no. 41 (Brepols, 1961), no. 46, chs 22–3, 548–50. See P. Brown, 'Religious coercion in the later Roman Empire: the case of North Africa' in his *Religion and Society in the age of Saint Augustine* (New York, 1972), 315.

2. *Epistolae*, no. 185, ch. 7, ed. A. Goldbacher, *Corpus Scriptorum Ecclesiasticorum Latinorum*, vol. 57 (Leipzig, 1911), 6, trans. as *Letters*, vol. 4, by W. Parsons, in the *Fathers of the Church* series (Washington, 1955), 148.

3. Roman penalties for heresy are conveniently summarised in *Theodosiani Libri xvi cum constitutionibus Sirmondianis*, eds P. Krueger and T. Mommsen (Berlin, 1954), 16:5:52, 872–3, trans. as *The Theodosian Code and novels and the Sirmondian Constitutions*, ed. C. Pharr (New York, 1952), 459.

4. J. A. Brundage, *Medieval Canon Law* (Harlow, 1995), 94–5, 147–50: J. H. Arnold, *Inquisition and Power* (Philadelphia, 2001), 30.

5. M. Lambert, *The Cathars* (Oxford, 1998), 118–21; Alberic des Trois Fontaines, *Chronica*, ed. P. Schefer-Boichorst, *MGH SS* 23, 931–2 (brief John of Vicenza ref. 933), *Gesta Treverorum*, ed. H. Cardauns, *MGH SS* 24, 400–2, trans. *WEH*, 267–9; new edn of Gregory's commission to Conrad of Oct. 11, 1231 by L. Kolmer in P. Segl (ed.), *Die Anfänge der Inquisition* (Köln, 1993), 190–3.

6. Ripoll, *Bullarium*, I, 45–6.

7. The symbolic significance of Robert's choice of centres of heresy first reported in the mid twelfth century has been brought out in Malcolm Barber's as yet unpublished article, 'Northern Catharism'. My thanks to Prof. Barber for letting me see a draft.

8. The classic article on Robert is C. H. Haskins, 'Robert le Bougre and the beginnings of the inquisition in northern France' in his *Studies in Medieval Culture* (New York, 1929), 212–17, 225–7; Alberic, *Chronica*, 940 and 944–5, Philippe Mousket, *Historia Regum Francorum*, ed. A. Tobler, *MGH SS* 26, 804–6, Matthew Paris, *Historia Anglorum*, and *Abbreviatio Chronicorum Anglie*, ed. F. Madden, Rolls Series, 44, 3 vols (London, 1869), vol. 2, 338, 415; vol. 3, 278, respectively. Gerard de Fracheto, *Vitae fratrum Ordinis Praedicatorum*, ed. Reichert (Rome, 1897), 292.

9 E. Graham-Leigh, 'Hirelings and shepherds. Archbishop Berengar of Narbonne (1191–1211) and the ideal bishop' in *English Historical Review*, 116 (2001), 1083–102.

10 K.-V. Selge (ed.), *Texte zur Inquisition* (Gütersloh, 1967), 45–6.

11. Selge, ibid., 30.

12. Ripoll, *Bullarium*, I, 47–8.

13. There are parallels here with the enthusiastic response for the perils of a mission to the Cumans in 1253. Gerard de Frachet, *Lives of the Brethren*, trans. P. Conway (London, 1955), 135–6.

14. Guilhem Pelhisson, *Chronicle*, trans. in W. L. Wakefield, *Heresy, Crusade and Inquisition, 1100–1250* (Berkeley, 1974), 228–33 and see Wakefield's own account, 140–9.

15. Innocent III, in *PL*, 214, cols 537–9. See also M. Bévenot, 'The Inquisition and its Antecedents' in *Heythrop Journal* 7, 3 (1966), 257–68; 7, 4 (1966), 381–93; 8, 1 (1966), 52–69; 8, 2 (1966): 152–68 and H. Maisonneuve, *Etudes sur les origines de l'inquisition* (Paris, 1960), 151–98, 243–368. Imperial legislation in Selge, op. cit., 35–40, esp. 40.

16. Thomas Aquinas, *Summa Theologiae*, 2. 2. Q11. [a]3, Benziger Bros., edn 1947 in Christian Classics Ethereal Library, Calvin College, Grand Rapids, Michigan, on website: http://www.ccel.org. *Theodosiani Libri*, 9:21:5, 473, trans. *Theodosian Code*, 243.

17. Guillaume de Puylaurens, *Chronique*, ed. J. Duvernoy (Paris, 1976), 160–1.

18. A. Dondaine, 'Le Manuel de l'inquisiteur (1230–1330), *AFP*, 17 (1947)', 88–9, 99, also in his *Les hérésies et l'Inquisition, XIIᵉ–XIIIᵉ siècles*, III (Aldershot, 1990), *WEH*, 160–7.

19. Trans. in Wakefield, op. cit., 252–3.

20. Council of Narbonne, Mansi, *Concilia*, xxiii, 356–7.

21. Doat MS 21: 196r–v, 18r–v.

22. J. H. Mundy, 'Charity and social work in Toulouse, 1100–1250' in *Traditio*, 22 (1966), 209–10, n. 19.

23. Council of Béziers, Mansi, *Concilia*, xxiii, 721, cap. 28.

24. *Monumenta diplomatica Sancti Dominici*, ed. V. J. Koudelka (*MOPH* xxv, 1966), 17–18. I am grateful to Dr Simon Tugwell for allowing me to look at his unpublished edition of the text. See also M. G. Pegg, *The Corruption of Angels: the great inquisition of 1245–46* (Princeton, 2001), 126–7.

25. In Italy attitudes to cross-wearing were often still more casual. See C. Lansing, *Power and Purity: Cathar heresy in medieval Italy* (Oxford, 1998), 146–7.

26. *Rule of Saint Benedict*, ed. and trans. J. McCann (London, 1952), ch. 25, 75; C. Douais, 'Saint Raymond de Peñafort et les hérétiques: directoire à l'usage des inquisiteurs aragonais, 1242' in *Moyen Âge*, 12 (1899), 317.

27. A. Roach, 'Penance and the making of the Inquisition' in *JEH*, 52 (2001), 426.

28. Pegg, op. cit., 40–3, e.g. Wakefield, op. cit., 238–9.

29. For confiscation see Mansi, *Concilia*, vol. 23, cols 719–21; P. Timbal 'La confiscation dans le droit français de xiiie et de xive siècles' in *Revue historique de droit français et d'étranger*, 22 (1943), 44–79 and 23 (1944), 35–60. Generally, see J. Given, *Inquisition and medieval society: power, discipline and resistance in Languedoc* (Ithaca, NY, 1997), 62–5, 79–83.

30. G. W. Davis, *The Inquisition at Albi, 1299–1300* (Columbia, 1948), 281–2.

31. J. Given, 'The inquisitors of Languedoc and the Medieval technology of power' in *American Historical Review*, 94 (1989), 336–59, Pegg, op. cit., 28, Moneta, *Adversus Catharos*, ed. T. Ricchini (Rome, 1743), lib. V, cap. 13, 509.

32. For inquisition in Orvieto see Lansing, op. cit., 57–9. For confraternities and Peter in Florence see Lambert, op. cit., 177, 182–3 and J. Duvernoy, *Le catharisme: II L'Histoire*, (Toulouse, 1979), 180–3.

33. Ripoll, *Bullarium*, I, 192–3.

34. E. Peters, *Torture* (Oxford, 1985), 44–60; K. Pennington, *The Prince and the Law, 1200–1600* (Berkeley, California, 1993), 156–60.

35. R. Fraher, 'Preventing Crime in the Middle Ages: the medieval lawyers' search for deterrence' in *Popes, Teachers and Canon Law in the Middle Ages*, eds J. R. Sweeney and S. Chodorow (Ithaca, NY, 1989), 230; Pennington, ibid., 41–2.

36. *Ad extirpanda*, Mansi, *Concilia*, 23, cols 571–5, *Ut negotium fidei* in H. C. Lea, *A History of the Inquisition in the Middle Ages*, 3 vols (London, 1888), vol. 1, 575 and *Magnum Bullarium Romanum*, ed. L. Cherubini, 8 vols, vol. 1 (Luxemburg, 1727), 132.

37. Bernard Gui, WEH, 411 *Manuel de l'Inquisiteur*, ed. G. Mollat, 2 vols (Paris, 1926–7), I, 104–7; Vienna, Peters, op. cit., 60, Given, op. cit., 54.

38. J. Arnold, *Inquisition and Power: Catharism and the confessing subject in medieval Languedoc* (Philadelphia, 2001), 100, citing Doat MS 26: 1215v–16v, 220v–21r.

39. Doat MS 25: 298v–300r for the start of Peire's evidence. *Notai Liguri del secolo XII e del XIII: (6) Lanfranco (1202–26)*, ed. Krueger & Reynolds, I (Genoa, 1952), 120, 209, 234–5, 241–2, 243, 375, 376, 377; for troubadours see above, Ch. 2, 48–9; Boutière and Schutz, *Biographies des Troubadours*

(Paris, 1964) 252–3, 236–8, 434–5, 508–9, 503–4. A. Dupont, *Les Relations Commerciales entre les Cités maritimes de Languedoc et les Cités Mediterranéen d'Espagne et d'Italie du Xème au XIIIème siècles* (Nîmes, 1942), 122–3.

40. Doat MS 25: 299r–304v.

41. Archives Départmentales de la Haute-Garonne, MS 124: 201r, 76v, 210v.

42. Doat MSs 25:322r–v, 26:32r–33r, 25:7v–8r.

43. Lambert, op. cit., 183–5.

44. Ripoll, *Bullarium*, vol. 1, 400–1, 242–3. Haute-Garonne, MS 124: 20r, and see A. Roach, 'Relationship of the Italian and Southern French Cathars' (Oxford, D.Phil., 1990), 170–1, 177.

45. L. Astegiano, *Codex Diplomaticus Cremonae, 715–1334*, 2 vols, vol. 1 (Cremona, 1895–98), 287–8, 290–1; B. Pullan, *History of early Renaissance Italy* (London, 1973), 135. A third treaty with Venice in 1258 strengthened links with the north-east and Adriatic coast, perhaps allowing contact with dualist heretics in eastern Europe.

46. R. S. Lopez, 'Back to Gold, 1252' in *Economic History Review*, 9 (1956–7), 231; 'Le trasformazioni sociali del XIII secolo' in *Storia di Piacenza*, 8 vols, vol. 2 (Piacenza, 1984), 196, 199; Y. Renouard, *Les hommes d'affaires italiens du moyen âge* (Paris, 1949), 66–9.

47. *Annales Placentini Gibellini* in *Monumenta Historica Parmae et Placentiae* (Parma, 1869), 'Chronica Placentinorum', vol. 5, 227–35.

48. N. J. Housley, 'Politics and heresy in Italy: anti-heretical crusades and confraternities, 1200–1500' in *JEH*, 33 (1982), 204.

49. WEH, 369. Dondaine, 'La Hiérarchie cathare', III, 316–17, and see above, 225n.56.

50. 'Chronica Placentinorum', op. cit., 273–4.

51. Verona residents were required to approve the alliance of their lord, Ezzelino da Romano, with Oberto Pallavicini in 1254. These lists give us six people with the name *de Provenza* or *Provenzalus*, the Italian term for all southern French, and three others probably from the Marseilles area. Archivio di Stato di Cremona, Fondo segreto, diplomatico, docs nos 2341, 2346, 2348, 2351, 2352, 2355, 2356, 2360, 2361, 2364, 2367.

52. Doat MS 25: 145r–146r, 25:246r–47v, 26:15v.

53. C. Cipolla, 'Il Patarenismo a Verona nel secolo XIII' in *Archivio Veneto*, vol. 25 (1883), 78–80, Biblioteca Comunale di Verona, MS 815, fol. 24v–25v, Doat MS 32:155r–156v.

54. Doat MS 25:323r, 25:182v–87r, 25:142r–43r respectively. For the Sicilian venture see Duvernoy, op. cit., 301, 303, 308.

55. Doat MS 25:105v, 25:118v, 26:15v respectively.

56. Doat MS 26:23v–4r, 26:16r–19v.

57. Doat MS 25:307v–309r.

58. Doat MS 25:266r; 'quod valde erant boni homines et multum valebat minus terra ista quia non audebant in ea morari.'

Chapter 7

1. J. A. F. Thomson, *The Western Church in the Middle Ages* (London, 1998), 163–5.
2. For instance, *FAED*, vol. 3, 123–37, 110–12.
3. Salimbene de Adam, *Chronicle*, trans. J. L. Baird, G. Baglivi and J. R. Kane (Binghamton, NY, 1986), 215.
4. Salimbene, op. cit., 229–30, B. McGinn (ed.), *Encyclopedia of Apocalypticism*, vol. 2 (New York, 1998), 93.
5. For Joachim's influence on the Franciscans see M. Reeves, *Joachim of Fiore and the Prophetic Future* (London, 1976), 29–31.
6. Salimbene, op. cit., 217–22, esp. 219.
7. Salimbene, op. cit., 226–7.
8. Salimbene, op. cit., 252–62.
9. P. S. Clasen, 'Tractatus Gerardi de Abbatisvilla "Contra adversarium perfectionis christianae"' in *AFH*, 31 (1938), 276–329 and 32 (1939), 89–200, lib. I pt. iii, 304–10. See also D. L. Douie, *The Conflict between the Seculars and Mendicants at the University of Paris in the Thirteenth Century*, Aquinas Paper No. 23 (London, 1954).
10. Clasen, op. cit., *AFH*, 32 (1939), 98–103, 136–40.
11. Clasen, op. cit., *AFH*, 32 (1939), 125 and esp. 197–8.
12. *Defense of the Mendicants*, trans. J. de Vinck (Paterson, NJ, 1966). Food (2nd point of Second Answer), 79–88. Wealth (1st point of Fourth Answer), 220–1.
13. Salimbene, op. cit., 249.
14. Salimbene, op. cit., 477–8, N. J. Housley, 'Politics and Heresy in Italy: anti-heretical crusades and confraternities, 1200–1500' in *JEH*, 33 (1982), 206.
15. Humbert's report in *De corrigendis in ecclesia Latinorum* printed in *Sanctorum Conciliorum et decretorum Collectio Nova: Supplementum ad concilia*, eds. Veneto and Labbeana, 6 vols (Lucca, 1749), vol. 3, cols 1–28. Council legislation in C. J. Hefele (ed.), *Histoire des conciles d'après les documents originaux* (Paris, 1914), vol. 6, pt 1, 181–209.
16. Olivi's *De usu paupere: the Quaestio and the Tractatus*, ed. D. Burr (Florence and Perth, 1992); 'Tractatus', Qs. 9 and 15 are discussed in detail in D. Burr, *Olivi and Franciscan Poverty* (Philadelphia, 1989), 66–73.
17. Jacopone of Todi, *The Lauds*, trans. S. and E. Hughes (London, 1982), 109–14.
18. J. R. H. Moorman, *A History of the Franciscan Order from its origins to the year 1517* (Oxford, 1968), 309–11.
19. B. Borngässer, 'Gothic architecture in Italy' in *The Art of Gothic: architecture, sculpture, painting*, ed. R. Toman (Köln, 1998), 245–6.
20. M. Carlin, 'Fast food and urban living standards in medieval England' in M. Carlin and J. T. Rosenthal (eds), *Food and Eating in Medieval Europe* (London, 1998), 27–51, although I take her point that some of the customers would be too poor to afford their own cooking equipment.
21. P. Chorley, 'The cloth exports of Flanders and northern France during the thirteenth century: a luxury trade?' in *Economic History Review*, 40 (1987), 368–71. R. H. Bautier, *The Economic Development of medieval Europe* (London, 1971), 117–18.

22. N. J. G. Pounds, *An Economic History of medieval Europe*, 2nd edn (London, 1994), 414, Bautier, ibid., 152–3.
23. Pounds, op. cit., 145–7 for population; P. Jones, *Italian city state: from commune to signoria* (Oxford, 1997), 232–4. C. Dyer, *Making a Living in the Middle Ages* (New Haven, 2002), 246–63 offers an up-to-date overview from a British perspective.
24. Dyer, ibid., 195, Reynolds, *Kingdoms* 69–70, quoting G. H. Martin, 'The English borough in the thirteenth century' in *TRHS*, ser. 5, 13 (1963).
25. For Perugia guild see G. G. Meersseman, *Ordo Fraternitatis: Confraternite e Pietà dei Laici nel Medioevo* (Rome, 1977), vol. 2, 1063–6, conveniently translated in J. Shinners (ed.), *Medieval popular religion, 1000–1500* (Peterborough, Ontario, 1997), 300–3. For Norwich see T. Smith (ed.), *English Guilds*, Early English Text Society (London, 1870), 19–21. For use of fraternity for credit checking see G. Rosser, 'Crafts, guilds and the negotiation of work in the medieval town' in *Past and Present*, 154 (Feb. 1997), 3–31.
26. Reynolds, op. cit., 92, Meersseman, ibid.
27. Smith, op. cit., 19. D. R. Dendy, *The Use of Lights in Christian Worship* (London, 1959), 50–3.
28. Reynolds, op. cit., 93–4, Morris, op. cit., 536–7.
29. Fourth Lateran Council, c. 32 and R. A. R. Hartridge, *A History of Vicarages in the middle ages* (Cambridge, 1930), 67–70, for Simplevelt 140–1.
30. M. Rubin, *Corpus Christi: the Eucharist in late medieval culture* (Cambridge, 1991), 60–5.
31. J. D. C. Fisher, *Christian Initiation: baptism in the medieval West: a study in the disintegration of the primitive rite of Initiation* (London, 1965), 123–4.
32. J. A. Brundage, *Law, Sex and Christian Society* (Chicago, 1987), 431–2, 442–4. C. Klapisch-Zuber, 'Zacharias or the ousted father: nuptial rites in Tuscany between Giotto and the Council of Trent' in her *Women, Family and Ritual in Renaissance Italy* (Chicago, 1985), 195.
33. M. Robson, 'A ministry of preachers and confessors: the pastoral impact of the friars' in G. R. Evans, (ed.), *A History of Pastoral Care* (London, 2000), 132; Salimbene, op. cit., 414–15.
34. M. Mansfield, *The Humiliation of Sinners: public penance in thirteenth-century France* (Ithaca, NY, 1995), 71–2.
35. P. Adam, *La Vie Paroissiale en France au XIV siècle* (Paris, 1964), 237–8, B. Poschmann, *Penance and the Anointing of the Sick*, trans. F. Courtney (London, 1964), 243–4.
36. E. Cohen, '"*In haec signa*": pilgrim-badge trade in southern France' in *Journal of Medieval History*, 2 (1976), 193–5, D. Webb, *Pilgrims and Pilgrimage in the medieval West* (London, 2001), 15, Shinners, op. cit., 380.
37. Webb, ibid., 64–6, 77, 89; D. Birch, *Pilgrimage to Rome in the middle ages* (Woodbridge, 1998), 199–201.
38. P. M. Costa, *Guglielma la Boema, l' 'eretica' di Chiaravalle* (Milan, 1985), 34–41.
39. Costa, ibid., 55.
40. L. Muratori (ed.), *Antiquitates Italicae Medii Aevi*, vol. 5 (Milan, 1741), cols 96–110 deal with canonisation proceedings, 111–14 allegations of

the confession, 117–18 the cathedral's defence of Punzilupo, 118–40 the Inquisition interrogations. See also Lambert, op. cit., 281–2 and Lansing, op. cit., 92–5.

Chapter 8

1. C. Erickson, *The Medieval Vision: essays in history and perception* (Oxford, 1976), 198–9. Translated extracts from Jerome and Augustine on virginity and marriage in E. Amt (ed.), *Women's Lives in Medieval Europe: a sourcebook* (New York, 1993), 23–8.

2. J. C. Dickinson, *Origins of the Austin Canons and their Introduction into England* (London, 1950), 137, 142 and 286–99, Barber, *Cathars*, 35.

3. Vicaire, *Saint Dominic and his times* (London, 1964; earlier edn of work cited in ch. 4), 271; N. Georges, *Blessed Diana and Blessed Jordan* (Somerset, Ohio, 1933), 17–19, 25.

4. S. Cohn, *Women in the Streets: essays on sex and power in Renaissance Italy* (Baltimore, 1996), 90–2. S. Epstein, *Genoa and the Genoese, 958–1528* (North Cardina, 1996), 92–4, 117–19, 129–33, 185–6, J. H. Mundy, 'Charity and social work in Toulouse, 1100–1250' in *Traditio*, 22 (1966), 230–1.

5. A. Brenon, *Les femmes cathares* (Paris, 1992), 14, Doat MS 22:9v–10r, WEH, 331, 337.

6. Doat MS 22: 124v–25r, 23, fos 46v–7r respectively.

7. Archives Départmentales de la Haute-Garonne ms 124:76v. Cf. Doat MS vol. 21 fo. 226, vol. 25 fo. 322. In this last case the woman changed her mind about the journey, but her mother was already in Italy as a *perfecta*.

8. S. Murk-Jansen, *Brides in the desert* (London, 1998), 26–7.

9. P. Galloway, 'Neither miraculous nor astonishing. The devotional practice of Beguine communities in French Flanders' in *New Trends in Feminine Spirituality: holy women of Liège and their impact*, eds J. Dor, L. Johnson and J. Wogan-Broune (Amsterdam, 1999), 112–17.

10. Mechtild of Magdeburg, *The Flowing Light of the Godhead*, trans. F. Tobin (New York, 1998), Book V; ch. 13, 191–2. VI; ch. 3, 229–30.

11. B. M. Kienzle, 'The prostitute-preacher: patterns of polemic against medieval Waldensian women preachers' in *Women, preachers and prophets through two millennia of Christianity*, eds Kienzle and Pamela J. Walker (Berkeley, California, 1998), 99–103; Jezebel's career; 3 Kings chs. 16, 18, 21 and 4 Kings 9 (Douai version).

12. P. Biller, 'The preaching of the Waldensian sisters' in his *The Waldenses, 1170–1530* (Aldershot, 2001) esp. 133–7. Biller has reprinted the references from Doat MS vol. 21 fos 228r–v, 248r and 282r–v.

13. A. Blamires, 'Women and preaching in medieval orthodoxy' in *Viator*, 26 (1995), 135–52.

14. The *De Vita et actibus, de fide et erroribus haereticorum, qui se dicunt Pauperes Christi seu Pauperes de Lugduno*, ed. W. Preger, as part of 'Über die Verfassung der französischen Waldesier in der älteren Zeit' in *Abhandlungen der bayerischen Akademie der Wissenschaften*, 19 (1890), 709 and see below ch. 9, n. 27.

15. *De Vita et actibus*, ed. Preger, 709, M. T. Clanchy, *From Memory to Written Record*, 2nd edn (Oxford, 1993), 270; Jacoba; *Fournier*, 512–14 and see below ch. 9, n. 27. Both cases summarised by Biller, op. cit., 137–8.

16. Reims case, Ralph of Coggeshall, *Chronicon Anglicanum*, ed. J. Stevenson (London, 1875), 123, WEH, 252. To this should probably be added Stephen of Bourbon's Waldensian woman 'priest' who must have acquired a degree of maturity and learning, WEH, 348. The question of education of children is in J. H. Mundy, *Men and women at Toulouse in the age of the Cathars* (Toronto, 1990), 38–9, 109–10.

17. D. Herlihy, 'Land, family, and women in continental Europe, 701–1200' in S. M. Stuard (ed.), *Women in Medieval Society* (Pennsylvania, 1976), 25–6, 30. B. Hanawalt, 'Peasant women's contribution to the home economy' in her *Women and work in preindustrial Europe* (Bloomington, Indiana, 1986), 7–8. Cf. R. I. Moore, 'Family, community and cult on the eve of the Gregorian Reform' in *TRHS*, 30 (1980).

18. See above ch. 5, n. 13 and A. Roach, 'The Cathar economy' in *Reading Medieval Studies*, 12 (1986), 62–3.

19. *De vita et actibus*, 711, 709. P. Biller and J. N. Green, 'The *De Vita et actibus pauperum de Lugduno*' in Biller's, *The Waldenses*, 1170–1530 (Aldershot, 2001), 229–30. I translate *agulherios/achalberios* as 'needleboxes'; they could be 'pins'.

20. Murk-Jansen, op. cit., 29–30.

21. *Fontes*, 2500, quoted in C. Gennaro, 'Clare, Agnes and their earliest followers: from the Poor Ladies of San Damiano to the Poor Clares' in *Women and Religion in Medieval and Renaissance Italy*, eds D. Bornstein and R. Rusconi (orig. 1992, trans. Chicago, 1996), 46.

22. J. Coakley, 'Gender and the authority of the friars: the significance of holy women for thirteenth-century Franciscans and Dominicans' in *Church History*, 60 (1991), 445–60.

23. For Clare of Montefalco see E. Menestò, 'The apostolic canonisation proceedings of Clare of Montefalco' in Bornstein and Rusconi (eds), op. cit., 104–29 and L. Mo, 'Public Bodies and Private Spaces: locating cloistered contemplative discourses in female Franciscan spirituality in thirteenth century Umbria' (Ph.D dissertation, University of Glasgow, 2002), 158–80.

24. M. Goodich (ed.), *Other Middle Ages: witnesses at the margins of medieval society* (Philadelphia, Pennsylvania, 1998), 218–19.

25. Menestó, op. cit., 110–12, 121, n. 22.

26. *Fontes*, 2487 (witness 9.3), 'molti beni havemo recevute da questa cità, et imperò devemo pregare Dio che epso la guarde.'

Chapter 9

1. J. A. F. Thomson, *The Western Church in the Middle Ages* (London, 1998), 166–70, J. R. H. Moorman, *A History of the Franciscan Order from its origins to the year 1517* (Oxford, 1968), 265.

2. The only version of the letter which has survived is a summary by the inquisitor Bernard Gui, in *Rerum Italicarum Scriptores (RIS)* IX.5, ed. A. Segarizzi (Città

di Castello, 1909), 19–21 translated into Italian by R. Orioli, *Fra Dolcino; nascita, vita e morte di un'eresia medievale* (Novara, 1988), 117–21.

3. C. Backman, *The Decline and Fall of Medieval Sicily; politics, religion and economy in the reign of Frederick III, 1296–1337* (Cambridge, 1995), 192–9.

4. Gui, *RIS*, 22.

5. 'Historia Fratris Dulcini Heresiarche', *RIS*, 9.

6. L. Paolini and R. Orioli, (eds) *Acta sancti officii Bononie ab anno 1291 usque ad annum 1310: fonti per la storia d'Italia no. 106*, 3 vols, continuous pagination (Rome, 1982), 432.

7. Gui, *RIS*, 25, cf. Bernard Gui, *Practica Inquisitionis*, WEH, 405–7, or Manuel de l'Inquisiteur, ed. G. Mollat, 2 vols (Paris, 1926–7), I, 86–94, 'Historia', *RIS*, 4.

8. Paolini and Orioli, op. cit., 389–90. ' . . . orare, contemplari vitas et passiones sanctorum et, cum est hora necessitatis conmedendi, mendicari et petere ellemosinas et fundamentum vite et status dictorum apostolorum est servare paupertatem et omnia vendere et dare pauperibus et bona propria non habere nec possidere.'

9. Paolini and Orioli, op. cit., 391.

10. 'Ego nolo iudicare, set credo vos pocius bonos quam malos esse.' Paolini and Orioli, op. cit., 407.

11. Paolini and Orioli, op. cit., 423–4.

12. Paolini and Orioli, op. cit., 404–5 and cf. 408.

13. Gui, *RIS*, 22–3: Dante Alighieri, *The Divine Comedy, Hell*, Canto 28, ll. 55–60, ed. and trans. G. L. Bickersteth (Oxford, 1981), 200–3.

14. 'Historia', *RIS*, 5.

15. Gui, *RIS*, 24, cf. *Manual* in WEH, 405–6; Mollat (ed.), op. cit., 88–90.

16. 'Historia', *RIS*, 9–10, Gui, *RIS*, 26–8. For the possible third letter see Orioli, op. cit., 22–3.

17. 'Processo Trentino', *RIS*, 80. The witness is Margarita's brother who suggests she might have escaped death and was living in Vicenza around 1330.

18. 'Waldensianisms', E. Cameron, *Waldenses: rejections of holy church in medieval Europe* (Oxford, 2000), 139, quoting Grado Merlo. Stephen of Bourbon in WEH, 346–51.

19. Stephen of Bourbon, WEH, 348, Cameron, op. cit., 71–8.

20. A. Dondaine, 'La hiérarchie cathare en Italie, II' in *AFP*, 20 (1950), 319. Cf. Francis's 'Testament', '. . . they gave to the poor; and they were content with one tunic . . . with cord and short trousers. And we did not want to have more. The clerks among us said the office like other clerks, the laymen said the "Pater Noster". And I worked with my hands, and I still want to work with my hands. And I certainly wish all the other brothers to work in labour which pertains to honesty. Let those who do not know how to work, learn, not on account of the desire to receive the price of their labour, but because it's an example and to drive away idleness. And when the price of our labour is not given to us, let us return to the Lord's table by seeking alms from door to door.' *Fontes*, 229 (my trans.), *FAED*, 125.

21. Dondaine, ibid., 317–21, M. Lambert, *Medieval Heresy: popular movements from the Gregorian Reform to the Reformation*, 2nd edn (Oxford, 1992), 149–52.

22. Archivio Segreto Vaticano (ASV), Collectoriae 133, fos 28–37, partially edited by G. Biscaro, 'Inquisitori ed eretici Lombardi, (1292–1318),' *Miscellanea Storia*

Italiana, 50 (1922), 503–16; Malixia, fo. 28 (505), James of Lumello 29 (505–6) and cf. fo. 36 on 513 which looks as if Lanfranco describes the case as being Poor of Lyon, Peter of Martinengo, fo. 36 (513).

23. Philippus van Limborch, *Historia Inquisitionis. Cui subjungitur Liber Sententiarum inquisitionis Tholosanae* (Amsterdam, 1692), textile refs 221–2, 224; opposition to clerics, 223, 226; Cameron, op. cit., 78–87.

24. Limborch, ibid., 201, 221, 222; Cameron, op. cit., 82–3.

25. J. Duvernoy (ed.), *Le Registre d'Inquisition de Jacques Fournier*, 3 vols (Paris, 1978), education and Franciscans, vol. 1, 99–102; supporters spinning, vol. 1, 44–5. Cameron, op. cit., 87–92.

26. Duvernoy (ed.), ibid., vol. 1, 512–13, 81 respectively. R. Weiss, *The Yellow Cross* (London, 2000), 256.

27. ASV, Collectoriae 133, fos 29, 37–8, Biscaro, op. cit., 506, 514–15 respectively. The *De Vita et actibus, de fide et erroribus haereticorum, qui se dicunt Pauperes Christi seu Pauperes de Lugduno*, ed. W. Preger, as part of 'Über die Verfassung der französischen Waldesier in der älteren Zeit' in *Abhandlungen der bayerischen Akademie der Wissenschaften*, 19 (1890), 708–11. Redated and located by P. Biller and J. N. Green, 'The *De Vita et actibus pauperum de Lugduno*' in Biller's *The Waldenses, 1170–1530* (Aldershot, 2001), 225–31, 299–300. Bernard Gui, *Practica* in WEH, 393; Mollat (ed.), op. cit., 50–2.

28. Dondaine, op. cit., II, 324.

29. Mariano da Alatri, 'Inquisitori veneti del Duecento' in *Collectanea Francescana*, 30 (1960), 398–452; A. Murray, 'The medieval inquisition: an instrument of secular politics' in *Peritia*, 5 (1986), 161–200.

30. ASV, Collectoriae 133, fos 28–37, Biscaro, op. cit., 503–16. By my calculations, September 1292–June 1295, income exceeded expenditure by just £29 (c.£671/£642). For June 1295–October 1296, the figures are less reliable, but the inquisitor had vastly increased his income and was only required to hand over £18 4s. 11d. Evidence of renewed financial zeal in Boniface's pontificate in T. S. R. Boase, *Boniface VIII* (London, 1933), 126.

31. ASV Collectoriae, fos 29–31, Biscaro, op. cit., 505–8.

32. ASV Collectoriae, fo. 33, Biscaro, op. cit., 510; ASV Collectoriae, fo. 32.

33. ASV Collectoriae, fos 33, 34, 37, Biscaro, op. cit., 510, 511, 514. Also 'Arnaud the Provençal, likewise poor, fos 48 and 51, 521, 523.

34. ASV Collectoriae, fos 32–3, Biscaro, op. cit., 509–10 and see P. Ormerod and A. P. Roach, 'The Medieval Inquisition: scale-free networks and the suppression of heresy' in *Physica A*, 339 (2004), 650–1. I underestimated Lanfranco's expenses there. I now put the cost of the operation at £33 7s. *libri imperiales* plus supplying a vicar to replace Lanfranco in Pavia, the cost of which is not stated.

35. ASV Collectoriae, fo. 30, Biscaro, op. cit., 507. For the Oliba brothers in Pavia in the 1260s see Doat MS, vol. 23, 94r–96r; 25, 303r–4r.

36. Lambert, op. cit., 232–3, Duvernoy (ed.), op. cit., 566–7, 604–5, 609. J-L. Biget, 'L'extinction du catharisme urbaine: les points chauds de la répression in *Cahiers de Fanjeaux*, 20 (1985), 312–15.

37. Lambert, op. cit., 233; I. Von Döllinger, *Beiträge zur Sektengeschichte des Mittelalters* (Munich, 1890), 'Dokumente', 21–3.

38. Döllinger, ibid., 19–20, 27; Lambert, op. cit., 234, 240–1.

39. Döllinger, ibid., 23, 28–9. Biscaro, op. cit., 520–31, esp. 531.

40. See J-L. Biget, 'Un procès d'inquisition à Albi en 1300' in *C de F*, 6 (1971), 273–341, G. W. Davis, *The Inquisition at Albi, 1299–1300* (Columbia, 1948), 165–8, 189–90, S. Bonde, *Fortress Churches of Languedoc* (Cambridge, 1994), 44–6.

41. Davis, ibid., 253–4, 135, 126–7, 131–2 respectively.

42. Duvernoy (ed.), op. cit., 700, Biget, op. cit., 318–19, Lambert, op. cit., 235, J. Mathorez, 'Notes sur les Italiens en France du XIIᵉ siècle jusqu'au régne du Charles VIII', pt. 2, in *Annales de la Faculté des Lettres de Bordeaux: Bulletin Italien*, 7 (1917–18), 86.

43. L. Paolini and R. Orioli (eds), op. cit., vol. 1, 20–1; Lambert, op. cit., 284–5 and Paolini's 'Bonigrino da Verona e sua moglie Rosafiore' in O. Capitani (ed.), *Medoevo ereticale* (Bologna, 1977), 213–16.

44. Paolini and Orioli (eds), ibid., 13–14. Lambert, op. cit., 284–6, C. Lansing, *Power and purity: Cathar heresy in medieval Italy* (Oxford, 1998), 91.

45. M. T. Clanchy, *From Memory to Written Record*, 2nd edn (Oxford, 1993), 266. Dante Alighieri, *De vulgari eloquentia*, ed. and trans. S. Botterill (Cambridge, 1996), 2–3, 20–1, 34–5.

46. L. Paolini and R. Orioli, *L'eresia a Bologna fra XIII e XIV secolo* (Rome, 1975), 172–4, 95. Bompietro's testimony in their *Acta*, 1; op. cit., 31–3. Dissatisfaction at burning of dead, 215.

47. A. Friedlander, *Processus Bernardi Delitiosi: the trial of Fr Bernard Délicieux*, Transactions of the American Philosophic Society, vol. 86, pt 1 (Philadelphia, 1996), 173–4.

48. Gui, *De fondatione et prioribus conventuum*, ed. Amargier (Rome, 1961), 103 quoted in J. Duvernoy, op. cit., 319, my emphasis; ASV, Collectoriae 133, fo. 156, Biscaro, op. cit., 547.

49. 'Ego fr. Franciscus habui necesse emere equos sine quibus inquisitio non potest fieri convenienter in partibus Pedemontis propter loca multum [sic] distancia et periculosa in quibus habitant heretici et Valdenses.' ASV, Collectoriae 133, fo. 149, Biscaro, op. cit., 545; *Fournier*, 985–6, 992.

FURTHER READING

I have concentrated on modern literature in English, mentioning older works and foreign language literature where relevant.

General

The subject of heresy has been well served in recent years and the starting point must be Malcolm Lambert's *Medieval Heresy* (Oxford, 2002), currently in its third edition and rightly termed by one reviewer 'a masterpiece of its kind'. Overshadowing the present volume is the work of R. I. Moore, the most important historian of heresy of his generation. His *Origins of European Dissent* (London, 1978) provided a narrative thread for the arrival of the Cathars amid a climate of dissatisfaction with the Church which still seems a broadly valid interpretation. In subsequent work Moore has emphasised the subjectivity of heresy. His *Formation of a Persecuting Society* (Oxford, 1987) linked the classification of heretics with that of Jews and lepers. More recently he has proposed 970–1215 as *The First European Revolution* (Oxford, 2000), bringing the *clerici* to the forefront of society and all but suggesting that the threat of heresy was largely exaggerated to help this class achieve power. I disagree with this interpretation, but the breadth of vision makes compelling reading. In the last fifteen years two conferences have had an important influence on the direction of heresy studies; the first took place in Oxford in 1992 and was published as *Heresy and Literacy, 1000–1530* (Cambridge, 1994) eds P. Biller and A. Hudson. The second was at York in 2000 and appeared as *Texts and the repression of medieval heresy*, eds C. Bruschi and P. Biller (Woodbridge, 2003). The titles reflect the darkening mood, as heresy specialists become more interested in persecution.

Of older works perhaps the most important is Herbert Grundmann's *Religiöse Bewegungen im Mittelalter* (Berlin, 1935, 2nd edn, Darmstadt, 1961) translated into English as *Religious Movements in the Middle Ages* as late as 1995. In terms of sources for the reader of English an immeasurable debt is owed to W. L. Wakefield and A. P. Evans whose collection *Heresies of the High Middle Ages* (Columbia, 1969) is still in print. By its nature no work of translation will satisfy all readers, but Wakefield and Evans strove hard to be transparent, giving many variant readings in their footnotes. This can be supplemented by R. I. Moore's own collection, *The Birth of Popular Heresy* (London, 1975) and E. Peters, *Heresy and Authority in Medieval Europe* (London, 1980).

Chapter 1

The best account of the medieval Church at this period is Colin Morris's, *The Papal Monarchy: the Western Church from 1050 to 1250* (Oxford, 1989). J. A. F. Thomson's *Western Church in the Middle Ages* (London, 1997) takes a broader overview and has the advantage of being a history of the Church written by a specialist in heresy. Local studies of the Church on the ground in this period are rare. C. E. Boyd's *Tithes and Parishes in Medieval Italy: the historical roots of a modern problem* (Ithaca, NY, 1952) is still valuable as is J. Becquet, 'La paroisse en France aux XIe et XIIe siècle' in *Atti della sesta settimana internazionale di studio, Milano, 1–7 settembre, 1974: Le istituzioni ecclesiastiche della "societas christiana" dei secoli xi–xii: diocesi, pievi e parrochie* (Milan, 1976). The parish as a basic structure of medieval life is considered by Susan Reynolds and her *Kingdoms and Communities in Western Europe, 900–1300* (Oxford, 1984) has valuable comments.

For individual sacraments M. Searle and K. W. Stevenson's *Documents of the Marriage Liturgy* (Collegeville, Minnesota, 1992) is a valuable resource and J. D. C. Fisher, *Christian Initiation: baptism in the medieval West* (London, 1965), a useful commentary. Confession and penance have attracted more attention from historians with *Handling Sin: confession in the middle ages*, eds P. Biller and A. J. Minnis (Woodbridge, 1998) bringing together modern scholarship, to which should be added A. Murray, 'Confession before 1215', *Transactions of the Royal Historical Society* 6th ser. 3 (1993). That having been said, there is no adequate study of the sacraments in the middle ages and readers may have to fall back on the relevant entries in the *Dictionary of the Middle Ages*, ed. J. R. Strayer (New York, 1982–89), the *New Catholic Encyclopedia* (2nd edn, Detroit, 2003) or the learned, if venerable, version online at www.newadvent.org/cathen/ (New York, 1907–14). For pilgrimage documents, commentary and bibliography see D. Webb, *Pilgrims and Pilgrimage in the medieval West* (London, 1999). The article which started me thinking about religion and consumer choice was E. Cohen's study of the economics of pilgrimage, ' "In haec signa": the pilgrim-badge trade in southern France', *Journal of Medieval History*, 2 (1976).

The preachers of the eleventh century attracted much attention from the 1960s to the 1980s, but rather less since. For Milan, H. E. J. Cowdrey's articles on 'Archbishop Aribert', *History*, 51 (1967) and 'The Papacy, the Patarenes and the Church of Milan', *Transactions of the Royal Historical Society* 5th ser. 18 (1968) suggested that early heresy was linked to calls for reform of the Church; Moore's contemporary work suggested a link in France and Flanders. B. Stock's *The Implications of Literacy* (Princeton, 1983) is the most substantial work in English and with its explanation of 'textual communities' gave a powerful tool for the study of later heretical movements. The preachers of northern Europe are put in a different context by C. Dereine, 'Les prédicateurs "apostoliques" dans les diocèses de Thérouanne, Tournai, et Cambrai-Arras durant les années 1075–1125', *Analecta Praemonstratensia*, 59 (1983), who looks closely at how preachers dealt with local clergy and sometimes needed papal protection to avoid charges of heresy. To some extent the study of eleventh-century religion was drawn into work on the first millennium such as T. Head and R. Landes, *The Peace of God: social violence and religious response around the year 1000* (Ithaca, 1992).

Chapter 2

The medieval economy is currently the subject of much debate. Older theories that it was dominated by subsistence are being challenged by views of it as a more sophisticated entity in which markets played a greater role. Because of the preponderance of sources, many of the detailed studies come from Britain. An account of the various theoretical approaches applicable to Britain and Europe can be found in *Modelling the Middle Ages*, by John Hatcher and Mark Bailey (Oxford, 2001). On the growing commercialisation of the economy see R. H. Britnell, *The Commercialisation of English Society* (Cambridge, 1993). The clearest introduction to the medieval European economy, with some relevant material on southern France, is N. J. G. Pounds's *An Economic History of Medieval Europe*, 2nd edn (London, 1994). C. M. Cipolla's *Before the Industrial Revolution*, 3rd edn (London, 1993) has more on Italy.

For the economic and social background to the troubadours see Linda Paterson's *The World of the Troubadours* (Cambridge, 1993). Self-explanatory but no less interesting is *Love for Sale: materialist readings of the troubadours* (New York, 1997) by William E. Burgwinkle on the economics of poetry and performance. Views on the troubadours are changing rapidly, but *The troubadours: an introduction* edited by Simon Gaunt and Sarah Kay (Cambridge, 1999) is a good starting point on current thinking. There are innumerable collections of Provençal verse in translation.

On medieval universities the ancient classic is Hastings Rashdall's *The Universities of Europe in the Middle Ages*, 2nd edn (London, 1936) edited by F. M. Powicke and A. B. Emden, still useful as a work of reference. The biography *Abelard: a medieval life* by Michael Clanchy (Oxford, 1997) is good on all aspects of social context, and Abelard himself is a key source in his *Historia Calamitatum*, translated by Betty Radice in *The Letters of Abelard and Heloise*, new edition by M. T. Clanchy (London, 2003). For the later period there is G. Leff, *Paris and Oxford Universities in the thirteenth and fourteenth centuries* (New York, 1968) and J. W. Baldwin, *Masters, Princes and Merchants*, 2 vols (Princeton, 1970) and also his 'Masters at Paris from 1179 to 1215: a social perspective' in *Renaissance and Renewal in the Twelfth Century*, eds R. L. Benson and G. Constable (Cambridge, Mass. 1982).

Chapter 3

The study of the western Cathars must still start with the Bogomils of the Byzantine Empire. Doubters as to any link with the West include Angold, Pegg and now Moore (see ch. 3 n.10). The most persuasive proponent to the contrary is Bernard Hamilton, whose detailed studies on many aspects of East–West relations appear in his two collections, *Monastic Reform, Catharism and the Crusades* (London, 1979) and *Crusaders, Cathars and the Holy Places* (Aldershot, 1999). The best synthesis is Y. Stoyanov, *The Hidden Tradition in Europe* (London, 1994), republished as *The other God: dualist religions from antiquity to the Cathar heresy* (New Haven, Conn., 2000). Both authors build on the work of D. Obolensky, *The Bogomils* (London, 1948), modified in his article 'Papa Nicetas: a Byzantine dualist in the land of the Cathars', *Harvard Ukrainian Studies*, 7 (1983). An unjustly neglected article by Boris Primov makes some pertinent remarks on heresy and puts them into a wider context of trade and cultural connections: 'The spread and influence of Bogomilism in Europe', *Byzantino Bulgarica*, 6 (1980). Fortunately, the Bogomil sources are now available in scholarly English translation by Janet and Bernard Hamilton as *Christian Dualist Heresies in the Byzantine World, c.650–c.1405* (Manchester, 1998). Recent eastern European work is considered in M. Angelovska-Parova's *Bogomilism in the Macedonian Spiritual Culture* (in Macedonia, Skopje, 2004). There is also a decade's new work on Bulgaria, its relations with Byzantium and its links with the West: Jonathan Shepard's authoritative articles, 'Slavs and Bulgars', and 'Bulgaria: the other Balkan "empire"' in vols 2 and 3 respectively of the *New Cambridge Medieval History* (Cambridge, 1995) should be followed by Paul Stephenson's *Byzantium's Balkan Frontier* (Cambridge, 2000) and K. Ciggaar, 'Western travellers to Constantinople' in her *The West and Byzantium, 962–1204: cultural and political relations* (Leiden, 1996). On Byzantine orthodox religious culture see M. Angold, *Church and Society in Byzantium under the Comneni, 1081–1261* (Cambridge, 1995).

For the Cathars themselves, M. Lambert, *The Cathars* (Oxford, 1998) is a good, scholarly introduction. A more populist approach is taken by Stephen O'Shea, *The Perfect Heresy* (London, 2000). For southern France, Malcolm Barber's *The Cathars: Dualist Heretics in the Middle Ages* (Harlow, 2000) is excellent. Italian Catharism has never been as well covered, although there are some pertinent comments in Lambert. Less easy to compartmentalise than heresy in Languedoc, the Italian scene awaits a historian who can combine a knowledge of heresy with that of the Italian political context. Carol Lansing goes some way towards this, from the perspective of Orvieto, with her *Power and Purity: Cathar heresy in medieval Italy* (Oxford, 1998). Two exhaustive works in other languages should be mentioned: G. Rottenwöhrer, *Der Katharismus*, 4 vols (Bad Honnef, 1982–93) and J. Duvernoy, *Le Catharisme*, 2 vols (Toulouse, 1976–9).

On the Waldensians, G. Audisio's *Les Vaudois* (Turin, 1989) has been translated as *The Waldensian Dissent: persecution and survival: c.1170–1570* (Cambridge, 1999) and Euan Cameron has produced his *Waldenses: rejections of holy church in medieval Europe* (Oxford, 2000). Both are fine works, but the longevity of the Waldensian movement mean that neither author can devote the same attention to this period as writers on Catharism. Peter Biller's very specific studies of aspects of the sect are collected in his *The Waldensians, 1170–1530* (Aldershot, 2001). Beyond this, there is a paucity of scholarship in English. E. S. Davison's *Forerunners of Saint Francis* (London, 1927), comparing saint and heretic, remains perceptive for its time. The most stimulating challenge to current orthodoxy is M. Rubellin, 'Au temps où Valdes n'était pas hérétique' in M. Zerner (ed.) *Inventer l'hérésie* (Nice, 1998).

Chapter 4

All the main sources for the Albigensian Crusade are now available in translation. The remarkable team of W. A. and M. D. Sibly have now added *The Chronicle of William of Puylaurens* (Woodbridge, 2003) to their excellent rendering of Peter of les Vaux-de-Cernay's *Historia Albigensis* as *The History of the Albigensian Crusade* (Woodbridge, 1998).

Janet Shirley has translated the Provençal poem about the crusade as *The Song of the Cathar Wars* (Aldershot, 1996). The best modern secondary work is probably M. D. Costen, *The Cathars and the Albigensian Crusade* (Manchester, 1997), but Jonathan Sumption's *The Albigensian Crusade* (London, 1978) can still be read with profit as a military account of the campaign. J. R. Strayer, *The Albigensian Crusades* (Ann Arbor, Michigan, 1971) looked at the political implications for the French kingdom. The second edition has a useful extended epilogue by Carol Lansing (1992). Historians have long debated to what extent the campaign was really a crusade and the latest contribution is from Malcolm Barber, 'The Albigensian crusades: wars like any other?' in *'Dei gesta per Francos': Etudes sur les croisades dédiées à Jean Richard/Crusade Studies in Honour of Jean Richard*, eds M. Balard, B. Z. Kedar and J. Riley-Smith (Aldershot, 2001). A significant view from the periphery in more senses than one comes from Nicholas Vincent who, although not a historian of heresy, suggests some cogent reasons shaping the attitudes of English chroniclers to reports of heresy in southern France. His essay 'England and the Albigensian Crusade' is in *England and Europe in the Reign of Henry III*, eds B. K. U. Weiler and I. F. Rowlands (Aldershot, 2002). The historiography of the crusade is considered in my 'Occitania past and present: Southern consciousness in medieval and modern French politics', *History Workshop Journal*, 43 (1997).

Dominic

For Dominic and the early Order of Preachers, there is a good collection of sources in translation, *Early Dominicans: selected writings* (New York, 1982) and especially Jordan of Saxony's *On the Beginning of the Order of Preachers* (Dublin, 1982), both produced by Simon Tugwell OP. The standard biography is by M-H. Vicaire OP, *Histoire de Saint Dominique* (Paris, 1957), translated by K. Pond as *Saint Dominic and his Times* (London, 1964). Readers should be aware that Vicaire made substantial amendments to the work and the most recent edition was published in French with a preface by G. Bedouelle as recently as 2004 (Paris). An essential supplement to this are the three substantial 'Notes on the life of St Dominic' by Tugwell in the *Archivum Fratrum Praedicatorum*, vols 65, 66, 67 (1995, 1996, 1997). It is to be hoped that the author will synthesise these articles or publish them in a collected volume. A brief biography of Dominic for the general reader is *Dominic* by V. J. Koudelka OP (London, 1997). Older literature includes the monumental *History of the Dominican Order* by W. A. Hinnebusch OP, 2 vols (New York, 1965, 1973) and the shrewd *The Early Dominicans* by R. F. Bennett OP (Cambridge, 1937).

Francis
Scholarship on the saint has been bedevilled by the so-called 'Franciscan problem', the degree to which the succeeding collections of reminiscences of the saint made throughout the thirteenth and even fourteenth centuries can properly be called biographical material or were fabrications for contemporary ends. While the problem will never be completely resolved, readers now have every opportunity to make up their own minds. In the original languages the *Fontes Franciscani* (Assisi, 1995) eds E. Menestò OFM *et al.*, provides an extensive edition of Francis's works and early material about the order. This is matched in English by *Francis of Assisi: Early Documents*, edited in four volumes by R. J. Armstrong, J. A. W. Hellmann and W. J. Short, all OFM (New York, 1999–2002). It supercedes *St Francis of Assisi: writings and early biographies* by M. A. Habig OFM (4th ed., Quincy, Illinois, 1991). Biographies of Francis are legion and vary greatly in quality: Michael Robson's *St Francis of Assisi: the legend and the life* (London, 1997) is a reliable recent production. See also J. Le Goff, *Saint Francis of Assisi* (London, 2004, originally Paris, 1999) and A. House, *Francis of Assisi* (London, 2001). D. Webb's article, 'The pope and the cities: anticlericalism and heresy in Innocent III's Italy' in *Studies in Church History*, Subsidia, 9 (1991) also known as *The Church and Sovereignty, c.590–1918: essays in honour of Michael Wilkes*, ed. D. Wood (Oxford, 1991) points out how important it was not to offend Assisi for papal territorial ambitions. At the other end of the scale J. R. H. Moorman's *A History of the Franciscan Order* (Oxford, 1968) is a clear guide to the complex history of the order throughout the medieval period.

Fourth Lateran Council
The most accessible text in English is online at: www.fordham.edu/halsall/basis/lateran4.html as part of Paul Halsall's *Internet Medieval Source Book* at Fordham University, but it is old. More recent translations are available in *English Historical Documents, 1189–1327*, ed. H. Rothwell (London, 1975) and P. J. Geary, *Readings in Medieval History* (Peterborough, Ontario, 1989). The intellectual roots of the council are surveyed in J. W. Baldwin, *Masters, Princes and Merchants*, 2 vols (Princeton, 1970) and its effects examined by P. B. Pixton, *The German Episcopacy and the Implementation of the Decrees of the Fourth Lateran Council, 1216–45: Watchmen on the Tower* (Leiden, 1995). On Innocent III Jane Sayers's *Innocent III: Leader of Europe, 1198–1216* (Harlow, 1994) is a brief but comprehensive study. Brenda Bolton's excellent studies of both pope and council are brought together in *Innocent III: studies on papal authority and pastoral care* (Aldershot, 1995). The

proceedings of an important 1997 conference were published as *Pope Innocent III and his world* (Aldershot, 1999) ed. J. C. Moore.

Chapter 5

The thirteenth century, in general, is not as well covered as the twelfth and there is little between the broad overviews mentioned under Chapter 3 and specialist articles. C. H. Lawrence's *The Friars: the impact of the early mendicant movement* (Harlow, 1994) provides a good account of the friars and this largely replaces Rosalind Brooke's *The Coming of the Friars* (London, 1975), although the latter is still valuable for its translated documents. On thirteenth-century mendicant sermons see D. L. D'Avray, *The preaching of the friars* (Oxford, 1985). For the Cathars, the general works should be supplemented by Hamilton's article on 'Wisdom from the East' in Biller and Hudson for intellectual developments and my article on 'The Cathar economy', *Reading Medieval Studies*, 12 (1986). I stand by most of the latter, but it does seem idealistic. I suspect that the social pressures on those who did not give to the Cathars were quite severe, while I would now look more closely for ties of family or village between *perfecti* and donors. Mark Pegg's *The Corruption of Angels* (Princeton, 2001) offers a wider study of relations between believers and *perfecti* along with much else. The many works of J. H. Mundy on Toulouse comprise the best case study of 'the competition for souls', most recently *Men and women at Toulouse in the age of the Cathars* (Toronto, 1990) and *Society and government at Toulouse in the age of the Cathars* (Toronto, 1997).

Chapter 6

The most flourishing aspect of the study of heresy is the Inquisition. Portentous reflections on the *Zeitgeist* apart, the most obvious reason is that the search for new sources on heresy has been comparatively unsuccessful in the last 30 years and so attention has turned to the more abundant stock of inquisitorial material. John Arnold's *Inquisition and Power* (Philadelphia, 2001) provided a severe and intelligent critique of Inquisition records as a source for examining heresy. They are after all a 'discourse of power' and it is all too easy for the historian to assimilate the inquisitor's point of view. In contrast, James Given's sociological approach provides a systematic account of *Inquisition and Medieval Society: Power, Discipline and Resistance in Languedoc* (Ithaca, 1997), building on his perceptive articles in the *American Historical Review*, 94 (1989), 'The Inquisitors of Languedoc and the medieval technology of power' and 'Social stress, social strain, and the inquisitors of Languedoc' in *Christendom and its Discontents: exclusion, persecution and rebellion* eds S. L. Waugh and P. D. Diehl (Cambridge, 1996). Finally, Mark Pegg has emphasised the impact of the inquisitors in the Lauragais of the 1240s in his *Corruption of Angels*, using Toulouse MS 609, a document once considered unreadable and so little used by previous generations of scholars.

Of the older works, W. L. Wakefield's *Heresy, Crusade and Inquisition, 1100–1250* (Berkeley, 1974) provides a lucid exposition of the origins of 'the Inquisition' and gives translations of an early inquisitor's handbook and the fragmentary chronicle of Guilhem Pelhisson. Richard Kieckhefer then challenged the idea of the Inquisition, preferring to refer to separate inquisitions in his *The Repression of Heresy in Medieval Germany* (Liverpool, 1979), a position he modified somewhat in his article in *Journal of Ecclesiastical History*, 46 (1995), 'The Office of Inquisition and Medieval Heresy'. To some extent my 'Penance and the making of the Inquisition in Languedoc', *Journal of Ecclesiastical History*, 52 (2001) is a response to his ideas and those of Bernard Hamilton. The latter's *The Medieval Inquisition* (London, 1981) provided the necessary antidote to the blood-curdling prevailing visions of inquisitors by stressing the origins of their procedure in the sacrament of confession and penance.

The writers of all the above have their mutual disagreements which are carried out more or less amicably in the academic press. The sunlight of late twentieth-century liberalism has illuminated a subject all too often clouded by prejudice. Yet many of the seminal texts are sprung from this earlier era. H. C. Lea's *A History of the Inquisition in the Middle Ages*, 3 vols (New York, 1888) remains the most complete history of the institution in English and the most uncompromising condemnation of it. Jean Guiraud's scholarly, yet chilling, pre-war defence of its goals and methods was reprinted as *Elogio della Inquisizione* (*In praise of the Inquisition*) as recently as 1994 (Milan). Lea's righteous shade haunts Edward Burman's otherwise clear account of *The Inquisition: the Hammer of Heresy* (London, 1984) which covers the institution from medieval to modern times and has been recently reissued (Stroud, 2004), unfortunately without any updating of text or bibliography. The most recent reflections on the power relations of the Inquisition have been published as *Inquisition et pouvoir*, ed. G. Audisio (Aix-en-Provence, 2003).

Chapter 7

On the later Franciscans see David Burr's *The Spiritual Franciscans: from protest to persecution* (Philadelphia, 2001) and *Olivi and Franciscan poverty: the origins of the "usus pauper" controversy* (Philadelphia, 1989). A selection of sources in translation from Joachim of Fiore and the Spirituals is available in a volume of *Apocalyptic Spirituality*, trans. B. McGinn (New York, 1979).

On later medieval markets see C. Dyer's two works, *Standards of Living in the Later Middle Ages* (Cambridge, 1989) and *Making a Living in the Middle Ages* (New Haven, 2002). To them should be added Peter Spufford's *Power and Profit: the merchant in medieval Europe* (London, 2002), W. C. Jordan's *The Great Famine* (Princeton, 1996) and the essays in *Food and Eating in Medieval Europe*, edited by Martha Carlin and Joel T. Rosenthal (London, 1998).

Popular religion in the later Middle Ages is far better served than the earlier period. Hugely influential on perceptions of the late medieval Church has been Eamon Duffy's *The Stripping of the Altars* (New Haven, 1992) which depicted it as a successful vehicle for popular spirituality in England. R. N. Swanson takes broadly the same line in *Religion and Devotion in Europe, c.1215–c.1515* (Cambridge, 1995). On individual sacraments see *Handling Sin: Confession in the Middle Ages*, edited by Peter Biller and A. J. Minnis (York, 1998). Almost as influential as Duffy is Miri Rubin's *Corpus Christi: the Eucharist in the late middle ages* (Cambridge, 1991). *The History of Pastoral Care* edited by Gillian Evans (London, 2000) is useful, as is John Shinners's excellent collection of sources, *Medieval Popular Religion, 1000–1500: a reader* (Peterborough, Ontario, 1997).

Chapter 8

Women and heresy have been two of the great research areas in medieval history over the last 40 years. Our knowledge of the role of the women in the Church is now lending perspective to scholarship on heresy. While most general works on medieval religion now give due weight to women's contribution, specialist works tend to concentrate on the later period when the profile of female religion is rather higher. As a starting point for the twelfth century there is still Brenda Bolton's *Mulieres sanctae*, originally published in *Studies in Church History*, 10 (1973) or her *The Medieval Reformation* (London, 1983) and Caroline Walker Bynum's *Holy feast and holy fast: the religious significance of food to medieval women* (Berkeley, 1987). Janet Burton's excellent chapter on nunneries in *Monastic and Religious Orders in Britain, 1000–1300* (Cambridge, 1994) highlights many of the problems also found in the European context. For the role of lay women see P. Biller, 'The common woman in the Western Church in the thirteenth and fourteenth centuries' in *Women in the Church*, eds W. J. Sheils and D. Wood, *Studies in Church History*, 27 (1990).

The borders of later women's monasticism and heresy are explored by Frances Andrews, *The Early Humiliati* (Cambridge, 1999), Saskia Murk-Jansen's excellent concise *Brides in the Desert: the spirituality of the Beguines* (London, 1998) and the volume of essays edited by Danielo Bornstein and Roberto Rusconi, *Women and Religion in Medieval and Renaissance Italy* (Chicago, 1996). Traditionally, women were supposed to have taken a role in Catharism more equal with men than in the orthodox Church. This position was scientifically examined by R. Abels and E. Harrison, 'The participation of women in Languedocian Catharism', *Medieval Studies*, 41 (1979), whose statistical analysis of Inquisition depositions stripped away many illusions. However, it is impossible to deny the accumulation of evidence in M. C. Barber's sober article, 'Women and Catharism', in *Reading Medieval Studies*, 3 (1977), reprinted in his *Crusaders and Heretics, 12th–14th Centuries* (Aldershot, 1995) and the distinctive contribution of women is now emphasised by most scholars including Barber himself in his book on the Cathars and the leading French authority, Anne Brenon, in her *Les femmes cathares* (Paris, 1992). Women and the Bogomils are considered by Maja Angelovska-Panova's article 'The Role of the Woman in Bogomil Circles', in *Balkanistic Forum: Custom and Law on the Balkans* (Blagoevgrad, 2002). For women in the Waldensians see Biller's 'The preaching of the Waldensian sisters', *Heresis*, 30 (1999) reprinted in his *The Waldenses* (see above Chapter 3) and B. M. Kienzle, 'The prostitute-preacher: patterns of polemic against medieval Waldensian women preachers', in *Women, preachers and prophets through two millennia of Christianity*, eds Kienzle and Pamela J. Walker (Berkeley, 1998). A good cross-section of primary sources on women and heresy was brought together by M. Goodich in his sourcebook *Other Middle Ages* (Philadelphia, 1998).

Chapter 9

There is little on Fra Dolcino in English and readers have to make do with Marjorie Reeves, *The Influence of Prophecy in the later Middle Ages: a study in Joachimism* (Oxford, 1969), a good book now showing its age. Lambert's few pages on the subject are also helpful (see General). For the Waldensians during this period Biller's work comes into its own and there are some pertinent remarks from Cameron (see above Chapter 3 for both).

Work on the later Cathars dwarfs that on both the above groups which is surprising since dualism had almost reached the end of the road in the West. Its popularity as a subject of study is partly explained by the copious quantity of edited Inquisition material. The most famous use of it was by Emmanuel Le Roy Ladurie whose *Montaillou: village occitan de 1294 à 1324* (Paris, 1975) was translated and abridged as *Montaillou* (Harmondsworth, 1980). It became a bestseller in both languages. This remains one of the great works of medieval social history, but Le Roy Ladurie ruthlessly applied his own agenda to the material and was not particularly interested in Catharism. Using the same material René Weis's *The Yellow Cross* (London, 2000) vividly tells 'the story of the last Cathars' and is particularly good on the geography of the area. Barber (see above Chapter 3) is also good on the Autier revival. How the inquisitiors perceived these last heretics is touched on by P. Ormerod and A. P. Roach, 'The medieval inquisition: scale-free networks and the suppression of heresy', *Physica A*, 339 (2004) with an earlier non-technical draft in the *The Times Higher Education Supplement,* No. 1593, 13 June 2003, p. 21. Readers can get a flavour of the records produced by the Fournier Inquisition by reading the testimony of the widow Beatrice in *Readings in Medieval History,* ed. and trans. P. J. Geary (Peterborough, Ontario, 1989) or online at the site of Nancy P. Stork of San Jose State University, California at http://www2.sjsu.edu/depts/english/Fournier/jfournhm.htm.

INDEX

Index of modern authors in text and Further Reading